❧ Doing Conceptual History in Africa ❧

MAKING SENSE OF HISTORY
Studies in Historical Cultures
General Editor: Stefan Berger
Founding Editor: Jörn Rüsen

Bridging the gap between historical theory and the study of historical memory, this series crosses the boundaries between both academic disciplines and cultural, social, political and historical contexts. In an age of rapid globalization, which tends to manifest itself on an economic and political level, locating the cultural practices involved in generating its underlying historical sense is an increasingly urgent task.

For a full volume listing, please see back matter

DOING CONCEPTUAL HISTORY IN AFRICA

Revised Edition

Edited by Axel Fleisch and Rhiannon Stephens

berghahn
NEW YORK · OXFORD
www.berghahnbooks.com

First published in 2016 by
Berghahn Books
www.berghahnbooks.com

© 2016, 2018 Axel Fleisch and Rhiannon Stephens
Revised paperback edition published in 2018

All rights reserved. Except for the quotation of short passages
for the purposes of criticism and review, no part of this book
may be reproduced in any form or by any means, electronic or
mechanical, including photocopying, recording, or any information
storage and retrieval system now known or to be invented,
without written permission of the publisher.

Library of Congress Cataloging-in-Publication Data

Names: Fleisch, Axel, editor. | Stephens, Rhiannon, editor.
Title: Doing conceptual history in Africa / edited by Axel Fleisch and
  Rhiannon Stephens.
Other titles: Making sense of history; v. 25.
Description: New York: Berghahn Books, 2016. | Series: Making sense of
  history; v. 23 | "This volume is the product of a series of collaborative
  meetings and workshops between 2010 and 2014."--Acknowledgements.
  | Includes bibliographical references and index.
Identifiers: LCCN 2015045891 | ISBN 9781785338625 (paperback : alk.
  paper) | ISBN 9781785339523 (ebook)
Subjects: LCSH: Africa--Intellectual life--History. | Semantics,
  Historical. | African languages--Semantics, Historical. | Social
  change--Africa--History.
Classification: LCC DT14 .D65 2016 | DDC 960--dc23 LC record
  available at http://lccn.loc.gov/2015045891

British Library Cataloguing in Publication Data
A catalogue record for this book is available from the British Library

ISBN 978-1-78533-862-5 paperback
ISBN 978-1-78533-952-3 ebook

Contents

List of Maps, Figures and Tables   vii
Acknowledgements   viii
Notes on Language   x

Introduction. Theories and Methods of African Conceptual History   1
   Rhiannon Stephens and Axel Fleisch

Chapter 1. 'Wealth', 'Poverty' and the Question of Conceptual History in Oral Contexts: Uganda from c. 1000 CE   21
   Rhiannon Stephens

Chapter 2. Conceptual Continuities: About 'Work' in Nguni   49
   Axel Fleisch

Chapter 3. Tracking the Concept of 'Work' on the North-Eastern Cape Frontier, South Africa   73
   Anne Kelk Mager

Chapter 4. Understanding the Concept of 'Marriage' in Afrikaans during the Twentieth Century   91
   Marné Pienaar

Chapter 5. Male Circumcision among the Bagisu of Eastern Uganda: Practices and Conceptualizations   115
   Pamela Khanakwa

Chapter 6. The Concept of 'Land' in Bioko: 'Land as Property' and 'Land as Country'   138
   Ana Lúcia Sá

Chapter 7. Conceptualizing 'Land' and 'Nation' in Early Gold Coast Nationalism 162
  Pieter Boele van Hensbroek

Chapter 8. An Untimely Concept: Decolonization and the Works of Mudimbe, Mbembe and Nganang 185
  Pierre-Philippe Fraiture

Index 209

Maps, Figures and Tables

Maps

Map 1.1	Linguistic Landscape of Eastern Uganda	25
Map 3.1	North-Eastern Cape Frontier, South Africa, c. 1865	75
Map 5.1	Bugisu, Eastern Uganda	116
Map 6.1	Bioko, Equatorial Guinea	139
Map 7.1	The Gold Coast in the Nineteenth Century	164

Figures

Fig. 1.1	Classification of Eastern Nilotic	28
Fig. 1.2	Sub-classification of North Nyanza within Great Lakes Bantu	29
Fig. 7.1	Linkages between the concepts 'territory', 'land', 'access to land', 'political identity'	169

Tables

Table 1.1	The root *-can- in Eastern Nilotic languages	31
Table 1.2	The root *-kuly- in Eastern Nilotic languages	32
Table 1.3	The root *-ták- in North Nyanza languages	34
Table 1.4	The root *-(w)avu in North Nyanza languages	35
Table 1.5	The root *-naku in North Nyanza languages	36
Table 1.6	The root *-ker- in Eastern Nilotic languages	38
Table 1.7	The root *-bar- in Eastern Nilotic languages	39
Table 1.8	The root *-gaiga in North Nyanza languages	41

Acknowledgements

This volume is the product of a series of collaborative meetings and workshops between 2010 and 2014. A number of colleagues participated in those meetings who are not represented in the chapters collected here. Their contributions were invaluable in shaping *Doing Conceptual History in Africa* by pushing us to engage critically with new methodologies and to cross disciplinary boundaries. We are, therefore, very grateful to: Abdullah An Na'im, Inge Brinkman, Andreas Eckert, Lwazi Lushaba, Lars Magnusson, Valentin-Yves Mudimbe, Terje Østigård, Simphiwe Sesanti and Holger Weiss. We wish to acknowledge Terje Østigård in particular for hosting one of our meetings at the Nordic Africa Institute in Uppsala and for obtaining the necessary funding for that meeting. The original input for this project came from Bo Stråth, who did much of the fund-raising and was a key member of all meetings.

STIAS, the Stellenbosch Institute for Advanced Study in Stellenbosch, South Africa, has contributed greatly to the success of the project by hosting Bo Stråth and Axel Fleisch as research fellows and providing the logistics for several workshops. We thank the STIAS board and its entire staff for their sustained support. We had the opportunity to present our work to other fellows at STIAS on many occasions and acknowledge their valuable comments, criticisms and encouragement, in particular Anne Allison, Antjie Krog, Rosalind C. Morris and Charles Piot.

For reading all or part of the manuscript and their valuable input, we thank David Schoenbrun, Henrik Stenius and three anonymous reviewers for Berghahn Books. We offer a special thank you to Chris Chappell, our editor at Berghahn, for his enthusiasm for the project and for shepherding us through the publication process so ably. We are grateful to Eileen Quam who prepared the index. We also thank Joaquín Fanego Palat who produced all five of the maps that appear here.

All books owe their existence to financial and institutional support of some kind. That is most especially the case for this one, being as it is the product of four collaborative meetings and three further workshops, held in South Africa, Sweden and Finland. We acknowledge the support of the Department of Afrikaans, University of Johannesburg, South Africa; the Nordic Africa Institute in Uppsala, Sweden; the Riksbanken Jubileumsfond, Sweden; the Centre for European and Nordic Studies, University of Helsinki, Finland; and the Kone Foundation, Finland. We also express our appreciation to the Schoff Fund at the University Seminars at Columbia University for their help in publication. Material in this work was presented to the University Seminar: Studies in Contemporary Africa.

Last, but not least, we are grateful to Joaquín Fanego Palat and Jarod Roll for their support throughout this long process.

Notes on Language

The contributions in this book deal with the history of people in various parts of Africa. These people use different languages. Some chapters rely mostly or exclusively on sources in Indo-European languages: Afrikaans, English, French and Spanish. Several chapters draw on sources in African languages: interviews, reconstructed and elicited data and corpus data. Given the broad variety of languages used in the original sources, the following notes will make the African language data more accessible for readers less familiar with these languages.

A big group of languages represented in this book belong to the Bantu family: isiXhosa, isiZulu, isiNdebele in Southern Africa, but also Kiswahili, Luganda, Lugwere, Lusoga, Lugisu, etc. in East Africa. Nouns in these languages have prefixes that affect the meaning of the word, e.g. *Mswahili* 'a Swahili person', *Waswahili* 'Swahili people', *Kiswahili* 'the Swahili language'. The prefix indicates that the respective noun belongs into a particular noun class. There are more than twenty noun classes; not all of these are present in each individual language. Nilotic languages (see Rhiannon Stephens's chapter) also use prefixes, albeit fewer in number, which distinguish between related meanings, e.g. Iteso for the people who speak the language called Ateso.

For ease of reference and comparison across Bantu languages, their noun classes are numbered according to a conventionalized system. The shape of the prefix may vary from one language to another (for instance *ki-* in Kiswahili corresponds to *isi-*, *si-* or *se-* in other languages), but the overall classification into numbered noun classes is fairly robust throughout Bantu. In glosses, the numbers are usually given in brackets after the word, for the Swahili example above then: *Mswahili* (cl. 1) 'a Swahili person', *Waswahili* (cl. 2) 'Swahili people', *Kiswahili* (cl. 7) 'the Swahili language'.

When using Bantu or Nilotic terms, we generally keep the noun class prefixes, because these prefixes are not only grammatical markers, but contain significant semantic information. For a range of language names, then, we use siSwati, not Swati or Swazi (otherwise widely used in English), isiZulu, not just

Zulu, etc. In certain contexts, however, the prefix is dropped, e.g. in adjectival use (so 'isiXhosa' for the language, but 'Xhosa farmers'). Note that the spelling conventions differ with regard to the use of capital letters; sometimes the initial letter of the stem is capitalized, sometimes the initial letter of the prefix (Setswana, but siSwati). We adhere to the language-specific orthography where possible.

INTRODUCTION

Theories and Methods of African Conceptual History

Rhiannon Stephens and Axel Fleisch

What does it mean to do conceptual history? And what is particular about doing conceptual history in Africa? Some forty years ago, Terence Ranger described conceptual history in Africa in the following terms: 'Conceptual history is … the difficult study of ideas of causation in each region over the past decades'.[1] In this he was largely in agreement with Reinhart Koselleck and the other editors of the monumental *Geschichtliche Grundbegriffe* (*Basic Concepts in History*), who argued that concepts are far more than merely 'indicators of change', marking historical shifts that have already happened. Rather, concepts 'affect political and social change because it is through concepts that a horizon is constituted against which structural changes are perceived, evaluated, and acted upon'.[2] Conceptual history thus offers an opportunity to take seriously peoples' intellectual activity as part of historical processes; it is a way of expanding the horizons created by social, environmental and economic history. And it is an approach that has not been much taken advantage of in African history.[3]

A central motivation for Koselleck and his co-editors was to move beyond the elite circles of intellectual history and understand the use and meaning of different concepts across all levels of society. To achieve such an understanding, conceptual historians need to search for usages of these concepts in as wide a range of sources as possible.[4] This is a particularly compelling approach for historians of Africa on two grounds. First, because the available source base so often requires a catholic approach, ranging from the written to the oral to the material. This need for eclecticism becomes ever more acute the further back in time one wishes to research. Second, because the dominance of social history in

Notes for this section begin on page 16.

African history over the past decades has richly documented the manifold ways in which people from all strata of society have shaped that history.[5] Conceptual history enables us to build on this work by offering the opportunity to engage with people's intellectual lives and explore how their ideas shaped their history without the reductionism of exclusively studying elite thought.

But before going further, let us start with the 'us': we are scholars based in Eastern and Southern Africa, Northern and Southern Europe and North America; we come from a range of disciplines: history (conceptual and otherwise), linguistics, philosophy, literature and sociology; our work (at least for this project) spans sub-Saharan Africa from Ghana and Equatorial Guinea to Uganda and South Africa. We have been exploring how to do conceptual history in Africa since February 2010 when we first gathered as a group at the Stellenbosch Institute for Advanced Study. Since then, over the course of three meetings and a series of workshops dealing with individual chapters, we have collaborated to bring our different perspectives to bear on this project. We have sought to develop a new methodology for conceptual history in the frequent absence of the conventional extensive written sources used by Koselleck and others in Europe and Asia. The chapters that emerged from this do not follow a single methodological approach, but all are informed by the collaborative spirit of our attempt. The historians among us most comfortable with documentary sources have taken seriously linguistic questions, the literary scholars have engaged with historical perspectives and the linguists have analysed their data with the constant objective of relating them to historical time and space. The epistemological and methodological differences between our disciplines are considerable, and collaboration across these boundaries has proved challenging yet immensely enriching. In this introduction we set out the theoretical and methodological basis of our cross-disciplinary endeavour.

The concepts we decided to explore in this research network are ones that exist at the interface of the social and the economic and which, as a result, have been sites of contestation and struggle. But they also reflect important continuities, thereby anchoring them in historical perspective. The initial impetus for the focus on the social and economic came from Bo Stråth, who instigated the 'ConceptAfrica' research network as part of a broader effort to expand conceptual history beyond its primary habitat in Western Europe in a manner that pushed back against 'the economic reductivism of the globalisation narrative since the early 1990s'.[6] This volume includes histories of the concepts 'poverty', 'wealth', 'work', 'marriage', 'circumcision', 'land' and 'decolonization'. Over the course of our meetings we explored several other concepts: 'communication', 'water', *ujamaa,* 'citizenship', *umkhosi womhlanga* ('reed festival'), 'knowing', 'belonging' and 'national identity'.[7] Our discussions on how to think historically about these concepts were invaluable in pushing those of us represented in this volume to consider more critically the ways in which historical actors worked both to contest meanings and to ensure continuity of meaning.

Language and Conceptual History in Africa

In its original context of continental Europe, conceptual history relies on a specific method and set of sources: a reflection on key concepts used in public debate, concepts that proved significant in galvanizing popular support for certain views and actions. The questions pursued in the European context focus predominantly on the debates and contestations over concepts, and on how concepts that seemed clear to every actor – but could in fact be understood in different ways – have shaped political debate.[8] Identifying and describing similar debates (representing different historical actors' expectations and illusions) in African history helps foreground the ways in which the intellectual work of Africans shaped their worlds. A conceptual history approach ensures that those actors – even when their names are lost to us – are seen as having performed that intellectual work and are not relegated to a reactive position. As with social history and intellectual history, conceptual history places Africans at the centre of their own history, but it does so by emphasizing language as a historical source.[9] And while it is not alone in this, other approaches – such as the history of ideas and studies drawing on evidence from historical linguistics – use language in rather different ways from us. Since we both draw on and diverge from these approaches, a discussion of our methodological underpinning is necessary.

Historians of Africa have long recognized the value of language as a source and the value of evidence drawn from linguistic data.[10] Conceptual historians, too, rely strongly on language in their approach because language offers us access to concepts that have characterized historical political debates. In this sense, then, African historians and conceptual historians working elsewhere appear to be close in spirit and stance. Yet conceptual historians have usually focused on a specific kind of context, namely language cultures and nation states. Even if in practice the notion of coinciding national and linguistic boundaries was more often an ideal rather than a factual situation in, for instance, nineteenth-century Europe, the idea serves as a heuristic starting point for conceptual historians. Such an isomorphism – even if idealized – between language, culture and nation state is almost entirely absent on the African continent.[11] Most modern nation states on the continent are relatively young. Their citizens use several languages in different functional domains. The languages have different geographic ranges. Some might be restricted to a single town or even village, others (like Kiswahili) stretch across thousands of kilometres and some (like English) reach across the world. While language certainly plays a role in identity politics in Africa as it does elsewhere, the ways in which this happens are considerably more complex than the simplified model originating in nineteenth-century European nationalism. In order to assess the possibilities and limits of a conceptual history approach, a sense of these linguistic realities in Africa is necessary.

The linguistic landscape in Africa is rich and diverse. Based on models developed in and for the context of European language studies, linguists have devised genealogical family trees that indicate long-term histories for the demographics and settlement of Africa. Two main phyla are widely accepted among African linguists: Niger-Congo and Afro-Asiatic. Both are very large families in terms of speaker numbers with estimates of over 435 million speakers for Niger-Congo and nearly 375 million speakers for Afro-Asiatic.[12] The more than 1,500 Niger-Congo languages are used in a geographic area stretching from Senegal in West Africa across to Kenya in East Africa and all the way to South Africa, while Afro-Asiatic spreads beyond the African continent into Southwest Asia. A third phylum is Nilo-Saharan, although there is ongoing debate about its status as a genealogical entity and, especially, about the exact historical links among the two hundred or so languages classified under it. Finally, there are the languages spoken in Southern Africa (with outliers in Tanzania) that used to be grouped together as Khoisan, but that are now considered to be several unrelated families. The sociolinguistic settings across Africa are also varied. Some areas are relatively homogenous in linguistic terms and some languages have millions of speakers (such as Gĩgĩkũyũ, Wolof and Hausa). The more typical scenario, though, is of smaller speaker communities numbering from just a few hundred people up to hundreds of thousands. Multilingualism is common, both at the societal and the individual level. People usually speak several African languages and often know one or more Indo-European languages, the latter being a legacy of colonial rule. Furthermore, most language use remains oral rather than written, although this fact should not be overstated; after all, literacy in the European context has not made oral communication less significant. Moreover, there is a long tradition of writing in African languages in several places on the continent and the practice has become increasingly common since the nineteenth century.

For a conceptual history approach, this diverse language scenario and the primacy of orality hold particular challenges, but they also open up new possibilities. With regards to orality, the main challenge lies in sources. Conceptual history has relied on written documents from the public sphere – on pamphlets, newspapers and parliamentary records – to trace emerging conflicts and contestations within concepts, whether the concept of tyranny during the French Revolution or that of democracy in interwar Sweden.[13] Pieter Boele van Hensbroek can demonstrate the radical shifts in the meaning of 'land' for members of the Gold Coast elite. By contrast Ana Lúcia Sá, facing a shortage of written texts in Bubi, the language of the people of Bioko in Equatorial Guinea, has turned to transcribed oral literature, including songs, as a means of accessing a fuller conceptual history of 'land'.[14] Rhiannon Stephens, writing about a period for which we have no contemporaneous documentation, draws on comparative historical linguistics and diachronic semantics to uncover the history of peoples' concepts of 'wealth' and 'poverty' in Uganda over the past millennium. Offering another approach, Axel Fleisch draws on both historical linguistics and the analysis of contemporary written corpora, to trace long- and short-term patterns in the concept of 'work' among Nguni speakers.

Translation

Koselleck was sceptical about the translatability of concepts between languages that shared European cultural historical legacies;[15] the African linguistic landscape presents yet more complications. Does this complex linguistic landscape offer merely a highly fragmented picture with manifold local traditions? Or does it provide exactly those examples in which conceptual trends and ideas transcend language boundaries and afford the possibility of studying concepts that are constantly being translated? Viewing individual languages as essentially different systems leads to the question of what happens when communication crosses language boundaries. And ultimately, translation is not just a matter of language, but also of cultural or temporal distance between people. (Even within the same community and linguistic tradition, using anachronistic terms is a common error.) We do not see translation simply as a conversion process between two linguistic systems; that is, we do not believe that a translation simply expresses the exact same content in different words. Rather, translation always involves understanding and interpreting a text and re-expressing it in a different language.[16] In this sense, meanings are always renegotiated in the process of translation – as they are in historical interpretations that aim to explain past situations. Since our approach relies so fundamentally on language data and their historical interpretation, a closer look at what is involved in translating is apt.

Full equivalence in translation is impossible; a certain degree of mismatch cannot be avoided. Denotational meaning (the informative content), connotations, metaphors and pragmatic usage patterns of translation equivalents will often not match perfectly: Koselleck, Ulrike Spree and Willibald Steinmetz grappled with the English 'citizen', German *Bürger*, and French *citoyen*, whose meanings correspond to one another, but are not entirely co-extensive.[17] The connotations of words like these differ between languages, as do their pragmatic usage patterns, including the aesthetic values speakers attach to them. It is often possible to remain loyal to one of these layers in translation only for it to be necessary to compromise on another. Linguists have proposed models to help us analyse these translation mismatches. Anna Wierzbicka, for example, breaks lexical meaning into what she considers the smallest constituents of meaning, that is, parts of meaning that cannot be further analysed and are, in her analysis, universal.[18] She claims that even concepts that appear to be highly language- and culture-specific can thereby be transferred and analytically replicated into any target language. Yet although her approach aims for universality at the deepest analytical level, there remains ample space for cultural relativism engrained in language. This has a simple explanation: the level of linguistically-mediated cognition is not that of the smallest building blocks of meaning, but rather of bigger segments of meaning. Even words like 'fairness' in English or *Schadenfreude* in German are not understood through an analysis of their component parts, but – if they are known to speakers of other languages – as holistic concepts. They are more generic cultural scripts and semantic concepts and constitute the generic level of linguistic meaning. It is at this level that speakers access semantic meaning, that they try to translate and make meaning more explicit; this is also the space for the engrained cultural differences that make the translation process a challenging task. This is the case not just for the analyst, but also for speaker communities who constantly mediate between languages in the linguistically-diverse African context. Indeed, psycholinguists offer a growing body of evidence in support of the view that languages can be so incommensurate that translation becomes next to impossible in some areas of human experience, cognition and some cultural domains.[19]

Yet people translate constantly. In this sense we cannot speak of the impossibility of translation, since it is a practice that almost everyone is engaged in. It is precisely because of that permanent and continual practice of translation that concepts are debated and contested and so subject to change in a way that the uncontested is not. Some contributions in our volume focus on historical actors who chose to use a language other than their own. Boele van Hensbroek focuses on nineteenth and early twentieth-century Gold Coast intellectuals and nationalists who chose to speak, correspond and publish newspapers in English, rather than Akan or any other of their 'mother tongues'. He looks precisely at the continual acts of translation of this group of political actors in their articulations of the concept of 'land' against growing colonial encroachment. These articulations drew on 'indigenous' concepts of 'land' found in the various languages spoken by these intellectuals, as well as on concepts they encountered in European texts. Their articulations of these concepts in English underscore the possibilities, rather than the limitations of translation. *Doing Conceptual History in Africa* thus offers a glimpse into the possibility of acknowledging linguistic relativity without essentializing languages and without attempting to corral historical actors into ethnolinguistic boxes.[20]

Temporal Layers: Conceptual Shifts and Continuities

The overall linguistic complexity in Africa may appear daunting, yet it is exactly this complexity that holds the key to alternative methodological opportunities that can be explored for tracing conceptual continuities and changes.

One method that has long been used to write history using language evidence is 'words-and-things'. In its origins, this method relied on lexicography and the endeavour to comprehensively record and reflect conventionalized word meanings. The focus, thus, is on the shared meaning of relevant terms, assuming mostly shared understandings among members of the same speaker community. By identifying the terminology that was available to speakers of earlier languages, we can learn about their material culture, technological innovations and also their social institutions and political organization. Two of the pioneers of this methodology in African history, Christopher Ehret and Jan Vansina, have worked to write histories of religion and political traditions as well as of agriculture, pastoralism and other economic activities.[21] Subsequent generations of historians have explored histories of political authority and social identity, of the creation of ethnicity and of gender.[22] Even where the linguistic picture is highly fragmented, such as in coastal West Africa, this methodology offers the possibility to, at least partially, reconstruct knowledge about the past, as Edda Fields-Black demonstrated in her work on rice farming and its broader cultural and economic ramifications.[23]

By their nature, the reconstructed vocabularies that form the basis of these histories tend to pick out enduring conventional meanings, thereby stressing the long-term and the collective. Enduring meanings – sometimes in the face of dramatic historical developments – are a key component to conceptual history. But changes, including rapid, short-term changes that emerge out of immediate conflict, changes that may become long-term or may simply disappear, are also an essential element, and one that must be addressed if we are serious about bringing in the intellectual input of historical actors. Enduring conventional understandings emphasize linguistic legacies and continuities that are a product of both conscious decisions to assert continuity and less conscious inertia; episodes of more rapid change and crisis point to different historical forces at work, whether efforts to change from within or new engagements with another speaker community. Both mechanisms – endurance and change – are at work at the same time.

It is therefore important to pay attention to how different temporal layers can be at work simultaneously. Longer trends and stable conceptual conventions (as favoured by conventional historical linguists) do not preclude rapid change and dramatic events. For us, the integration of cognitive semantic insight with a conceptual historical approach is an important methodological advance. Cognitive semanticists understand lexical meaning as an encyclopaedic repertoire that speakers draw on when they construe actual meaning during a specific speech event or act of writing.[24] The lexical repertoires of speakers (i.e., historical actors) are not best understood as a mental lexicon containing a list of well-defined entries with clear denotations. Speakers may have acquired such technical knowledge for some lexical items, but this is clearly not what characterizes the mental lexicon at large. Furthermore, there is no difference in principle between different kinds of meaning: lexical-denotational, historical, connotational and so on. Even 'stable meanings' do not have to be agreed on in lexicographic fashion by the members of a speaker community; they do not need to be crystallized through inclusion in a dictionary. In fact, the contrary often applies: inherent contestation serves to keep concepts alive and allows for different temporal layers of meaning to coexist. It is therefore important not to choose one temporal granularity at the expense of the other, not to choose between the long and short term. Rather we need to view these together. Various methods for the analysis of linguistic data afford this possibility.

Some of our core techniques are well-developed instruments: the comparative method enabling the historical linguistic reconstruction of lexical items and the careful semantic analysis of relevant vocabulary. There is, however, a crucial difference between our approach and how these techniques are used by philologists, historical linguists and even in the original words-and-things approaches: we are less interested in clearly conventionalized meanings that can be rendered with a definition. Our emphasis is on those items that defy clear lexicographic characterization.[25] Reconstructing history on the basis of lexical items that are the loyal reflexes of past experience is one necessary component of this, but it does not end there. It is also necessary to flesh out the competing meanings that the key terms under study may have had, because it is in those competing meanings that the potential for active contestation lies. When speakers draw fundamental and significant concepts and ideas to the level of conscious debate, or act with them in new ways, or juxtapose them with new kinds of material or bodily practice, dissonance is part of the very make-up of such concepts.[26] They can thus serve as pointers to historical dynamics not readily accessible through static understandings of word meaning.

Marné Pienaar, in her chapter on 'marriage' in Afrikaans, points to these various layers. On the one hand, 'marriage' is a clearly defined, legal concept. As such, it should lend itself to conventional reconstruction and, indeed, the historical comparative methods she draws on shed light on the etymologies of relevant terms. On the other hand, Pienaar shows how problematic it is to assume a consensual understanding of what 'marriage' is. Taking a theoretical impetus from innovative cognitive semanticists allows her to establish conceptual links to terms less engrained in the language of marriage that were, and still are, nonetheless meaningful concepts for Afrikaans speakers and that clearly pertain to the domain of 'marriage'. Through this approach, Pienaar opens up conventional lexicography towards pragmatics and towards a discourse-oriented construal of meaning. In their chapters, Fleisch and Stephens use a similar approach to write the history of the concepts 'work', 'wealth' and 'poverty' and to push beyond the limits of the lexicographic record.

Mechanisms of Language Change

Pienaar's study of 'marriage' illustrates how attempts at reconstructing past meanings can benefit from recent insights in cognitive linguistics, in particular cognitive semantics. Many cognitive linguists have abandoned the distinction between lexical and encyclopaedic knowledge; indeed George Lakoff and Mark Johnson questioned the usefulness of this distinction back in 1980.[27] Their work helped catalyse diachronic interest in linguistics by countering the predominant synchronic formal approaches in the linguistic mainstream at the time.[28] Linguistic approaches such as grammaticalization theory rely on ideas of language change driven by pragmatic requirements (the things one needs to do with language in particular circumstances of communication), but constrained by our nature and physiology – our perceptual-cognitive apparatus. These are admittedly 'outside language', but since the cognitive constraints are universal, they necessarily lead to systematic patterns of linguistic change seen in language after language.[29] In this view linguistic change is a product of features in languages, rather than a product of human thought and action, implying that language-internally motivated change is universal and hence not historically relevant. As long as this was the dominant view of language, the only real possibility for language change resulting in linguistic data that could serve as a historical source was through external contact. That is, change resulting from contact with the speaker community of a different language.[30] This somewhat limiting view changed only with a more wholehearted adoption of the important insight that the trigger of language change is located outside of language. As such, language change internal to a speaker community is also a historical phenomenon.

Let us illustrate these thoughts with a more detailed example. Someone tells her assistant: 'Please find a better copy of this book!' The use of the verb 'to find' instead of 'to search', or 'to look for' is motivated by the speaker's interest in the outcome, rather than the search conducted by the assistant. Linguists would interpret this as an instance of subjectification. In an instruction, a result-oriented verb is preferred over a process verb, even though this forces a sense onto the verb 'to find' which is not part of its original semantic make-up. Its meaning changes from an accidental event to 'making something happen'. Note that the goal-oriented, non-accidental sense of 'to find' applies most often in phrases where it is accompanied by a beneficiary: 'Find me a better copy!' sounds even more natural. Such constructions that orient the action toward a beneficiary are arguably the starting point for this semantic extension. What subjectification means then is that a subjective interest in a situation is expressed by a term that originally has, in terms of semantic denotation, a slightly different meaning. The subjective interest is a sufficient pragmatic trigger to make the semantic change effective. While this trigger is external to the grammatical system of the language, as a mechanism it is arguably regular, and we can expect other languages to show similar semantic developments. A comparative linguist or historian might reach similar insight, but would typically follow a different path. For instance, coming across the words 'finds' or 'findings' for archaeological remains in a given language would indicate that the speakers must have engaged in archaeological research. For comparative semanticists, this indexical level is not the endpoint. Instead, the history of the terms would be traced by comparing them with the semantic extension of cognate terms in related languages. Such careful philological and comparative work can lead to a rich history of the ideas behind the term, and some of the contributions in our volume rely on this methodology as well.

In his study of the concept of 'work' in the Nguni languages of Southern Africa, Fleisch draws on a range of linguistic methodologies, including synchronic corpus analysis and comparative semantic reconstruction. This enables him, for example, to show how in isiNdebele, it is *ukuberega*, the term borrowed from Afrikaans (< *werk*), that captures the everyday notion of 'work' (such as performing chores), whereas *ukusebenza*, inherited from their Nguni-speaking ancestors, is more closely associated with employment or paid labour. The etymological origins are thus reversed compared to the expected range of meaning. This suggests both a persistence in the need to distinguish between different modes of 'working' and that contact with Afrikaans was more complex than an intense one-time episode during the 'colonial encounter' between isiNdebele speakers and Afrikaans speakers. In a similar manner to the example of 'finds' and 'findings', philological work, comparison across language boundaries and high-resolution semantic analysis of actual language use can identify cases like these, cases that highlight continuities as well as semantic change not necessarily reflected in the actual word form (e.g., *ukusebenza* has different meanings related to 'work' in other Nguni languages).

In the absence of contemporary language corpora for the period studied, Stephens explores the ways in which the comparative historical linguistic data can be approached in a manner that draws on cognitive semantics to write conceptual history. This involves looking for the widest possible sets of meanings for a particular word that has, as one of its glosses, the meaning 'wealth' or 'poverty' or 'rich person' or 'poor person'. Tracing all of those across the relevant languages of Eastern Uganda, and their ancestral or proto-languages, brings to light important changes in the concepts that reflect conflict or struggles within the speaker communities. This approach also enables us to see continuities in these concepts, continuities that endured radical changes in terms of environment, economy and social relations. The continuities allow for shifting semantic meanings that over time reflected those radical changes. One might say, the concepts remained but their meanings changed. For example, the concept of 'poverty' for Nilotic speakers represented by the root *-can-* retained its negative associations across very long stretches of time. But the nature of those associations – part of the meaning given to the concept – changed sharply; speakers shifted their negative views from recognizing the impact of poverty on the poor to expressing anxiety about the impact of the poor on the wider community. This suggests moments of confrontation around wealth inequalities in communities, confrontations that challenged the meanings of key concepts like 'poverty'.

Ultimately, then, we are interested in the contestations around the ideas behind the word. The German adjective *findig* 'resourceful' relates to the verb *finden* 'to find' and refers to a person who can rely on her abilities to find a solution to problems when they occur, or find an easy way to avoid them. Labelling a candidate as *findig* in an interview is ambiguous: some would interpret this positively as resourcefulness, others would think of the person as imaginative, but also insufficiently conscientious. What comes into play here is the accidental aspect of being lucky that is evoked by the verb 'to find'. These different understandings can remain implicit, but can also be drawn to the level of conscious debate. Higher-level concepts ('marriage', 'masculinity', 'decolonization', etc. – the kinds of concepts that our contributions address and that are intrinsically contested) carry the potential of greater historical currency. Their contested meanings are laid bare by those engaging in open debate. This is what a conceptual approach to history targets, and what determines its way of drawing on linguistic sources for the writing of history.

Addressing the semantic domain of work and labour, Anne Kelk Mager's chapter shows a competition for semantic ground between two main concepts pertaining to the domain of 'work' among isiXhosa speakers. This competition takes place against the backdrop of their being increasingly affected by European notions of 'work' and 'labour'. As Mager's analysis demonstrates, the renegotiation of ideas of 'work' in isiXhosa was a much more complex process than colonial notions unilaterally affecting pre-existing concepts. Indeed, labour and employment are not just abstract ideas, but concrete arenas of negotiation of economic conditions. Mager shows how linguistic understandings of concepts of 'work' were shaped by the events of the nineteenth century, including the expansion of colonial rule, but also how these concepts themselves influenced isiXhosa speakers' decisions and actions during this period. This bidirectional view was possible because Mager adopted three different perspectives: the cognitive/linguistic, the historical and the conceptual. Cognitivists tend to focus on the systematic aspects of change; human agency is viewed as relevant (pragmatics triggers all change), but constrained. Historians explore in great detail the indexical possibilities that the lexicon affords.[31] Language in this perspective is mainly viewed as pointing to past experiences, but not so much as a tool that could be used to discover how these experiences were brought about. Our approach in *Doing Conceptual History in Africa* adds precisely this idea of the actively pursued debate, of the contestation of key concepts as a trigger for change.

The resulting conceptual conflicts can be made explicit; intellectuals can scrutinize them and in so doing further challenge the concepts at stake. Pierre-Philippe Fraiture's chapter is a case in point. Taking 'decolonization' as a key concept that has preoccupied intellectuals and philosophers since the mid-twentieth century, Fraiture shows how far the concept is from its denotational meaning, which attributes agency to colonial powers. Valentin Mudimbe, Achille Mbembe and Patrice Nganang, in their often conflictual writing, contest the notion that 'decolonization' is a process whereby withdrawal results in independence, with a clear end point and a neat reversal of the act of colonizing. Instead, it falls as much on the formerly colonized and subsequent generations to decolonize themselves, a process that is ongoing and that includes the appropriation of European intellectual production for Africa's own ends. What exactly 'decolonization' means and what it looks like, however, both remain the focus of intense debates, particularly so in the wake of some of the important disappointments of independence.

Conceptual Affordances and Constraints

Conceptual history offers an approach to Africa's past that can also foreground the intellectual work of ordinary people; it is about all kinds of people shaping powerful concepts, such as 'land' or 'wealth', and doing so through language. Because in *Doing Conceptual History in Africa* we work from the assumption that language is inherently social and produced by people, we place human agency firmly at the centre of the narrative. Here then, people are not constrained by hegemonic discourses that limit their agency, nor are they instrumentally acted upon by lineage systems or traditions or the fact of living on a frontier. Neither does the 'harsh environment' or 'rich volcanic soil' determine their life trajectory from start to finish. Rather we see them creating, contesting and reshaping key concepts, sometimes in a context of struggle and hardship, sometimes not.

Placing language at the centre of our analysis, especially as we emphasize translation, necessitates a discussion of our stance towards linguistic relativity. Language is not only a reflection of lived experience, not just a record of events that have left their imprint in language as a conventionalized inventory. It is this, to some extent: we can trace changes in agriculture from linguistic evidence because the adoption of new crops is marked in language yet does not entirely displace the language for older forms of food production. But language serves also to enable speakers both to make sense of the world and to shape the world. Key concepts are those that enable speakers to do the latter; they are those concepts that drive actors towards a certain course of action. People's expectations are phrased in these concepts, and so language becomes a tool for manipulating debates in particular directions. Of course, this does not always work. Others are also seeking to use language in this way and ultimately a certain consensus must emerge if one interpretation of a key concept is to become dominant and hence effective.

In her chapter on the concept of 'land' in colonial Bioko (Equatorial Guinea), Sá offers a powerful example of a concept enabling speakers – and writers – to shape the world they inhabit, or at least to make a concerted effort to do so. By tracing the ways in which the concept of 'land' shifted from one grounded in the specificity of life on Bioko to include core colonial concepts, such as the plantation, her chapter offers another example of the entanglements and contestations wrought by colonialism in Africa. But she goes further. Writing about a group of Bubi farmers who named themselves collectively as 'sons of the country' and who submitted a petition to the colonial government, Sá shows how they appropriated the colonial concepts of 'land' and *indígenas*. They did so to assert their rights to land expropriated from them and given to settlers and to assert their vision for a different future in which past and ongoing abuses would be undone.

Language is created through speech and through social interaction and so the creating, contesting and reshaping of key concepts is done performatively. Speech necessarily occurs within a context and that context can determine the kind of speech that is acceptable or appropriate or even possible. What is more, certain kinds of actions can form part of the struggle over the meaning of concepts. For example, a person officiating at the marriage of two men, through her actions, engages in the ongoing debate over the concept of 'marriage' in South Africa.

Pamela Khanakwa's chapter effectively demonstrates the ways in which actions as well as language form part of the debate over particular concepts, in her case concepts of 'circumcision', of 'group identity' and of 'masculinity'. Indeed, the key concept in the chapter – *imbalu*, with circumcision as the central event – is a ritual rather than a lexical concept. The performance of that ritual, and efforts to control the nature of that performance, established a number of other highly significant contested concepts, such as 'masculinity' and 'ethno-national belonging'. The shape of the scar left by a surgeon performing circumcision in colonial Bugisu mattered, as did the stance of the person being circumcised, whether he was lying down or standing upright. Struggles over these kinds of aspects were central to debates over the meaning of 'circumcision' and all its related concepts in Eastern Uganda, especially from the 1930s to the 1960s. When bands of men abducted and forcibly circumcised Bagisu and non-Bagisu men, they violently contested the notion that 'being Bagisu' could involve not being circumcised. At the same time, the public performance of circumcision during *imbalu* established a particular concept of 'manhood', one that was continually challenged and reframed over the course of the twentieth century. Khanakwa's chapter offers a striking example of ritual as the expression of a concept and thus of ritual as history. This is internal Gisu history, but it is also the history of cultural encounters, of missionaries seeking to recreate rites in a manner compatible with their interpretation of Christian values. This approach does not reify the cultural encounters as a simple binary between Gisu and Western, but demonstrates the plasticity of such encounters and the malleability of contentions over the meaning given to rituals and the appropriation of their interpretive power.

This inclusion of ritual practice as an expression of a concept brings us back to the questions of what constitutes a key concept and what concepts have been significant in African history. Historians of Africa, and other scholars, have long grappled with the latter question. For example, histories of public healing make the case that it is a key concept. Steven Feierman's work speaks to this with his argument that the dual concepts of 'healing the land' and 'harming the land' are the lens through which we can understand Shambaa history over the past two centuries or more.[32] John Janzen meanwhile shows how *ngoma* healing helped structure economic and social life across central and southern Africa.[33] Because we came at this as a group of scholars focused on exploring how to do conceptual history in Africa, we are not claiming that the concepts set out here represent all the fundamental concepts of African history, but they are among them. They are at once universal and specific and, after Nietzsche,[34] they are all undefined, or at least resist any straightforward definition, no matter what dictionaries may tell us to the contrary. Concepts that have a history are, according to Nietzsche, not possible to define from some overall 'objective' point of view, since *history* means that they are continuously contested. Starting from the framework of the social and economic, the concepts we explore here tend towards those that transcend ethnolinguistic, even regional, boundaries.

Unsurprisingly, perhaps, much focus is on the nineteenth and twentieth centuries and their history of colonialism and independent nation states. But this is less about the 'colonial encounter' and the reification of that experience (as one between two coherent and bounded sides) as it is about showing how colonialism and missionary Christianity contributed to the contestations over concepts – whether 'work' among isiXhosa speakers (Mager, and also Fleisch) or 'circumcision' among Lugisu speakers (Khanakwa) – and the continuities in those concepts despite the profound ruptures of the last centuries. Or the ways in which Africans sought to mobilize concepts such as 'decolonization' (Fraiture) or 'land' (Sá and Boele van Hensbroek) to bring about the future they imagined for themselves at independence or to navigate the disappointments of the years since. But these conceptual histories are not limited to the relatively recent past. People have debated, for example, the meaning of 'wealth' or of 'poverty' for the past millennium and more (Stephens). Such debates continue, as struggles to redefine 'marriage' in the twentieth and twenty-first centuries demonstrate (Pienaar). The utility of the key concepts that we chose to explore in our chapters stems from this double-sidedness: they result from past experiences, but are also reshaped in order to better explain past experience. And they contribute to people's visions of future possibilities, thereby influencing historical actors whose actions are built on their expectations for the future, rather than emerging mechanically from past experiences. We must bear these thoughts in mind when returning to Ranger's statement: 'Conceptual history is … the difficult study of ideas of causation'.

Conclusion

In *Doing Conceptual History in Africa*, we adhere to a view of temporality that goes beyond a plain sequence of cause and effect, and two aspects of temporality are particularly important to us. The first has to do with the moment of the colonial encounter, without doubt a highly significant moment for African history, but one that has gained an unjustified currency as a foundational moment for the entire enterprise of writing history in Africa. The second has to do with the understanding of time and temporality for the writing of history. Both help us to clarify where we see the novelty and additional explanatory force of a conceptual history approach in the African context and beyond.

Relying on linguistic data in addition to the more conventional historical documentary sources enables us to overcome the enshrined divide of precolonial versus colonial and postcolonial.[35] This is about more than simply developing a richer understanding of the interface at which precolonial becomes colonial. It is also about more than finding new ways to push further back in time, given the limitations of sources for Africa's history beyond the past two centuries. We do not write back into the past; the histories included here are not about explaining how the world today came into being, but rather explore different sets of expectations at historically significant moments, to study the past futures in the sense offered by Koselleck.[36] Broadening the range of instruments available to us, by adopting theoretical impetus and methodological aid from conceptual history and linguistics, is not aimed at improving our analysis of the impact of colonialism on African societies. Instead, a conceptual historical approach opens the possibility for a more radically different way of writing history, one closer to what scholars of the subaltern studies collective have long debated.[37] This includes the possibility of placing the colonial relationship in its wider and deeper historical context. Conceptual history is about understanding discursive formations at a given point in time. It is about the prevalent views held and interpretations made by people at that time, including the expectations upon which they acted.[38] As such it emphasizes the contingencies and contestations that surround historical events, asserting an explicitly anti-teleological approach.

The methodological tool of conceptual history not only helps to transcend the divide between postcolonial, colonial and precolonial. It also holds the opportunity to transcend the distinction between African history and the history of other regions. The methods invoked here are certainly not restricted to their application in an African context. We chose the continent because of our familiarity with that context, and also because of the often-reiterated specificities (scarcity of written sources, specific socio-political settings, diversity, etc.) that are used to question the feasibility of doing this kind of African history, hoping that thereby the possibilities, and perhaps limits, of our methodological proposals would become most evident. There is not anything intrinsic to our approach that would necessarily confine it to being applied exclusively to African history. In fact, transporting it to, for example, an Asian or European setting is tempting. There is a clear potential for this approach to enhance our knowledge about non-elite intellectual thought in contexts where the availability of written sources may have led to specific biases. In this sense, our methodological proposal ties in with the renewed interest in global history, but a global history without a Western centre, and without elite actors as its necessary protagonists.

Notes

1. T.O. Ranger, 'Towards a Usable African Past', in C. Fyfe (ed.), *African Studies since 1945: A Tribute to Basil Davidson* (London: Longman for the Centre of African Studies, Edinburgh, 1976), 26.

2. M. Richter, '*Begriffsgeschichte* and the History of Ideas', *Journal of the History of Ideas* 48(2) (1987): 255.

3. Although they have not explicitly taken a conceptual history approach, Africanist historians have written histories that examine particular concepts, some of which are discussed below.

4. Although for Koselleck and his colleagues these were limited to written sources. Richter, '*Begriffsgeschichte* and the History of Ideas', 253.

5. The list is far too long to include here, but see the many contributions in the Social History of Africa series published by Heinemann and the New African Histories series published by Ohio University Press.

6. Bo Stråth, 'Towards a Global Conceptual History', keynote address at National and Transnational Notions of the Social Seminar, Helsinki, 21 August 2008. Retrieved 12 May 2015 from http://www.helsinki.fi/conceptafrica/theory_method_literature/towards_a_global_conceptual_history.html. See also H. Schulz-Forberg (ed.), *A Global Conceptual History of Asia, 1860–1940* (London: Pickering & Chatto, 2014).

7. These were in papers by Inge Brinkman, Lwazi Lushaba, V.Y. Mudimbe, A.A. An Na'im, Terje Østigård and Holger Weiss, as well as members of the group represented in this volume.

8. Carol Gluck, drawing on Wittgenstein, describes this as seeing either the rabbit or the duck in the entwined gestalt; both are there but cannot be perceived simultaneously. C. Gluck, '*Sekinin*/Responsibility in Modern Japan', in C. Gluck and A.L. Tsing (eds), *Words in Motion: Toward a Global Lexicon* (Durham: Duke University Press, 2009), 90–91.

9. In this there is some overlap between conceptual history and the history of ideas. See Richter, '*Begriffsgeschichte* and the History of Ideas', for a discussion of that relationship.

10. One of the earliest historians to embrace the possibilities of linguistic evidence for writing African history was Roland Oliver, the first person to hold a lectureship in African History (specifically 'East African Tribal History') at the School of Oriental and African Studies in London. See R. Oliver, 'The Problem of the Bantu Expansion', *Journal of African History* 7(3) (1966): 361–76. While his work has since been superseded, the recognition of language as a historical source has remained important for subsequent scholars.

11. In sub-Saharan Africa potential exceptions to this include Amharic in Ethiopia, an autochthonous imperial language with a long tradition in writing, and countries such as Somalia, Burundi and Cape Verde with a dominant language spoken as a first language by practically all inhabitants. Today, we could also include Tanzania and the Central African Republic, where African linguae francae (Kiswahili and Sango respectively) have developed into nationwide means of communication.

12. 'Statistical Summaries: Summary by Language Family, Table 5. Major Language Families of the World', in M.P. Lewis, G.F. Simons, and C.D. Fennig (eds), *Ethnologue: Languages of the World*, 17th ed. (Dallas, Texas: SIL International, 2014). Retrieved 21 July 2014 from http://www.ethnologue.com.

13. R. Monnier, 'Use and Role of the Concepts of Tyranny and Tyrannicide during the French Revolution', *Contributions to the History of Concepts* 2(1) (2006), 19–41; A. Friberg, 'Democracy in the Plural? The Concepts of Democracy in Swedish Parliamentary Debates during the Interwar Years', *Contributions to the History of Concepts* 7(1) (2012), 12–35.

14. On the definition of oral literature, see R. Finnegan, *The Oral and Beyond: Doing Things with Words in Africa* (Oxford: James Currey, 2007).

15. R. Koselleck, U. Spree and W. Steinmetz, 'Drei bürgerliche Welten? Zur vergleichenden Semantik der bürgerlichen Gesellschaft in Deutschland, England und Frankreich', in H.-J. Puhle (ed.), *Bürger in der Gesellschaft der Neuzeit. Wirtschaft-Politik-Kultur* (Göttingen: Vandenhoeck & Ruprecht 1991), 14–58.

16. Translation can also be 'political argumentation'. D.R. Peterson, *Creative Writing: Translation, Bookkeeping, and the Work of Imagination in Colonial Kenya* (Portsmouth: Heinemann, 2004), 9 (quote), 80–85.

17. Koselleck, Spree and Steinmetz, 'Drei bürgerliche Welten?'.

18. A. Wierzbicka, 'Translatability and the Scripting of Other Peoples' Souls', *Australian Journal of Anthropology* 24 (2013): 1–21.

19. S.C. Levinson, *Space in Language and Cognition: Explorations in Cognitive Diversity* (Cambridge: Cambridge University Press, 2003).

20. On the danger of an ethnographic approach, see V.-Y. Mudimbe, 'Meditations on *Eikones* (Questions on "À Propos un Passe-Vue Conceptuel")', keynote address, ConceptAfrica workshop, Helsinki, 26 May 2011. Retrieved 9 May 2015 from http://www.helsinki.fi/conceptafrica/theory_method_literature/meditations_on_eikones.html.

21. C. Ehret, *Southern Nilotic History: Linguistic Approaches to the Study of the Past* (Evanston, Illinois: Northwestern University Press, 1971); C. Ehret, *An African Classical Age: Eastern and Southern Africa in World History, 1000 B.C. to A.D. 400* (Charlottesville: University of Virginia Press, 1998); J. Vansina, *The Children of Woot* (Madison: University of Wisconsin Press, 1978); J. Vansina, *Paths in the Rainforest: Toward a History of Political Tradition in Equatorial Africa* (Madison: University of Wisconsin Press, 1990); J. Vansina, *How Societies Are Born: Governance in West Central Africa before 1600* (Charlottesville: University of Virginia Press, 2004).

22. D.L. Schoenbrun, *A Green Place, A Good Place: Agrarian Change, Gender, and Social Identity in the Great Lakes Region to the 15th Century* (Portsmouth: Heinemann, 1998); K.A. Klieman, *'The Pygmies Were Our Compass': Bantu and Batwa in the History of West Central Africa, Early Times to c. 1900 C.E.* (Portsmouth: Heinemann, 2003); R. Stephens, *A History of African Motherhood: The Case of Uganda, 700–1900* (New York: Cambridge University Press, 2013).

23. E.L. Fields-Black, *Deep Roots: Rice Farmers in West Africa and the African Diaspora* (Bloomington: Indiana University Press, 2008). For other works on the history of economic activities see, for example R. Klein-Arendt, *Die traditionellen Eisenhandwerke der Savannen-Bantu:*

Eine sprachhistorische Rekonstruktion auf lexikalischer Grundlage (Frankfurt: Peter Lang, 2004); K. Bostoen, *Des mots et des pots en bantou: une approche linguistique de l'histoire de la céramique en Afrique* (Frankfurt: Peter Lang, 2005).

24. V. Evans and M. Green, *Cognitive Linguistics: An Introduction*. (Mahwah: Lawrence Erlbaum, 2006).

25. By this, we do not mean dictionary definitions, but rather those terms for which speakers of a language could offer a straightforward definition.

26. These are similar to Gallie's understanding of essentially contested concepts. W.B. Gallie, *Philosophy and the Historical Understanding* (London: Chatto & Windus, 1964), Chapter 8.

27. G. Lakoff and M. Johnson, *Metaphors We Live By* (Oxford: Oxford University Press, 1980).

28. An example of cognitive linguistic work in this tradition that also addresses the question of (pragmatic) triggers for linguistic change is E. Sweetser, *From Etymology to Pragmatics: Metaphorical and Cultural Aspects of Semantic Structure* (Cambridge: Cambridge University Press, 1991); see also E. Closs Traugott and R.B. Dasher, *Regularity in Semantic Change* (Cambridge: Cambridge University Press, 2001).

29. B. Heine and T. Kuteva, *Language Contact and Grammatical Change* (Cambridge: Cambridge University Press, 2005).

30. In *Language Contact and Grammatical Change*, Heine and Kuteva go so far as to claim that even in contact situations, linguistic change can only occur according to paths of language change that also apply to individual languages not (or only minimally) influenced by other languages: 'transfer [of grammatical meaning and structures] is essentially in accordance with principles of grammaticalization' (p. 1), and 'grammatical replication is independent of the particular sociolinguistic factors that may exist in a given situation of language contact' (p. 260). That implies that language contact may accelerate the pace of change, but not radically alter its course.

31. This approach is neatly summarized by Vansina: 'Words are the tags attached to things'. Vansina, *Paths in the Rainforest*, 11.

32. S. Feierman, *Peasant Intellectuals: Anthropology and History in Tanzania* (Madison: University of Wisconsin Press, 1990), 69–93.

33. J.M. Janzen, *Ngoma: Discourses of Healing in Central and Southern Africa* (Berkeley: University of California Press, 1992).

34. F. Nietzsche, 'Zur Genealogie der Moral: Eine Streitschrift. Zweite Abhandlung: Schuld, schlechtes Gewissen und Verwandtes', in *Philosophische Werke in sechs Bänden*. Bd. VI. (Munich: Carl Hanser, 1980 [1887]), 820.

35. See also F. Cooper, *Africa since 1940: The Past of the Present* (Cambridge: Cambridge University Press, 2002), 4; S. Ellis, 'Writing Histories of Contemporary Africa', *Journal of African History* 43(1) (2002), 5–6.

36. R. Koselleck, *Futures Past: On the Semantics of Historical Time*, trans. K. Tribe (Cambridge, Massachusetts: MIT Press, 1985). Original publication: *Vergangene Zukunft: Zur Semantik geschichtlicher Zeiten* (Frankfurt am Main: Suhrkamp, 1979).

37. D. Chakrabarty, *Provincializing Europe: Postcolonial Thought and Historical Difference* (Princeton: Princeton University Press, 2007); R. Majumdar, *Writing Postcolonial History* (London: Bloomsbury Academic, 2010, Bo Stråth).

38. L. Schneider, *Government of Development: Peasants and Politicians in Postcolonial Tanzania* (Bloomington: Indiana University Press, 2014) offers an example of this kind of approach.

References

Bostoen, K. *Des mots et des pots en bantou: une approche linguistique de l'histoire de la céramique en Afrique*. Frankfurt: Peter Lang, 2005.

Chakrabarty, D. *Provincializing Europe: Postcolonial Thought and Historical Difference*. Princeton: Princeton University Press, 2007.
Closs Traugott, E. and R.B. Dasher, *Regularity in Semantic Change*. Cambridge: Cambridge University Press, 2001.
Cooper, F. *Africa since 1940: The Past of the Present*. Cambridge: Cambridge University Press, 2002.
Ehret, C. *Southern Nilotic History: Linguistic Approaches to the Study of the Past*. Evanston: Northwestern University Press, 1971.
———. *An African Classical Age: Eastern and Southern Africa in World History, 1000 B.C. to A.D. 400*. Charlottesville: University of Virginia Press, 1998.
Ellis, S. 'Writing Histories of Contemporary Africa'. *Journal of African History* 43(1) (2002), 1–26.
Evans, V. and M. Green. *Cognitive Linguistics: An Introduction*. Mahwah: Lawrence Erlbaum, 2006.
Feierman, S. *Peasant Intellectuals: Anthropology and History in Tanzania*. Madison: University of Wisconsin Press, 1990.
Fields-Black, E.L. *Deep Roots: Rice Farmers in West Africa and the African Diaspora*. Bloomington: Indiana University Press, 2008.
Finnegan, R. *The Oral and Beyond: Doing Things with Words in Africa*. Oxford: James Currey, 2007.
Friberg, A. 'Democracy in the Plural? The Concepts of Democracy in Swedish Parliamentary Debates during the Interwar Years'. *Contributions to the History of Concepts* 7(1) (2012), 12–35.
Gallie, W.B. *Philosophy and the Historical Understanding*. London: Chatto & Windus, 1964.
Gluck, C. '*Sekinin*/Responsibility in Modern Japan', in C. Gluck and A.L. Tsing (eds), *Words in Motion: Toward a Global Lexicon*. Durham: Duke University Press, 2009, 83–106.
Heine, B. and T. Kuteva. *Language Contact and Grammatical Change*. Cambridge: Cambridge University Press, 2005.
Janzen, J.M. *Ngoma: Discourses of Healing in Central and Southern Africa*. Berkeley: University of California Press, 1992.
Klein-Arendt, R. *Die traditionellen Eisenhandwerke der Savannen-Bantu: Eine sprachhistorische Rekonstruktion auf lexikalischer Grundlage*. Frankfurt: Peter Lang, 2004.
Klieman, K.A. '*The Pygmies Were Our Compass*': *Bantu and Batwa in the History of West Central Africa, Early Times to c. 1900 C.E*. Portsmouth: Heinemann, 2003.
Koselleck, R. *Futures Past: On the Semantics of Historical Time*, trans. K. Tribe. Cambridge: MIT Press, 1985. Original publication: *Vergangene Zukunft: Zur Semantik geschichtlicher Zeiten*. Frankfurt am Main: Suhrkamp, 1979.
Koselleck, R., U. Spree and W. Steinmetz. 'Drei bürgerliche Welten? Zur vergleichenden Semantik der bürgerlichen Gesellschaft in Deutschland, England und Frankreich', in H.-J. Puhle (ed.), *Bürger in der Gesellschaft der Neuzeit. Wirtschaft-Politik-Kultur*. Göttingen: Vandenhoeck & Ruprecht, 1991, 14–58.
Lakoff, G. and M. Johnson. *Metaphors We Live By*. Oxford: Oxford University Press, 1980.
Levinson, S.C. *Space in Language and Cognition: Explorations in Cognitive Diversity*. Cambridge: Cambridge University Press, 2003.
Lewis, M.P., G.F. Simons and C.D. Fennig (eds). *Ethnologue: Languages of the World*, 17th ed. Dallas, Texas: SIL International, 2014. Retrieved 21 July 2014 from http://www.ethnologue.com.
Majumdar, R. *Writing Postcolonial History*. London: Bloomsbury Academic, 2010.
Monnier, R. 'Use and Role of the Concepts of Tyranny and Tyrannicide during the French Revolution', *Contributions to the History of Concepts* 2(1) (2006), 19–41.
Mudimbe, V.-Y. 'Meditations on *Eikones* (Questions on "À Propos un Passe-Vue Conceptuel")', keynote address, ConceptAfrica workshop, Helsinki, 26 May 2011. Retrieved 9 May 2015 from http://www.helsinki.fi/conceptafrica/theory_method_literature/meditations_on_eikones.html.
Nietzsche, F. 'Zur Genealogie der Moral: Eine Streitschrift. Zweite Abhandlung: Schuld, schlechtes Gewissen und Verwandtes', in *Philosophische Werke in sechs Bänden*. Bd. VI. Munich: Carl Hanser, 1980 [1887].
Oliver, R. 'The Problem of the Bantu Expansion', *Journal of African History* 7(3) (1966), 361–76.

Peterson, D.R. *Creative Writing: Translation, Bookkeeping, and the Work of Imagination in Colonial Kenya*. Portsmouth: Heinemann, 2004.

Ranger, T.O. 'Towards a Usable African Past', in C. Fyfe (ed.), *African Studies Since 1945: A Tribute to Basil Davidson*. London: Longman for the Centre of African Studies, Edinburgh, 1976, 17–30.

Richter, M. '*Begriffsgeschichte* and the History of Ideas', *Journal of the History of Ideas* 48(2) (1987), 247–63.

Schoenbrun, D.L. *A Green Place, A Good Place: Agrarian Change, Gender, and Social Identity in the Great Lakes Region to the 15th Century*. Portsmouth: Heinemann, 1998.

Schulz-Forberg, H. (ed.). *A Global Conceptual History of Asia, 1860–1940*. London: Pickering & Chatto, 2014.

Stephens, R. *A History of African Motherhood: The Case of Uganda, 700–1900*. New York: Cambridge University Press, 2013.

Stråth, B. 'Towards a Global Conceptual History', keynote address at National and Transnational Notions of the Social Seminar, Helsinki, 21 August 2008. Retrieved 12 May 2015 from http://www.helsinki.fi/conceptafrica/theory_method_literature/towards_a_global_conceptual_history.html.

Sweetser, E. *From Etymology to Pragmatics: Metaphorical and Cultural Aspects of Semantic Structure*. Cambridge: Cambridge University Press, 1991.

Traugott, E.C. and R.B. Dasher. *Regularity in Semantic Change*. Cambridge: Cambridge University Press, 2001.

Vansina, J. *The Children of Woot*. Madison: University of Wisconsin Press, 1978.

———. *Paths in the Rainforest: Toward a History of Political Tradition in Equatorial Africa*. Madison: University of Wisconsin Press, 1990.

———. *How Societies Are Born: Governance in West Central Africa before 1600*. Charlottesville: University of Virginia Press, 2004.

Wierzbicka, A. 'Translatability and the Scripting of Other Peoples' Souls', *Australian Journal of Anthropology* 24 (2013), 1–21.

CHAPTER 1

'Wealth', 'Poverty' and the Question of Conceptual History in Oral Contexts
Uganda from c. 1000 CE

RHIANNON STEPHENS

'Wealth' and 'poverty' are concepts that appear to be constant. That is, although the quantity of the wealth held by individuals might vary across societies and across time, it remains recognizable. The same is true of poverty, which might, too, reflect varying degrees of abjection. This chapter challenges this perception with reference to Uganda over the past millennium, with a particular focus on Ateker Eastern Nilotic and North Nyanza Bantu languages.[1] It seeks to trace continuities and changes in the concepts of 'wealth' and 'poverty' in diverse linguistic and cultural communities over several centuries to uncover the multiple and dynamic ways in which people in this one small corner of the world have conceived of the 'poor' and 'rich'. A focus on concepts and their history enables us to move beyond the economic determinism of labelling a society as pastoralist, agricultural, mercantilist, etc., and the binary of wealth in people or wealth in things.[2] We can thus see other social aspects that intersect with wealth and its absence, notably, power and gender relations.

In 1974 Terence Ranger addressed the question of producing a 'usable past' for Africans to draw on as they sought to reimagine their futures in the wake of the disappointments of the first decade or so of independence.[3] This move towards a usable past grew out of the critiques of the first wave of writings by professional African historians after the Second World War, notably that African historiography to that point had 'contributed exclusively to cultural nationalism'. 'But, the young radicals object', continued Ranger, 'the poor and hungry cannot *eat* past cultural achievements'.[4] A productive reaction to this criticism, he argued, would focus on the history of poverty to work towards a

---

Notes for this section begin on page 43.

solution for this seemingly intractable problem; a problem, economic historian A.G. Hopkins has argued, that appears to have worsened over the past five decades. In his view, historians have not taken up Ranger's call to focus on poverty, but have instead simply 'taken it off the agenda'.[5] While the extent to which historians have ignored African poverty is subject to debate, it is true that other topics have received considerably more attention. Hopkins lays the blame at the door of postcolonial theory, but paradoxically it may be the dominance of social history that is most responsible. While Ranger saw promise for the study of poverty in the advent of social history, the focus on broader processes of social change (marriage, work, political movements, popular culture, etc.) has instead hidden the poor from direct view.[6]

The twin concepts of 'wealth' and 'poverty' must be a central focus of any consideration of the social and the economic in African history. The degree of access to wealth by members of a society is inextricably linked with that society's economy. But categories of 'rich' and 'poor', of 'wealth' and 'poverty' are rarely, if ever, only about economic status. Rather they remain in a dynamic relationship with the social: social status creates or reinforces economic status and vice versa. And defining who is poor and who wealthy – and the struggles over such work of definition – is as much about the ideological basis for these categories as it as a question of quantification. In this way, 'poor' and 'rich', 'poverty' and 'wealth', become concepts that are contested within and across communities. This is why a conceptual history approach is productive for studying topics that at first glance would seem to be contained within economic history. Ranger realized this long ago: 'An answer to the problem of poverty is not to be found by means of an exclusive concentration upon production history. The study of changing concepts is also very relevant. African history needs to make a connection not only with the material way of life of the people but also with their modes of thought'. Such an approach, he believed, was productive precisely because 'Conceptual history is no longer a business of "Bantu Philosophy" – great schemes of African metaphysics – but of the difficult study of ideas of causation in each region over the past decades'.[7]

This study is interested in more than the past decades. It seeks to trace the evolution of the concepts of 'wealth' and 'poverty' and of 'the wealthy' and 'the poor' over the course of the past millennium. Because the twentieth century was a period of such dramatic changes in economy, in political formations and in transportation (and hence space and time) in East Africa and elsewhere, there is a danger of perceiving it as a fundamental rupture from a static deeper past. By looking beyond the twentieth century, we uncover the ways in which key concepts such as these were contested, as the communities that developed them transformed their economic, political and social institutions long before the violent advent of capitalism, colonialism and Christianity. But, importantly, we also see continuities in concepts that have endured, sometimes from ancient times, although certainly not without change, through the turmoil of the nineteenth and twentieth centuries.[8] Such a time frame requires an adaptation of the methodology of conceptual history, which is heavily focused on literate contexts.

Conceptual History in Oral Societies

Conceptual history is about translation and the shifts in meaning and use that occur in key concepts across time and across languages. We can thus explore the extent to which different communities – separated in space or time or by language – can share common concepts. It is in the lack of one-to-one translations, in the fact that two words in different languages may share one meaning but not others, where we find the rich possibilities of conceptual history. As Bo Stråth has noted, conceptual history focuses on the tension that arises in the simultaneous agreement and disagreement over particular concepts and 'the variety of approaches that emerge out of this point of departure'.[9] It is in the complexity of a concept that history can be found. Friedrich Nietzsche asserted that 'all ideas, in which a whole process is promiscuously comprehended, elude definition; it is only that which has no history, which can be defined'. Nietzsche was writing about 'punishment' and of how it is only by disentangling its various components at an earlier stage in their historical development that it becomes possible to conceive of it historically. It thus becomes possible to recognize that 'the idea of punishment ... is not content with manifesting merely one meaning, but manifests a whole synthesis "of meanings"'.[10] It is productive to extend this analysis to other concepts, including those of 'wealth' and 'poverty' explored here.

Reinhart Koselleck demonstrated the potential of comparative conceptual history in his study of 'crisis', which traced the shifting intellectual history of the term from its medical and juridical application in classical Greece to its political and economic application in revolutionary Europe.[11] He not only showed that the term had changed in meaning and application – a rather unsurprising finding – but how those changes were embedded in and reflective of social, political and economic developments. Indeed, Koselleck noted, the very imprecision of the term 'crisis' in late twentieth-century Europe, 'may itself be viewed as a symptom of a historical crisis that cannot as yet be fully gauged'.[12] This offers us a model of using conceptual history in a comparative context, but one nonetheless firmly grounded in European commonality. As Stråth argued, 'despite the European diversity, our conceptualisation of the political, the economic, the social, the religious, and so on, and the semantic fields which this conceptualisation has built up, in many respects rely on a Greek and Roman origin'.[13] The challenge is to move beyond this rather narrow space and open up a more diverse perspective.

One approach is to look at the introduction of foreign concepts into societies, especially in contexts of colonial conquest. Two recent studies explore the ways in which missionaries and their interlocutors introduced new religious concepts into the languages of the Americas and Africa. Focusing on the role played by Franciscan friars in Yucatán, William Hanks shows how the transcription and description of Maya facilitated conquest through the inscription of Spanish ideas of society, governance and religion into the language itself. Through a process of *reducción* of Maya to grammars and dictionaries, the friars sought to organize the language and introduce new concepts into it, concepts taken up by Maya authors. Despite their foreign origins, these concepts did not take the form of loan words in Maya – borrowed items identifiable as alien – but were rather created through transcription and description, through *reducción*. In this way, the concept of an omnipotent God – one so deeply entrenched in the European colonial project as to be almost impossible to disentangle from it – became part of Maya.[14] Missionaries in Southern Africa also sought to introduce this concept. Paul Landau shows how Christian missionaries took an existing word and gave it this new meaning. The word they chose – *modimo* 'ancestor' – was tied to people's political identity, as well as their lineal one, because they referred to the founder of their polity as their *modimo*. Having taken an existing word and changed the concept it referred to, missionaries claimed the existence of the word proved that people speaking Bantu languages already knew God. In other words, having appropriated the form to describe their concept, missionaries argued that the existence of the form demonstrated the prior existence of the concept. Because they were also the ones who made a *reducción* of the languages by writing grammars and dictionaries, as in Yucatán, they and literate Christian South Africans ensured the new meaning took hold.[15]

These are both cautionary tales for a historian working without contemporary documentation. They underline the mutability of language and the ways in which evidence of change can be submerged from view. For Koselleck, Hanks and Landau, the possibility of tracing change is a result of copious documents produced, in the case of the latter two, by missionaries and their literate converts. Uganda – and its eastern region in particular – is another case altogether. The earliest documents written in Luganda, spoken in the central region, date to the last quarter of the nineteenth century. To the east we find few documents in the languages spoken there before the first quarter of the twentieth century and in some cases they remain sparse. This presents a fundamental challenge to conceptual history: how is it even possible without documentary evidence of changes and continuities in meanings and uses of particular concepts? But to yield in the face of that challenge is, in some sense, to accept Hegel's view that Africa has no history before its encounter with Europe and, to his mind, the advent of literacy. A solution lies in a greater attention to cognitive semantics in historical linguistics. But first, let us pay attention to the societies in question.

Eastern Uganda

Eastern Uganda encompasses a remarkable degree of linguistic diversity (see Map 1.1). Judging by linguistic boundaries (avoiding the arbitrary division of speech communities created by national boundaries), the region stretches from the Nile River in the west to the Nzoia River in the east and from Lake Victoria-Nyanza in the south to Mount Moroto in the north. The terrain shifts from mountains and foothills to dry plains to small hills interspersed by swamps and rivers. Partly due to this ecological variation, it has historically been home to a range of economic activities, including the cultivation of crops, raising livestock, hunting, fishing and gathering wild foods. While often depicted as entirely separate economic systems – practised by 'pastoralists', 'farmers', 'fishers' – in reality communities historically drew on combinations of these. The region has also historically been diverse in its political organization, with polities centred around royal families to others based in chiefly authority and to political activity occurring through age-grade systems or within lineages.

While the region was the focus of several historical studies in the 1960s and 1970s, more recent work has tended to examine contemporary crises, whether the war in Teso in the late 1980s or even more recent violence and

Map 1.1 Linguistic Landscape of Eastern Uganda

social dislocation in Karamoja. Much of the historical work has focused on the important changes of the twentieth century, notably colonial conquest, the dramatic uptake of cash-cropping, the spread of school-based education and Christianity, and the complications of independent Uganda. The earlier historians, interested in what had happened before conquest, worked in the school that sought to legitimize oral traditions as historical sources and write histories of particular peoples, such as 'the Jie' or 'the Teso'.[16] In large part because of the sources and the approach, these histories tended to focus on migration narratives. These narratives are a critical part of the history of the region because it has long formed what has been described as a 'migration corridor', but which might more accurately be described as a 'shatter zone', a place where diverse people have moved into and found themselves living together before sometimes moving on.[17]

There are some fourteen languages spoken in Eastern Uganda. They fall into two main linguistic groups: Great Lakes Bantu and Nilotic. The focus here is on the North Nyanza and Eastern Nilotic languages spoken in the region. By around 1200 CE, people speaking South Kyoga, the ancestral language to Lusoga, Lugwere and Rushana, and descended from North Nyanza, lived in the south-western area of the region. South Kyoga diverged into Lusoga and East Kyoga (or pre-Lugwere) by c. 1500, with the latter spoken to the northeast of its ancestral language. Rushana and Lugwere emerged from East Kyoga in the early nineteenth century, as a result of movement into the foothills of Mount Masaaba following drought and war.[18] Some two thousand years ago, proto-Ateker speakers – a language descended from Eastern Nilotic – settled on the northern edge of Eastern Uganda.[19] Despite this early settlement on its fringe, people speaking Ateker languages only began establishing themselves in the heart of the region from around 1500. People who came to speak Ateso moved into the area somewhat later; they appear to have established homesteads in the region from c. 1600. This gradual movement took place in the form of a series of new settlements back and forth, into new and established lands, over more than two centuries.[20]

For all the number and variety of languages spoken in the region, there have historically been high levels of social and economic interactions between members of different speech communities. Exogamous marriage practices, for example, tend to result in households composed of individuals with different first languages. While it is complicated to reconstruct such patterns historically, the nature of loanwords borrowed between Great Lakes Bantu and Nilotic languages strongly suggests that this is a long-standing phenomenon.[21] A comparative conceptual history that explicitly looks across linguistic divides enables us to uncover the intellectual products of those interactions, rather than viewing speech communities as bounded and coherent and tied to ethnicity.

Semantics, Conceptual History and Tracing Change

Scholars working in Bantu historical linguistics have tended to focus on phonetic changes and, as Axel Fleisch has noted, have tended to ignore 'the fact that meaning as well as form undergoes change'.[22] While historians of the deeper past have drawn on semantic change to trace historical developments, they have not always paid the same attention to the reconstruction of changes in meaning as they have to form. If we are to convincingly move beyond reconstructing past material worlds and into the reconstruction of past cognitive or conceptual worlds, paying close attention to changes in meaning is essential. Schoenbrun's recent turn to conceptual metaphors is one approach that has shown great potential for opening up past intellectual worlds.[23] Diachronic semantics is another productive approach and the one drawn on here.

Dirk Geeraerts's prototype theory in the field of diachronic semantics offers a useful model. Members of a semantic category 'can be graded in terms of their typicality'.[24] For example the category 'bird' encompasses a wide range of meanings, some of which are more typical than others. In English, we would place sparrow, eagle, and even ostrich towards the centre of typicality, and female humans and prisoners more on the periphery. This is as true of apparently simple words, such as bird, as it is of words that describe more complex concepts, such as 'wealth' or 'poverty'. Geeraerts uses prototype theory to explore semantic change because the prototype model is a better reflection of our semantic worlds than any attempt at fixed definition. Prototypicality also provides a model for explaining why meanings change and the ways in which they can change. Speakers can develop 'peripheral nuances within given categories' in response to 'changing cognitive requirements' as well as material and intellectual changes. Because 'marginally deviant concepts can be peripherally incorporated into existing categories', those existing categories can remain stable even as they undergo change.[25] That is, a category can be expanded to include a meaning that is peripheral while holding on to its more central meanings. Over time, a peripheral meaning may become more central, thereby shifting what we think of as the 'meaning' of a word.

How, though, can it be possible, in a context of limited written documentation with a shallow time span to trace changes in the semantic categories of 'poverty' and 'wealth'? Scholars such as Hanks and Landau have benefitted from literary texts contemporary to the period they wrote about. The Eastern Ugandan context does not allow this; some languages have barely been documented at all and others inconsistently and for less than a hundred years. The solution lies in historical linguistics, which enables us to trace words back in time, by first developing a genetic classification of the relevant languages, that is, establishing which languages share a common ancestral or proto-language at one stage remove, two stages remove, and so on. Such genetic classifications rely on phonological, morphological and lexical data in particular. The genetic

Eastern Nilotic
   A. Bari
   B. Tung'a
      i. Lotuko-Maa
         a. Lotuko
         b. Maa
         c. Ongamo
      ii. Ateker
         a. Turkana
         b. Ngakarimojong
         c. Ateso
         d. Toposa

Figure 1.1 Classification of Eastern Nilotic
This draws on both Bender and Ehret.

classification can then be used to reconstruct various elements of those ancestral languages, including the lexicon.

Despite early and misguided efforts to squeeze the Nilotic languages into the racial – not linguistic – classification of Nilo-Hamitic, their coherence is well established and widely accepted.[26] The genetic classifications of the Nilotic languages reflect a three-way split from proto-Nilotic into Western Nilotic, Eastern Nilotic and Southern Nilotic. Eastern Nilotic split in two: Bari and Tung'a, with Tung'a in turn yielding Lotuko-Maa and Ateker (Figure 1.1). The Eastern Nilotic languages spoken in Eastern Uganda are Ngakarimojong and Ateso.[27]

The classification of the Great Lakes Bantu languages spoken in Eastern Uganda (North Nyanza), although not without any controversy, is rather more straightforward. The sub-classification of North Nyanza and its relationship to Great Lakes Bantu is shown below (Figure 1.2). The relevant languages here are Lusoga, Lugwere and Rushana.

With the linguistic classifications in hand, the next stage is to develop the most detailed possible maps of the prototype categories of 'wealth' and 'poverty' for each modern-day language within the area of study and for a number of related languages outside the area, including an emphasis on homonyms and synonyms.[28] This is done by collecting data from speakers of the languages and from published sources, such as dictionaries. It is then possible to use the genetic linguistic classifications to reconstruct inherited forms back to proto-languages, thereby generating a relative chronology for changes in the concepts of 'wealth' and 'poverty'. The relative chronology emerges from innovations and borrowings and the determination of at what stage in the history of these linguistic families they occurred. As Geeraerts highlights, it is essential to trace

Great Lakes Bantu
    A. East Nyanza
    B. Greater Luhyia
    C. Rugungu
    D. Western Lakes
    E. West Nyanza
        I. Rutara
        II. North Nyanza
            a. Luganda
            b. South Kyoga
                i. Lusoga
                ii. East Kyoga
                    α. Lugwere
                    ß. Rushana

Figure 1.2 Sub-classification of North Nyanza within Great Lakes Bantu
Derived from D. Schoenbrun, 'Great Lakes Bantu: Classification and Settlement Chronology', *Sprache und Geschichte in Afrika* 15 (1994): 91–152, and Stephens, *A History of African Motherhood*. Schoenbrun's 'Great Lakes Bantu' builds on Yvonne Bastin's work, which classified many of the languages as Zone J. There has been some criticism of Schoenbrun's classification, although none that affects the North Nyanza branch. See D. Nurse, 'Towards a Historical Classification of East African Bantu Languages', in J.M. Hombert and L.M. Hyman (eds), *Bantu Historical Linguistics: Theoretical and Empirical Perspectives* (Stanford: Center for the Study of Language and Information, 1999), 1–42, and D. Nurse and H. Muzale, 'Tense and Aspect in Lacustrine Bantu Languages', in Hombert and Hyman, *Bantu Historical Linguistics*, 517–44.

essential to trace both the creation or borrowing of new forms and changes in meaning of existing forms.[29] This makes it possible to trace interactions between speakers of different languages and, therefore, processes of translation of the concepts of 'poverty' and 'wealth' between them.

Concepts of 'Wealth' and 'Poverty' in Eastern Nilotic and North Nyanza Bantu

Eastern Nilotic: 'Poverty'

The various glosses for 'wealth' and 'rich person' and for 'poverty' and 'poor person' across the Eastern Nilotic and North Nyanza languages point to a dynamic and complex history with important continuities across long periods of time. One way this is apparent is in the remarkable diversity of words people had to talk about these concepts and the range of associations we can trace for those words. Looking at the Eastern Nilotic languages first, there are at least fourteen separate roots for the English glosses 'poverty' and 'poor person', often among other meanings.[30] In Ateso, there is *ican* 'poverty', *ibakor* 'poverty, misery', and *amule* 'poor woman, unmarried woman staying alone, widow living in solitude', and Ngakarimojong gives *akulyako* 'poverty, abject poverty'. The Eastern Nilotic languages spoken in Kenya offer further roots, such as the adjectives *aisínànì* 'poor', *aiterani* 'lacking in cattle', *okishi* 'poor' and *suuji* 'poor, ugly, dirty, menial' in Maa, along with the noun *ol-kirikoi* 'a man who is not established, has no home, no cows, no women, not necessarily without means but travels around and lives on others'. And in Turkana, there are the nouns *eboot* 'poverty', *ekewan* 'pauper', *ekelipan* 'beggar' and *ekabangibangat* 'pauper', along with the adjective *ejutarit* 'poor'. All but two of these appear to be limited to single languages, reflecting a high degree of innovation in the language for 'poverty' after the emergence of the modern Eastern Nilotic languages. These terms hold a range of meanings, including a lack of people as well as of material goods and point to the contingencies of life cycle dynamics.

In spite of this innovation, there is an important continuity in negative associations with 'poverty' in these languages. This is evident from the one root that has a wide enough distribution to make it possible to reconstruct a proto-form, *-can-,[31] which has cognates in both branches of Tung'a (Ateker and Lotuko-Maa). While there do not appear to be cognates in Bari, the other branch of Eastern Nilotic, there are cognates in the Southern Luo languages of West Nilotic. The distribution of these latter cognates across the Southern Luo languages from Acoli to Dholuo favours inheritance from proto-Nilotic as an explanation. If it is an inherited form from proto-Nilotic, this would suggest the antiquity of the related concepts 'poverty' and 'poor person' among the ancestors of speakers of Nilotic languages, dating back over three thousand years.

That this root, *-can-, appears to be so ancient is particularly striking because of the highly negative connotations that it holds, connotations that come through clearly in its homonyms (see Table 1.1). The root clusters together a number of negative meanings with the meaning 'poverty'. These include meanings that apply to the subject – to the person who is poor. The nouns *ican* in Ateso and *ngican* in Ngakarimojong and Turkana are the most obvious examples of this, with the meanings poverty, trouble, misery, distress, affliction, hardship, suffering, grief, adversity, calamity, grievance, misfortune and torture, although it comes across clearly in other reflexes of the root in all three languages represented here and in the Southern Luo languages. In addition to negative meanings applied to the subject herself, there are also meanings that suggest the person who is poor inflicts negative consequences on others. These include, to trouble, afflict, disturb and annoy, as can be seen with the Ngakarimojong verb *akicanut*. 'Poverty' therefore needs to be understood not only in terms of the physical, social and emotional consequences of poverty

Table 1.1 The root *-can- in Eastern Nilotic languages

Root: *-can-

Ngakarimojong

ŋican, ngican n. trouble, affliction, hardship, suffering, grief, poverty, adversity, calamity
acanaanu n. poverty
akicana v.i. lack, be lacking
akicanut v.tr. trouble, disturb, annoy, molest, afflict, cause to be sad
akisican v.tr. to afflict (ailment), punish

Ateso

ican n. poverty, trouble, misery, distress
ecanit (pl. *ican*) n. poverty
aicanakin v.i. become poor
aitican v.tr. maltreat, punish, torture
aiticanet n. punishment, penalty, inconvenience
aiticanio n. punishment
araut na ican being poor
icana adj. (of person) poor, destitute; (of anything) rare, scarce
itunganan yeni ican, itunganan yeni ican adepar, itunganan yeni ican noi n. poor person
aberu na ican n. poor woman
ikoku yen ican n. poor child

Turkana

ngican n. adversity, grief, grievance, hardship, misery, misfortune, poverty, torture, trouble
akican v.tr. annoy, disturb, grieve, trouble
akisicanakin v.tr. & i. grieve
akicane v.tr. & i. lack
akicanakin v.tr. & i. lack; v.i. trouble
acanakinet n. lack, poverty
akicanut n. poverty
icana (pl. *icanasi*) adj. destitute, miserable, needy, poor
icanana (pl. *icanaka*) adj. disturbing, troublesome

on the poor themselves, but also its social and economic consequences for the community. It is noteworthy, however, that this aspect of the range of meanings associated with poverty does not appear in the Southern Luo languages. Here, then, we can see a historical change whereby speakers of Ateker and Lotuko-Maa languages appear to have developed significantly more negative views of the impact of poor people on the wider community. This is further supported by the fact that it has been possible to identify fourteen separate roots for the concepts 'poverty' and 'poor person' in these languages, whereas only five such roots have been identified in Southern Luo languages, one of which is *-can-. Such growth in vocabulary in Tung'a languages to talk about this condition and those living in it strongly suggests that it was a serious concern for these

Table 1.2 The root *-kuly- in Eastern Nilotic languages

Root: *-kuly-
Ngakarimojong
akulyako n. poverty, abject poverty
akulyakanut n. poverty due to lack of cattle
ekulyakit adj. poor; n. pauper (pl. *ngikulyak*)
ekulyakana n. poor person
Turkana
ekulikit adj. destitute

speech communities. Why precisely this was the case is difficult to reconstruct but may be related to the particular ecologies their linguistic ancestors inhabited before moving into Eastern Uganda over the last five to six centuries.

Ethnographic data give us some insight into why poverty might have been so negatively viewed in these societies, although the evidence is from the twentieth century and so only suggestive. Ivan Karp argued that Iteso men, in particular, sought a balance between the heart (hot) and the head (cool) as part of being an adult. 'When adults achieve the ideal balance between heart and head they are described as "happy" (*elakara*). The happy man is someone who is controlled in his actions but open and sharing with other persons.' 'The happy man', for example, 'eats out of doors [i.e. openly], frequently brews beer for his neighbours, and is willing to cooperate in working parties and share his resources'.[32] A happy man was, therefore, someone who had enough wealth to be in a position to share food, beer and labour. By contrast, a man who ate 'hidden in the rear of his hut, rather than outside where anyone who passes by can share his meal' was negatively viewed as proud and selfish.[33] As others have also noted for Zambia and Malawi, eating alone has long been an important strategy of the poor, or almost poor, as they sought to conserve what little food they had until the next harvest.[34] Among the Iteso, poverty would have prevented a man from fulfilling his socially expected roles of generosity and openness, and happiness would therefore have eluded him.

In addition to this vocabulary for describing poverty and the poor in negative terms, people speaking Eastern Nilotic languages distinguished gradations of poverty. We can see this in the root *-kuly-, which has reflexes in Ngakarimojong and Turkana and so can be posited as an Ateker proto-form (see Table 1.2). The root describes people living in extreme poverty or destitution. This indicates that people speaking Tung'a languages and practising cattle pastoralism, possibly some two thousand years ago, distinguished degrees of poverty. At least for Ngakarimojong speakers in more recent times, this kind of poverty was defined by a lack of cattle. Unless further linguistic evidence can be uncovered in other Ateker languages, it will be almost impossible to establish when this definition came into being. It is nevertheless an important innovation that highlights how wealth and its absence was defined, but also how this was more complicated than simply a lack of cattle. A lack of cattle may have resulted in destitution, but there were other ways to be poor.

North Nyanza: 'Poverty'

Livestock also formed part of the economy for North Nyanza speakers as early as the eighth and ninth centuries CE, nonetheless this speech community measured wealth and its absence in other ways. Looking at the vocabulary that people speaking North Nyanza and its descendants developed to describe and talk about the poor and their condition, we can see a large and diverse set of roots that may well reflect growing economic distinctions between these societies. I have discerned fourteen separate roots for the concepts 'poverty' and 'poor person'. Of these, six are inherited forms. Of those that are unique to a language, we find the noun *mudambi* 'pauper' in Lugwere, and the nouns *obúghafú* 'poverty', *o'wêtaavú* 'being in dire need', and *omúghédhélé* 'very poor person, poor wretch, person in dire need' in Lusoga. There are a number of relevant nouns in Luganda across the Nile to the west and so beyond the geographical focus of this chapter, but of importance due to the close linguistic relationship with Lusoga and Lugwere. These are *òmùbulwa* 'needy, destitute person', *encwampa* 'very poor person', *òmùjega* 'poor, wretched person', and *òmùkuseerè* 'poor, wretched person'. While the North Nyanza languages share with the Ateker languages a plurality of terms to talk about 'poverty' and 'the poor', the emphasis here is on distinguishing gradations of poverty, although the terms are by no means value-free.

The language of 'poverty' used by North Nyanza speakers and their descendants is in part an ancient one, despite more recent innovation resulting in the diversity noted above. The root *-ták- appears in Lugwere and Lusoga where it is used to refer to a poor person or poor people and to the condition of being poor (see Table 1.3). In Lugwere there is a close connection with the older meanings of the verbal form, namely 'want', 'need' and 'like'.[35] Yvonne Bastin and Thilo Schadeberg list *-càk- as a proto-Bantu form with the glosses 'desire, wish; search for'. They also list a variant form *-tàk- 'desire, lack'.[36] This demonstrates a clear recognition by speakers of Lugwere of the relationship between unmet needs and poverty. It also suggests a conceptualization of poverty as a condition in which desires are unfulfilled. By contrast, the Lusoga nouns derived from this root are far more negative. They include the meanings 'miserable person', 'dejected person' and 'degraded person' alongside 'poor person' for *ómútáki*. These negative meanings are mirrored in the abstract noun *bútáki* with two sets of glosses 'deficiency in conduct, manners, money, etiquette' and 'physical, social and spiritual ineptitude'. These extensions in meaning appear to be specific to Lusoga, at least in connection to this root, and so are no older than the sixteenth century and some meanings likely more recent. The very particular connotations of 'spiritual ineptitude' and its

Table 1.3 The root *-ták- in North Nyanza languages

Root: *-ták-
Lugwere
óbútáki n. poverty
ókutakíwálá v.i. to become poor
ókutaká v.i. to want, need, like
ómúntu ómútáki n. poor person
mutaki n. poor person
Lusoga
óbútáki [Lulamoogi only] n. misery, degradation
butaki n. 1. being in need; deficiency in conduct, manners, money, etiquette; 2. physical, social and spiritual ineptitude
ómútáki n. poor person, miserable, dejected, degraded person

relationship to poverty, for example, strongly suggest that this is a development that has occurred since the advent of Christianity to Busoga in the closing years of the nineteenth century.

While the elaboration in meaning for the root *-ták- gives us a glimpse into the ways in which people's conceptualizations of poverty could shift in the face of social and economic change, another equally ancient root is rather more opaque. The root *-(y)olo has also been reconstructed as a proto-Bantu noun with the form *-jódò (cl. 1) and the glosses 'weak; smooth; poor'. Bastin and Schadeberg also note a possible related form, *-bódó (cl. 1) with the gloss 'poor person'.[37] In North Nyanza the root appears in the nouns lukyôlo 'pauper' in Lusoga and òmwôlò 'destitute wretch, very poverty-stricken person' and òbwôlo 'poverty' in Luganda. There is little with reference to this root to provide insight into the concepts of poverty held by their speakers, although the associations with weakness and smoothness in proto-Bantu are intriguing.

North Nyanza speakers also drew on the vocabulary for poverty that their West Nyanza-speaking linguistic ancestors created. We see this in the root *-(w)avu which gives us the nouns omwâvú and obwâvú in Lusoga and òmwávù and òbwávù in Luganda, among other reflexes (Table 1.4). David Schoenbrun has reconstructed the root *-yábu to proto-West Nyanza with the meaning 'poverty by misfortune'.[38] This would make it some 1,500 to 2,000 years old. It is, however, rather difficult to find a continuation of the misfortune aspect in this form of poverty in the Luganda and Lusoga cognates and a survey of proverbs in the two languages yielded only one of very many addressing poverty that suggested misfortune could cause the condition. This is the Lusoga proverb: *Nályavú ow'éirá: yééna atí, 'Omúgandá yándékérá ki?'*, which has a literal translation of 'The person who has been poor since long ago speaks thus, "What did the Muganda leave me with?"'.[39] The proverb, collected only in the late

Table 1.4 The root *-(w)avu in North Nyanza languages

Root: *-(w)avu

Lusoga
obwâvú n. 1. poverty, neediness, being without food/money, destitution, indigence, pauperism; 2. indiscipline of manners, conduct
omwâvú n. pauper, destitute, indigent, needy, undisciplined or deficient person

Luganda
òbwavù n. poverty, destitution
kwàvùwala v.i. become poor
kwavùwaza v.tr. make poor, impoverish
-avù adj. poor, destitute
òmwávù n. poor person

---

twentieth century, references the prolonged period, from the early eighteenth to the late nineteenth century, during which the army of Buganda – and at times militias organized by chiefs – raided the Soga kingdoms to steal food and people.[40] Our ability to know when a proverb such as this originated is very limited, although it is almost certainly not more than two hundred years old. Nonetheless, we can appreciate that being the victim of such violence would surely constitute misfortune, and so the proverb enabled poor people to underscore the factors beyond their control that resulted in their condition. But while the Rutara languages, which form the other branch of West Nyanza languages, make connections with jealousy and thus, most likely, witchcraft, this is not the case in either Luganda or Lusoga, suggesting a different approach to the causes of poverty.

North Nyanza speakers and their linguistic ancestors appear to have connected particular emotions with 'poverty'. The root *-naku can also be reconstructed to proto-West Nyanza again dating it to almost two thousand years ago (Table 1.5). In North Nyanza, between the eighth and twelfth centuries, there was a direct connection drawn through this root between poverty and the negative emotions of grief, distress, anguish, sadness and the states of depression and misery. While the meaning 'poverty' has fallen away in Lugwere, the root retained the meaning of sadness in that language. This is a root that would appear to unproblematically fit into our modern vision of poverty as a condition of neediness and destitution causing suffering, anguish and misery. But there is another set of meanings for this root that disrupts this perception. These are meanings related to time and which can also be reconstructed to proto-West Nyanza. In Lusoga, for instance, olúnakú glosses as 'day' but its plural, énnakú, glosses both as 'days' and 'adversity, suffering, indigent'. This is repeated across the North Nyanza languages, as well as in the Rutara languages where, for example, in Runyankore obunáku glosses as 'time, season; trouble'. This suggests a possible conceptualization of poverty and suffering as

Table 1.5 The root *-naku in North Nyanza languages

Root: *-naku

Lugwere
ókunakúwálá v. feel sad
ólunáku n. day
énáku, nnaku n. days

Lusoga
obúnakú n. neediness, affliction, anguish, destitution, misery, misfortune, depression, grief, sorrow, suffering
énaku, énnakú n. adversity, anguish, depression, misery, grief, hardship, hapless, distress, days
olúnakú n. day

Luganda
-nakù adj. troubled, distressed, poor
ènnakù n. trouble, sorrow, days
òlùnakù n. day

---

related to a cyclical conception of time. Elias Mandala has written powerfully about the need to appreciate Malawian peasants' conceptualization of time as both cyclical and linear in order to understand the history of seasonal hunger in the Tshiri valley of Malawi and its relationship to poverty and episodic famine.[41] While seasonal hunger might have been less urgent in the banana-growing areas of regular rainfall inhabited by speakers of proto-North Nyanza and their descendants, there were nonetheless fluctuations across the year in terms of access to food and droughts could destroy banana groves with devastating effects. Furthermore, their West Nyanza-speaking ancestors, who relied more heavily on grain crops, would have been liable to suffer from scarcity in the months before the new crops could be harvested.

North Nyanza speakers also connected poverty to suffering in the root *-yinik-, but it was suffering of a particular kind. This root is derived from a proto-Bantu verb *-jìn- 'dislike', which shifted meaning in proto-Great Lakes Bantu to 'tease' or 'ridicule'. In the North Nyanza languages the root retains those meanings for the verb -yínà, but extends it to encompass poverty and troubles in the noun obúyiníké. The conceptual framing of poverty in this case is one in which the condition renders a person liable to be the subject of ridicule. This is reflected in Luganda proverbs that suggest that a poor person's inability to dress appropriately for communal events was a matter of shame:

> 'Nze embaga zantama': nga ne ky'ayambala talina
> 'I have tired of celebrations': says the one with nothing to wear
> 'Nze nnakula sizannya': nga ayambadde olukadde (olubugo)
> 'I grew up without dancing': says the one dressed in an old barkcloth

The explications of both of these proverbs note that the purpose was to find an excuse to avoid social situations.[42] The reference to barkcloth in the second proverb suggests it dates at least to the early nineteenth century and likely earlier. The linkage of poverty to harassment and teasing by others, however, created by the noun *obúyiníké* is older than that, perhaps dating to the turn of the millennium.

Gradations of poverty were also marked in the language. We see this in a noun common to the North Nyanza languages, *lúnkupe*, which describes a very poor person. The fact that it appears in identical form in these languages suggests it is an areal form that has spread since the twelfth century, rather than an inherited one. Other words are specific to the individual languages, such as the Lugwere adjective *kidoobi* 'destitute; being extremely poor and unable to provide'. It is in Luganda, however, that we find the greatest number of words to describe the poor and their poverty. This almost certainly reflects the socio-economic disparity that resulted from growing competition for control over the most productive lands, especially those most suited to banana cultivation, a process that started as early as the thirteenth century but became increasingly pronounced after the sixteenth. This struggle to control economic wealth went alongside the centralization of political power and the successful creation of kingdoms ruled by royal families that had an ideology of reproduction at their centre. This served to further sharpen distinctions between those with greater certainty of access to resources and those excluded from accessing them. These processes can be seen reflected in the elaboration of forms of marriage and, in particular, the naming of a form of marriage that resulted from a man working for his father-in-law, rather than paying bridewealth. In the patrilineal context of Buganda this was a stark marker of low social status.[43] The elaborate language developed by Luganda speakers to describe the poor and its overwhelmingly negative associations emerges from this context.

Eastern Nilotic: 'Wealth'

Moving from 'poverty' to the other end of the economic scale, we can trace a number of important developments in the lexicon for 'wealth' developed by speakers both of Eastern Nilotic languages and of North Nyanza languages. In a striking contrast with the terms for 'poverty', there is no Eastern Nilotic term for 'wealth' or 'wealthy person' that I have been able to reconstruct further back than proto-Tung'a (the 'parent' language of proto-Ateker). While one root, *-ker-, would seem to be a candidate for reconstruction to Eastern Nilotic, I have not been able to find attestations in Bari and so cannot posit it as having existed earlier. On the other hand, a strong similarity with the terms for 'poverty' lies in the size and diversity of the vocabulary to talk about the 'rich' and their 'wealth'.

The root *-ker- is of interest both because it would appear to be the oldest root used to form words about 'wealth' and the 'wealthy' in the Eastern Nilotic languages and because of its association with power (see Table 1.6).[44]

Table 1.6 The root *-ker- in Eastern Nilotic languages

Root: *-ker-

Maa
ol-kar n. richness
en-kársísìsho n. riches, wealth, richness
kársís (pl. kársísí) adj. rich, wealthy, affluent, well-to-do
ol-karsis (pl. il-karsis) n. a rich man
en-karsis (pl. in-karsis) n. a rich woman
ekarikon n. leader

Turkana
ekarikon (pl. ngikarikok) n. chief

Ateso
akerianut adj. successful (especially in business)
akerianut n. wealth, prosperity; economy
akerianut v.i. to be rich, skilful (ekeriaka kesi, they are rich; they are skilful)
akerianar v.i. to prosper

To date, I have found cognates in Maa, Turkana and Ateso. These languages belong to both language families descended from Tung'a and are not spoken in geographically adjacent areas. That does not mean that we can definitively rule out borrowing during a more recent period in the linguistic history, but the variation in meaning strongly militates against such an interpretation. There are two sets of meaning for words formed from this root. On the one hand are those that refer to 'wealth', for example, the Maa noun olkar 'richness' and the Ateso verb akerianar 'prosper'. On the other are those that refer to power, for example, the Turkana noun ekarikon 'chief'. If this is an inherited root, as I posit it to be, it suggests that in proto-Tung'a there was an association between wealth and political power, with the meanings narrowing over time. While the gloss 'chief' suggests this may be a recent innovation, the Maa noun glosses as 'leader' pointing to a less specific and likely older reference to political power.

A newer root, *-bar-, innovated by people speaking proto-Ateker perhaps some two thousand years ago, speaks to what constituted 'wealth' in their society (Table 1.7). There is a strong association between 'wealth' and possession of livestock with no clear division in meaning between 'wealth' and livestock. We can see, for example, that in Ateso, the noun for a rich man is ekabaran and the noun for a single head of cattle is ibarasit. Similarly in Turkana the single noun ngibaren holds the meanings 'wealth' and 'cattle'. It would appear, therefore, that the importance of cattle herding to the Ateker economy was directly, and in an uncomplicated manner, connected to distinctions of wealth. While this confirms a widely recognized fact in the literature on the Nilotic-speaking pastoralists of East Africa, it suggests that this happened rather early on in their history.[45]

Table 1.7 The root *-bar- in Eastern Nilotic languages

Root: *-bar-

Ngakarimojong
akabaran (pl. *ngikabarak*) n. wealthy person, rich man
abarit adj. wealthy
abaru n. riches, wealth
ibarasit (pl. *ŋibaren*) n. livestock, riches, good luck (pl. only)
ebarar v.i. be plenty, numerous
akibar, abarun v.i. become wealthy, get rich

Ateso
ekabaran (pl. *ikabarak*) n. rich man, wealthy man
abaran (pl. *abarak*) n. a rich man
ebarit adj. wealthy, rich in livestock, money, etc.
itunganan yeni ebarit, itunganan yeni ebarit adepar, itunganan yeni ebarit noi n. rich person
aberu na abaran n. rich woman
akilokit lo abaran n. rich man
abar n. wealth, treasure
abarit noi n. riches
ibarasit (sing.) n. head of cattle
ibaren (pl.) n. livestock, cattle, cow, goat, sheep etc., as wealth
aitabar v.tr. make rich, wealthy

Turkana
ebarit (pl. *ebarito*) adj. affluent, wealthy, rich
abaran adj. (attributive) affluent
ekabaran n. affluent man
abar(u) n. affluence, prosperity, wealth
ibarasit (pl. *ngibaren*) cattle, livestock
ngibaren n. prosperity
akibar v.i. prosper
ebarit (pl. *ngibarito*) n. prosperity, riches, wealth

A striking contrast to the strong linkage between possession of livestock and being regarded as 'wealthy' among speakers of the Ateker languages is the development by Ateso speakers – and only them – of vocabulary to describe wealth in crops. This vocabulary is derived from a single root, *-mi-*, yielding a range of nouns, verbs and adjectives: *amion* 'one wealthy in food', *amio* 'wealth in food', *aimi* 'be rich in crop products', and *emiyono* '[a person] tending to be wealthy in crops'. Whereas speakers of Ateker languages such as Maa, Ngakarimojong and Turkana continued to centre their economies primarily on livestock herding through the twentieth century – and even when this failed to be the case in practice, it remained ideologically true – speakers of Ateso embraced new economic specializations in Eastern Uganda and Western Kenya.

With a movement towards agricultural production, albeit alongside keeping livestock, we can see important shifts in conceptualizations of what was required to be wealthy. More research on dialects is required to come to any conclusions about when this linguistic change may have occurred, but it must have been in the past five hundred years.

While the basis of 'wealth' might change, there was conceptual continuity in what it could facilitate in terms of access to power. We saw, with reference to the root *-ker- above, that an association between 'wealth' and political power appears to date to the time when proto-Tung'a was spoken. That association remained strong in the Ateker languages, most notably in Turkana and Ngakarimojong. We can see it, for instance, in the root *-polo- which yields *apoloor* 'to prosper' in Ngakarimojong and the nouns *akapolon* 'chief' and *apolou* 'honour' in Turkana. We can also see it in the following related set of nouns, adjectives and verbs in Ngakarimojong and Turkana: *ejakaana* 'wealth, rich', *ejakait* 'chief', *ajakaanut* 'wealth', and *ajakanut* 'chieftaincy' in the former, and *ejok* 'rich' in the latter. The particular nature of power and its expression would have changed significantly over time, yet it is evident that, for speakers of these languages, those with wealth had access to power and, almost certainly, those with power had access to wealth. This association, perhaps obviously, was not limited to speakers of Eastern Nilotic or even Nilotic languages, but has parallels in Bantu languages all the way back to proto-Bantu and the root *-kúm-* 'be honoured; be rich' with the derived forms: *-kúmú* (cl. 1a) 'chief; medicine-man; rich person' and *-kúmú* (cl. 14) 'authority, kingship'.[46]

North Nyanza: 'Wealth'

This close linkage of 'wealth' and power continued into Great Lakes Bantu languages, such as proto-Forest and the root *-gale* or *-gala* (cl. 1) 'rich person, leader'.[47] But although for more recent times there is no shortage of evidence to show the wealth of chiefs and kings in the North Nyanza communities, the linguistic evidence does not reflect a conceptual linkage of the two. The only root for 'wealth' or 'wealthy person' that can be reconstructed to proto-North Nyanza is *-gaiga-* (Table 1.8). In the modern North Nyanza languages this yields a large number of nouns, verbs and adjectives, such as *óbugáigá* 'riches' in Lugwere, *-gaigaghala* 'get wealthy' in Lusoga, and *òmùgággà* 'rich person' in Luganda. There is no indication in these words of the basis or form of wealth they refer to or any suggestion of power deriving from wealth.

It is only in Lusoga, and so dating to the sixteenth century at the very earliest, that there is any real insight into the meaning and form of 'wealth' from the lexical data. The Lusoga cognate *omúgaigá*, for example, is glossed as 'rich man with many wives', and the same gloss is given for *omúkombé*, *omúfuní* and *ómulokí*. That the meaning is common to all but two of the Lusoga nouns for 'rich person' suggests two things. First, at some point after Lusoga emerged as a distinct language, its speakers began to talk of 'wealth' in gendered, and

Table 1.8 The root *-gaiga in North Nyanza languages

Root: *-gaiga-

Lugwere
óbugáigá n. riches
ókugaigáwála v.i. become rich
ómúntu ómugáigá n. rich person
mugaiga n. rich person

Lusoga
obúgaigá n. affluence, luxury, wealth, fortune, endowment, capital, riches
-gaiga adj. wealthy, rich
bugaiga bwa kitalo n. immense wealth
kugaigaghala v.tr. get wealthy
omúgaigá n. rich man with many wives; affluent person, magnate

Luganda
obugággà n. wealth, riches
bya bugagga n. riches, wealth
-gággà adj. rich
kugággàwala v.i. become rich
kugággàwaza v.tr. make rich, wealthy
òmùgággà n. rich person

specifically male, terms. Second, the way wealth was demonstrated, consolidated and increased was through polygynous marriage. This is further supported by the use of the colloquial phrase omúsaadhá byágí to refer to a 'rich man' when it has the literal meaning of 'man of granaries'. Each wife in a homestead would have her own granary, so a man with many granaries had wealth in the form of grain in the granaries and in the form of wives whose labour helped produce that grain.

In Luganda alone and with the noun òmùvundu can we see a specifically negative association with 'wealth'. This noun for a very wealthy person is derived from the intransitive verb -vunda 'rot, go bad'. Otherwise, across the North Nyanza languages the language used to describe wealth is generally value-neutral. But that is not to say that the relationship between rich and poor in these societies was not heavily freighted. Another proverb from Luganda gives us insight into that relationship: Akuwa okulya: y'akutwala omuluka 'The one who feeds you: makes you a client'.[48] Here we can see the oral literature presenting a social norm in which the materially wealthy took advantage of their situation to increase their wealth in people and, therefore, their power. That this was the case in Buganda with its highly differentiated society, from at least the seventeenth century, fits well with our knowledge of relations of power and of patrons and clients in the wider region.[49] Nonetheless, the fact that we can see associations in the linguistic evidence for Eastern Nilotic languages that make direct connections between power and wealth and that it is also apparently possible to reconstruct that connection back to proto-Bantu strongly indicates that this tension between 'rich' and 'poor' is both significantly older than the period of political centralization in Buganda and far more widespread, including in substantially less stratified societies.

Conclusion

Historians of Africa are increasingly studying poverty, whether its intersection with warfare or famine or the science of studying poverty.[50] Historians and anthropologists have shown how entering into poverty could threaten – or change entirely – a person's social and ethnic identity.[51] But while we have, for example, rich descriptions of exchange economies and of value in Luo society in Parker Shipton's work,[52] we know all too little about how people in different societies conceptualized 'poverty' and 'wealth' before the twentieth century and, especially, how such conceptualizations were contested. We are left with theoretical models, such as that of 'wealth in people', which offer valuable insight, but lack nuance when applied as universals.[53] This chapter has shown how the notion of 'wealth in people' was one of the meanings of 'wealth' in Eastern Uganda, in particular in Busoga since the sixteenth century. But it coexisted with a host of other meanings. Its absence in all but one of the languages focused on here shows the variation in people's and societies' concepts of 'wealth'. An examination of the ways in which modern communities and their linguistic ancestors in Eastern Uganda have conceived of the economic binary of 'wealth' and 'poverty' enables us to think more carefully about the dynamic relationships between the longer social, economic, and cultural histories of different groups in particular places.

The apparent tensions between 'rich' and 'poor' in societies that used to be described as acephalous or segmentary highlight the potential of conceptual history even in the absence of extensive documentation. The strong – and, in some cases, ancient – associations of 'wealth' and power and of 'poverty' and social unease foreground those tensions in particular ways. But the concepts explored here also highlight the potential benefits to the entire society of having wealthy members who might share food at meals or support a less fortunate person through the institution of clientship. They point to other tensions too, such as the gendering of the wealthy as male through valuing wealth in cattle or wives, above other forms. The kind of history produced in this way is one that explores social ideals, not the reality of daily life. But the changing definitions of who constituted the poor or the wealthy and how they came to be so were the products of changing political, economic and social realities. While we cannot achieve the same rich and fine-grained history of concepts that is possible for more recent times with better documentation (as in other chapters in this volume), the marked changes in the concepts discussed here are the product of contestations between members of these communities. A conceptual history approach enables us to uncover some of the intellectual work that has shaped the ways in which people have understood, and so have responded, to the rich and to the poor in their societies.

Notes

This chapter benefited from feedback at the African Studies Association Annual Meeting, Makerere Institute for Social Research, Princeton University's Fung Global Fellows Program and the Columbia University Seminar Studies on Contemporary Africa. Funding for the research was provided by the Department of History and the Summer Grant Program in the Social Sciences at Columbia University and the research was conducted with the approval of the Uganda National Council for Science and Technology.

1. In so doing I draw on debates over the definition of poverty. For an overview of these debates, see S. Beaudoin, *Poverty in World History* (Oxford: Routledge, 2007), 1–14.
2. See J.I. Guyer, 'Wealth in People, Wealth in Things – Introduction', *Journal of African History* 36(1) (1995): 83–90.
3. His revised conference presentation was published as T.O. Ranger, 'Towards a Usable African Past', in C. Fyfe (ed.), *African Studies Since 1945: A Tribute to Basil Davidson* (London: Longman, 1976), 17–30.
4. Ranger, 'Towards a Usable African Past', 22. Emphasis original.
5. A.G. Hopkins, 'The New Economic History of Africa', *Journal of African History* 50(2) (2009), 157.
6. Ranger, 'Towards a Usable African Past', 26–27.
7. Ranger, 'Towards a Usable African Past', 26.
8. Although heavily focused on the late twentieth century, Parker Shipton's work on entrustment in Western Kenya is illustrative of the potential of such a project as this: *The Nature of Entrustment: Intimacy, Exchange, and the Sacred in Africa* (New Haven: Yale University Press, 2007).
9. B. Stråth, 'Towards a Global Conceptual History', National and Transnational Notions of the Social, Helsinki: University of Helsinki, 21 August 2008.
10. F. Nietzsche, 'Second Essay: Guilt – Bad Conscience – And the Like', in *The Genealogy of Morals*, trans. H.B. Samuel (New York: Boni and Liveright, 1918), 70.
11. R. Koselleck, 'Crisis', trans. M.W. Richter, *Journal of the History of Ideas* 67(2) (2006), 357–400.
12. Koselleck, 'Crisis', 399.
13. Stråth, 'Towards a Global Conceptual History'.
14. W. Hanks, *Converting Words: Maya in the Age of the Cross* (Berkeley: University of California Press, 2010).
15. P. Landau, *Popular Politics in the History of South Africa, 1400–1948* (Cambridge: Cambridge University Press, 2010). See also W. Worger, 'Parsing God: Conversations about the Meaning of Words and Metaphors in Nineteenth-Century South Africa', *Journal of African History* 42(3) (2001), 417–47.
16. J. Lamphear, *The Traditional History of the Jie of Uganda* (Oxford: Oxford University Press, 1976); J.B. Webster et al., *The Iteso during the Asonya* (Nairobi: East African Publishing House, 1973).
17. I take the term shatter zone from J. Scott, *The Art of Not Being Governed: An Anarchist History of Upland Southeast Asia* (New Haven: Yale University Press, 2009), 7. But J. Vincent used it earlier in *Teso in Transformation: The Political Economy of Peasant and Class in Eastern Africa* (Berkeley: University of California Press, 1982), 64.

18. R. Stephens, *A History of African Motherhood: The Case of Uganda, 700–1900* (New York: Cambridge University Press, 2013), 34, 149.

19. R. Vossen, *The Eastern Nilotes: Linguistic and Historical Reconstructions* (Berlin: Dietrich Reimer, 1982), 472. Proto-Ateker is also referred to as proto-Teso-Turkana. See also C. Ehret, *Southern Nilotic History: Linguistic Approaches to the Study of the Past* (Evanston: Northwestern University Press, 1971).

20. J.B. Webster, 'The Karionga: The Westward Migration of the Ateker', in J.B. Webster et al., *The Iteso During the Asonya* (Nairobi: East African Publishing House, 1973), 11.

21. Stephens, *A History of African Motherhood*, e.g. 130–32.

22. A. Fleisch, 'The Reconstruction of Lexical Semantics in Bantu', in D. Ibriszimow (ed.), *Problems of Linguistic-Historical Reconstruction in Africa*, Sprache und Geschichte in Afrika 19 (Cologne: Rüdiger Köppe, 2008), 79.

23. D. Schoenbrun, 'Mixing, Moving, Making, Meaning: Possible Futures for the Distant Past', *African Archaeological Review* 29(2) (2012): 293–317.

24. W. O'Grady, M. Dobrovolsky and F. Katamba (eds), *Contemporary Linguistics: An Introduction*, 3rd ed. (London: Longman, 1996), 276.

25. D. Geeraerts, *Diachronic Prototype Semantics: A Contribution to Historical Lexicology* (Oxford: Clarendon Press, 1997), 15.

26. M.L. Bender, *The Nilo-Saharan Languages* (Munich: Lincom Europa, 1996); C. Ehret, *A Historical-Comparative Reconstruction of Nilo-Saharan* (Cologne: Rüdiger Köppe, 2001); J.H. Greenberg, 'Studies in African Linguistic Classification: V. The Eastern Sudanic Family', *Southwestern Journal of Anthropology* 6 (1950), 143–60. See C. Meinhof, *Die Sprachen der Hamiten* (Hamburg: L. Friederichsen, 1912) for a linguistic classification along racial lines. Bender and Ehret have classified Nilotic under Nilo-Saharan. Not all linguists agree with this, with others viewing Nilotic as an independent phylum, e.g. H. Hammarström et al. (eds), *Glottolog 2.4* (Leipzig: Max Planck Institute for Evolutionary Anthropology, 2015).

27. Bender, *The Nilo-Saharan Languages*, 25–37; Ehret, *A Historical-Comparative Reconstruction of Nilo-Saharan*, 70–71. Bender prefers non-geographical nomenclature, using E9b for Eastern Nilotic.

28. This method is similar in scope to the comprehensive approach of D. Schoenbrun in *The Historical Reconstruction of Great Lakes Bantu Cultural Vocabulary: Etymologies and Distributions* (Cologne: Rüdiger Köppe, 1997).

29. Geeraerts, *Diachronic Prototype Semantics*, 94–95.

30. The sources for all language data are listed in the references.

31. The asterisk denotes that this is a posited reconstructed form and not an attested one.

32. I. Karp, 'Morality and Ethical Values According to the Iteso of Kenya', in H.G. De Soto (ed.), *Culture and Contradiction: Dialectics of Wealth, Power, and Symbol* (San Francisco: EMTexts, 1992), 330.

33. Karp, 'Morality and Ethical Values According to the Iteso of Kenya', 331.

34. L. Cliggett, *Grains from Grass: Aging, Gender, and Famine in Rural Africa* (Ithaca: Cornell University Press, 2005); E.C. Mandala, *The End of Chidyerano: A History of Food and Everyday Life in Malawi, 1860–2004* (Portsmouth: Heinemann, 2005).

35. A similar semantic overlapping has occurred in English between 'want, need, desire'. See for example, A.L. Sihler, *Language History: An Introduction* (Philadelphia: John Benjamins, 2000), 118.

36. Y. Bastin and T. Schadeberg, 'Bantu Lexical Reconstructions 3' (Tervuren: Royal Museum for Central Africa, 2002, updated 2005), Main 418; Var 9606.

37. Bastin and Schadeberg, 'Bantu Lexical Reconstructions 3', Main 6938; (no label) 6924.

38. Schoenbrun, *The Historical Reconstruction of Great Lakes Bantu Cultural Vocabulary*, 245–46, no. 375.

39. *Ensambo edh'Abasoga dhakolebwa aba Cultural Research Centre Diocese of Jinja*, vol. 2 (Jinja: Cultural Research Centre, 2000), 67, no. 748. My translation from the Lusoga, which differs slightly from that offered in the volume.

40. For discussions of this period in Busoga-Buganda relations, see D.W. Cohen, *Womunafu's Bunafu: An African Community in the Nineteenth Century* (Princeton: Princeton University Press, 1977); H. Médard, *Le royaume du Buganda au XIXe siècle: Mutations politiques et religieuses d'un ancient État d'Afrique de l'Est* (Paris: Karthala, 2007); and R. Reid, *Political Power in Pre-Colonial Buganda: Economy, Society and Warfare in the Nineteenth Century* (Oxford: James Currey, 2002).

41. Mandala, *The End of Chidyerano*, especially 14–21.

42. F. Walser, *Luganda Proverbs* (Berlin: Dietrich Reimer, 1982), 304, no. 3392; 305, no. 3396. My translations vary slightly from those offered by Walser.

43. See Stephens, *A History of African Motherhood*, especially Chapter 3.

44. R. Vossen notes that 'languages of the MAA Group occasionally have a in place of ɛ~e'. The most plausible reconstruction of the root is thus the one offered (*The Eastern Nilotes*, 339).

45. See for example, D.M. Anderson and V. Broch-Due (eds), *The Poor Are Not Us: Poverty and Pastoralism in Eastern Africa* (Oxford: James Currey, 2000).

46. Bastin and Schadeberg, 'Bantu Lexical Reconstructions 3', Main 2113, DER 2118 and DER 3746.

47. Schoenbrun, *The Historical Reconstruction of Great Lakes Bantu Cultural Vocabulary*, 117–18, no. 170.

48. Walser, *Luganda Proverbs*, 30, no. 326. My translation, which differs slightly from Walser's.

49. For a somewhat later period, see C. Newbury, *The Cohesion of Oppression: Clientship and Ethnicity in Rwanda, 1860–1960* (New York: Columbia University Press, 1988).

50. See for example, V. Bonnecase, *La pauvreté au Sahel: du savoir colonial à la mesure internationale* (Paris: Karthala, 2011); C. Crais, *Poverty, War, and Violence in South Africa* (New York: Cambridge University Press, 2011); G. Davie, *Poverty Knowledge in South Africa: A Social History of Human Science, 1855–2005* (New York: Cambridge University Press, 2015); J. Kuhanen, *Poverty, Health and Reproduction in Early Colonial Uganda* (Joensuu: University of Joensuu, 2005); all of which follow in the footsteps of J. Iliffe, *The African Poor: A History* (Cambridge: Cambridge University Press, 1987).

51. Anderson and Broch-Due *The Poor Are Not Us*; T. Spear, '"Being Maasai", But Not "People of Cattle": Arusha Agricultural Maasai in the Nineteenth Century', in T. Spear and R. Waller (eds), *Being Maasai: Ethnicity & Identity in East Africa* (Oxford: James Currey, 1993), 120–36.

52. Shipton, *The Nature of Entrustment*.

53. And of course, the authors of this model didn't make such a claim, but it has become something of a truism in African history. S. Miers and I. Kopytoff (eds), *Slavery in Africa: Historical and Anthropological Perspectives* (Madison: University of Wisconsin Press, 1977); Guyer, 'Wealth in People, Wealth in Things'.

References for Language Data

Interviews and Personal Correspondence

Hihubbi Adam, Stephen Akabway, Gesa Aristarchus, Kasango Banuli, Jimmie Eribu, Gudoi Esau, Adyango Freda, Helen Kagino, Pamela Khanakwa, Joy Kisule, John Kunena, Samuel Luvunya, Masai Moses, Henry Aloysius Mafwabi, Samuel Mubbala, Peter Muloit, Laury Ocen, Robert Osega, Ephraim Talyambiri, Timothy Wangusa

Published Sources

Adong, J. and J. Lakareber. *Lwo-English Dictionary*. Kampala: Fountain Publishers, 2009.
Barrett, A.N. *English-Turkana Dictionary*. Nairobi: Macmillan Kenya, 1988.
Boot-Siertsema, B. *Masabe Word List: English-Masaba, Masaba-English*. Tervuren: Royal Museum for Central Africa, 1981.

Bukenya, A. and L. Kamoga. *Standard Luganda-English Dictionary*. Kampala: Fountain Publishers, 2009.
Tapsubei Creider, J. and C.A. Creider. *A Dictionary of the Nandi Language*. Cologne: Rüdiger Köppe, 2001.
Dictionary: Lusoga-English English-Lusoga. Jinja: Cultural Research Centre, Diocese of Jinja, 2000.
Dimmendaal, G.J. *The Turkana Language*. Dordrecht: Foris Publications, 1983.
Gulere, C.W. *Lusoga-English Dictionary*. Kampala: Fountain Publishers, 2009.
Guthrie, M. *Comparative Bantu: An Introduction to the Comparative Linguistics and Prehistory of the Bantu Languages*. Farnborough: Gregg, 1967-1971.
Hilders, J.H. and J.C.D. Lawrance. *An English-Ateso and Ateso-English Vocabulary*. Nairobi: Eagle Press, 1958.
Johnson, F. *A Standard Swahili-English Dictionary*. Dar es Salaam: Oxford University Press, 1939, reprint. 1996.
Kagaya, R. *A Gwere Vocabulary*. Tokyo: Research Institute for Languages and Cultures of Asia and Africa, 2006.
Kiingi, K.B. *Enkuluze y'Oluganda ey'e Makerere*. Kampala: Fountain Publishers, 2007.
Loyola, A.I. *Bi-lingual Ateso Dictionary*. Entebbe: Marianum Press, 2007.
Mol, F. *Maa: A Dictionary of the Maasai Language and Folklore English-Maasai*. Nairobi: Marketing and Publishing, Ltd., 1978.
Nabirye, M. *Eiwanika Ly'Olusoga*. Kampala: Menha Publishers, 2009.
Nakarimojoŋ-English and English-Nakarimojoŋ Dictionary. Verona: Comboni Missionaries – Verona Fathers, 1985.
Noonan, M. *A Grammar of Lango*. Berlin: Mouton de Gruyter, 1992.
Nzogi, R. and M. Diprose. *EKideero ky'oLugwere Lugwere Dictionary: Lugwere-English with English Index*. Budaka: Lugwere Bible Translation and Literacy Association with SIL International, 2011.
Odonga, A. *Lwo-English Dictionary*. Kampala: Fountain Publishers, 2005.
Oketcho, P. *Dero ma Dhopadhola*. Cape Town: Centre for Advanced African Studies, 2010.
Okonye, G. *Lango-English Dictionary*. Kampala: Fountain Publishers, 2012.
Ongodia, S.P. and A. Ejiet. *Ateso-English Dictionary*. Kampala: Fountain Publishers, 2008.
Orchardson, I.Q. *Kipsigis*, edited by A.T. Matson. Nairobi: Eagle Press, 1961.
Rottland, F. *Die Südnilotischen Sprachen: Beschreibung, Vergleichung und Rekonstuktion*. Berlin: Dietrich Reimer, 1982.
Snoxall, R.A. *Luganda-English Dictionary*. Oxford: Clarendon Press, 1967.
Tucker, A.N. and J.T.O. Mpaayei. *A Maasai Grammar with Vocabulary*. London: Longmans, Green and Co., 1955.

References Cited

Anderson, D.M. and V. Broch-Due (eds). *The Poor Are Not Us: Poverty and Pastoralism in Eastern Africa*. Oxford: James Currey, 2000.
Bastin, Y. and T.L. Schadeberg. 'Bantu Lexical Reconstructions 3', Tervuren, Belgium: Royal Museum for Central Africa, 2002, updated 2005. http://www.africamuseum.be/collections/browsecollections/humansciences/blr.
Beaudoin, S. *Poverty in World History*. Oxford: Routledge, 2007.
Bender, M.L. *The Nilo-Saharan Languages*. Munich: Lincom Europa, 1996.
Bonnecase, V. *La pauvreté au Sahel: du savoir colonial à la mesure internationale*. Paris: Karthala, 2011.
Cliggett, L. *Grains from Grass: Aging, Gender, and Famine in Rural Africa*. Ithaca: Cornell University Press, 2005.
Cohen, D.W. *Womunafu's Bunafu: An African Community in the Nineteenth Century*. Princeton: Princeton University Press, 1977.

Crais, C. *Poverty, War, and Violence in South Africa*. New York: Cambridge University Press, 2011.
Davie, G. *Poverty Knowledge in South Africa: A Social History of Human Science, 1855–2005*. New York: Cambridge University Press, 2015.
Ehret, C. *Southern Nilotic History: Linguistic Approaches to the Study of the Past*. Evanston: Northwestern University Press, 1971.
———. *A Historical-Comparative Reconstruction of Nilo-Saharan*. Cologne: Rüdiger Köppe, 2001.
Ensambo edh'Abasoga, vol. 2. Jinja: Cultural Research Centre, Diocese of Jinja, 2000.
Fleisch, A. 'The Reconstruction of Lexical Semantics in Bantu', in D. Ibriszimow (ed.), *Problems of Linguistic-Historical Reconstruction in Africa*, Sprache und Geschichte in Afrika, 19. Cologne: Rüdiger Köppe, 2008.
Geeraerts, D. *Diachronic Prototype Semantics: A Contribution to Historical Lexicology*. Oxford: Clarendon Press, 1997.
Greenberg, J.H. 'Studies in African Linguistic Classification: V. The Eastern Sudanic Family', *Southwestern Journal of Anthropology* 6 (1950): 143–60.
Guyer, J.I. 'Wealth in People, Wealth in Things – Introduction'. *Journal of African History* 36(1) (1995): 83–90.
Hammarström, H. et al. (eds). *Glottolog 2.4*, Leipzig: Max Planck Institute for Evolutionary Anthropology, 2015. Retrieved 13 May 2015 from http://glottolog.org/glottolog/family.
Hanks, W. *Converting Words: Maya in the Age of the Cross*. Berkeley: University of California Press, 2010.
Hopkins, A.G. 'The New Economic History of Africa'. *Journal of African History* 50(2) (2009): 155–77.
Iliffe, J. *The African Poor: A History*. Cambridge: Cambridge University Press, 1987.
Karp, I. 'Morality and Ethical Values According to the Iteso of Kenya', in H.G. De Soto (ed.), *Culture and Contradiction: Dialectics of Wealth, Power, and Symbol*. San Francisco: EMTexts, 1992.
Koselleck, R. 'Crisis', trans. M.W. Richter. *Journal of the History of Ideas* 67(2) (2006): 357–400.
Kuhanen, J. *Poverty, Health and Reproduction in Early Colonial Uganda*. Joensuu: University of Joensuu, 2005.
Lamphear, J. *The Traditional History of the Jie of Uganda*. Oxford: Oxford University Press, 1976.
Landau, P. *Popular Politics in the History of South Africa, 1400–1948*. Cambridge: Cambridge University Press, 2010.
Mandala, E.C. *The End of Chidyerano: A History of Food and Everyday Life in Malawi, 1860–2004*. Portsmouth: Heinemann, 2005.
Médard, H. *Le royaume du Buganda au XIXe siècle: Mutations politiques et religieuses d'un ancient État d'Afrique de l'Est*. Paris: Karthala, 2007.
Meinhof, C. *Die Sprachen der Hamiten*. Hamburg: L. Friederichsen, 1912.
Miers, S. and I. Kopytoff (eds). *Slavery in Africa: Historical and Anthropological Perspectives*. Madison: University of Wisconsin Press, 1977.
Newbury, C. *The Cohesion of Oppression: Clientship and Ethnicity in Rwanda, 1860–1960*. New York: Columbia University Press, 1988.
Nietzsche, F. 'Second Essay: Guilt – Bad Conscience – And the Like'. in *The Genealogy of Morals*, trans. H.B. Samuel. New York: Boni and Liveright, 1918, 40–93. Retrieved 29 April 2013 from http://solomon.tinyurl.alexanderstreet.com/ZX4Q.
Nurse, D. 'Towards a Historical Classification of East African Bantu Languages', in J.M. Hombert and L.M. Hyman (eds), *Bantu Historical Linguistics: Theoretical and Empirical Perspectives*. Stanford: Center for the Study of Language and Information, 1999, 1–42.
Nurse, D. and H. Muzale. 'Tense and Aspect in Lacustrine Bantu Languages', in J.M. Hombert and L.M. Hyman (eds), *Bantu Historical Linguistics: Theoretical and Empirical Perspectives*. Stanford: Center for the Study of Language and Information, 1999, 517–44.
O'Grady, W., M. Dobrovolsky and F. Katamba (eds). *Contemporary Linguistics: An Introduction*, 3rd ed. London: Longman, 1996.

Ranger, T.O. 'Towards a Usable African Past', in C. Fyfe (ed.), *African Studies Since 1945: A Tribute to Basil Davidson*. London: Longman for the Centre of African Studies, Edinburgh, 1976, 17–30.

Reid, R. *Political Power in Pre-Colonial Buganda: Economy, Society and Warfare in the Nineteenth Century*. Oxford: James Currey, 2002.

Schoenbrun, D.L. 'Great Lakes Bantu: Classification and Settlement Chronology', *Sprache und Geschichte in Afrika* 15 (1994): 91–152.

———. *The Historical Reconstruction of Great Lakes Bantu Cultural Vocabulary: Etymologies and Distributions*. Cologne: Rüdiger Köppe, 1997.

———. 'Mixing, Moving, Making, Meaning: Possible Futures for the Distant Past'. *African Archaeological Review* 29(2) (2012): 293–317.

Scott, J. *The Art of Not Being Governed: An Anarchist History of Upland Southeast Asia*. New Haven: Yale University Press, 2009.

Shipton, P. *The Nature of Entrustment: Intimacy, Exchange, and the Sacred in Africa*. New Haven: Yale University Press, 2007.

Sihler, A.L. *Language History: An Introduction*. Philadelphia: John Benjamins, 2000.

Spear, T. '"Being Maasai", But Not "People of Cattle": Arusha Agricultural Maasai in the Nineteenth Century', in T. Spear and R. Waller (eds), *Being Maasai: Ethnicity & Identity in East Africa*. Oxford: James Currey, 1993, 120–36.

Stephens, R. *A History of African Motherhood: The Case of Uganda, 700–1900*. New York: Cambridge University Press, 2013.

Stråth, B. 'Towards a Global Conceptual History', National and Transnational Notions of the Social, Helsinki, 21 August 2008. Helsinki: University of Helsinki. Retrieved 27 September 2013 from http://www.helsinki.fi/conceptafrica/theory_method_literature/towards_a_global_conceptual_history.html.

Vincent, J. *Teso in Transformation: The Political Economy of Peasant and Class in Eastern Africa*. Berkeley: University of California Press, 1982.

Vossen, R. *The Eastern Nilotes: Linguistic and Historical Reconstructions*. Berlin: Dietrich Reimer, 1982.

Walser, F. *Luganda Proverbs*. Berlin: Dietrich Reimer, 1982.

Webster, J.B. 'The Karionga: The Westward Migration of the Ateker', in J.B. Webster et al., *The Iteso During the Asonya*. Nairobi: East African Publishing House, 1973, 1–19.

Webster, J.B. et al. *The Iteso during the Asonya*. Nairobi: East African Publishing House, 1973.

Worger, W. 'Parsing God: Conversations about the Meaning of Words and Metaphors in Nineteenth-Century South Africa', *Journal of African History* 42(3) (2001): 417–47.

Rhiannon Stephens is an assistant professor of African history at Columbia University. Her work focuses on the longue durée history of East Africa, with a particular focus on Uganda. She is the author of *A History of African Motherhood: The Case of Uganda, 700–1900* (Cambridge University Press, 2013) and has published in the *Journal of African History* and *Past and Present*. Her current research is on people's conceptualizations of wealth and poverty in Eastern Uganda over the past millennium.

CHAPTER 2

Conceptual Continuities

About 'Work' in Nguni

AXEL FLEISCH

The Nguni languages isiXhosa and (South African) isiNdebele each have two items in their lexical inventory that refer to 'work': *ukusebenza* and *ukuphangela* in isiXhosa, and *ukusebenza* and *ukuberega* in isiNdebele. Why do these languages have competing words for work? And why, despite their fairly close linguistic relationship, do they have different words? One could argue that these lexicographic details are simply arbitrary labels, and ultimately only interesting to the historical linguist. Yet these contrasts are not just philological quibbling, but a significant pointer to the historical conditions of the respective speaker communities. Specific notions of 'work' in the Nguni language family have shaped the ways in which their speakers dealt with the economic constellations that resulted from colonial advances in South Africa. This chapter explains significant historical differences among Nguni-speaking communities with regard to their encounter with the expanding colonial labour system in the nineteenth century on the basis of linguistic data.

    The magnitude of those events makes it appear as if there was no continuity in conceptual understandings – a clear before and after. In economic terms, this rupture would be marked by the ending of sustainable subsistence economies and rise of the dominant model of migrant labour. But to what extent is this really true? The effects that these changing economic and political conditions had on social and economic traditions among Nguni speakers (and in fact most other African people in the region) were undoubtedly profound. It would still be inadequate to view this moment in South African history as one of total closure of traditional life and of modernity setting in all at once.

Notes for this section begin on page 65.

The semantic history of work-related concepts in Nguni is a good illustration that this was indeed not the case.

Linguistic inventories are a particularly suitable place to look to in order to get a better grasp of this. Lexical word meaning is constantly re-enacted and thereby reflects the non-linguistic real-life conditions of speaker communities. At the same time, it is highly conventionalized and serves as a structuring device for experienced reality and a tool for people to make sense of the world around them. The coexistence of constant renegotiation of meaning and 'semantic inertia' implies that linguistic data as a source for historical research entails a significance for different temporal scales and granularity, although each data point (reconstructed lexical item, recorded utterance, written statement, etc.) stems from a given moment in time. Its theoretical analogue in Koselleckian conceptual history is the coeval character of processes and ideas whose historical significance goes beyond plain temporal sequencing and causal motivation. This dual character of linguistic sources is reminiscent of postcolonial history-writing for which linear temporality is also too simple a model, and which incorporates countervailing perspectives on individual agency on the one hand, and persistent discursive formations (in the form of colonizing structures and postcolonial assemblages) on the other hand.

In this vein, John and Jean Comaroff posit a binary contrast in the concept of work among the Setswana-speaking Batshidi, with an 'indigenous' conceptualization on one side and a 'foreign' colonial import on the other. This is reflected in the linguistic labelling and etymological origin of the terms applied to the two opposing concepts of work. The Batshidi appear to have added a colonial-Western (= *Sekgoa*) concept of contract work (*go bereka*) to an 'autochthonous', genuinely Tswana concept (*go dira*).[1] Anne Kelk Mager (this volume) shows that current notions of work among isiXhosa speakers are not a one-time import of a colonial concept, but rather the product of an extended process in which new socio-economic realities and established (Nguni) conceptual patterns interacted in intricate ways toward the end of the nineteenth century.

This has a significant implication for language historians and historians working with linguistic data. The presence of borrowed lexical items in a language entails historical contact between different speaker communities. For isiXhosa it is not the presence of newly imported words from languages that, in the nineteenth century, were associated with the colonial sphere (mostly English and Afrikaans) that indicate historically interesting processes of adopting new, and adjusting earlier, notions of 'work' and 'labour'. Rather, semantic borrowing and competition has actually left an imprint in the usage patterns of the original Nguni terms *ukusebenza* and *ukuphangela*, both of which seem quite inconspicuous given that they occur (in near identical shape) in all Nguni languages. IsiNdebele shows what could be seen as an anomaly in a conventional perspective: the term *ukusebenza* refers to labour in the modern context, despite its etymological Nguni origins, and the term borrowed from Afrikaans, *ukuberega*, has become more general and applies to rather common types of work not linked to those that emerged in connection with the colonial situation, industrialization, modernization or formal employment.

There is a significant lesson to be learned from this. Historically relevant borrowing does not have to take place in the form of simple 'form + meaning'-transfer from a source to a target language. In fact, the case of semantic borrowing and conceptual adaptation may be technically more difficult to elucidate, but can often provide an even richer historical texture than attestations of fully fledged lexical transfer.

How conceptual change and continuity can coexist will be shown by way of a closer look into the lexical concepts relating to notions of 'work' in Nguni. In methodological terms, a crucial difference between the semantic analysis proposed here and more conventional historical lexical semantics exists: historical semantics often aims at reconstructing changes in word meaning as subsequent substitution of one meaning by another. However, as diachronically oriented linguists point out, multiple senses of a polysemous word can coexist for a long time.[2] Meaning in language does not result from the formal composition of words into a sentence. Words provide meaning purport,[3] but specific meaning is construed in real-time communication in a process by which words point to meaning, rather than denoting it. In this sense, they are a resource (rather than merely a repository of meaning) that can be drawn on according to situational demands, albeit within certain conventionalized boundaries. A diachronically relevant effect of this is that the semantic history of a word is not best characterized as a chronological sequence of static word meanings, but requires a much richer account of how the word under study has been utilized, and how its conventionalized range of possible meanings has changed.

It may now seem as if the task of a historical semanticist is therefore even more complicated than initially expected. This is not necessarily true, because an understanding of lexical meaning as a complex array of various senses – and to some extent malleable contents – affords a number of methodological options. Etymological histories, the comparison of semantic constellations across related or neighbouring languages and historical linguistics reaching into a more remote past all offer possibilities of insight for specific historical conditions and events.

Linguists have different specific techniques at their disposal with which they can approach these questions. This chapter uses a combination of various approaches: tracking relevant terminology in the (relatively few) historical documents available, searching digital text corpora, reading closely the available lexicons and dictionaries and conducting comparative semantic analyses of relevant cognate and equivalent terms.

The result of this linguistic approach to the history of the lexical concepts pertaining to the domain of work and labour is that, despite the dramatic changes in the socio-economic formations of Nguni-speaking communities in the nineteenth century, there are fundamental conceptual continuities that persist throughout times of dramatic change. The importation of a colonial labour notion is not a simple adoption of a new concept (along with its linguistic label) by Nguni speakers, but rather a drawn-out process in which earlier understandings of work turned out to be quite resilient. In this sense, the conceptual history of work among Nguni speakers is rather different from the binary opposition described by the Comaroffs for the Setswana-speaking Batshidi.

In the rest of this chapter I first briefly present relevant aspects concerning the historical settings that affected the Nguni languages. In discussing the linguistic relationship and historical scenarios I will focus on the period since the nineteenth century, emphasizing specifically the existence of public debate among members of the Nguni language communities – an aspect of particular relevance to conceptual history. How such conceptual contestations that existed prior to the colonial impact can be accessed from sources beyond the colonial archive is taken up in the following section. In that section, I present different domains in the study of language with their specific challenges and some relevant techniques that the linguistic tools afford a conceptual historical approach. Drawing on these techniques I then offer an analysis of two competing lexical concepts in the semantic domain of work, *ukuphangela* and *ukusebenza*, among Nguni languages. Drawing on Mager's insights on isiXhosa (this volume), I broaden the perspective to encompass other Nguni languages in order to disentangle short-term processes, conjunctural tendencies and *longue durée* processes in the semantic history of the terms under study.

The concluding section summarizes the possibilities that linguistic approaches – careful lexical semantic analyses, corpus work, comparative methods – afford, stressing conceptual continuities. These conceptual continuities are not a reflex of semantic determinism, not an attestation of naïve linguistic relativity. Rather, they are viewed as the outcome of semantic legacies rooted in language that can outlast substantial social transformations, but this historical linguistic resilience does not deny the significance of speaker agency and pragmatic requirements. Looking into the concepts of 'work' in Nguni, it is possible to illustrate an important methodological move in historical linguistics which, I hope, has the potential to make linguistic data a more widely used source for history: from historical semantics and meaning change to historical pragmatics, from the question of what a word means to the question of 'how it means'.

Nguni Languages: Historical Scenarios

The interest in work and labour emerges out of the historiography on mid-nineteenth-century Southern Africa. Colonial demands for African labour rose sharply during that time — a period characterized in South Africa by a number of dramatic events: colonial advances involving a frontier scenario in the Eastern Cape, major demographic shifts and migrations in the wake of the Mfecane/Difaqane,[4] white settler expansion, and the discovery of rich mineral resources. These had a lasting impact, affecting not only Nguni communities, but African populations across Southern Africa.

The Nguni languages are linguistically quite closely related, and one might expect the rise of colonial labour to be reflected in their lexical inventories in similar ways. This is not the case, however, despite some superficial formal similarities in the relevant terminology. While all Nguni communities were ultimately subjected to the same colonizing structure in the Southern African context, different groups experienced the colonial advances in the nineteenth century in their own specific ways. The task for this chapter is to bring to the fore the fine semantic differences in the domain of 'work' and 'labour', and to illustrate their bearing on the different experiences of various Nguni communities.[5]

Nguni varieties with higher speaker numbers include isiXhosa, isiZulu, siSwati, and (Zimbabwean) isiNdebele. Despite the similarity in name, the latter is rather distant from Southern isiNdebele, one of South Africa's official languages.[6] Several other Nguni languages, sometimes mutually intelligible with other varieties, exist in small geographic areas and whose speakers have been heavily influenced by neighbouring varieties.[7] Among language historians, several issues concerning the early history of the Nguni languages remain controversial.[8] Some of the differences are due to an emphasis on phonological properties as opposed to lexical evidence.[9] In addition, linguistic evidence and oral traditions are weighted differently in scholarly work on Nguni history.[10] The South African languages isiXhosa, isiZulu and (Southern) isiNdebele have been foregrounded here, since they represent relatively different experiences in terms of colonial encroachment and resistance strategies to colonial advances. Moreover, digital corpora are available for these languages, allowing for text searches. Additional contrastive insight comes from siSwati and Zimbabwean isiNdebele, where deemed relevant.

The approach advocated here is to look carefully at lexical data from the languages used by the historical actors and, in particular, the Nguni-speaking population, since it is their voice that is mostly lacking. In parts of the Eastern Cape, speakers of isiXhosa had to rebuild their lives in the late 1850s after a millenarian prophecy led to socio-economic disaster.[11] Speakers of isiZulu were mainly living in Natal or Zululand, some under colonial control in Natal, others beyond the borders of the colony in Zululand,[12] until political autonomy was fully lost following military conflict with Britain. The (Southern) isiNdebele in the Transvaal were affected by the expansion of Afrikaans-speaking settlers. These are quite different scenarios, yet ultimately all were affected by the growing demand for colonial labour, on farms and in the mines.

Some work and labour relations with the colonial sphere had existed before the 1850s, but with the discovery of diamonds in Kimberley in 1867 and gold on the Witwatersrand in 1886, the demand for labour rose at an unprecedented pace and transformed the social and economic character of Southern Africa.

Insufficient access to economic resources, colonial labour as a recourse, and ensuing socio-economic changes among Nguni communities have been central to the historical debate. This is why this chapter attempts to co-read the terminologies and concepts that Nguni languages encapsulate as gleaned from relevant texts and by means of a systematic lexicographic search. The perception of work and labour as a means to fulfil economic needs invokes a number of contentious issues in the African context. These strategies are the subject matter of many current development discourses on Africa. Such discourses are based on certain notions to which a conceptual history approach is diametrically opposed, such as teleological ideas of how history unfolds, or the insufficient explanation of how external, allegedly universal explanatory concepts motivate human behaviour in a given historical context.

Here, a more relativist approach is followed. It is important to understand that this does not mean a naïve use of emic categories. Such an approach can easily lead to a decorative use of indigenous labels that differs only superficially from using external explanatory concepts. Another risk is that of radical relativism — nihilistic and not likely to provide much insight. By idealizing a substantivist understanding of economics to an extreme degree, one could ultimately posit that economic notions are altogether quite insignificant in the context under study; as long as people pursue their livelihoods but do not engage in explicit debate on economic issues, why dedicate attention to them?

The reason why we should is because there have always been competing discourses and manifold debates, including those about how to address the social grievances and overcome economic challenges in light of the fast-changing historical conditions in the nineteenth century in Southern Africa. Two brief examples underscore this.

Several authors have rightly pointed out that the absorption of African workers into a far-reaching migrant labour system was not by any means an automatic process. People in search of work had different options, since demand for migrant labour was great. Charles van Onselen and Patrick Harries have looked into workers' decision-making processes and state very clearly that information-seeking and debate were crucial.[13] Van Onselen goes so far as to claim that Southern Rhodesian workers in the early twentieth century shared a worker consciousness, based on tracing information exchange and debate on labour options in different places across Southern Africa.[14]

The second, considerably earlier example that illustrates the significance of public debate and information-seeking in order to make informed decisions is discussed in detail by Jeff Peires.[15] In 1856/57, members of the Xhosa communities were divided about whether to follow a millenarian prophecy that required them to destroy their economic resources in expectation of redemption. Political leaders, local intellectuals and other influential members of various Xhosa communities sent emissaries for the purpose of information-seeking, investigating what was happening at the site of the prophecies. This gave rise to debate among Xhosa political leaders, but also among the general public in many parts of the isiXhosa-speaking areas. Xhosa opinions were split over whether to follow the instructions and these divisions ran through communities and families.[16] People spent time and effort to convince others of their respective view. This, in some cases, even resulted in surprising episodes, e.g. the attempt to convince Afrikaner farmers to join the cattle-killing movement.[17]

How can these public debates be made visible? A common way to access public debate is through the analysis of newspapers written in an African language. Early examples of such newspapers were circulated in the Eastern Cape between the 1830s and 1870s, but often only very few issues appeared before they were discontinued. In terms of content, they were mostly concerned with religious matters. In the 1880s, a black press was established that was independent of missionary control (e.g., *Imvo Zabantsundu* in 1884; its founder, John Tengo Jabavu, had earlier been the editor of the mission-dependent *Isigidimi sama-Xosa*, but was dissatisfied, since expressing critical views in the latter was impossible). The existence of newspapers and a readership in the Eastern Cape in the mid-nineteenth century may seem trivial, at best of anecdotal significance. Yet while their readership may have been small in number, and the contents biased towards religious topics, some like the *Imvo Zabantsundu* remained viable for several decades.[18] They included official communications and classified advertisements. These aspects taken together indicate that they enabled non-face-to-face communication, developing into a nascent written forum of debate, negotiation and contestation.

Until the end of the nineteenth century, though, newspapers tend to be limited in scope. Around the beginning of the twentieth century, working conditions in the colonial system become an issue in these journals. But in a sense, this is slightly too late if we want to learn about the formative period (1870s and 1880s) during which the significance and meaning of work was under debate among Nguni-language speakers. Moreover, the grievances expressed in newspapers beginning in the early twentieth century[19] are typically about general working conditions or unfair wages.[20] On the basis of this, it is difficult to reconstruct how Nguni and colonial notions of labour and work became entangled.

Exploring Linguistic Devices: The Potential of Language Data

The lack of textual evidence is challenging. One possibility for overcoming this problem is to turn to linguistic data. Languages reflect what is significant and relevant to a speaker community. Paying close attention to language and linguistic data for historical purposes offers a broad array of possible tools for historical investigation. Historical (and diachronically oriented cognitive) linguistics has several techniques and approaches in store: the history of word meanings as it can be gleaned from close readings of dictionaries, fine-grained analysis of polysemy patterns and other relevant semantic properties of the terms under study, the comparative dimension of the terms across language boundaries, and – in order to learn more about their pragmatic enactment – a look at how they are used at the present time. I will briefly discuss and, where possible, illustrate these with examples from the domain of 'work' and 'labour'.

By comparing the meaning of lexical items between related languages, some semantic changes can be reconstructed. This has long been explored by scholars of African history, e.g. in the tradition of Vansina who approaches the history of political institutions by way of the words-and-things method.[21] Relying mostly on reconstructed lexical data, this kind of work contains sound interpretations of lexical meaning. What is difficult to glean from that kind of data are the pragmatic usage patterns of these reconstructed lexical items: how were these words used in context? This question is particularly relevant for a conceptual approach to African history, but poses some methodological challenges. Different strategies and techniques are available, though, that may help to answer these questions.

The validity and explanatory strength of such reconstructions will increase if one takes into account not just lexical semantics, but also the ways in which the key terms are currently used. In a first step, this will yield a better understanding of contemporary usage patterns in an individual language, but comparing these across languages then allows us to access diachronic dynamics. The relative frequencies of occurrence of different meanings in actual language use are significant, as well as the co-occurrence patterns. Especially in the case of verbs that require some nominal arguments, the kind of attested nominal counterpart that occurs with the verb under question can shed much light on the semantic and pragmatic range of the verb.[22]

An example from the context of work-related notions illustrates this: in all Nguni languages, the verb *ukusebenza* 'work' also occurs in a derived form, *ukusebenzisa*. The extension -*is*- usually serves to express causative meaning, but the Nguni verb *ukusebenzisa* means 'to use' (rather than 'to cause to work', which is not ruled out, but less common).[23] In that sense, it has a much wider use and range of applications compared to e.g. the English 'work'. The verb *ukusebenzisa* 'use' applies to contexts where an abstract quality is used to do something ('she used her cunning to …'), or using ingredients and spice in cooking. Such considerations of usage patterns can be very important tools in historical interpretation when there are specific differences between such notions among related languages and for languages that have stood in different historical contact scenarios.

The fine-grained semantic analysis even of contemporary data, or data from a shallow past, allows us to move beyond synchronic semantic definition. In fact, what we are getting here is a pan-chronic characterization of the lexical item's meaning, which contains sufficiently rich texture for historical interpretation. The English verb 'to work' shows a rather extensive polysemy. Its lexical meaning contains many different senses: 'to be employed', 'to function', but also more peripheral, specialized senses, such as kneading (to work ingredients into a dough), exercising (to work out), or using a device (to work a machine). We can explain how these came into being by listing them all and arranging them into a network-like structure grouping similar lexical senses closer to each other The emerging network will help us understand which meanings are based on which other meanings, and provide us at least with a likely relative chronology of the semantic changes that the term under study must have undergone.[24] Admittedly, dating remains a problem, but by comparing relative chronologies across languages we at least gain a sense of temporal scales, and any further evidence (e.g. scarce mentions in datable texts) could then be read against a fuller, albeit undated, background.

For languages with a fairly long tradition of writing, like English, the emerging patterns can be scrutinized by looking into historical language use at different points in time – we can have synchronic usage patterns at different moments, and thereby corpora, which should confirm our analysis. In the African context, we usually do not have this opportunity, but we can of course turn to a comparative approach. In order to learn about the semantics of 'work' in English, comparison across language boundaries may yield valuable insight, e.g. by contrasting the semantic extensions of the cognate verbs English *work*, Afrikaans *werk*, or Dutch and German *werken*. Similar contrastive-comparative analyses are possible among the Nguni languages and will be illustrated in the next section.

Work in Nguni

Returning to the issue at stake, we can now look into notions relating to the semantic domain of work among nineteenth-century users of Nguni languages. Three terms are most relevant here: *ukusebenza*, *ukuphangela* and *ukuberega~ukubeleka*. John and Jean Comaroff, in their account of notions of work and labour among the Batshidi in the nineteenth century,[25] construe a binary contrast between an indigenous concept of *go dira* and *go berega*, a term borrowed from Afrikaans (< *werk*). While *go dira* evokes constructive work, implying an idea of creating wealth, or achieving some degree of stability, *go berega* applies to types of labour associated with the European/colonial sphere, e.g. on farms or in the mines. Theirs is a story of how this borrowed lexical item epitomizes a transfer from the colonial sphere: an adopted concept of 'work', and in connection with it very substantial socio-economic change for the Setswana-speaking Batshidi. The authors are certainly aware of the complexities of the European-Tswana (or Sekgoa-Setswana) encounters, and of the hybrid outcomes in Tshidi historical consciousness, but the central point of departure is a strong and clear binary opposition between these two political, social and cultural spheres. Comparable concepts in the Nguni languages attest to more protracted processes accompanying the adoption and adaptation of colonial labour notions.

Mager's account (this volume) includes moments of dramatic change, but also draws attention to how the entangled processes of conceptual transfer with regard to concepts of 'labour' and 'work' span a much longer period, and have been discursively contested ever since the colonial situation affected the speaker communities (in her case isiXhosa users in the Tambookie location near Queenstown). Both *ukusebenza* and *ukuphangela* are rooted in the lexical inventory of isiXhosa. No lexical borrowing is involved here. While *ukusebenza* carries a stronger idea of working for oneself, carrying out a task, *ukuphangela* implies completing a job that aims at fulfilling a responsibility towards shared necessities. Interestingly, in recent interviews with speakers, it appears that these terms have now converged in terms of their lexical meaning and their pragmatic range of use.[26] In the following, I broaden the angle and contrast work notions across Nguni languages.

Semantic Inertia

In the lexical sources that I have considered via the digital text corpora for isiZulu, isiXhosa and isiNdebele,[27] there is strong bias toward the use of *ukusebenza*. This term is commonly given in reference material as the closest translation equivalent of the English 'to work', and abounds in written material. For reference material, such as dictionaries, this might be a shallow effect of how these came into being: in most lexicographic work, there is a bias towards European-preferred understandings of work (missionaries and colonialists mostly selected *ukusebenza* in their interaction with isiXhosa speakers). Yet corpus searches on a much broader range of literary genres (the bulk of which stems from the last three decades) reveal that, in writing, *ukusebenza* is more commonly used in more recent times. Again, this does not necessarily mean that the term is overall more significant, broader in scope or in fact more widely used in spoken communication. It is very typical that contested concepts coexist with other semantically-overlapping lexical items in a language.[28] Both *ukusebenza* and *ukuphangela* are semantic formations with a considerable degree of conventional polysemy. But the kind of lexical polysemy differs between them, and the different kinds of polysemy attest to different historical legacies. We need to look at both words in turn, and across languages in order to learn more about this.[29]

Ukusebenza covers a range of meanings in various Nguni languages. These include 'to be employed', 'carrying out a job', etc. The verb *ukusebenza* also expresses that something is functional and is thus also used with non-human subjects: isiZulu *injini yesithathu ayisebenzi* 'the third engine doesn't work'.[30] This polysemy is likely to have been copied from the closest semantic equivalent in English and Afrikaans: *werk* 'work'. Even though the semantic extensions of English/Afrikaans *work/werk* and Nguni *ukusebenza* converge here, it is still useful and possible to distinguish two separate points of departure: utility versus functionality. We can trace this distinction in the Nguni languages because, interestingly, the utility aspect comes to the fore in the specific semantic valency of *ukusebenzisa* (with useful non-agent subjects), whereas the functionality interpretation is more commonly attested with the underived verb *ukusebenza*: its subject nouns are often machines. The distinction between possible subject nouns that fall into different semantic types with more than a chance distribution is evidence for two separate semantic strategies.

The overall range of meaning does not seem to differ substantially among the Nguni varieties. Both isiZulu and Southern isiNdebele *ukusebenza* have a similar semantic extension, but given that the use of *-phangela* is more restricted, *ukusebenza* is the more common term, covering a wide range of meanings. Southern isiNdebele and isiZulu appear not to show 'competition' between *ukuphangela* and *ukusebenza*, at least not to the same extent as isiXhosa. No direct equivalent for the isiXhosa term *ukuphangela* with the meaning 'to work' is recorded in the available lexical reference material.[31] But interestingly, the non-derived verb *ukuphanga* appears with some fairly specific meanings: 'to eat greedily/gluttonously', but also as 'to rob'.[32] In sum, the semantic extension attested for this root in isiZulu and Southern isiNdebele does not include the meaning of 'work', as in isiXhosa, but notions of 'plunder' and 'abduction'. While in isiZulu and isiNdebele these are clearly negatively connoted (isiZulu *isiphangwa* 'prisoner of war'; isiNdebele *ukuphangwa* 'to be hijacked, to be robbed'), this is not (consistently) the case in isiXhosa.

The semantic scope of *ukuphangela* in the Nguni languages is rather intriguing. The networks constituted by its related lexical meanings show a number of different meanings, many of which are only loosely connected, and the semantic bridges that one would assume to have served as pathways of meaning extensions often remain quite speculative. Current notions in isiXhosa include 'doing part-time work', or 'work hastily', in addition to those detected by Mager in her interviews. Also, when looking at related languages, the links between different senses of *-phangela* seem almost random and the etymological relationship has been blurred to the extent that no shared meaning is evident, such as the isiZulu examples *ukuziphangelana* 'to storm in; to swashbuckle'[33] or *phangeleyo* 'general, common'.[34] These lexical items whose semantic link is anything but obvious attest to the process by which *-phangela* has become what could be called a fractured lexical concept resulting from a formerly more coherent semantic network that has been encroached upon by competing lexical concepts. In the case of isiXhosa, this competition appears to have been a more prolonged, entangled process than in some other languages in the region.[35] A likely scenario of this semantic process and its relation to non-linguistic historical conditions is presented in the following section.

Conflicting Ideas of Work: Approaching Historical Usage Patterns

The semantics of *ukusebenza* and *ukuphangela* reflect how the colonial labour experience affected linguistic concepts. But lexical semantics is more than sedimented experience. The historical semantics of these isiXhosa terms attests to contestations, but also continuities in the understandings of 'work' and 'labour' in the colonial context.

Competition around access to labour – speaking from the perspective of colonial society – became particularly fierce with the discovery of diamonds in Kimberley in 1867 and, in 1886, gold in the Witwatersrand area. While initially small claims were held by different actors (foreigners as well as local people, of different cultural backgrounds) who worked as independent diggers, the mining industry consolidated quickly. The costs incurred in running mines rose sharply, although the gains were certainly also exorbitant. Mining magnates invested enormous sums and created a labour model that was to characterize migrant labour in the mines for most of the twentieth century.[36] Contract labourers were recruited and brought to the mines from all over South Africa, and beyond. For the migrant labourers, this kind of contract work was completely different from any economic activity experienced before.[37]

In one important sense, this marks a genuine turning point. For the isiXhosa-speaking migrants, the attempt to re-establish one's economic self-reliance, *uku[zi]busa*, does not correspond at all to the experience of contract labour. Life in the mines had nothing to do with the restitution of lost resources. Superficially, the fixed-term contracts with work remunerated at the end of the contract time may appear similar to some kind of tribute labour,[38] but in fact the payment schemes were designed to create total dependency on the mining companies. The mining companies restricted miners' mobility and forced them to acquire necessary commodities in the few outlets available to them. Consolidated mining companies exerted monopolies and pushed down wages. Large portions of income were spent on goods in the mining areas, reducing the miners' income and at the end of the day, little if any money was left when they returned home.[39] This clearly did not help much in getting back on one's feet, and this type of migrant labour is a far cry from goal-oriented service delivered along lines of personalized social relations.[40]

The general Nguni term used in this context is *ukusebenza*, a word whose origins are more problematic to trace. It is shared among Nguni languages and is therefore certainly not an invention of the nineteenth century, but it became much more widely used during the last decades of that century. Looking at its current semantic extension, the term is quite broad. It encompasses a variety of meanings that include 'exerting a professional activity' involving a notion of recurrent tasks and professional skills training. It can also refer to exercise, both in terms of physical and mental training. Commonly used derived nouns are *umsebenzi* (cl. 3/4, *imi-*) and *umsebenzi* (cl. 1/2, *aba-*). The former appears to have a meaning that can be more or less predicted compositionally – a nominalization of the verb 'to work' which can refer to a specific task or chore, to work in the form of employment, but also to types of work that create a specific domain of responsibilities (*umsebenzi wenkomo* 'work relating to cattle', used to label different ritualized functions that require cattle to be slaughtered).[41] In contrast, the agent noun *umsebenzi/abasebenzi* (cl. 1 and 2) has a more specialized meaning in most of its corpus occurrences, that of a worker (as opposed to other kinds of livelihood-securing strategies) in a sense of hired labour as a commodity. It can semantically contrast in this function with other professional actors (self-employed, farmers, service employees, etc.). This semantic extension is not necessarily predictable on the basis of its composition (verb root + agent noun ending and prefix): after all, representatives of other professions carry out work as well. The specialized meaning is in all likelihood a semantic extension inherited from European notions of workers in a context of industrial work.[42]

The verb *ukusebenza* is used in all Nguni languages, but not beyond that family. Two possibilities need to be considered. One is that this is an innovation in proto-Nguni, dating from anywhere between 900–1200 AD, before the family split up. Another possibility is that this term is actually a later innovation in one of the varieties, and has since spread into all different varieties of Nguni. Based on the fact that the distribution is so neatly Nguni, the first hypothesis seems more likely,[43] yet the second cannot be ruled out, because this particular Nguni term became the common term when Nguni varieties were used in multilingual settings. These often included non-Nguni speakers. The missionary context is significant here, because it is a plausible catalyst.

In the missionary context, these notions of work were coupled with an additional semantic ingredient of strain and work as self-improvement. It is also plausible to assume that Xhosa writers in the mission context formed an important nexus and, due to their position between the more close-knit Xhosa communities and the colonial sphere, could serve as linguistic innovators – individuals instrumental in the conceptual transfer that affected notions of work, and preferred usage patterns for the available competing terms. They had access to both spheres and expressed their ideas in writing, which facilitated the dissemination of conceptual innovations into wider communication. The missions were also instrumental in shaping the language, in a rather normative sense. New meanings were often inscribed into lexical items, and once written into reference material even somewhat contrived lexical choices for new concepts stood a chance of becoming conventional.[44]

This leads to an important question, that of the reliance on written language corpora as reliable testimony to historical semantics. This is not just a matter of scarce sources in the African context; even for languages with a more extensive and older written record, the question remains to what extent the written attestations reflect standard, mainstream or common uses of (spoken) language at the respective times. While historical written records afford the possibility of tapping into earlier meanings (which in the case of the Nguni language are mostly restricted to the twentieth century), there is a serious problem inherent in this. A semantic reconstruction based solely on the interpretation of such sources will overlook the important character of oscillating meanings, which find their space less in the written than in the oral domain. Especially in the case of languages like those of the Nguni group, the sole reliance on written sources (or a corpus based on written language) will necessarily tilt the interpretation toward a dated modernity in writing. I am thinking here of the challenging experience of bridging the gap between the language reduced to writing and that of oral use.[45] This contrast should not just be regarded as a conflict between spoken language and a written norm that can never catch up with the fast-changing creative oral twists. Both domains/modalities can lead an independent life, and -*phangela* in isiXhosa is a case in point.

In fact, one may wonder why a notion such as -*phangela*, arguably with goal-oriented aspects (achievements) and collective notions (contributing one's share to the communal requirements) would not catch on in the missionary context. It is important to bear in mind here that within colonial society, too, there was no one unified concept of work. Coloureds, British colonial administrators and Afrikaners, settlers and missionaries had different understandings about what 'work' signified, and what shape work relations should take (boss-subject; employer-employee; tutor-*Zögling*).[46] Lexical semantic differences between the English 'work' and 'labour', and the contrasting semantic extensions of Dutch/Afrikaans *werk* and German *Werk* and *Arbeit* (relevant for the missionary context) illustrate how contested these various fields were even among the users of European(-based) languages in South Africa.[47] It is actually interesting that German, in addition to *werken* (implying a notion of craftsmanship) and *arbeiten* (the term of wider application), certain regional varieties use a verb *schaffen* as the most common term to refer to 'work'. The verb *schaffen* carries strong ideas of 'bringing to completion, achieving, creating'. This may appear intriguingly close to certain notions of -*phangela*, yet in the mission context the work to be completed (leading people to conversion) was reserved for the missionaries; *ukusebenza*, the continued effort and repetitive carrying out of chores, best describes what the missionaries had in mind for the bulk of the population attached to the mission stations (whose importance as economic units and sites of labour often surpassed their function as religious centres).

Another trigger for the generalized use of *ukusebenza* among Nguni varieties is the mining context, in which often non-standard varieties were used. The mainly Nguni-based pidgin language Fanakalo was an important vehicular language in this context.[48] In such a sociolinguistic setting, the choice of one term for the concept 'labour', rather than an intricate coexistence of semantically near synonymous terms, is likely. This could have propelled the use of *ukusebenza* and led to its widespread use among all Nguni varieties.[49] In fact, it is quite possible that the term *ukusebenza* is a fairly recently dispersed term. Its homogenous and exclusive distribution in Nguni goes against this view. Yet there are smaller pieces of evidence that support this hypothesis.

Northern varieties of South African isiNdebele,[50] used in the vicinity of Mokopane, have a completely different term for 'to work', *kutjhuma*, in addition to *kusebenta*.[51] On the basis of the available material, it is impossible to say much about the pragmatic difference between both terms. The common Nguni word *ukusebenza* came to be used predominantly for notions of work introduced in a colonial context, which points to a later adoption (or at least revaluation) of that term. Southern isiNdebele uses *ukusebenza* in a similar way, but has another verb, *ukuberega*, borrowed from Afrikaans *werk*. In stark contrast to the situation in Setswana as used by the Batshidi, this term is not used predominantly to denote work contexts associated with colonial/Western notions of 'work'. Southern isiNdebele has thus inverted the association of etymological origin and semantic range. It is not the word of ultimately European origin, *ukuberega*, but the Nguni term *ukusebenza* that is used for 'work' notions that came into being in the colonial context.

The translation/transposition process between European views of work and African languages is therefore a complex mapping, not a unidirectional one-time transfer. Jean and John Comaroff – notwithstanding their explicit awareness about the hybridity and entanglements in such processes of meaning construal – analyse Batshidi understandings on the basis of a binary contrast in Tswana between Afrikaans-borrowed *go bereka* and original Setswana *go dira*.[52] In the isiXhosa context, assuming such a strict opposition following the Comaroffs would be too strongly dichotomous, and in isiNdebele, the etymological origin almost seems to reverse the picture: inherited forms express the novel notions, borrowed forms represent older understandings.

Semantic Analysis and Conceptual Continuities in Nguni

After analysing the lexicographic and, to the extent possible, the diachronic pragmatic information we can glean from linguistic data in the relevant semantic fields, the critical question that we need to deal with – if we hope to make a methodological contribution – is the following: is our approach simply embellishing historical insight that we have gained through other (more conventionally used) historical sources? Or can this contribute to an understanding of historical continuities and fissions in the past of communities using Nguni languages that would not have been possible, if it had not been for our conceptual approach? Obviously, our answer needs to be that the latter is the case. But how so?

An important aspect in the current contemplation of work in its historical Nguni ramifications is of great value: by relying on a contrastive semantic analysis, it has been possible to overcome or break with a tradition in research and lay understanding concerning the significance of the colonial encounter. While this moment is crucial, it has now become very clear that the work, even critical work, on this historical moment is bound to reproduce exactly what it criticizes.[53] To take an example, it is easy to get the impression that the Xhosa at the time preceding the cattle killing were not only largely pre-colonial but also pre-modern, and both changes occurred very quickly as a reaction to outside influence.[54] All accounts of Xhosa history imply a hidden change from pre-modern to modern that is located somewhere between the late nineteenth and the early twentieth centuries. It is accompanied by a change in text genres, professional activities, mobility patterns, etc. Yet this is a very problematic notion to begin with: its origins may be an effect of the kind of historical sources available; its significance and explanatory strength is dubious; its political implications in the twentieth century devastating.

It is important to ask which ruptures are established in Nguni notions of what happened in those decades from the second half of the nineteenth century into the early twentieth century. But we need to do so without dismissing or ignoring the long-term continuities in the semantic underpinnings of the crucial terms, in our case 'work'. This is where the historical semantic analysis of socially and economically relevant concepts comes into play. The relevant semantic fields are made up of lexical items used to address these notions by speakers of Nguni languages. Semantic analysis sheds light on longer-term historical continuities of central notions that shape and are being shaped by subsistence activities and aim at socio-economic well-being.

A linguistic look at cultural concepts works, therefore, against fragmentation. Cultural linguistics and historical semantics provide the empirical basis for a kind of historical insight that is very difficult to grasp in post-structuralist or deconstructivist analyses. In the present example, the semantic shaping of the domain of 'work' and 'labour' in Nguni has shown diachronic processes that are hardly visible to other techniques. The persistent distinction of work framed as either activity (chore or function) or as act or action (with an inherent understanding of completion) has been maintained among users of isiXhosa. In isiNdebele, matters are more reminiscent of what the Comaroffs describe for Setswana among the Batshidi: notions (and words denoting these) concerning kinds of work/labour associated with the colonial domain as more directly adopted from the colonial sphere together with the formal expression, *-berega* < Afrikaans *werk*. But, as we have seen, this comes with an interesting twist: despite its Nguni origin, *ukusebenza* applies to those kinds of work that are associated with modern life, urban settings and employment; the loanword (borrowed from Afrikaans, possibly with Sotho-Tswana as a catalyst) applies to longer-established kinds of work, such as agriculture, craftsmanship and animal husbandry.

The fact that here lexical contents and formal shape are borrowed is of some significance. A hypothesis currently strengthening with growing evidence is that those borrowings that occur in a form/meaning package are actually the more readily made ones. Those where form and meaning are not packaged attest to longer contestations and contentions.

This is an important point because, so far, much work relying on lexical evidence (comparative, reconstructed) for historical interpretation zooms in on those concepts that are prone to be of the first type. In fact, for conceptual history, what is more relevant are those concepts in which the translation process delinked form and meaning. This is what made the domain of 'work' so intriguing for the current purpose – a concept that is part of everyday parlance, common vocabulary and not easily suspected of being representative of, or instrumental in, historical drive.

By writing a conceptual history of such notions around 'work' and 'livelihood', we draw attention also to those things that remain otherwise unaccounted for – most importantly perhaps the resilience of the economic and the social among speakers of Nguni languages. The linguistic long term is a necessary heuristic to counterbalance what comes across as somewhat overly dramatic moments in time in many historical accounts.

Notes

1. J.L. Comaroff and J. Comaroff, 'The Madman and the Migrant: Work and Labor in the Historical Consciousness of a South African People', *American Ethnologist* 14(2) (1987), 191–209.

2. See for example D. Geeraerts, *Diachronic Prototype Semantics: A Contribution to Historical Lexicology* (Oxford: Clarendon Press, 1997).

3. For a detailed discussion of recent understandings of lexical meaning, see D.A. Cruse, 'Aspects of the Microstructure of Word Meanings', in Y. Ravin and C. Leacock (eds), *Polysemy: Theoretical and Computational Approaches* (Oxford: Oxford University Press, 2000), 30–51; W. Croft and D.A. Cruse, *Cognitive Linguistics* (Cambridge: Cambridge University Press, 2004); V. Evans, *How Words Mean: Lexical Concepts, Cognitive Models, and Meaning Construction* (Oxford: Oxford University Press, 2009).

4. In the first half of the nineteenth century, the Zulu kingdom under Shaka had become militarized and sparked raids and military expeditions affecting neighbouring groups. As a result, violent conflicts emanated from the Zulu kingdom as the epicentre across wide swaths of Southern Africa.

5. See W. Beinart, 'Labour Migrancy and Rural Production. Pondoland c. 1900–1950', in P. Mayer (ed.), *Black Villagers in an Industrial Society* (Cape Town: Oxford University Press, 1980),

81f., who warns against generalization: '[T]he process of capitalist penetration, the response of rural producers, and patterns of migrancy varied considerably from area to area.'

6. In fact, there are several linguistic varieties under the same name, isiNdebele, in South Africa. In this chapter, I refer to the Southern isiNdebele variety that forms the basis of the official language since it is this variety that is represented in the Pretoria Ndebele Corpus (D. Prinsloo, University of Pretoria). For more on the linguistic setting, see P.B. Skhosana, 'The Linguistic Relationship between Southern and Northern Ndebele' (Ph.D. dissertation, University of Pretoria, 2009).

7. Other varieties (Phuthi, Lala, Bhaca, Hlubi, Northern (Transvaal) Ndebele, etc.) are of great significance when it comes to disentangling the history of the entire family, but they are badly documented. Some of them are extinct, others highly endangered. For the present work, these varieties have not been considered because of the lack of data. The current most reliable overview of the internal classification of the Nguni varieties is J.F. Maho's 'New Updated Guthrie List: A Referential Classification of the Bantu Languages', last updated 2009.

8. There is some controversy over whether isiZulu should be grouped closer to siSwati or isiXhosa, about the position of the isiNdebele varieties, and other details of the proposed classification. For the current purpose, it may suffice to bear in mind that all Nguni varieties (except for the late emergence of Zimbabwean isiNdebele in the aftermath of the Mfecane) had separated long before the nineteenth century. They have since influenced each other in various ways, but had developed into discernible entities not later than the fifteenth century. M. Wilson, 'The Nguni People', in M. Wilson and L. Thompson (eds), *The Oxford History of South Africa* (Oxford: Clarendon Press, 1969), 75–130; C.P. Ownby, 'Early Nguni History: The Linguistic Evidence and its Correlation with Archaeology and Oral Tradition' (Ph.D. dissertation, University of California, Los Angeles, 1985).

9. For more on this, see Ownby, 'Early Nguni History', 28–37.

10. Ownby, 'Early Nguni History'; S. Marks and A. Atmore, 'The Problem of the Nguni: An Examination of the Ethnic and Linguistic Situation in South Africa before the Mfecane', in D. Dalby (ed.), *Language and History in Africa* (London: Cass, 1970), 120–32; Wilson, 'The Nguni People'.

11. J. Peires, *The Dead Will Arise: Nongqawuse and the Great Xhosa Cattle-Killing Movement of 1856–57* (Bloomington: Indiana University Press, 1989). For more on this, see Mager this volume, and references therein.

12. For an in-depth analysis of the Natal case see K. Atkins, *The Moon is Dead! Give Us Our Money! The Cultural Origins of an African Work Ethic, Natal, South Africa, 1843–1900* (Portsmouth: Heinemann, 1993).

13. P. Harries, *Work, Culture and Identity: Migrant Laborers in Mozambique and South Africa c. 1860–1910* (Portsmouth: Heinemann, 1994); C. van Onselen, *Studies in the Social and Economic History of the Witwatersrand, 1886–1914* (London: Longman, 1982 [reprint 2001]).

14. C. van Onselen, 'Worker Consciousness in Black Miners: Southern Rhodesia, 1900–1920', *Journal of African History* 14(2) (1973), 237–55.

15. Peires, *The Dead Will Arise*.

16. Interestingly, the resulting antagonism between believers and non-believers led to social rifts that Zakes Mda's novel *The Heart of Redness* describes as of very current relevance (New York: Farrar, Straus & Giroux, 2002). Mda writes the distinction between believers and non-believers into his account of current contestations around modernity. He unmasks the idea of belief in progress as dated modernity.

17. Peires, *The Dead Will Arise*, 128.

18. L. Switzer and D. Switzer, *The Black Press in South Africa and Lesotho: A Descriptive Bibliographic Guide to African, Coloured, and Indian Newspapers, Newsletters, and Magazines, 1836–1976* (Boston: Hall & Co., 1979).

19. Early newspapers in Nguni languages that expressed social and economic grievances were the African-owned and controlled *Imvo Zabantsundu* ('Native Opinion', in isiXhosa, since 1884) and *Ilanga laseNatal* ('The Natal Sun', in isiZulu, since 1903).

20. Peter Limb recalls Sol Plaatje who published newspapers in Setswana: 'In comparison with more conservative black newspapers, such as *Ilanga laseNatal* or *Imvo Zabantsundu*, Plaatje's newspapers give relatively more consistent representations of black workers'. (P. Limb, 'Sol Plaatje Reconsidered: Rethinking Plaatje's Attitudes to Class, Nation, Gender, and Empire', *African Studies* 62(1) (2003), 40.) The Nguni-language newspapers appear comparably silent on worker concerns.

21. J. Vansina, *Oral Tradition as History* (London: James Currey, 1985); J. Vansina, *Paths in the Rainforest: Toward a History of Political Tradition in Equatorial Africa* (Madison: University of Wisconsin Press, 1990). The methodology has since been developed further. For an application, see Stephens' chapter on poverty and wealth across several Ugandan languages, this volume.

22. This kind of information can be obtained from larger text corpora. Such corpora are available and have been consulted for isiXhosa, isiZulu and (South African) isiNdebele at the University of Pretoria. The corpora that have been compiled by D. Prinsloo and his co-workers contain a variety of text material. For my corpus searches I have excluded translated material (much of which stems from a religious or legal context) in order to minimize unwanted translation effects in the semantic make-up and to avoid thematic distortion toward specific text genres that make up a large portion of the written material, but reflect rather special jargon. For the present purpose, it appeared more appropriate to rely on newspaper texts, fiction and some other smaller text genres like bulletins on public health issues or security at the workplace, or political pamphlets.

23. Earlier reference material gives the translations 'help' and 'make to work'; J.W. Colenso, *Zulu-English dictionary* (Pietermaritzburg: Davis, 1884). It is not possible to tell with certainty whether the term took on the more specific meaning 'to use' since then, but in light of the otherwise fairly adequate character of Colenso's dictionary, it would seem so. This gives us a hunch of the pace with which the term has undergone semantic modification.

24. See D. Jurafsky, 'Universal Tendencies in the Semantics of the Diminutive', *Language* 72 (1996): 533–78; A. Fleisch, 'A Cognitive Semantic Approach to the Linguistic Construal of upper space in Southern Ndebele', *Southern African Linguistics and Applied Language Studies* 23(2) (2005), 139–54.

25. Comaroff and Comaroff, 'The Madman and the Migrant'.

26. Mager (this volume) presents a fuller discussion of this.

27. These corpora were compiled, and are maintained at the University of Pretoria, by D. Prinsloo and his team. They include different text genres, although they are not well balanced in terms of temporal coverage (most texts from the 1970s onwards) and text genre (educational, religious, official documents are over-represented). It is, however, possible to recompile source texts that feed into the corpora so that these variables can be controlled for to some extent, which lends plausibility to arguments based on frequency changes in different genres or over the course of time.

28. At this stage it is very difficult to say, to what extent both Xhosa notions, *ukusebenza* and *ukuphangela*, represent essentially contested concepts in Gallie's sense. See W.B. Gallie, 'Essentially Contested Concepts', in *Philosophy and the Historical Understanding* (London: Chatto & Windus, 1964), 157–91. It is tempting to see some of the semantic developments that affected both terms as a direct outcome of evaluative contestations and ideological motivations, e.g. when worker (*umsebenzi*) status becomes an identity marker and politically mobilizing at the latest in the early twentieth century in connection with the rise of trade unions, see below.

29. An additional term of some relevance here is *-busa*. In isiXhosa, its meaning covers the notion of rendering service/work to a ruler (or other person) in hope of compensation. This is rather different from isiZulu. Here, *ukubusa* is usually understood as 'rule, govern'. In combination with the reflexive morpheme *-zi-* it yields *ukuzibusa*, serving to express an idea of autonomy, also in economic terms ('be self-supportive'). The derived causative verb form *ukubusisa* in isiZulu means 'to make prosperous', developed from what would, in terms of purely compositional semantics, be expected to mean 'to make/cause to rule' (possibly an interesting connection to an idea of 'wealth in people'). In isiXhosa, this term has been recorded by Mager, but has interestingly apparently vanished from the record. While the *Greater Dictionary of isiXhosa* lists *-búsisa* as a possible derivation, this form has not been attested in the Pretoria Xhosa corpus.

30. 'Ukwenza Ukuhamba Ngezindiza Kuphephe Kakhudlwana'. Retrieved 25 November 2013 from http://wol.jw.org/zu/wol/d/r28/lp-zu/102000686.

31. For isiNdebele: *IZiko lesiHlathululi-mezwi sesiNdebele/IsiNdebele/English Dictionary* (Cape Town: Phumelela Books, 2006). For isiZulu, C.M. Doke et al., *English-Zulu, Zulu-English Dictionary* (Johannesburg: Witwatersrand University Press, 1990) [1st combined version]; Colenso, *Zulu-English Dictionary*.

32. These are attested also as starred forms *C.S. 1439/1440 in M. Guthrie, *Comparative Bantu: An Introduction to the Comparative Linguistics and Prehistory of the Bantu Languages*, vol. 2 (Farnborough: Gregg Press, 1971). 'Bantu Lexical Reconstructions 3', a Tervuren-maintained database, has two possibly relevant entries: 2396 *pàng* 'plan, intend to'; 2397 *páng* 'act; make'. None of them is attested in zone S, though. Y. Bastin and T.L. Schadeberg, 'Bantu Lexical Reconstructions 3' (Tervuren: Royal Museum for Central Africa, 2002, updated 2005). Retrieved 10 September 2014 from http://www.africamuseum.be/collections/browsecollections/humansciences/blr.

33. Pretoria Zulu Corpus, Source text: nasi-kei.txt, sentence 41. Accessed Nov 2012.

34. https://www.facebook.com/permalink.php?id=226920520799147&story_fbid=229187637239102.

35. That this process of constant semantic re-evaluation involves speaker agency, and is far from over at present, is clear when one looks into current use of *-phangela* in a sense that is often closer to 'job' than to 'work'. This lexical concept has remained available as a way of expressing speakers' ideas about different 'ways of working'.

36. van Onselen, *Studies in the Social and Economic History of the Witwatersrand*; Harries, *Work, Culture and Identity*, 66–71.

37. See various contributions in Mayer, *Black Villagers in an Industrial Society*.

38. Keletso Atkins also describes the mismatch between the workers' understanding of the working relationship and the colonial notion of labour: 'Migrant workers initially perceived themselves in a patron-client arrangement.' Atkins, *The Moon is Dead!*, 76.

39. Harries, *Work, Culture, and Identity*, 69, 173–182. Moreover, there were systems in place whereby the migrant worker would receive advance pay in kind in the rural home areas in which case there was little cash money involved; William Beinart, "Labour Migrancy and Rural Production: Pondoland c. 1900–1950," in Mayer, *Black Villagers in an Industrial Society*, 81–108.

40. For crucial distinctions in the conceptualization of work along service/outcome-centred and personal relations, see G. Spittler, 'Arbeit – Transformation von Objekten oder Interaktion mit Subjekten?', *Peripherie* 85/86 (2002), 9–31.

41. As an example, see 'Umsebenzi wenkomo kumasiko ekiXhosa', a blog entry on *Intlalo Neengcambu Zamaxhosa Akwantu*, 26 July 2012. Retrieved 3 December 2013 from http://fubustyle.blogspot.com/2012/07/xhosa-cow-slaughtering-rituals.html.

42. Charles van Onselen discusses the rise of worker consciousness among black miners in Zimbabwe (then Southern Rhodesia) and argues for its existence despite the absence of worker associations or unions in the first two decades of the twentieth century, even among miners from Matabeleland (Zimbabwean isiNdebele is also a Nguni language); van Onselen, 'Worker Consciousness', 237–55. These workers are referred to as *zhuwawo* 'ordinary labourer', i.e. by a chiShona term. Apparently, the rise of a worker identity (and the noun designating a worker) was mobilized independently from the related verb. See also N.M. Shamuyarira, *Crisis in Rhodesia* (London: Deutsch, 1965), 51.

43. In addition to the distribution, a phonological property comes into play: in siSwati, the word is pronounced *-sebenta*, which is a completely regular sound correspondence in terms of historical sound change and would thus support the first hypothesis, an early exclusive Nguni innovation. However, languages with highly regular sound correspondences can adapt the sound shape of borrowed terms, so this argument could be refuted.

44. While language planners' efforts to bring newly coined terms into acceptance may often have failed, experiences with the development of grammars, dictionaries and schoolbooks show that first reference material can have a major impact on future language use in languages with a limited writing tradition.

45. W. Hanks, *Converting Words: Maya in the Age of the Cross* (Berkeley: University of California Press, 2010) contains an insightful discussion of this *reducción* in the Spanish-Mayan contact. Aspects of the process of reducing to written norm apply also in the context of isiXhosa and other Nguni languages.

46. How European understandings, including those of early anthropologists, intersect with African notions is also discussed in G. Spittler, 'Beginnings of the Anthropology of Work: Nineteenth-Century Social Scientists and their Influence on Ethnography', in J. Kocka (ed.), *Work in a Modern Society: The German Historical Experience in Comparative Perspective* (Oxford: Berghahn, 2010), 37–53.

47. See W. Conze, Arbeit', in O. Brunner, W. Conze and R. Koselleck (eds), *Geschichtliche Grundbegriffe. Historisches Lexikon zur politisch-sozialen Sprache in Deutschland, Vol. 1 A-D* (Stuttgart: Klett Cotta, 1979); B. Stråth, 'The Concept of Work in the Construction of Community', in B. Stråth (ed.), *After Full Employment: European Discourses on Work and Flexibility* (Brussels: PIE-Peter Lang, 2000), 62–105; J. Kocka, 'Mehr Last als Lust: Arbeit und Arbeitsgesellschaft in der europäischen Geschichte', in *Kölner Vorträge zur Sozial- und Wirtschaftsgeschichte*, vol. 44 (Forschungsinstitut für Sozial- und Wirtschaftsgeschichte an der Universität zu Köln, 2006).

48. R. Mesthrie, 'The Origins of Fanagalo', *Journal of Pidgin and Creole Languages* 4(2) (1988), 211–40; R. Aderdorff, 'Fanakalo in South Africa', in R. Mesthrie (ed.), *Language and Social History: Studies in South African Sociolinguistics* (Cape Town: David Philip, 1995), 176–92.

49. 'Bantu Lexical Reconstructions 3', though, includes an entry 7765 *cébenj* 'work' with an attestation in Guthrie's zone M (mainly Eastern Zambia, neighbouring areas), but here it is possibly a later borrowing through extensive involvement of speakers from these areas in migrant labour.

50. South African isiNdebele is mainly used in north-eastern parts of present-day Gauteng (including speakers in and close to Pretoria) and the neighbouring Mpumalanga and Limpopo provinces. The relevant contact languages for South African isiNdebele have been varieties of the Sotho-Tswana group (since at least the seventeenth century) and Afrikaans, since the nineteenth century. Also in the nineteenth century, during the time of the *imfecane*, speakers of other Nguni varieties (closer to present-day isiZulu and Zimbabwean isiNdebele) came from the current KwaZulu-Natal region and stayed for some time in the area inhabited by the ('Transvaal') Ndebele under Mzilikazi. This further complicated the historical sociolinguistic constellation for that language.

51. The form *ukusebenza* corresponds regularly to *kusebenta* in the Northern Ndebele varieties spoken in the South African Limpopo province; D. Ziervogel, *A Grammar of Northern Transvaal Ndebele (A Tekela Nguni Dialect Spoken in the Pietersburg and Potgietersrus Districts of the Transvaal Province of the Union of South Africa)* (Pretoria: van Schaik, 1959); Skhosana, 'The Linguistic Relationship between Southern and Northern Ndebele', 61, 107.

52. Comaroff and Comaroff, 'The Madman and the Migrant'.

53. Among many others, Rochona Majumdar discusses this insightfully in *Writing Postcolonial History* (London: Bloomsbury Academic, 2010).

54. On this issue, the mechanism by which scholarly work on the nineteenth century in South Africa limits Xhosa agency (or rather, its significance in their works), more needs to be done; see P.S. Landau, *Popular Politics in the History of South Africa, 1400–1948* (New York: Cambridge University Press, 2002), on European views of parallel times, different stages of development. This is what leads to the possibility to create a myth of a pre-modern Xhosa society later exploited in the nationalist project.

References

Language resources

Pretoria Ndebele Corpus. Dept. of African Languages (D. Prinsloo). University of Pretoria.
Pretoria Xhosa Corpus. Dept. of African Languages (D. Prinsloo). University of Pretoria.

Pretoria Zulu Corpus. Dept. of African Languages (D. Prinsloo). University of Pretoria.

Dictionaries

Colenso, J.W. *Zulu-English Dictionary*. Pietermaritzburg: Davis, 1884.
Davis, W.J. *A Dictionary of the Kaffir Language: Including the Xosa and Zulu Dialects*. London: Wesleyan Mission House, 1872.
Döhne, J.L. *A Zulu-Kafir Dictionary: Etymologically Explained with Copious Illustrations and Examples, Preceded by an Introduction on the Zulu-Kafir Language*. Cape Town: Pike, 1857.
Doke, C.M. et al. *Zulu-English/English-Zulu Dictionary*. Johannesburg: Witwatersrand University Press, 1990.
Elliott, W.A. *Notes for a Sindebele Dictionary and Grammar*. Bristol: Sindebele Publishing Company, n.d. [shortly after 1910].
IZiko lesiHlathululi-mezwi sesiNdebele/IsiNdebele/English Dictionary. Cape Town: Phumelela Books, 2006.
Kropf, A. and R. Godfrey. *A Kafir-English Dictionary*, 2nd ed. Lovedale: Lovedale Mission Press, 1915.
Pelling, J.N. *A Practical Ndebele Dictionary*. Salisbury: Longman, 1971.
Shabangu, T.M. and J.J. Swanepoel. *Isihlathululimezwi: An English-South Ndebele Dictionary*. Cape Town: Maskew Miller Longman, 1989).
The Greater Dictionary of IsiXhosa. 3 vols. University of Fort Hare, 1989–2006.

Other Works

Adendorff, R. 'Fanakalo in South Africa', in R. Mesthrie (ed.), *Language and Social History: Studies in South African Sociolinguistics*. Cape Town: David Philip, 1995, 176–92.
Atkins, K.E. *The Moon is Dead! Give Us Our Money! The Cultural Origins of an African Work Ethic, Natal, South Africa, 1843–1900*. Portsmouth: Heinemann, 1993.
Bastin, Y. and T.L. Schadeberg. 'Bantu Lexical Reconstructions 3'. Tervuren: Royal Museum for Central Africa, 2002, updated 2005. Retrieved from http://www.africanmuseum.be/collections/browsecollections/humansciences/blr.
Beinart, W. 'Labour Migrancy and Rural Production: Pondoland c. 1900–1950', in P. Mayer (ed.), *Black Villagers in an Industrial Society*. Cape Town: Oxford University Press, 1980, 81–108.
Comaroff, J.L. and J. Comaroff. 'The Madman and the Migrant: Work and Labor in the Historical Consciousness of a South African People', *American Ethnologist* 14(2) (1987), 191–209.
Conze, W. 'Arbeit', in O. Brunner, W. Conze and R. Koselleck (eds), *Geschichtliche Grundbegriffe. Historisches Lexikon zur politisch-sozialen Sprache in Deutschland, Vol. 1 A-D*. Stuttgart: Klett Cotta, 1979.
Croft, W. and D.A. Cruse. *Cognitive Linguistics*. Cambridge: Cambridge University Press, 2004.
Cruse, D.A. 'Aspects of the Microstructure of Word Meanings', in Y. Ravin and C. Leacock (eds), *Polysemy, Theoretical and Computational Approaches*. Oxford: Oxford University Press, 2000, 30–51.
Evans, V. *How Words Mean: Lexical Concepts, Cognitive Models, and Meaning Construction*. Oxford: Oxford University Press, 2009.
Fleisch, A. 'A Cognitive Semantic Approach to the Linguistic Construal of upper space in Southern Ndebele', *Southern African Linguistics and Applied Language Studies* 23(2) (2005), 139–54.
Gallie, W.B. 'Essentially Contested Concepts', in *Philosophy and the Historical Understanding*. London: Chatto & Windus, 1964, 157–91.
Geeraerts, D. *Diachronic Prototype Semantics. A Contribution to Historical Lexicology*. Oxford: Clarendon Press, 1997.
Guthrie, M. *Comparative Bantu: An Introduction to the Comparative Linguistics and Prehistory of the Bantu Languages*, vol. 2. Farnborough: Gregg Press, 1971.
Hanks, W. *Converting Words: Maya in the Age of the Cross*. Berkeley: University of California Press, 2010.

Harries, P. *Work, Culture, and Identity: Migrant Laborers in Mozambique and South Africa, c. 1860–1910*. Portsmouth: Heinemann, 1994.
Jurafsky, D. 'Universal Tendencies in the Semantics of the Diminutive'. *Language* 72 (1996), 533–78.
Kocka, J. 'Mehr Last als Lust: Arbeit und Arbeitsgesellschaft in der europäischen Geschichte', in *Kölner Vorträge zur Sozial- und Wirtschaftsgeschichte*, vol. 44. Forschungsinstitut für Sozial- und Wirtschaftsgeschichte an der Universität zu Köln (Research Institute for Social and Economic History, University of Cologne), 2006.
Landau, P.S. 'An Amazing Distance: Pictures and People of Africa', in P.S. Landau and D.D. Kaspin (eds), *Images & Empires: Visuality in Colonial and Postcolonial Africa*. Berkeley: University of California Press, 2002, 1–40.
———. *Popular Politics in the History of South Africa, 1400–1948*. New York: Cambridge University Press, 2002.
Limb, P. 'Sol Plaatje Reconsidered: Rethinking Plaatje's Attitudes to Class, Nation, Gender, and Empire', *African Studies* 62(1) (2003), 35–52.
Maho, J.F. 'New Updated Guthrie List: a Referential Classification of the Bantu Languages'. Last updated 2009. Retrieved 1 March 2014 from http://goto.glocalnet.net/mahopapers/nuglonline.pdf.
Marks, S. and A. Atmore. 'The Problem of the Nguni: An Examination of the Ethnic and Linguistic Situation in South Africa before the Mfecane', in D Dalby (ed.), *Language and History in Africa*. London: Cass, 1970, 120–32.
Majumdar, R. *Writing Postcolonial History*. London: Bloomsbury Academic, 2010.
Mda, Z. *The Heart of Redness*. New York: Farrar, Straus & Giroux, 2002.
Mesthrie, R. 'The Origins of Fanagalo', *Journal of Pidgin and Creole Languages* 4(2) (1988), 211–40.
Ownby, C.P. 'Early Nguni History: The Linguistic Evidence and its Correlation with Archaeology and Oral Tradition (South Africa)'. Ph.D. dissertation. University of California, Los Angeles, 1985.
Peires, J. *The Dead Will Arise: Nongqawuse and the Great Xhosa Cattle-Killing Movement of 1856–57*. Bloomington: Indiana University Press, 1989.
Rycroft, D.K. *Concise Siswati dictionary: Siswati-English, English-Siswati*. Pretoria: Van Schaik, 1995.
Shamuyarira, N.M. *Crisis in Rhodesia*. London: Deutsch, 1965.
Skhosana, P.B. 'The Linguistic Relationship between Southern and Northern Ndebele'. Ph.D. dissertation. University of Pretoria, 2009. Retrieved 24 February 2014 from http://upetd.up.ac.za/thesis/available/etd-10092010-130514/.
Spittler, G. 'Arbeit – Transformation von Objekten oder Interaktion mit Subjekten?', *Peripherie* 85/86 (2002), 9–31.
———. 'Beginnings of the Anthropology of Work: Nineteenth-Century Social Scientists and their Influence on Ethnography', in J. Kocka (ed.), *Work in a Modern Society: The German Historical Experience in Comparative Perspective*. Oxford: Berghahn, 2010, 37–53.
Stråth, B. 'The Concept of Work in the Construction of Community', in B. Stråth (ed.), *After Full Employment: European Discourses on Work and Flexibility*. Brussels: PIE-Peter Lang Publishing, 2000, 62–105.
Switzer, L. and D. Switzer. *The Black Press in South Africa and Lesotho: A Descriptive Bibliographic Guide to African, Coloured and Indian Newspapers, Newsletters and Magazines 1836–1976*. Boston: Hall & Co., 1979.
Van Onselen, C. 'Worker Consciousness in Black Miners: Southern Rhodesia, 1900–1920'. *Journal of African History* 14(2) (1973), 237–55.
———. *Studies in the Social and Economic History of the Witwatersrand, 1886–1914*. London: Longman 1982.
Vansina, J. *Oral Tradition as History*. London: James Currey, 1985.
———. *Paths in the Rainforest: Toward a History of Political Tradition in Equatorial Africa*. Madison: University of Wisconsin Press, 1990.

Wilson, M. 'The Nguni People', in M. Wilson and L. Thompson (eds), *Oxford History of South Africa*. Oxford: Clarendon Press, 1969.

Ziervogel, D. *A Grammar of Northern Transvaal Ndebele (A Tekela Nguni Dialect Spoken in the Pietersburg and Potgietersrus Districts of the Transvaal Province of the Union of South Africa)*. Pretoria: van Schaik, 1959.

Axel Fleisch is a professor of African studies at the University of Helsinki, Finland. His regional focus area is Southern Africa, with research interests including the description and analysis of African languages, historical linguistics and the intersection of language and history. Among his published works are *Lucazi Grammar: A Morphosemantic Analysis* (Cologne: Köppe 2000), and *Grandmother's Footsteps: Oral Tradition and South-East Angolan Narratives on the Colonial Encounter* (Cologne: Köppe, 1999; co-edited with Inge Brinkman).

CHAPTER 3

Tracking the Concept of 'Work' on the North-Eastern Cape Frontier, South Africa

Anne Kelk Mager

Conceptual history, a new field for African history, draws on methodologies developed in Europe, and while this is sometimes a controversial starting point for African scholars, this initiative opens up possibilities for thinking about the complex history of everyday concepts. Bo Stråth in particular has shown the value of conceptual history as a heuristic tool, a means for adding scope and depth to broader historical questions in postcolonial contexts. By extending Reinhart Koselleck's approach to the previously colonized world, Stråth demonstrates that tracing the contextual history of concepts is critical to coming to terms with social change and to problem solving.[1] This chapter takes its cue from Stråth's insights and builds on four key premises. Firstly, since language is rooted in social interaction and communication that is contextually bound, concepts are developed by social actors. Secondly, colonial encounter, not unlike revolution, is a powerful moment for the exploration of the conflict and contestation of concepts across linguistic and cultural boundaries. Thirdly, while the outcome of conceptual conflicts is open-ended, it produces interests and further conflicts since ideological power 'derives from power over concepts and categories of meaning'. Fourthly, since concepts are grounded in agency and action, time and space, and since they intermingle and undergo change through a complex series of interactions over time, 'linguistic transformation' and meaning need to be mapped 'empirically in the context of sociopolitical struggles' while concepts must be relativized and historicized.[2]

Stråth's approach is innovative for African history. The questions of conceptual history – what new concepts were introduced by whom, to what

Notes for this section begin on page 86.

purpose, through which contestations and with what effect – are yet to be systematically explored. While historical linguists have established a strong interest in the reconstruction of language in Africa, they have paid less attention to the interaction between language and the actions of people. Social historians on the other hand have shown little interest in how language and concepts have changed in relation to social and economic change. Only a few scholars have hinted at the possibility of conceptual contestations in the colonial period. In his essay on colonizing time, Fred Cooper argues that the notion of industrial time and the work rhythms of capitalism were instilled in a limited way and in the specific locality of the port of Mombasa. He demonstrates that colonial intervention led to the development of 'a sociological and political language in which the African worker stood as a universal, cultureless being' apart from the social milieu beyond the workplace.[3] However, Cooper stops short of examining how those construed as 'cultureless beings' might bring culture with them to the workplace and how this might have shaped concepts in everyday life. More recently, Paul Landau has examined missionary translations of the Christian concept of God in African languages. He shows how missionaries grafted their concept of God onto the notion of ancestors, displacing the historical discourse of ancestors as men and replacing it with the idea of God as spirit. This mutation-facilitated communication in colonial contexts provided potential converts with a pathway to conversion.[4] In this exploration, Landau comes closer to the idea of conceptual history as set out by Stråth.

In exploring the concept of 'work', this chapter fills a gap in a historiography replete with studies of labour in colonial contexts but few on the notion of 'work'. The North-Eastern Cape frontier – comprised of various rural native locations, mission stations, a white frontier town and its farming district – constituted a particularly intense site of struggles over ideological and material power between indigenous people, missionaries and colonists (see Map 3.1). At the centre of these conflicts was the colonial settler demand for labour and, as this chapter shows, the meaning of 'work'. Conflicts were framed by wider social and economic upheavals, which periodically erupted into war before the area was subjugated by the end of the century. Pivotal to the colonial project on this frontier were endeavours that sought to recast everyday life so that indigenous notions of 'work' would be replaced by the conceptions, and needs, of colonial masters.

Since the notion of 'frontier' itself is contested, the concept immediately implies unsettled states of meaning. In Southern African studies, 'frontier' has been perceived as a zone in which conflicts and contestations are never finally settled.[5] It has also been understood as a short period of relative openness in social and economic relations preceding tight closure as colonial power takes hold.[6] Recently, the term 'borderlands', borrowed from American scholarship, has been deployed in an African context to suggest 'a space governed by

Map 3.1 North-Eastern Cape Frontier, South Africa, c. 1865

interactive, overlapping, and incomplete authorities'.[7] In this chapter the term 'frontier' is used in order to indicate the indeterminate character of authority, entanglements between authorities, and crucially, conflicts and contestations over the meaning of authority.

Sources are a challenge. While there are no written texts for oral societies and no 'big texts' that might be used as a reference point, historical sources such as missionary and colonial documents and early colonial dictionaries provide a useful starting point. These texts need to be read both with and against the grain of their interlocutors and producers. Both Kropf's *Kaffir-English Dictionary* and McLaren's *Xhosa-English Dictionary* rely on Gaika (Ngqika) isiXhosa and might be criticized for 'mistranslating' cultural concepts. This begs the question: how does one differentiate between cultural and non-cultural concepts? Indeed, since these dictionaries are also cultural constructions, exploring the interactions and identifying the overlaps between concepts takes us further than a straightforward linguistic approach.[8] Colonial records such as administrators' reports and the frontier press convey a colonial understanding of 'work' while the Moravian concept of 'work', so central to their evangelical project is conveyed in the reports and biographies of their missionaries. By drawing on these sources to construct a sense of everyday life in the midst of the colonial encounter, it is possible to arrive at an understanding of the processes through which indigenous concepts of 'work' displayed both mutable and durable characteristics.

Colonial Dictionaries as a Source for the Concept of 'Work': *Ukusebenza* and *Ukuphangela*

Delineating an isiXhosa concept of 'work' is not straightforward. There is no pristine isiXhosa concept of 'work'. However, colonial reports and missionary writing indicate that two key terms *ukusebenza* and *ukuphangela* were used at the moment of colonial encounter in the mid-nineteenth century and provide important semantic fields for our inquiry.

Ukusebenza is translated by colonial lexicographer McLaren in 1915 as a transitive verb meaning 'to work, labour, operate'. It comes from the verb *uku-enza* 'to make, do, perform, execute'. As a noun, *intsebenzo* means 'use, utility; work, occupation; reward, wages'. *Umsebenzi* (cl. 1) is a worker or labourer; *umsebenzi* (cl. 3) is work, labour, trade or occupation.[9] *Ukusebenzela* is to work for. *Ukusebenzisa* is to employ and *umsebenzisi* is an employer. Work carried on around the homestead was described as *umsebenzi* and encompassed construction and maintenance of dwellings, cattle rearing, cultivating crops, making pots and weaving baskets.

Ukusebenza was used by colonists for physical work and derived its meaning from the concept of 'work' spelled out in the Masters and Servants Act (see below); it was a restricted and utilitarian concept. In contrast, isiXhosa speakers had a somewhat different understanding of the meaning of work for wages or reward. *Ukusebenza*, as activity that results in a reward (*ubaso*), derives a key element of its meaning from the term *ukuphangela*, derived from *ukuphanga*, and is translated by McLaren as 'to do with speed or force or violence; to hasten; do hurriedly, eagerly; to take by force, rob, plunder from'.

The conceptual link between *ukusebenza* and *ukuphangela* requires an understanding of context. In the Xhosa conceptual universe in the mid-nineteenth century, every man was expected to do his share for the homestead by joining in action beyond the homestead and bringing home the reward, i.e. *ukuphangela*. This meant responding to the defence of the chief, the principal protector of the clan or tribe and engaging in cattle raids as ordered by the chief. A man's share of the spoils in a successful cattle raid was a principal means of wealth acquisition. Cattle raids were also a means of demonstrating and establishing power relations and of summoning opponents or troublemakers to negotiation. Men were to maintain themselves in readiness to play their part and receive their share of the spoils. Young boys practised the art of riding and driving cattle at speed and men were admired for their skill and prowess in raiding.[10] There was no sense of criminality in this activity; it was carried out at the chief's behest and the spoils were apportioned to those who took part with the chief receiving the greatest share. *Ukuphangela* did not apply to someone who plundered unjustly; such a person was not respected, but condemned as one who injured (*ukuoona*) someone else.

There is an implicit gendered element in the originating distinction between *ukusebenza* and *ukuphangela*. While women did not participate in plundering and raiding cattle or the negotiations that followed this action (and so did not receive a share of the reward), their labour in tilling the soil, collecting fuel, building houses and cooking was described as *umsebenzi*. Women were not permitted to accumulate *impahla* (material goods) but they were expected to perform work (engage in necessary labour) that carried little status.

These concepts and the distinction between them shifted in the course of the colonial encounter, nudged by limited opportunities for raiding and increased recourse to wage work. With the extension of the colonial economy, *ukuphangela* came to mean going to work in the colony and returning with wages that contributed directly or indirectly to the well-being of the household. Loosely translated, it meant having a job or going to work. In time it came to be used interchangeably with *ukusebenza*. However, the originating distinctions persisted and different usages indicate an uneasy and incomplete convergence between these terms and between missionary and colonial concepts of 'work'.

Moravian Missionaries and the Concept of 'Work'

The colonial concept of 'work' has two originating moments – colonial desire to put indigenous people to work (for their own and for colonial benefit) and colonial contempt for indigenous concepts of 'work'.

Missionary observations of daily life in and around Shiloh in the mid-1830s identify women as burdened by work and men as idle, exploiting women and parasitic on their labour. Using middle-class European experience as a lens, the Moravians designated domestic work as the appropriate sphere for female activity and looked to African men for productive activity. What they saw did not fit this pattern and they were endlessly disappointed in their observations of indigenous men's occupations. Brother Bonatz's description of men's daily routine in the mid-nineteenth century is one such example:

> The occupations of the men are, to milk the cows, to hunt game, or else to sit the whole day in the kraal, reciting news and adventures, and likewise to carry on war. At sunrise, they creep out of their round huts, each with a milking basket in his hand, skilfully manufactured by the women, and hasten to the cattle kraal. Everyone pays the greatest attention to his cows, and endeavours to obtain from them as much milk as possible.

Once the cattle had been attended to, 'the rest of the day is commonly spent by the men in idleness', the Moravians observed, 'they either sit gossiping in the cattle kraals, or lie sleeping in the sun'.[11] This 'idleness' of African men is a trope of missionary and colonial discourse, constructed through a desire to see African men labouring in the service of the modernist and Europeanizing ambitions of Moravian and other missionaries and colonists.

African men were mindful of the difference between their own view of work and that of the Moravians. Missionary writing sets out how unimpressed African people were with their attempts to build a mission station. Wilhelmina Stompjes, interpreter for the Shiloh Moravians, commented in her auto-obituary (so heavily edited by Brother Bonatz that it may be read as an official Moravian text) that the Tambookies 'gibed at everything' the missionaries attempted:[12]

> When they saw the men work with pick and spade, they said: 'You are such stupid people, to work so hard – we would never do that! We would rather die than put our body through such hard labour!' When they watched how clay was thrown against the walls of the pole houses, they laughed and said: 'Look here! They do it like swallows, they learnt from them. Oh they are so stupid! They will all die here on the cold plain if we do not take care of them'.[13]

Writing in his own name, Brother Bonatz celebrates hard-working African women and chastises African men for an idleness sustained by the attitude that they purchased the right to female labour through *ukulobola* (the customary practice of exchanging cattle for a bride):

> The Tambookie [the San name for abaThembu] women are considered as the slaves of their husbands, because the latter have bought them, and it is they who have to perform manual labour of every kind ... On arriving at a new dwelling place, the women must build the round huts, a work which they understand well. The cultivation of the gardens is likewise their incumbency. This labour they perform on their knees, with wooden spades. A yet severer duty is the gathering of firewood on the neighbouring hills. The women also manufacture baskets of various kinds, which will hold both milk and water, and round earthenware pots which they mould and bake with great cleverness. For the grinding of Caffre-corn, they use a flat stone, crushing the corn against it by the help of another pointed stone, or iron pestle. It is astonishing to see, in what a short time they are able to fill a large jar with flour, by means of such an imperfect apparatus.[14]

This discourse of the uncivilized but industrious heathen woman served to provide the missionaries with hope. However, this African gender division of labour set up a conflict for the patriarchal German missionaries. In their view, men should lead the way to modernity by embracing Christianity and practising sedentary agriculture based on the application of technology. This discursive tension is captured in Moravian accounts of African responses to new technologies such as the new watermill at Shiloh:

> The Africans were amazed, and exclaimed: 'What a diligent woman is this mill, she works day and night, never gets hungry and drinks only water'. Others said: 'How the Whites do manage to subjugate everything; not only human beings are to be their servants but even water is made to serve their needs'.[15]

While the Moravian concept of 'work' was tightly linked to discipline and control, in the Xhosa conceptual universe these concepts were associated not with 'work' but with gendered adulthood. Thus, *ubudoda*, what it meant to be a man, implied forbearance, controlling one's temper, ability to strategize, courage in conflict, loyalty to one's chief and the ability to keep order in the homestead, particularly control over one's wives. Ultimately, the missionary project sought to remove these values from gendered authority and to graft them onto the meaning of work. For in the Moravian's Germanic, Protestant view, the process of work would bring uncivilized heathens closer to God. Their mission stations provided the model: tireless effort, perfection, resilience, orderliness and improvement:

> The missionaries were tireless in their efforts to improve the station. The water furrow which brought water for the gardens and fields from the dam at a distance of about half-an-hour's journey on foot, was a great blessing, but also involved much work, as crabs dug holes into its sides, causing water to escape, or cattle broke it down when walking across it. Gardens and fields yielded more and more as the years went by. Groves of oaks and poplars were planted and even walnut trees flourished. The smithy, the carpentry and wheelwright shops were centres of activity. Other workers learnt how to shape and fire bricks and build substantial houses.[16]

In 1853, Shiloh was visited by Sir George Grey, colonial governor and champion of a 'civilizing' approach to 'native policy'. According to the Moravians, Grey was 'happy to see young Africans in the smith, the joinery and at the building site of the new water mill' where their work involved deploying technology to tame nature and so to bring modernity to the frontier.[17] However, if Grey envisaged that Africans might deploy these skills for their own account, this was not the model of colonialism that European settlers would allow.

In the meantime, the missionary experience augmented the vocabulary of work: *ukukhanda* to repair, to work as a blacksmith'; *ikhuba* 'a plough'; *isichwelo* 'a carpenter's plane'. Some new words were borrowed, for example, *ifotsholo* 'a shovel'. While this vocabulary remained within the asymmetrical binary of the cultured, hard-working society envisaged by the missionaries and the uncivilized, unskilled and labour of indigenous people, a significant isiXhosa vocabulary points to the development of a more complex and nuanced attitude to work. The notion of 'unskilfulness' *ubuqhitala* and an 'unskilled person' *iqhithala* set against *ukuqiliza* 'to be enterprising, to desire to work' and *iqili* 'an enterprising man' and *iqilizana* 'an enterprising woman' suggest that isiXhosa speakers reserved respect for those who worked hard. However, it is not clear how widely used these terms were among isiXhosa speakers. This vocabulary was laden with the values of missionaries bent on furthering their own concept of 'work'.

Colonial Concepts of 'Work' and Attempts at Conceptual Engineering

For the colonized, the notion of 'work' was defined by the Masters and Servants Act. In terms of this act (Act no. 15 of 1856, promulgated on 4 June 1856), the concept was intertwined with the concept of 'servant':

> The word 'servant' shall be construed and understood to comprise any person employed for hire, wages or other remuneration, to perform any handicraft or other bodily labour in agriculture or manufactures, or in domestic service, or as a boatman, porter, or other occupation of a like nature.

The act defined 'master' as an employer of servants or apprentices. A later amendment (Act no. 30 of 1889) extended the term 'servant' to apply to 'any man-servant employed as a domestic servant or to perform any bodily labour in manufactures, or as a boatman, porter, groom, stablekeeper, gardener, or other occupation of a like nature'.

This legislation specified that work to be carried out by the colonized would be defined as 'bodily labour'. Indigenous men were servants to the colonizers. The contract of service could be 'oral or written, expressed or implied' and the reward so vague as to extend to unspecified wages or 'other remuneration'. The Masters and Servants Act, and any transgression of its provisions, embedded the concept of 'work' in colonial relations of domination and subordination.

Most Africans experienced work in the colony as aligned with punishment; for them 'free labour' was often indistinguishable from the 'hard labour' meted out by colonial courts. 'Hard labour' was performed in contexts very similar to those of waged work – on roads, farms and municipal projects. Also, the food rations of farm and construction workers were so similar to those of prisoners that farmers complained of the luxury of prison life. Rather than providing prisoners with food, offenders should be flogged with sufficient violence to scar their bodies and sent back to work for their masters, they argued.[18] In a society where status was not signified by clothing, people wore their bodies with pride. A branded body lost its status, its capacity for beauty and the punished man lost his self-esteem. Unable to persuade the magistrates to favour lashing over hard labour, farmers took it upon themselves to thrash suspected stock thieves.

This notion, applied to the colonized, was not the only concept of 'work' present on the frontier. A revised and updated edition of the *Standard Dictionary of the English Language* in use on the frontier soon after it was published in 1903 defines 'work' as 'physical or mental effort and exertion'; 'work' as necessary for livelihood and 'work as the usual price of success'.[19] 'Work' was a means of accumulating wealth. Indeed, the choice to emigrate to the frontier – at least for the British settlers of 1820 and those recruited later to provide strategic services on this frontier – might be read as representing the desire for new opportunities for accumulation. Aside from a handful of rogues, most settlers sought an opportunity to use whatever skill they had to enhance their livelihoods. Colonists could presume that their hard work would lead to reward; the logo of a pharmacy established in a frontier town in the 1870s read *Labor Omnia Vincit* 'Work Overcomes All'.[20]

However, colonial success also depended on the labour of others – the African men whom they believed were inherently idle, living off plunder and the labour of their wives. Thus the colonial challenge was to transform African idleness into effective labour, and also to ensure that the desire for gain (the motivation for work) did not reach beyond what might be contained in the framework of the Masters and Servants Act. This challenge entailed devising strategies to force indigenous people to take up employment as servants in the colony (social engineering) in the belief that this would inculcate the right mindset and concept of 'work' (conceptual engineering). Thus the processes of social and conceptual engineering were intertwined on the frontier.

The first step towards this conceptual engineering was to ensure that African people on the frontier lost their independent livelihoods, i.e. they became separated from the means of production. By the mid-nineteenth century the colonists had seen how those displaced through the *mfecane* wars had lost their economic footing and so had become more dependent on colonial service.[21] AmaMfengu (Fingoes in colonial parlance) was a generic term for poor people that came to be deployed by colonists as an ethnic category; the concept served to meld together disparate individuals into a coherent body that might be named and controlled. Dispossessed of their livestock and without chiefs to protect them, amaMfengu accepted their dependent status and found the colonists their most willing protectors. Colonial employment provided these refugees with security and a steady supply of food, and their proximity to the colonists placed them at the forefront of the new experience of work.

Acknowledging their interdependence, the colonists referred to the amaMfengu as 'allies' or 'friends'. They were expected to adopt a colonial conception of 'work' as livelihood. 'I see no other way than for [the Fingoes] to turn out and get their own living, as Europeans do', said the superintendent of the Tambookie location. 'They must send their children to learn trades, civilise them, and put them into a position to get a living. They must not depend exclusively on a pastoral or agricultural way of living – just growing a few mealies, feeding stock, and so forth.'[22] Colonists celebrated this civilizing contact and exclaimed how, once 'poor and broken-spirited and now, under the fostering care of our government, they stand first on the list of border tribes for wealth and civilisation, and with all this can we say that their existence is inseparable with ours?'[23]

The largest Mfengu settlement on this frontier was at Oxkraal, adjacent to Shiloh, where 3,200 people, described as 'mostly Fingoes' lived. The superintendent reported that his efforts and those of colonially-appointed headmen transformed attitudes to the work of farming and that the people were 'fairly prosperous and contented'.[24] In this discourse, indigenous people properly supervised would acquire the appropriate concept of 'work' and the related concept of civilization.

But colonial attitudes changed when the amaMfengu demonstrated a desire to be independent of the colonists. In 1854, the municipality of a frontier town invited people from Oxkraal to assist in the construction of the town and several families were allocated plots on the commonage. Unimpressed by the slow returns on their labour in building the town, some of these families gave up their wage work, preferring to tend their livestock. The magistrate instructed them to desist from farming on the commonage claiming that their invitation to the town was as workers and not as 'squatters' on municipal property. Their welcome was determined by their ability 'to supply labour for the town, and not to keep large herds of cattle or to cultivate whatever ground they pleased'.[25] Cast in the asymmetries of the frontier, independent livelihoods would not be permitted, not even among allies and friends.

In 1857, in the district beyond this frontier town, many amaXhosa and abaThembu slaughtered their cattle in the hope that the millenarian prophesy of Nongqawuse and her uncle Mhlakhaza would come true and that African people would be relieved of the horror of colonial oppression. Tens of thousands of cattle were slaughtered. But white people were not driven into the sea and the cattle did not rise from the dead.[26] Nor did the colonial government intervene to provide famine relief. Rather, the colonial authorities celebrated the way in which the millenarian prophesy played into their hands. This mass slaughter of cattle destroyed the economic independence of thousands of African people. It weakened chiefly authority and brought mass starvation. Thousands of people made their way to white towns, farms and mission stations in desperate search of food. Colonial authorities and missionaries saw their task as managing the fallout and setting the starving to work. Thus the superintendent of the Tambookie location warned the colonial secretary of the need to protect the frontier from hungry people seeking to 'plunder'.[27] The colonial government was warned to create employment along this frontier so that the starving learned to work for their food. A public works programme of road building was duly initiated.[28] In contrast to the missionary ideals, there was no pretence that this work would serve as a means of civilizing people or advancing the cause of Christianity. Rather, work conducted in response to the failure of 'the cattle-killing delusion' would strengthen the colonist's arm and facilitate the construction of the colonial order.

Less than a decade after the cattle-killing fiasco, the superintendent of a large rural location in the district reported that it had become a labour reservoir for white farmers. 'The number who take colonial service during the year is from 6 to 900', he wrote: 'They are generally employed as farm servants and herds. Their remuneration varies from £3 to £6 per annum, but they are generally paid in live stock'.[29] Significantly, residents of the location continued to hold onto the prospect of working for themselves and saw employment as a short-term strategy, a means of regaining their lost cattle. Some succeeded in achieving this goal. Over a decade later, the superintendent reported that residents returned to the location after a period of service in the colony with large amounts of stock; indeed, they were 'rich in stock, all certified in their discharge papers as their lawful property'. In one season, 'returning servants brought into the location no less than 16,000 sheep and goats besides other stock, all properly certified'. Some of these 'servants' were independent farmers. Indeed, they were so successful that white merchants were buying wool produced by sheep farmers in this location.[30] It was evident that these farmers entered the modern colonial economy under the Masters and Servants Act with a view to regaining the means to re-establish their independence. As their livestock were replenished, so they regained their status as patriarchs. Their aim was to raise their children in independent, self-sufficient households in accordance with indigenous values.

This independence was perceived with ambivalence by the colonists. While the location superintendent accepted this approach to work, as it created a layer of yeoman farmers and entrepreneurs who set an example in his location, white farmers were more critical. Those farmers who wanted a stable labour force railed against men who returned to the location content with 'a few head of cattle'. A letter to the editor of a local colonial newspaper gave expression to this view:

> A native man when he is at home, never works; the little work that is done at all is performed by the women and children; he is either drinking, sleeping or fighting, and he will never work unless he is compelled to do so by starvation, &etc. I know of thousands of natives who have grown up or stayed a large number of years with English or Dutch farmers; they were during this time obliged to assume civilised customs; they can speak English and Dutch fluently; but all of them have thrown civilisation to the winds and have gone back to the red clay, beer drinking, &etc. There is no progress with these tribes if they are left to do as they choose, and they will be in the same barbarous state after centuries if they are not interfered with.[31]

Clearly, this settler perspective left no space for the idea that once a man had brought home his share of sustenance for the household, he was entitled to rest, respite and reintegration as a patriarch. When resources ran out, he might take up employment for another once again, but in the meantime there was, to his mind, no need to do so.

Cecil John Rhodes, Prime Minister of the Cape (1893–1896) put an end to this doubling of lifestyles and values. In the 1890s, Rhodes presented to parliament his idea for inducing into 'the African mind' a British colonial notion of 'work'. In the parliamentary debates on the Glen Grey Act (Act no. 25 of 1894), Rhodes outlined how the inhabitants of 'Tambookieland' would be provided with 'some gentle stimulants to go forth and find out something of the dignity of labour' in the form of a labour tax.[32] This tax would be used to fund industrial schools, which would provide instruction in 'useful trades'.[33] In return, those who lived under the Glen Grey Act would be eligible for freehold tenure. The pressure to meet tax obligations further encouraged the trend for rural patriarchs to send young men to work in the colony; their exhortations at male initiation ceremonies are well recorded:

> From today you must work for your living. You will leave for distant places. You will work far, far away from your people, where your customs are not known. Be thus always faithful to the customs of your people. You will go out to work on the farms of the white man. Let obedience to your masters be your first consideration.[34]

This exhortation marked a significant shift in indigenous meaning. It downplayed the idea that masculine self-esteem emanated from authority over the labour of others, (principally women) and promoted the idea of using one's own labour to achieve masculine status. However, this shift was not accomplished by exhortation or legislation. In its implementation, the Glen Grey Act generated more resentment than opportunity and to a large extent failed to enhance the value of productive labour. While men laboured to meet tax obligations, their communities received little in return. Rhodes' 'gentle stimulant' failed to elevate the concept of 'work' to that of noble endeavour. Rather than deepening the links between 'work', self-esteem and masculine identity, this social engineering hardened the association of 'work' with punishment.[35]

African Intellectuals and the Notion of 'Work' in Xhosa Fiction

Colonists complained bitterly that by concentrating on academic skills, British missionary institutions failed to convey the Protestant concept of 'work' and produced individuals who could make no contribution to the colony. Even magistrates deplored their efforts. One newspaper correspondent railed: 'The dignity of labour is lost sight of altogether in these schools, and the result is that children return to their homes more useless than when they left'.[36] Useless from the perspective of colonists who wanted manual labourers, these schools produced an African intelligentsia that was exposed to a wider world and was soon talking back to colonial power. Employed as teachers, preachers and clerks, African intellectuals saw themselves as engaging in mental rather than manual labour and came to embrace a concept of 'work' as both intrinsically satisfying, providing social status and materially rewarding. For them, the meaning of 'work' came close to the definition in the *Standard Dictionary* and was valued as a means of social uplift. It is through their work and that of later generations of mission-educated thinkers and writers that we glean tensions between competing conceptions of 'work'.

Well into the twentieth century, Xhosa writers and poets continued to describe colonial employment as a temporary measure. Thus Mqhayi's nostalgic poem 'Emakhayeni' laments the departure of migrant workers from the homestead and celebrates the self-sufficiency of the precolonial economy. F. Nomvete in his poem 'Sebenza' urges his son to *sebenza*, to work with his head (*intloko*) and to develop self-discipline in order to acquire cattle.³⁷ While nostalgia for an independent mode of life dominates much of isiXhosa literature, J.J.R. Jolobe's essay, 'Umsebenzi wabafazi kwisizwe esiNtsundu' ('The Work of the Women of the Black Nation') echoes the views of the missionaries in its criticism of the heavy burden placed on women by the division of labour in a cattle economy. The work of tilling the soil was far harder than watching cattle he observed.³⁸ Mission-educated, these men use *ukusebenza* as the generic term for 'work'.

Following the collapse of reserve agriculture in the mid-twentieth century, tens of thousands of men and women moved to the cities and towns. Increased urbanization, proletarianization and trade unionism led to new meanings of 'work'. Apart from a handful of professionals, African people became dependent on wage labour. While South Africa remained a labour surplus economy and wages remained low, there was no scarcity of employment until the 1970s when the needs of the economy began to change. As industry made more extensive use of technology, fewer workers were required and restructuring of the workplace led to retrenchments. Writing in the late twentieth century, L.E. Menze spells out the destructive outcomes of unemployment in his novel, *Iziphumo Zodendo*. He suggests that without legitimate work, i.e. a job, people would be forced to plunder, and to become thieves. In this novel, the meaning of *ukuphangela* returns to its roots.³⁹ Menze may have been proffering an explanation for the coterminous increase in unemployment and crime in the late 1990s.

Conclusion

This chapter has demonstrated, firstly, that the limited mutability of indigenous conceptions of 'work' in colonial South Africa was due to the refusal of people to embrace a notion of 'work' that denied indigenous values and restricted agency and experience. Over time, and as colonialism strangled the possibility of living outside its orbit, indigenous concepts of 'work' became more entangled with colonial concepts. However, their original meanings were not entirely displaced and remain imbricated in contemporary usages of terms such as *ukuphangela* and *ukusebenza*. Secondly, this chapter has shown that colonial and missionary records serve as useful texts for conceptual history. These texts enable us to see how indigenous Xhosa concepts interacted with colonial and missionary concepts and how indigenous actors developed a concept of 'work' both in relation to precolonial notions and through a colonial experience of work. Thirdly, by deploying the method of conceptual history, we are able to develop a more complex understanding of social change and continuity than might be possible with the conventional tools of social history or linguistics.

Notes

1. B. Stråth, 'Introduction: Production and Meaning, Construction of Class Identities, and Social Change', in B. Stråth and C. Homberg (eds), *Language and the Construction of Class Identities: The Struggle for Discursive Power in Social Organisation. Report from the DISCO II Conference on Continuity and Discontinuity in the Scandinavian Democratisation Process in Kungälv, 7–9 Sept 1989* (Gothenburg: Department of History, Gothenburg University, 1990), 2–9.
2. Stråth, 'Introduction', 7.
3. F. Cooper, 'Colonizing Time: Work Rhythms and Labor Conflict in Colonial Mombasa', in N.B. Dirks (ed.), *Colonialism and Culture* (Ann Arbor: University of Michigan Press, 1992), 209–45.
4. P.S. Landau, *Popular Politics in the History of South Africa, 1400–1948* (Cambridge: Cambridge University Press, 2010), 74–107.
5. M. Legassick, *The Struggle for the Eastern Cape 1800–1854: Subjugation and the Roots of South African Democracy* (Johannesburg: KMM Review, 2010).
6. R. Elphick and H. Giliomee, *The Shaping of South African Society 1652–1820* (Cape Town: Longman Penguin, 1979).
7. Landau, *Popular Politics*, 3.
8. A. Kropf, *Kafir-English Dictionary* (Alice: Lovedale Press, 1899); see also K. Moropa and A. Kruger, 'Mistranslation of Culture-specific Terms in Kropf's *Kafir-English Dictionary*', *South African Journal of African Languages* 20(1) (2000), 70–79.
9. J. McLaren, *A Concise Kaffir-English Dictionary* (London: Longman, 1915).
10. Brother A. Bonatz, 'Description of the Mission-Settlement at Shiloh, in the Country of the Tambookies: With Some Account of the Manners, Customs etc. of the Neighbouring Tribes', *Periodical Accounts Relating to the Missions of the Church of the United Brethren Established Among the Heathen* 13 (1834), 351–52.
11. Bonatz, 'Description of the Mission-Settlement at Shiloh'.
12. Wilhelmina Stompjes, born and raised as Ngqika Xhosa fled the Eastern Cape war zone in the early nineteenth century and found herself on the Moravian mission station at Genadendal where she converted to Christianity and married Carl Stompjes, a Khoi man.
13. 'Curriculum Vitae of Wilhelmina Stompjes, Kaffer-interpreter and national Helper, passed away in Shiloh on 9 July 1863', Moravian Archives, Herrnhut, Germany. Translated by Annette Behrensmeyer, German Department, University of Cape Town.
14. Bonatz, 'Description of the Mission-Settlement at Shiloh', 350–52.
15. E. van Calker, 'A Century of Moravian Mission Work in the Eastern Cape Colony and Transkei, 1828–1928', in T. Keegan (ed.), *Moravians in the Eastern Cape 1828–1928: Four Accounts of Moravian Mission Work on the Eastern Cape Frontier*, trans. F.R. Baudert (Cape Town: van Riebeeck Society, 2004), 29–30.
16. van Calker, 'A Century of Moravian Mission Work', 29–30.
17. Stompjes, 'Curriculum Vitae', 19.
18. Cape of Good Hope. *Proceedings of, and Evidence Taken by, Commission on Native Affairs* (Grahamstown: Godlonton and Richards, 1865), evidence of A.N. Ella, Field Cornet, 37.
19. *A Standard Dictionary of the English Language*, vol. 2 (New York: Funk and Wagnalls, 1903), 2,079.
20. See announcement of registered trademark for 'Aerated Waters' by Messrs Mager and March, *Queenstown Free Press*, 20 July 1894.
21. Political and economic pressures resulted in conflict that spread south-eastwards from the Zulu kingdom between 1815 and 1835, see C. Hamilton, *The Mfecane Aftermath: Reconstructive Debates in Southern African History* (Pitermaritzburg: University of Natal Press, 1995).
22. Cape of Good Hope. *Proceedings of, and Evidence taken by, Commission on Native Affairs*, evidence of J.C. Warner, superintendent of Tambookie location, 67–83.

23. 'Frontier Affairs', reprinted from the Cradock News, *Queenstown Free Press*, 23 March 1859, 2.

24. Editorial, *Queenstown Free Press*, 24 January 1893, 3.

25. Cape Archives. Records of Colonial Office. Charles Brownlee, Chairman Municipal Commission Queenstown, to Richard Southey Resident Secretary, King William's Town, 26 November 1856.

26. The literature on the cattle-killing episode is extensive. See for example, J.B. Peires, *The Dead Will Arise: Nongqawuse and the Great Xhosa Cattle Killing Movement of 1856–57* (Johannesburg: Ravan Press, 1989); J.B. Peires, 'The Central Beliefs of the Xhosa Cattle Killing', *Journal of African History* 28(1) (1987), 43–63; J.B. Peires, 'Suicide or Genocide? Xhosa Perceptions of the Nongqawuse Catastrophe', *Radical History Review* 46(7) (1990), 47–57; J. Zarwan, 'The Xhosa Cattle Killings 1856–57', *Cahiers d'études africaines* 16(63–64) (1976), 519–39; L. Mpande, 'Cattle Killing as Resistance: The Dead Will Arise Reconsidered', *Research in African Literatures* 22(3) (1991), 171–81; G.T. Sirayi, 'The African Perspective of the 1856/1857 Cattle Killing Movement', *South African Journal of African Languages* 11(1) (1991), 40–45; A. Ashforth, 'The Xhosa Cattle Killing and the Politics of Memory', *Sociological Forum* 6(3) (1991), 581–92; J. Lewis, 'Materialism and Idealism in the Historiography of the Xhosa Cattle Killing Movement 1856–7', *South African Historical Journal* 25(1) (1991), 244–58; T.J. Stapleton, '"They No Longer Care for Their Chiefs": Another Look at the Xhosa Cattle Killing of 1856–1857', *International Journal of African Historical Studies* 24(2) (1991), 383–92; T.J. Stapleton, 'Reluctant Slaughter: Rethinking Maqoma's Role in the Xhosa Cattle Killing (1853–1857)', *International Journal of African Historical Studies* 26(2) (1993), 345–69; H. Bradford, 'Women, Gender and Colonialism: Rethinking the History of the British Cape Colony and its Frontier Zones c. 1806–70', *Journal of African History* 37(3) (1996), 351–70; H. Bradford, '"Akukho Ntaka Inokubhabha Ngephiko Elinye" (No Bird Can Fly on One Wing): The Great "Cattle Killing Delusion" and Black Intellectuals c. 1840–1910', *African Studies* 67(2) (2008), 209–32; B. Carton, 'The Forgotten Compass of Death: Apocalypse Then and Now in the Social History of South Africa', *Journal of Social History* 37(1) (2003), 199–218; S.B. Davies, 'The Cattle Killing as Propaganda: Leon Schauder's Nonquassi (1939)', *African Studies* 67(2) (2008), 183–208; S.B. Davies, 'Raising the Dead: the Xhosa Cattle Killing and the Mhlakaza-Goliat Delusion', *Journal of Southern African Studies* 33(1) (2007), 19–41; J. Wenzel, 'The Problem of Metaphor: Tropic Logic in Cattle Killing Prophecies and Their Afterlives', *African Studies* 67(2) (2008), 143–58; A. Offenburger, 'The Xhosa Cattle Killing Movement in History and Literature', *History Compass* 7(6) (2009), 1,428–43.

27. Cape Archives. Records of Colonial Office, correspondence J.C. Warner, Tambookie Agent, letter to Richard Southey, Resident Secretary King William's Town, 11 March 1857.

28. Cape Archives. Records of Colonial Office.

29. Cape of Good Hope. *Proceedings of, and Evidence Taken by, Commission on Native Affairs*, 79.

30. Cape of Good Hope. *Proceedings of, and Evidence taken by, Commission on Native Affairs*, 82.

31. Letter to editor from C.A.S. Tembuland, 23 February 1891, *Queenstown Free Press*, 3 March 1891, 4.

32. Cape of Good Hope. *Debates in the House of Assembly, in the First Session of the Ninth Parliament of the Cape of Good Hope, 17th May to 18th August 1894* (Cape Town: Cape Times Publishing Works, 1894), 368.

33. Cape of Good Hope. *Debates in the House of Assembly*, 366.

34. Quoted in B.J.F. Laubscher, *Sex, Custom and Psychopathology: A Study of South African Pagan Natives* (London: George Routledge and Sons, 1937), 132.

35. See W.E.M. Stanford, *The Reminiscences of Sir Walter Stanford*, vol. 2. J.W. Macquarrie (ed.) (Cape Town: van Riebeeck Society, 1962), 197.

36. Charles J. Levey, Resident Magistrate of Cala made this statement at a school in Xhalanga. Reprinted from frontier Guardian, *Queenstown Free Press*, 20 March 1891.

37. S.E.K. Mqhayi, *Inihobe Nemhongo: Xhosa Poetry* (Lovedale: Lovedale Press, 1929), 38–39.

38. J.J.R. Jolobe, *Amavo* (Johannesburg: Witwatersrand University Press, 1973, first published 1940).

39. L.E. Menze, *Iziphumo Zoderdo* (Pretoria: van Schaik, 1998).

References

Archives and Newspapers
Cape Archives, Records of Colonial Office, Cape Town, South Africa.
Moravian Archives, Herrnhut, Germany.
Queenstown Free Press.

Published Works
Ashforth, A. 'The Xhosa Cattle Killing and the Politics of Memory', *Sociological Forum* 6(3) (1991), 581–92.

Bonatz, Brother A. 'Description of the Mission-Settlement at Shiloh, in the Country of the Tambookies: With Some Account of the Manners, Customs etc. of the Neighbouring Tribes', *Periodical Accounts Relating to the Missions of the Church of the United Brethren Established Among the Heathen* 13 (1834), 351–52.

Bradford, H. 'Women, Gender and Colonialism: Rethinking the History of the British Cape Colony and its Frontier Zones c. 1806–70', *Journal of African History* 37(3) (1996), 351–70.

———. '"Akukho Ntaka Inokubhabha Ngephiko Elinye" (No Bird Can Fly On One Wing): The Great "Cattle Killing Delusion" and Black Intellectuals c. 1840–1910', *African Studies* 67(2) (2008), 209–32.

van Calker, E. 'A Century of Moravian Mission Work in the Eastern Cape Colony and Transkei, 1828–1928', in T. Keegan (ed.), *Moravians in the Eastern Cape 1828–1928: Four Accounts of Moravian Mission Work on the Eastern Cape Frontier*, trans. F.R. Baudert. Cape Town: van Riebeeck Society, 2004.

Cape of Good Hope. *Proceedings of, and Evidence Taken by, Commission on Native Affairs*. Grahamstown: Godlonton and Richards, 1865.

———. *Debates in the House of Assembly, in the First Session of the Ninth Parliament of the Cape of Good Hope, 17th May to 18th August 1894*. Cape Town: Cape Times Publishing Works, 1894.

Carton, B. 'The Forgotten Compass of Death: Apocalypse Then and Now in the Social History of South Africa', *Journal of Social History* 37(1) (2003), 199–218.

Cooper, F. 'Colonizing Time: Work Rhythms and Labor Conflict in Colonial Mombasa', in N.B. Dirks (ed.), *Colonialism and Culture*. Ann Arbor: University of Michigan Press, 1992, 209–45.

Crais, C.C. *The Making of the Colonial Order in the Eastern Cape 1770–1865: White Supremacy and Black Resistance in Pre-Industrial South Africa*. Johannesburg: Witwatersrand University Press, 1992.

Davies, S.B. 'Raising the Dead: The Xhosa Cattle Killing and the Mhlakaza-Goliat Delusion', *Journal of Southern African Studies* 33(1) (2007), 19–41.

———. 'The Cattle Killing as Propaganda: Leon Schauder's *Nonquassi* (1939)', *African Studies* 67(2) (2008), 183–208.

Elphick, R. and H. Giliomee. *The Shaping of South African Society 1652–1820*. Cape Town: Longman Penguin, 1979.

Guy, J. 'Jeff Peires's "The Dead Will Arise": A Landmark, Not a Breakthrough', *South African Historical Journal* 25(1) (1991), 227–31.

Hamilton, C. *The Mfecane Aftermath: Reconstructive Debates in Southern African History*. Pitermaritzburg: University of Natal Press, 1995.

Jolobe, J.J.R. *Amavo*. Johannesburg: Witwatersrand University Press, 1973, first published 1940).

Keegan, T. (ed.) and F.R. Baudert (transl.), *Moravians in the Eastern Cape 1828–1928: Four Accounts of Moravian Mission Work on the Eastern Cape Frontier* (Cape Town: Van Riebeeck Society, 2004),

Kropf, A. *Kafir-English Dictionary*. Alice: Lovedale Press, 1899.
Landau, P.S. *Popular Politics in the History of South Africa, 1400–1948*. Cambridge: Cambridge University Press, 2010.
Laubscher, B.J.F. *Sex, Custom and Psychopathology: A Study of South African Pagan Natives*. London: George Routledge and Sons, 1937.
Legassick, M. *The Struggle for the Eastern Cape 1800–1854: Subjugation and the Roots of South African Democracy*. Johannesburg: KMM Review, 2010.
Lewis, J. 'Materialism and Idealism in the Historiography of the Xhosa Cattle Killing Movement 1856-7', *South African Historical Journal* 25(1) (1991), 244–68.
McLaren, J. *A Concise Kaffir-English Dictionary*. London: Longmans, 1915.
Menze, L.E. *Iziphumo Zodendo*. Pretoria: van Schaik, 1998.
Moropa, K. and A. Kruger. 'Mistranslation of Culture-Specific Terms in Kropf's *Kafir-English Dictionary*', *South African Journal of African Languages* 20(1) (2000), 70–79.
Mpande, L. 'Cattle Killing as Resistance: The Dead Will Arise Reconsidered', *Research in African Literatures* 22(3) (1991), 171–81.
Mqhayi, S.E.K. *Imihobe Nemibongo: Xhosa Poetry*. Lovedale: Lovedale Press, 1929.
Offenburger, A. 'The Xhosa Cattle Killing Movement in History and Literature'. *History Compass* 7(6) (2009), 1,428–43.
Peires, J.B. 'Nxele, Ntsikana and the Origins of the Xhosa Religious Reaction', *Journal of African History* 20(1) (1979), 51–61.
———. 'Sir George Grey versus the Kaffir Relief Committee', *Journal of Southern African Studies* 10(2) (1984), 145–69.
———. 'The Late Great Plot: The Official Delusion Concerning the Xhosa Cattle Killing 1856–1857', *History in Africa* 12 (1985), 253–79.
———. '"Soft" Believers and "Hard" Unbelievers in the Xhosa Cattle Killing', *Journal of African History* 27(3) (1986), 443–61.
———. 'The Central Beliefs of the Xhosa Cattle Killing', *Journal of African History* 28(1) (1987), 43–63.
———. *The Dead Will Arise: Nongqawuse and the Great Xhosa Cattle-Killing Movement of 1856–57*. Johannesburg: Ravan Press, 1989.
———. 'Suicide or Genocide? Xhosa Perceptions of the Nongqawuse Catastrophe', *Radical History Review* 46(7) (1990), 47–57.
Sirayi, G.T. 'The African Perspective of the 1856/1857 Cattle Killing Movement', *South African Journal of African Languages* 11(1) (1991), 40–45.
A Standard Dictionary of the English Language, vol. 2. New York: Funk and Wagnalls, 1903.
Stanford, W.E.M. *The Reminiscences of Sir Walter Stanford*, vol. 2. J.W. Macquarrie (ed.). Cape Town: van Riebeeck Society, 1962.
Stapleton, T.J. '"They No Longer Care for Their Chiefs": Another Look at the Xhosa Cattle Killing of 1856–1857', *International Journal of African Historical Studies* 24(2) (1991), 383–92.
———. 'Reluctant Slaughter: Rethinking Maqoma's Role in the Xhosa Cattle Killing (1853–1857)', *International Journal of African Historical Studies* 26(2) (1993), 345–69.
Stråth, B. 'Introduction: Production and Meaning, Construction of Class Identities, and Social Change', in B. Stråth and C. Homberg (eds), *Language and the Construction of Class Identities: The Struggle for Discursive Power in Social Organisation. Report from the DISCO II Conference on Continuity and Discontinuity in the Scandinavian Democratisation Process in Kungälv, 7–9 Sept 1989*. Gothenburg: Department of History, Gothenburg University, 1990, 2–9.
Wenzel, J. 'The Problem of Metaphor: Tropic Logic in Cattle Killing Prophecies and Their Afterlives', *African Studies* 67(2) (2008), 143–58.
Zarwan, J. 'The Xhosa Cattle Killings 1856–57', *Cahiers d'études africaines* 16(63–64) (1976): 519–39.

Anne Kelk Mager teaches history in the Department of Historical Studies at the University of Cape Town, where her interests encompass economic and social history and gender history. Her publications include articles in *Past and Present*, the *Journal of Southern African Studies* and the *Journal of African History* (on whose editorial board she served from 2003 to 2009) and two books, *Gender and the Making of a South African Bantustan: A Social History of the Ciskei, 1945–1959* (Heinemann, 1999) and *Beer, Sociability and Masculinity in South Africa* (Indiana University Press, 2010). Her current research is on the history and significance of the chieftaincy for South Africa.

CHAPTER 4

Understanding the Concept of 'Marriage' in Afrikaans during the Twentieth Century

MARNÉ PIENAAR

Trou is nie perdekoop nie.
'Marry in haste, repent at leisure', or literally 'to marry is not to buy horses'.

Between 1985 and 2006 a number of changes took place in the legislation that governs marriage in South Africa. South Africans currently have three laws under which they may choose to get married, with one reflecting the more conventional European notion of one man, one woman, another allowing polygamous marriages and yet a further that *inter alia* provides for same-sex marriages. The mere fact that there are three laws regulating the institution of marriage points towards a history of tension, contestation and varying practices in the country. This chapter focuses on the way the Afrikaans-speaking community[1] in South Africa has understood the concept of 'marriage' in the twentieth century by scrutinizing lexical items that have a bearing on the notion of marriage.[2]

The heterogeneous nature of the Afrikaans speech community (one of many heterogeneous speech communities in South Africa) in itself suggests a diversity of social practices, and marriage is no exception. The reason for this is to be found in the origins of the Afrikaans-speaking community that dates back to 1652 when Jan van Riebeeck settled in the Cape. From 1676 to 1838 marriage in the Cape involving colonists (Dutch, German, French and Danish to name a few) had at various times been both a religious and a civil ceremony. Scully notes that from 1676 couples had to have their marriages certified as

Notes for this section begin on page 109.

legally valid by a matrimonial court prior to being married in church.³ In 1804 the Batavian government instituted the civil celebration of a marriage by council members, but this was ended in 1806 when the British retook control of the Cape, and for the next thirty years marriages were again solemnized in church. In 1818 and 1827 legislation introduced the issuing of special marriage licences by new matrimonial courts and, on payment of a fee, people were permitted to marry without the publication of banns.⁴ In 1838 ministers of religion remained the only officials who could legally solemnize marriages.

In 1838 the *de facto* marriages of slaves, which had never previously been sanctioned by any public ceremony or formally registered, were finally recognized by a Marriage Order in Council. In the same year (after the abolishment of slavery) former slaves' demand to marry grew in order to secure their relationships and to demonstrate their participation in the free world.⁵ This is of particular importance in understanding the historical meaning of 'marriage', as a large segment of the Afrikaans-speaking community are descended – in part – from former slaves. The concept of 'marriage' that grew out of this history and its particular gender dimensions differs from that present in the marriages of colonists.⁶ In the words of Scully, 'the meanings of marriage and the importance of marriages in conceptualizing freedom arose from very particular gender experiences constituted under slavery'.⁷ Freed women married in order to protect themselves from sexual abuse, as the legal and social status of being married made them respectable women in the eyes of society. Freed men, on the other hand, married legally as such marriage meant that a man's relationship to his family was recognized by law. It was the only way in which freed men could control access to the body and labour of their wives and gain legal authority over their children.

From 1836 the Great Trek into the interior brought Afrikaans-speaking colonists into closer contact with the Nguni and Sotho groups who had their own concepts of marriage, which contrasted with those held by the colonists; marriage had nothing to do with the state or the church and certainly bore no notion of freedom, as was the case with former slaves. Historically, marriage between people of African descent in South Africa has allowed for polygamy. This, too, is important in understanding what marriage means in Afrikaans, as although only a small percentage of the primary speech community is black, the broader community is familiar with the concept of polygamy, and it also ties in with another subsection of the Afrikaans-speaking community, namely the Cape Malay, who are also descended from freed people, but who adhere to Islam. It is clear, then, that by 1840 at least three possibly conflicting ideas concerning marriage prevailed, with the first linked to religion, the second to freedom and emancipation and the third to polygamy. This of course does not mean that there were no similarities between the various ideas of marriage and it might be readily assumed that aspects such as economics, sexuality and reproduction had some role to play in all three.

In the first half of the twentieth century, concepts of marriage were directly affected by new legislation that sought to regulate sexual conduct in manifold ways, including outlawing sexual contact between people of different races and sex between men. The adoption of the Immorality Act (1927)[8] and the Immorality Amendment Act (1950)[9] prohibited sex between a white person and a person of another race. This act was once more amended in the Amended Immorality Act (1969), which included section 20A prohibiting men from engaging in any same-sex erotic conduct when there were more than two people present.[10] (This did not apply to women.) Finally, the Prohibition of Mixed Marriages Act (1949) prohibited interracial marriages.[11]

In the twenty-first century the institution of marriage is perceived to be in a crisis in South Africa. A report on marriage and divorce issued by Statistics South Africa shows a consistent decline in the registration of marriages in South Africa during the period 2002 to 2011.[12] The same report states that in 2011, 54.7 per cent of the divorcees had children younger than eighteen. At a conference on child abuse held in Pretoria on 26 June 2012, Sue Krawitz, the Chairperson of the National Adoption Coalition and the Director of Impilo Children Protection Services and Adoption Services said that only 33.5 per cent of South African children live with both parents. She attributed this to what she called 'the low prevalence of marriages'.[13] Various factors contribute to this state of affairs, such as a lessened influence of traditional churches, economic circumstances and political changes. The fact remains that marriage as the stronghold of the family and society is contested in the South African and in the Afrikaans speech communities. In order to ascertain the nature of this contestation, I will attempt to delineate the changing meanings of the concept of 'marriage' within the Afrikaans speech community during the twentieth century. To do this the construction of meaning, as such, needs discussion.

The Construction of Meaning

In 'About Key Concepts and How to Study Them', Jan Ifversen argues that instead of accepting Reinhart Koselleck's understanding of basic concepts as oscillating between a linguistic approach and a non-linguistic, contextual approach (as is evident from the *Geschichtliche Grundbegriffe*) the two viewpoints can be linked because a study of concepts must be seen as more than the mere study of semantic change.[14] He draws both on the paradigm of social constructivism and the idea that not all reality is social and thus constructed. Referring to the work of John Searle, Ifversen points out that:

> A feature is observer dependent if it could not exist without there being observers intentionally thinking about it and doing things with it. This is the difference between on the one hand, mountains, rivers and gravitational attraction and marriage and property on the other hand. Without a social decision of some kind, a

convention – or an institution as the sociologists would say – money would only be paper, and complex social institutions like marriage and property would not make any sense.[15]

This idea ties in closely with the cognitive semantic perspective, which also presupposes that the understanding of a concept is embedded in time and is culturally specific. But how do we construct meaning?

According to Evans and Green, 'meaning construction is the process whereby language encodes or represents complex units of meaning'.[16] They argue that words are prompts for meaning construction rather than containers that carry meaning. Meaning is thus seen as encyclopaedic. The encyclopaedic approach holds that there is no principled distinction between semantics and pragmatics. That is, the idea that a principled distinction exists between core meaning on the one hand and pragmatic, social or cultural meaning on the other hand is rejected. According to this view knowledge of what words mean and knowledge about how words are used are both semantic.

Encyclopaedic knowledge is further seen as a structured system of knowledge, organized in a network. In this network not all knowledge accessed by a single word has equal standing. For example, the words *bride* or *groom* include information concerning our ideas of what a bride or groom looks like, her or his role, reasons for becoming a bride or a groom, pictures we have seen, whether we have been a bride or a groom and everything else we associate with a bride or a groom.[17]

Of particular importance for this chapter is the view that lexical items are points of access to encyclopaedic knowledge. Lexical items are not containers that present clear pre-packaged bundles of information. Rather, they provide access to a vast network of encyclopaedic knowledge. Apart from long-term semantic changes, lexical items also provide insight into the way in which meaning is developed synchronically. This can be seen in the dissonances that appear in terminology where, for instance a lesbian bride is still tied to a particular speech community and culture. The extent to which she or others see her as a bride can be contentious at various levels.

The encyclopaedic understanding of meaning forms the background for this investigation into the shifting meanings of the concept of 'marriage' in both earlier stages of and present-day Afrikaans. In accordance with the notion that lexical items are points of access to encyclopaedic knowledge, the words *huwelik, eg* and *trou* (partial synonyms of each other and translation equivalents of the English term 'marriage') are used to explore the concept of marriage. In accepting the dynamic nature of encyclopaedic knowledge, I am taking the concept to be open-ended, flexible and multidimensional. I also take it to be simultaneously emerging from the Afrikaans speech community's experience of the world and shaping those experiences.

Before discussing the lexical items *huwelik*, *trou* and *eg*, the changed socio-political context in which these words have been used needs attention. We need to understand the history of marriage and the contestations from various sectors of society against the apartheid state's efforts to control sexuality and marriage. These contestations came from internal and external pressure to end apartheid – and therefore limitations on interracial sexual relations and marriage – and from the gay community, starting in the 1970s. They contributed to the changes in legislation from 1985 to 2006 outlined above. But these contestations also shaped and were shaped by the shifting meanings of the concept of 'marriage' in Afrikaans. It is thus not possible to understand the concept in the absence of its context nor the context in the absence of the concept.

The notion of lexical items as points of access to encyclopaedic knowledge ties in with Koselleck,[18] as quoted by Ifversen, who makes it clear that concepts are more than words: 'The concept is bound to a word, but is at the same time more than a word: a word becomes a concept when the plenitude of politico-social context of meaning and experience in and for which a word is used can be condensed into one word. ... Concepts are thus the concentrate of several substantial meanings'.[19]

Legal Language and Practices of Marriage

The current context in which the concept of 'marriage' is constructed and contested in the Afrikaans speech community is particularly clear if one looks at the recent changes in legislation and the debates on practices such as polygamy, same-sex marriages and cohabitation. The first of the recent changes in legislation pertaining to marriages in South Africa was the Immorality and Prohibition of Mixed Marriages Amendment Act of 1985.[20] This repealed the Prohibition of Mixed Marriages Act (1949), which prohibited interracial marriages, the Immorality Act (1927) and the Immorality Amendment Act (1950), which prohibited extramarital sex between white people and people of other races.

Three laws thus currently provide for the status of marriage in South Africa. These are the Marriage Act (1961),[21] reflecting the Eurocentric notion of marriage involving one man and one woman, the Customary Marriages Act (1998),[22] which provides for the civil registration of marriages solemnized via the traditional African custom and which may include polygamy, and the Civil Union Act (2006).[23] South Africans may choose under which of these laws they wish to be married, but may be married in terms of only one at any given time. The Civil Union Act (2006) is of particular significance as it provides for both opposite-sex marriage and same-sex marriage. Same-sex marriages are only allowed in terms of the Civil Union Act (2006). Couples marrying in terms of the act have to choose whether their union is called a civil partnership or a marriage partnership. Couples joined in a marriage partnership in terms of that act enjoy the same privileges as couples married in terms of the Marriage Act (1961). If it can be proven that a couple is married in terms of any of these three acts, that marriage is legally valid and may not be regarded as an invalid marriage or a non-marriage by anyone or any organization. It is therefore illegal for any organization to treat any such married persons as if they were unmarried.

As legislation does not necessarily initiate changed practices and conceptualizations but rather, often, follows them, the discussion now turns to three aspects reflected in current legislation, namely polygamy, same-sex marriage and *saambly* (the notion of living together as a couple in the same physical residence but not being legally married).[24]

Although polygamy has long been accepted in certain sections of South African society, President Jacob Zuma's widely publicized polygamous marriages have recently led to robust debate with some claiming the practice to be part of culture and others denying it to be so. Various feminist voices are also heard rejecting the practice of polygamy.[25]

In 2011 Statistics South Africa (SSA) released a report showing a decrease in customary marriages during the period 2003 to 2011. In 2003, 17,283 customary marriages were registered at the Department of Home Affairs, in 2009, 15,506 and in 2010, 9,996. In 2011, the number dropped even further to 5,084.[26] In contrast to the decrease in customary marriages, the report shows an increase in civil marriages from 134,581 in 2001 to 170,826 in 2010. Civil unions increased from 80 in 2007 (the first year of record keeping) to 888 in 2010. This perceived rise in the number of civil marriages and civil unions does not refute the earlier reference to the decline of marriage in South Africa, but is simply indicative of population growth. Dorrit Posel and Stephanie Rudwick state that, historically, non-marriage among Africans in South Africa seems to have been rare, but they note a drop in marriage rates at least since the 1960s. They ascribe this decrease to various factors, namely the ravaging effects of apartheid policies on family structure, rising levels of education and increased economic opportunities for African women as well as the difficulty of accumulating bridewealth or *lobola*.[27]

As far as Afrikaans speakers are concerned, Erasmus is of the opinion that they generally agree with the dominant Christian religious view that does not accept polygamy as part of the institution of marriage.[28] Her research suggests that polygamous marriages are strictly condemned by the church and by the majority of this community. This is likely broadly true among the 90.6 per cent of the Afrikaans speech community who view themselves as Christian. However, apart from the 4.6 per cent of Afrikaans-speaking people who have no religious affiliation, Van der Merwe and Van der Merwe also note the 3.1 per cent of non-Christian religious Afrikaans speakers, which includes a section of the Muslim Cape Malay community.[29]

The practice of polygamy, albeit acceptable in terms of the Muslim religion, is not a common occurrence among Afrikaans-speaking South African Muslims. In an interview, Professor Farid Esack, Head of the Department of Religious Studies at the University of Johannesburg went so far as to suggest that the word *poligamie* was, until very recently, not known or used in the Cape Malay community.[30] This was confirmed in further interviews. For example, a sixty-nine-year-old woman in a polygamous marriage, whose father had four wives indicated that she knew the word but had only learned it approximately five years ago. When asked what the word meant, she said, *Jy't gekrap in iemand se huwelik* 'you fiddled in someone's marriage'.[31] She further noted that according to her it was *'n nuwe Ingelse word* 'a new English word'. The term used with reference to polygamy in the Cape Malay Community is *maro*. This word only relates to marrying a second or further wife and can be approximated with the term 'co-wife' or 'co-spouse'; in the case of marriage to a first wife *trou* 'marry' is used. The word *maro* can be used in various senses. As a verb it takes the following forms and meanings: *hulle maro* 'they marry', *hulle het gemaro* 'they married', *hy het haar gemaro* 'he married her' and *sy het hom gemaro* 'she married him'. It can also be used as a noun: *sy is my maro* 'she is my maro'. Here it has a double meaning in that it can either refer to a second or further wife from the husband's perspective or to the first wife from the second or further wives' perspective(s). That is, if Fatima is Shaid's first wife and Katie is his second wife then Katie will be Shaid's *maro* and Fatima will be Katie's *maro*. Taking a second or further wife can also be expressed as: *Hy't 'n tweede/nog 'n vrou gevat* 'he took a second or further wife'.

While polygamy has remained limited among Cape Malay Muslims, a small group of Afrikaans-speaking Muslims do practise this form of marriage. In interviews, people in polygamous marriages explained their choices with reference to their religious beliefs.[32] Polygamy has become increasingly contested and the practice seems to be dwindling in the country as a whole, but it remains legal.

Similarly, the fact that legislation allowing for same-sex marriages was adopted does not mean that it is an uncontested part of the concept of 'marriage' in South Africa. Various religious organizations, in particular, still object to the idea as is *inter alia* evident from an incident in January 2010 when a gay minister of the Methodist Church, Ecclesia de Lange, was expelled by her church following her marriage to her life partner.[33] While marriage between people of the same sex is legally possible, its inclusion in the concept of 'marriage' is still challenged. Earlier, I noted how legal instruments negotiate two aspects: regulating a wished-for social way of being, and reflecting prevalent social norms at given times. Here an additional aspect becomes evident: legal measures are not just a technical implementation of either or both of those two aspects. They are also catalysts for further contestation and debate in public opinion.

If one looks at the history of marriage in the Afrikaans speech community, all notions of the concept (be they religious, Eurocentric, state-regulated, indigenous or polygamous) had one aspect in common, namely opposite sexes. Same-sex marriages are thus conceptually different from these other forms, yet now form part of the concept of 'marriage' in Afrikaans. The question that still remains to be answered is how the notion of *saambly* 'cohabitation' differs from the concept of 'marriage'. Generally speaking, South African family law does not grant any legal status to relationships where people live together but are not married in terms of the legislation mentioned above. In exceptional situations, however, particular legislation can revoke the differences between marriages and situations where unmarried people (including same-sex couples) live together, such as the Domestic Violence Act (1998).[34]

In this act the term 'domestic relationship' is defined as meaning a relationship between a complainant and a respondent in any of the following ways:

> (a) they are or were married to each other, including marriage according to any law, custom or religion; (b) they (whether they are of the same or of the opposite sex) live or lived together in a relationship in the nature of marriage, although they are not, or were not, married to each other, or are not able to be married to each other; (c) they are the parents of a child or are persons who have or had parental responsibility for that child (whether or not at the same time); (d) they are family members related by consanguinity, affinity or adoption; (e) they are or were in an engagement, dating or customary relationship, including actual or perceived romantic intimate or sexual relationship of any duration; and (f) they share or recently shared the same residence.[35]

These definitions are important as they reflect the many variations in relationships between cohabiting people and as such give a much clearer indication of the various practices in society and move away from the strict binary opposition between being married and cohabiting. They acknowledge various kinds of marriages (including customary marriages and, therefore, polygamy), same-sex relationships, parental relationships, relationships based on affinity, irrespective of it being romantic or sexual, and cohabitation. Of particular interest are the words 'in a relationship in the nature of a marriage'. It seems as if the legislators also find the concept of 'marriage' evasive and thus support the thesis of this chapter, namely that the boundaries between marriage and cohabitation is increasingly becoming blurred, yet they remain different.

As in the case of same-sex marriages, the religious community does not necessarily approve of the arrangement of people cohabiting and engaging in sexual relations without being married. In 2009, Professor Piet Strauss, the moderator of the Dutch Reformed Church (although speaking in his personal capacity), issued a statement rejecting the practice of cohabitation as not in accordance with the Church's notion of morality. This caused an outcry in the media and in the broader Church with strongly opposing views being voiced by both the religious Christian and the secular communities.[36] Part of the debate focused on the economic advantages and disadvantages associated with marriage vs. cohabitation and arguments such as women suffering financially when not officially married, came to the fore. An aspect that is seldom officially raised in these debates, but that certainly forms part of the Christian subtext, is the issue of extramarital sex, and in particular, resultant pregnancies and children born out of wedlock.[37] The issue of illegitimacy is also evident in the many pejorative terms used to refer to children born out of wedlock, e.g. *grasgeldkind* 'a grass money child' (referring to a child for whom maintenance has to be paid and who was sired while his parents were lying on the grass, i.e. had sex without being married), a *hoerdop* 'a whore's drink', a *opslagkoeël* 'a ricochet bullet', a *valkind* 'fall-child' (referring to the mother who fell from grace) and a *voorkind* 'a child that came before [a wedding]'.[38]

Irrespective of whether or not the religious community accepts or rejects the practice of cohabitation, it is a growing phenomenon (compare the notion of 'the low prevalence of marriage' in South Africa above) and the Afrikaans speech community is not excluded from this tendency.[39]

The Meaning of 'Marriage' in Afrikaans: Definitions and Etymology

It is against this background that I now turn to a discussion of the words *huwelik*, *trou* and *eg*. As stated above, a concept is more than a word. However, the lexical meaning, denotations, connotations, the diachronic and the synchronic meaning, lexical relations, syntagmatic as well as paradigmatic relations all have bearing on that which ultimately constitutes the meaning of a concept. A closer look at the linguistic make-up of the relevant terms allows us to gain a fuller understanding of what the concept 'marriage' entails in Afrikaans. Because lexical meaning is a point of access into the broader encyclopaedic meaning, I consulted a variety of dictionaries, word lists, idioms and proverbs in order to ascertain the broader lexical meaning of the word.[40] In addition, I investigated the syntagmatic and paradigmatic relations of the lexical item 'marriage'.[41]

In Afrikaans, marriage has three close equivalents: *huwelik*, *trou* and *eg*. The nouns *huwelik* and *eg* approximate the English noun 'marriage'. The process of marrying is expressed by means of verbs as in *om te trou*, *om in die huwelik te tree* and *om in die eg verbind te word*, and the related nominal concept of the act of marriage – the ritualized ceremony – by the nouns *huweliksbevestiging* 'marriage ceremony', *troue* 'wedding' and *bruilof* 'wedding'. The state of being married is conveyed by the expressions *om getroud te wees* 'to be married' and *om in die eg verbind te wees* 'to be bound in matrimony'.

The etymology of the lexical items *huwelik*, *trou* and *eg* adds to our understanding of the diachronic roots of the concept of 'marriage' in Afrikaans. According to Van Wyk, the noun *huwelik* has the following two definitions. First, *die wettige verbintenis tussen man en vrou om lewenslank saam te leef, of die troue self* 'the legal commitment between a man and a woman to live together for life, or the wedding itself'. And second, *toestand van in die eg verbind wees* 'the state of being united in matrimony'.[42] The word *huwelik* is derived from the Dutch word *huwelijk* with the first meaning already in use in Middle Dutch and the second meaning first recorded in 1658. The Dutch word *huwelijk* is itself a compound word consisting of *huwen* 'marry' and *-lijk*. The latter relates to, among other things, the Old High German *leih* 'game; melody' and the Gothic *laiks* 'dance', referring to the festive nature of the wedding ceremony.

As explained in note 40 the word *trou* has not yet been processed in the *Woordeboek van die Afrikaanse Taal*. It is, however, recorded in the database with the oldest written source being the first Afrikaans newspaper *Die Afrikaanse Patriot*, published in 1876. The standard Afrikaans dictionary *Handwoordeboek van die Afrikaanse Taal* (HAT)[43] defines the verb as 1. *in die huwelik tree* 'to step into marriage', 2. *in die huwelik bevestig* 'to unite in matrimony' and 3. *in die huwelik as vrou of man neem* 'to take a man or woman into marriage'. The verb is, however, derived from the noun *trou* or the Dutch form *trouw*, which is defined as the predisposition to maintain a bond, obligation or relationship, or loyalty.[44]

Trouw (as a noun, the verb in Dutch is *trouwen*) is also recorded in Middle Dutch as *trouwe* and *trûwe*, as *treuwa* in Old Saxon, as *triuwa*, in Old High German, *treue* in New High German, *trêow* in Old English, *triggwa* in Gothic, *trewwô in Germanic and *trewâ in Indo-Germanic. According to De Vries and Tollenaere, the Middle Dutch verbs *betrouwen* and *betrûwen* can be traced to the Indo-Germanic *dreu, *drou or *dru with the adjectival meaning of being as hard as oak or unbreakable.[45]

In Afrikaans *trou* is also found in derivatives such as *getroud* 'married', *troue* 'wedding', *getrou* 'faithful' and a seemingly endless number of compound words such as *trourok* 'wedding dress', *troupak* 'wedding suit', *troukoek* 'wedding cake', *troukar* 'bridal car', *troukaartjies* 'wedding invitation cards', etc.

Finally, the noun *eg* is defined as *huwelik* 'marriage', and stems from the Dutch *echt* (and Middle Dutch *echt(e)*). *Eg* is also found in the words *eggenoot* 'husband' and *eggenote* 'wife', *ega* 'husband' or 'wife' as well as *egbreuk* 'adultery', with the literal meaning 'to break the marriage'. *Eg* also has an additional (polysemic) meaning as an adjective and adverb giving 'true, real, not faked'. The *Handwoordeboek van die Afrikaanse Taal* (HAT) confirms this relationship with *eg* 'marriage' by distinguishing between *egte kind* 'true child', i.e. born in wedlock, and *onegte kind* 'untrue child', i.e. born out of wedlock.[46]

From the above certain (diachronic) entailments of the concept of 'marriage' emerge, namely: a legal bond, an arrangement between a man and a woman, a ceremony, a festivity, an obligation, a bond and loyalty. None of the entries in the *Etimologiewoordeboek van Afrikaans* mention the religious aspect of marriage, love or infatuation, nor do they acknowledge same-sex marriage or include polygamous marriage.[47] I can only speculate about the reasons for the absence of references to love or infatuation and even the religious aspect of marriage.

In terms of same sex marriage the reason might well be that it is a very recent (legal) practice.[48] As noted before, polygamy is known in the Afrikaans speech community but not commonly practised. It should, however, be noted that none of these aspects or possibilities is explicitly ruled out in these definitions.

The etymological dictionary gives insight into the diachronic development of words and the comprehensive Afrikaans dictionary combines two interests, one more normative-prescriptive geared towards standardization, the other more descriptive, gathering actual language use. In order to truly assess usage patterns, and how sedimented meaning is employed, another route has been explored.

The Meaning of 'Marriage' in Afrikaans: Proverbs and Expressions

As idioms, proverbs and expressions often provide conventional understandings of social life, I envisaged that they might provide further insight into the concept of 'marriage' in Afrikaans. An investigation into these provided further entailments of the concept 'marriage'. The first of these refers to the practice of people cohabiting as couples without being legally married: *Oor die puthaak trou* 'to marry over the well hook',[49] *Agter die bos getroud* 'married behind the bush'[50] and *Getroud maar nie gekerk nie* 'married but not churched'.[51] These expressions also allude to sexuality as they imply that the marriage has been consummated (behind the bush), without it being legal or condoned by the religious community. By contrast, we also find that marriage entails a religious aspect in references to marrying at the altar: *Voor die altaar* 'at the altar',[52] *Gebooie laat loop* 'to have the banns published'[53] and *Voor die kansel staan* 'to stand at the altar'.[54]

A number of idioms, expressions and proverbs also point towards the commonly understood complications associated with marriage. One entailment is that marriage causes disillusionment, as seen in the following proverbs: *Die bruid is in die skuit, nou is die mooi praatjies uit*[55] 'the bride is gotten, the promises forgotten', or literally 'the bride is on the boat, the sweet talk is over'[56] and *Trou is nie perdekoop nie*[57] 'marry in haste, repent at leisure', or literally 'to marry is not to buy horses'. A second is that marriage entails trouble: *Jou kop in die strik/strop steek* 'to put one's head into the noose'[58] and *Vars botter en warm brood is 'n ou man se bittere dood* 'a sweet young thing is the death of an old man',[59] or literally 'fresh butter and warm bread are the bitter death of an old man'. The following image of marriage as a thorn tree, and hence as entailing trouble, is a direct translation from an Owambo idiom into Afrikaans: *Trou is nie om bessies te gaan pluk nie, maar dit is om die haakdoring se vrugte te pluk* 'to marry is not to pick berries, but to pick fruit from the hook thorn tree'.[60] And finally, there is the work to be completed before getting married because marriage entails (material) preparation, such as having a house to live in: *Eers die koutjie dan die vroutjie* 'be sure before you marry of a house wherein you tarry',⁶¹ or literally 'first the (little) cage, then the (little) woman'. This particular proverb touches on an aspect that is not that evident in the other data, namely the responsibility that is placed on the groom to provide for his bride economically. These proverbs are extremely gendered in that they are admonitions directed at the potential groom. As such they also echo the idea of a rite of passage to manhood with certain preparatory steps indicated, such as individual and financial preparation and careful consideration for a ritualized ceremony, a ceremony marking not only a legal agreement, but also steps towards adulthood.⁶²

Imagery that centres on the idea of forming a household appears in proverbs that refer to a pot: *Mens moenie almal uit een pappot eet nie* 'everyone should not eat out of the same pot',⁶³ meaning that the same families should not be intermarrying. *Elke pot kry sy deksel* 'every pot gets its lid',⁶⁴ meaning 'every Jack has his Jill'. And *Al is 'n pot nog so skeef, hy kry 'n deksel* 'irrespective of the crookedness of a pot, it still gets a lid',⁶⁵ again meaning 'every Jack has his Jill'. The notion of herding is present in *Die skapies bymekaar jaag* 'to herd sheep together',⁶⁶ meaning 'to be married'. The idea of communal living is clear in *Velletjies bymekaar gooi* 'to throw your hides together',⁶⁷ meaning 'to get married' or 'to tie the knot'. These images of herding, hides and pots emphasize the importance of creating a household as well as the historical, economic and social aspects of marriage.

While working through the unprocessed card system of the comprehensive Afrikaans dictionary *Woordeboek van die Afrikaanse Taal*,⁶⁸ it soon became apparent that the additional (polysemic) meaning of *trou* as adjective, adverb and noun had a particularly high occurrence in the citations dating between 1938 and 1983, in other words in the ten years before the election of the National Party and through the heyday of apartheid. This meaning of *trou* can be summarized using the entry in the *Pharos Bilingual Afrikaans-English Dictionary*:

> *trou* n. faith(fulness), fidelity, loyalty, fealty, constancy; *goeie (kwade)* – good (bad) faith, bona (mala) fides; *te goeder (kwader)* – in good (bad) faith, bona (mala) fide; *sweer* – swear allegiance, the oath of allegiance, plight one's troth (faith). *trou* a. faithful; loyal (subject); firm; constant; staunch; true; trusty; devoted.⁶⁹

The particularly high frequency noted in the *Woordeboek van die Afrikaanse Taal* database of this meaning of *trou* can be attributed to the use of the word in the Afrikaner nationalist context. The following example quoted from the architect of apartheid and Afrikaner nationalism, H.F. Verwoerd, is typical of the kind found in the database: *'En as u terugkyk na die verlede en vorentoe na die toekoms, u trou bind u aan u eie land alleen, 'n eie Republiek van Suid-Afrika'* 'and if one looks back into the past and forward into the future one's loyalty binds one to one's own country only, a Republic of South Africa of our own'.⁷⁰

Although this polysemic meaning of *trou* does not, strictly speaking, impact the concept of 'marriage', it should be noted that this meaning is also under contestation. When the new democratic government came into power in 1994, the 'common sense' assumption held by some people of *trou aan God en land* 'faithfulness/loyalty to God and country', i.e. loyalty to the Church and to the National Party, was challenged. This was particularly the case insofar as the Afrikaans churches' justification of apartheid on a biblical basis was concerned. This led to a widespread turning away from the traditional Afrikaans churches and South Africa is now a secular state.[71]

Returning to *trou* 'marriage', the *Woordeboek van die Afrikaanse Taal* database confirms the entailments set out above and offers additional ones, including emotions and economics.[72] For example, marriage should entail love and one should not enter into marriage solely for perceived financial gain: *Trou vir liefde en werk vir geld* 'marry for love and work for money', *Honger trou met dors* 'hunger marries thirst', meaning both parties are equally poor and *Ek weet niks van jou trousake af nie, dis sommer in die algemeen dat ek die opmerkinkie maak, en dit is: As jy 'n arm man is, pasop daarvoor om 'n ryk vrou te trou* 'I know nothing about your marriage and it is only in general that I make the following comment, and that is: if you are a poor man, be careful to marry a rich woman'.

Despite economic or other difficulties, marriage is understood to last forever: *Kolganse 'trou' ook soos baie ander diere en bly aan vir die res van hul lewe bymekaar* 'Egyptian geese like many other animals also "marry" and stay together for the rest of their lives'[73] and *Trou is niks nie, maar die lank hou* 'marriage is nothing but the lasting thereof', implying that it lasts forever and that the parties will tire of one another.

At the same time, marriage is seen as an ailment: *Troukoors* 'marriage fever', meaning an urgent (feverish) need to get married. It is also a biological urge: *Trou kom soos 'n groot kak* 'marriage comes like a big shit'. To get married before breakfast (*Voor brekfis trou*) is to hastily enter into marriage without looking into the consequences. Nonetheless, marriage entails happiness with the prerequisite that a person with marriageworthy characteristics is found: *Kry u dit reg om ... so 'n trouwaardige (as huweliksmaat) raak te loop, is jul geluk verseker* 'if you manage to meet a person worthy of marriage, your happiness is guaranteed'.[74]

Apart from the additional entailments of the concept 'marriage' that emerged from the *Woordeboek van die Afrikaanse Taal* database, two further images were noted. The first is the notion of *lobola* (bride price or bridewealth): *Uiteindelik was dertien beeste in Jabulanie se pa se kraal en het hy laat weet dat hy oor ses maande ook nog genoeg kontantgeld sal hê om te kom trou* 'finally the thirteen pieces of cattle were in Jabulanie's kraal and he had let them know that he would also have enough cash in six months' time to come and get married' and *As dit net nie die troubeeste is nie – dan is daardie vrou los. 'n Ander man kan haar trou. Maar die troubeeste hou haar vas* 'if it weren't for the wedding cattle – then the woman would be free. Another man can marry her. But the wedding cattle ties her down'. The idea of *lobola* (*lobolo* (noun) and *lobola* (verb) in Afrikaans and derived from *ilobolo* in Zulu)[75] is not foreign to the Afrikaans speech community, as it is commonly practised in South Africa. It also bears a resemblance to the Malay community's tradition of *maskawie* (derived from the Malayu word *masawin*)[76] although *maskawie* is not bride price in same sense as *lobola*, but rather a token amount (around fifty South African Rand, or five U.S. dollars) given to the prospective bride by her prospective husband upon engagement, and is defined as a *pligsgeskenk aan die bruid* 'a gift of obligation to the bride'.[77] The point, however, remains that both *lobola* and *maskawie* relate to the economic aspect of marriage, and as such they tie in with the material preparation that a man has to complete before entering into marriage, and by extension also to a rite of passage and manhood.

One further polysemic meaning of *trou* emerged from the *Woordeboek van die Afrikaanse Taal* database, namely the idea of putting things together. This meaning is especially prevalent in entries that deal with food and wine as can be seen in the following examples. First, on food: *Die vleis kook lynsag en trou goed met die groente* 'the meat cooks until very soft and marries well with the vegetables' and *Die geure het tot heerlikheid getrou* 'the flavours married to splendour'. Second, on wine: *Met die metode waar die gas verkry word van 'n tweede gisting wat in die wyn plaasvind, is wyn en gas beter getroud sodat pragwyne dikwels al volgens hierdie prosedure verkry is* 'with the method where the gas is obtained from a second fermentation taking place in the wine, the wine and gas are better married resulting in beautiful wines being made according to this procedure'.[78] Given that marriage can be seen as the founding moment of a household which implies *inter alia* eating and drinking, this polysemic extension to wine and food is not all that surprising. The sentiment conveyed seems positive in the sense of the vegetables and the meat being well married, the flavours married to splendour and the marriage between the wine and the gas resulting in beautiful wine. The underlying idea of compatibility as well as the idea of a whole being worth more than its parts is also evident.

The idea of 'putting things together' in a political sense as the marriage of ideas, was also found: *'Die Nasionale Party daarenteen het gister in die debat oorgekom as die gematigde party wat streef na oplossings waarin groepsbelange laer gestel word as nasionale belange, wat idealisme probeer trou met realisme, wat besef dat demokrasie nie net deur die woorde van 'n grondwet omvat kan word nie, maar dat dit die gesindheid is wat die deurslag gee'*[79] 'in contrast the National Party yesterday came across as the moderate party that strives to obtain solutions where group interests are placed below national interests, that tries to marry idealism with realism, that realizes that democracy cannot only be embraced by the words of the constitution, but that the attitude is decisive'. I have deliberately included this example as it relates to the idea of loyalty to the state noted above. The excerpt dates to 1983, the heyday of the apartheid system. The National Party is here depicted as a moderate party, which wants to enter into the right kind of marriage, and in doing so is prepared to place its own interest on hold for the better good of all.[80]

As stated above, the *Woordeboek van die Afrikaanse Taal* strives to be as comprehensive as possible and seeks to incorporate all the varieties of Afrikaans but is not yet completed. It was therefore also necessary to consult other sources. In 2010 Anton F. Prinsloo published *Annerlike Afrikaans*, focusing on regional varieties of Afrikaans.[81] No new entailments of marriage were found in this work but it is worth mentioning the ironic and euphemistic use of the word *trou* as adultery or fornication amongst the speakers of Griqua-Afrikaans. *Saamsit* 'sitting together' is also indicated as a synonym of *trou* 'marry'. *'n Buitevuurtjie* 'an outside fire' is a euphemism for a lover. The idea of the household (founded on marriage) is clear yet again, with those who are a part of it being on the inside and those who are not, on the outside. This is important as it underscores the conceptual difference between relationships in and out of wedlock, or with reference to note 24 at the very least it informs our knowledge of what marriage is not.

The Meaning of 'Marriage' in Afrikaans: Syntagmatic and Paradigmatic Relations

So far, I have looked into semantic characterizations insofar as they can be established by way of a close reading of dictionaries, including etymological information, but also corpus-based analysis of larger contexts in which these terms are used. This leads to broader semantic fields and domains that are viewed as related, for example marriage and economy/household or marriage and sexuality. A final analytical tool to be used here is that of syntagmatic relations and compounding and paradigmatic relations. The systematic co-occurrence of words can be of great value for a finer understanding of what meanings a concept entails. Syntagmatic relations need to be borne in mind when considering the concept of 'marriage', as these relations are definitive in distinguishing a formal marriage from the informal (not legally recognized) arrangement of living together. In other words, the differences in the syntagmatic relations of *trou* 'marriage' and *saambly* 'cohabitation' respectively, point towards a conceptual difference in the two notions. For example, not all the possible compound words that have *trou* as their basis (in this instance 'wedding' or 'marriage' in English) can substitute *trou* with the word *saambly* 'cohabitation'. This can be seen in the compounds *troumars* 'wedding march', *trouplanne* 'wedding plans' *trou-album* 'wedding album', *troudag* 'wedding day', etc. Two other cases in point would be *trouman* and *trouvrou* (referring to a man or a woman one could marry in the sense that they meet the criteria one has set for oneself in terms of the attributes that a life partner should have).

Some terms generally reserved for marriage partners are occasionally usurped by the *saambly* option. Examples would be *man* and *vrou* 'man' and 'woman', but also 'husband' and 'wife', where some couples who live together will refer to their partners as their *meisie* or *kêrel/ou* 'girlfriend' or 'boyfriend' or as their *vrou* or *man* 'wife' or 'husband'. The opposite, however, does not occur, where a wife or husband is referred to as a girlfriend or boyfriend. Afrikaans does not have an equivalent for the gender-neutral English word 'partner' in the sense of someone with whom one is in a romantic or sexual relationship.

Paradigmatic relations include synonyms, antonyms, complementary pairs, opposites, homonyms, part-whole relations, ordered series and unordered series. Above, I indicated that *eg*, *huwelik* and *trou* act as synonyms for 'marriage' in Afrikaans. *Eg* has the additional polysemic meaning of 'true' (as in 'not fake') that is also elicited in compound words related to marriage such as *onegte kind* 'untrue child' or a child born out of wedlock. This is relevant for our understanding of what the concept 'marriage' means in Afrikaans, as it is portrayed as the real thing, as opposed to living together, which apparently is not.

Trou has two additional polysemic meanings, namely loyalty (to God and country) and joining (things or ideas). *Skei* 'split' or 'divorce' acts as a non-gradable antonym (or member of the complementary pair) of *trou* in the sense that a comparative structure such as married/divorced, more married/divorced, most married/divorced is not possible and the negative of the one (being married) implies the existence of the other (divorced). As in the case of syntagmatic relations, *saambly* 'cohabitation' is once more excluded from the paradigm as *skei* 'divorce' does not act as an antonym or form a complementary pair with *saambly* 'cohabitation'. The terms *uitmaak* 'to break up' or *uitmekaar* 'to split up' are used to indicate a break-up between people living together. However when it comes to hyponymic relations *geskei* 'divorced' can also be viewed as a co-hyponym for both *saambly* 'cohabitation' and *trou* 'marriage'. Hyponymy can be defined as a semantic relation of inclusion, where a more general word includes the meaning of a whole series of more specific words. The word *huwelikstatus* 'marital status' can therefore be seen as the superordinate of, for instance *enkel* 'single', *getroud* 'married', *geskei* 'divorced', *saambly* 'cohabitation', *weduwee* 'widow' and *wewenaar* 'widower', which act as hyponyms of the superordinate *huwelikstatus* 'marital status' and thereby also as co-hyponyms of each other.

The most important implication of the various paradigmatic relations of *trou* is that they support the conceptual difference between *trou* and *saambly*. Linguistically they are not synonyms, nor is 'divorce' an antonym of 'living together' as it is not (linguistically) possible to divorce someone after having lived together. *Trou* and *saambly* are co-hyponyms of each other, which also implies a conceptual difference in the same way as for instance 'bride' and 'groom' differ on the basis of gender. They may even be seen to lie on a continuum of falling in love, living together and marriage. The point remains that the two terms are not equivalent on a linguistic level.

The derivative of *trou* 'marriage', *troue* 'wedding' designates the wedding ceremony, for which no equivalent exists for *saambly* 'cohabitation'. *Om getroud te wees* 'to be married' indicates a state as *saambly* does. *Eg* is highly formal and used in fixed expressions such as *om in die eg verbind te word* 'to get bound in matrimony' or *om in die eg verbind te wees* 'to be bound in matrimony', and also refers to a state of being (married). The derivative *ega* denotes the term 'spouse' in English that is reserved for a marriage partner. Sexual engagement outside of marriage, or adultery, is *egbreuk* 'to break the marriage'. This term cannot be used in a context where people are living together. The term *verneuk* 'cheat' is used. *Verneuk* can be used to indicate adultery or unfaithfulness in any romantic relationship, but *egbreuk* 'adultery' only applies to marriage.

It could be argued that the institutional nature of marriage with its associated prescribed rituals are to blame for the discrepancies in terminology and that the trend towards living together as well as the institutionalization thereof via new legislation may erode the difference in the future. For the moment, however, *huwelik*, *trou* and *eg* are conceptually different from *saambly* and the Afrikaans language mirrors this difference.

Conclusion

At the outset of this chapter it was envisaged that the words *huwelik*, *trou* and *eg* could act as points of access to the encyclopaedic knowledge on 'marriage' embedded in the Afrikaans speech community. The encyclopaedic approach was chosen as it holds that there is no principled distinction between semantics and pragmatics and that both inform our understanding of meaning. The objective was to gain an understanding of what the concept 'marriage' used to mean and currently means in Afrikaans, given that it is a contested concept. Marriage is at the same time a simple and an immensely complex concept. Most people will have no problem in answering the question 'What does "marriage" mean?' and yet an investigation into the historical and current practices surrounding the concept indicates a very dynamic semantic environment. As such is it very difficult, if not impossible, to define the concept of 'marriage' in Afrikaans. As noted above, the meaning of the oldest traceable form of the noun *trou* (from which the verb is derived) – namely the presumed *dreu, *drou and *dru in Indo-Germanic – was 'unbreakable', implying loyalty. The derived verb first recorded in Middle Dutch found its way via seventeenth-century Dutch into what eventually became Afrikaans.

The Afrikaans speech community is not homogenous, and since 1652, when the first permanent European settlers brought Dutch to the Cape region, various diverse practices concerning marriages have occurred. Yet standard Afrikaans dictionaries do not reflect these diverse practices and consequently do not answer the question as to the meaning of the concept of 'marriage' in Afrikaans. Rather, they give a very narrow and now outdated Eurocentric view of one man and one women legally committing to live together for life. This definition excludes polygamy, same-sex marriage and cohabitation. Given the historic framing of these dictionaries (produced mainly in the 1960s) the underlying suggestion is also that this legal commitment does not pertain to interracial relationships.

At least one of the alternative practices is, however, reflected in proverbs and idioms on marriage, namely cohabitation. Homosexuality and marriages between whites and people of other races are reflected in colonial, and in particular, apartheid legislation that attempted to lay down rules to engineer the institution of marriage, namely the Immorality Act (1927), the Prohibition of Mixed Marriages Act (1949), the Immorality Amendment Act (1950), the Marriage Act (1961) and the Amended Immorality Act (1969). The important difference between these pieces of legislation and those that came later lies in the fact that they did not reflect current practices but forced changes in existing practices. It is also important to remember that the three largest Afrikaans churches (collectively known as the sister churches) endorsed apartheid on biblical grounds and thus supported this restrictive legislation.

External and internal pressure (including from within the Dutch Reformed Church by prominent clergy such as Beyers Naudé) however, led to the adoption of the Immorality and Prohibition of Mixed Marriages Amendment Act (1985), which decriminalized marriages between whites and people of other races. At the time the absurdity of apartheid became even more evident as the Group Areas Act (1950) was still in place. This act regulated the areas where people lived according to race and was only repealed on 5 June 1991. Between 1985 and 1991 marriages between whites and people of other races were therefore legal, but such couples were not legally allowed to live together in the same place. The democratization of South Africa in 1994 and the consequent adoption of the new constitution paved the way for legislation that mirrored various practices in society with the adoption of the Customary Marriages Act (1998), which regulates polygamy, and the Civil Union Act (2006). Yet certain anomalies remain that point towards the concept of 'marriage' still not being quite clear in the minds of the legal fraternity. The first being that the Civil Union Act (2006) gives couples the choice as to whether they want to refer to their union as being a civil partnership or a marriage partnership. The mere fact that such a choice is given implies a difference between a marriage and something else that is a legal bond, but not a marriage. The second is the wording in the Domestic Violence Act (1998) that *inter alia* defines a domestic relationship as a relationship that exists between people who 'live or lived together in a relationship *in the nature of marriage*, although they are not, or were not, married to each other, or are not able to be married to each other', which implies continued uncertainty over what the term means.

The question that still remains is whether changes in legislation reflect a changed context and, therefore, a change in meaning? In terms of the concept of 'marriage' in Afrikaans it is not so clear-cut, as the context within which the concept functioned was not necessarily reflected in the legislation of the first three quarters of the twentieth century but rather forced upon the broader Afrikaans speech community. The changes in the legislation towards the end of the century better portray the various practices and at the same time also reiterate different choices and practices and, therefore, underscore the dynamic nature of the concept of 'marriage' in Afrikaans.

Native speakers of Afrikaans simply 'know' the senses associated with *trou, eg* and *huwelik*, as they also 'know' the difference between 'marriage' and 'cohabitation'. They understand the range of possibilities 'in the nature of a marriage' and within the group they have preferences for certain practices rather than others. And so the concept of 'marriage' remains contested in the Afrikaans speech community and impacts on the economic, moral, religious and family life of the community as is reflected in the language used to talk, debate, relate, describe and argue about it.

Notes

1. The Afrikaans speech community is not a homogenous grouping. The primary speech community totals 5.98 million speakers, whereas the secondary speech community consists of 6.75 million speakers (including primarily first-language speakers of English, the Nguni and Sotho languages). Afrikaans is the third-largest speech community in South Africa (preceded by isiZulu and isiXhosa) and the dominant language in two provinces, namely the Western and Northern Cape. Afrikaans is spoken across all socio-economic groupings and Afrikaans-speaking people have an older age and higher education profile than the South African average. Apart from English, Afrikaans is the only other South African language that is used as a medium of learning and teaching in secondary and tertiary education. The Afrikaans speech community represents a large variety of religious affinities varying from a range of Protestantism, Roman Catholicism, Islam and others with 90.6% of the group who consider themselves Christian, 3.1% as non-Christian and 4.6% who do not belong to any affiliation. Afrikaans is used as a primary language across the range of ethnicities in South Africa, with 4.2% of the speakers being black African, 42.2% white and 53.2% coloured. In absolute terms, most Afrikaans speakers live in the urban metropoles – Cape Town and Gauteng. Port Elizabeth, Bloemfontein and Kimberley are secondary foci. I.J. Van der Merwe and J.H. Van der Merwe (eds.), *Linguistic Atlas of South Africa: Language in Space and Time* (Stellenbosch: Sun Press, 2006).

2. Afrikaans only became an official language in 1926. The oldest written data used are from 1902, when a word list was compiled based on the first published Afrikaans newspaper *Die Afrikaanse Patriot* (1876).

3. P. Scully, *Liberating the Family? Gender and British Slave Emancipation in the Rural Western Cape, South Africa, 1823–1853* (Cape Town: David Philip Publishers, 1997), 112.

4. The publication of banns refers to the public announcement in a Christian church of an impending marriage between two specified persons. The purpose of the banns is to enable

anyone to raise any legal impediment to the marriage, so as to prevent marriages that are invalid. Such impediments could for example include a pre-existing marriage that has been neither dissolved nor annulled, a lack of consent, or the couple being related within the prohibited degrees of kinship.

5. Scully, *Liberating the Family?* 110.

6. See S. Coontz, *Marriage, A History: How Love Conquered Marriage* (London: Penguin Books, 2005).

7. Scully, *Liberating the Family?* 110.

8. Republic of South Africa, Immorality Act (Act no. 5 of 1927).

9. Republic of South Africa, Immorality Amendment Act (Act no. 21 of 1950).

10. Republic of South Africa, Amended Immorality Act (Act no. 57 of 1969).

11. Republic of South Africa, Prohibition of Mixed Marriages Act (Act no. 55 of 1949).

12. Statistics South Africa, 'Statistical Release P0307. Marriages and Divorces' (2011), 2 and 4.

13. Versluis, 'Pa's Meer Afwesig By Kinders', *Beeld*, 27 June 2012, 7.

14. J. Ifversen, 'About Key Concepts and How to Study Them', *Contributions to the History of Concepts* 2(2) (2009), 2.

15. Ifversen, 'About Key Concepts', 2.

16. V. Evans and M. Green, *Cognitive Linguistics: An Introduction* (Mahwah: Lawrence Erlbaum, 2006), 214.

17. Some of this knowledge is more central, some more peripheral. The place in the network depends on the kind of knowledge: conventional knowledge (widely known), generic knowledge (general rather than specific in nature), intrinsic knowledge (deriving from the form of an entity or relation in question) and characteristic knowledge (relatively unique to the entity or the relation in question).

18. R. Koselleck, 'Crisis', trans. M.W. Richter, *Journal of the History of Ideas* 67(2) (2006), 84.

19. Ifversen, 'About Key Concepts', 7.

20. Immorality and Prohibition of Mixed Marriages Amendment Act (Act no. 72 of 1985).

21. Marriage Act (Act no. 25 of 1961).

22. Customary Marriages Act (Act no. 120 of 1998).

23. Civil Union Act (Act no. 17 of 2006).

24. Megan Vaughan notes units of analysis such as community or household are often problematic as socio-economic realities and the cultural expression thereof often do not fit. One solution to the problem is to analyse relationships and transactions that function alongside certain practices. The case in point here is that the notion of living together needs to be scrutinized as it serves to inform our knowledge of what marriage is not. M. Vaughan, 'Which Family? Problems in the Reconstruction of the History of the Family as an Economic and Cultural Unit', *The Journal of African History* 24(2) (1983), 275–83.

25. 'South Africa and Polygamy: Swimming against the Tide', *The Economist*, 28 April 2012.

26. Statistics South Africa, 7.

27. D. Posel and S. Rudwick. 'Marriage and ilobolo [Bridewealth] in Contemporary Zulu Society', *African Studies Review* 2 (2014), 53.

28. C. Erasmus, 'Die Vergestalting van die Sleutelkonsep *Huwelik* in Agaat deur Marlene van Niekerk' (M.A. dissertation, University of Johannesburg, Auckland Park, 2012), 157.

29. Van der Merwe and Van der Merwe, *Linguistic Atlas of South Africa*, 17.

30. Interview, Prof. Farid Esack, 23 October 2012.

31. Interview, Mrs Amina Linneveldt, 23 October 2012. I have to admit that I, too, only got to learn the word 'polygamy' later in life. Although it was common knowledge that the practice existed amongst black South Africans, the word *veelwywery* 'having many wives' was generally used and in a context that did not include South Africans, but was rather used to refer to the Mormon society in the United States.

32. Mrs Suaad Bower, a married young Afrikaans-speaking Muslim woman, clearly stated her disregard for what she called 'cultural' marriages. In getting married, she and her husband

followed the prescribed religious route and only met each other once three weeks before they got married. According to her beliefs, love has no role to play in finding a husband or getting married. When asked how she would react to her husband taking a second wife, she responded that she had discussed it with her husband and that her only condition would be that he should be forthright with her. She acknowledged that it might be hard to accept at first but was sure that she would get used to it. Interview, Mrs Suaad Bower, October 15, 2012.

33. N. Jackson, 'Gay Predikant Geskors Omdat Sy met Haar Lewensmaat Trou', *Beeld*, 17 February 2010, 3.

34. Domestic Violence Act (Act no. 116 of 1998). See also Erasmus, 'Die Vergestalting van die Sleutelkonsep *Huwelik*', 143.

35. Domestic Violence Act (Act no. 116 of 1998).

36. J. de Villiers, 'Storm in Kerk oor Saambly', *Rapport*, 15 December 2009.

37. Although abortion is now legal, the extreme negative evaluation of extramarital sex and resulting pregnancy in particular can be illustrated by the uproar caused by an Afrikaans film *Debbie*, that was released in 1965. The story is about a young girl from the countryside who falls pregnant and is subsequently rejected by her parents. She is confronted with a choice between an (illegal) abortion and adoption. The film was first released with an age restriction of 16, which was later raised to 21.

38. A.F. Prinsloo, *Annerlike Afrikaans* (Pretoria: Protea Boekehuis, 2010), 109.

39. Although precise statistics are hard to come by, the trustees of Salomo Trust, an Inter Vivos Trust that specializes in settling asset disputes following a break-up between couples who lived together but were not married, suggests that more than two million South Africans live with a partner without being married. Source: 'Eerste Saamblytrust vir Ongetroude Paartjies in Suid-Afrika'. Retrieved 11 March 2014 from http://link2media.co.za.

40. The *Woordeboek van die Afrikaanse Taal* was used as a point of departure as it is the oldest and only comprehensive dictionary in Afrikaans. Work on the dictionary started in 1926 (when Afrikaans became an official language) and volume X1V (S – Skool) was published in 2013. As *trou* 'marriage' falls under 'T', which is yet to be processed and published, I manually worked though the database consisting of mostly handwritten cards in the old library-like catalogue at the WAT. The oldest entry is dated 1902. The *Etimologiewoordeboek van Afrikaans* (Etymological Dictionary of Afrikaans) does not list remote etymologies as the assumption is that these can be obtained by accessing the source languages such as Dutch or English. As the words *huwelik*, *trou* and *eg* are all derived from Dutch, I relied on the Dutch Etymological Dictionary (*Etymologisch Woordenboek*) when necessary. The standard dictionary consulted, *Die Handwoordeboek van Afrikaans*, was first published in 1965. I consulted the 1985 and 2000 editions. A.F. Prinsloo (1997, 2004 and 2010) formed the basis for the research into proverbs and idioms and are mainly (but not exclusively) based on oral records. The oldest word list consulted is that of Van der Merwe, H.J.J.M. Although only published in 1968 it provides a bilingual list (Afrikaans-English) of words found in what is widely accepted as the first concerted attempt to write Afrikaans in 1876 with the publication of the first Afrikaans newspaper, *Die Afrikaanse Patriot*. This list, originally published in 1902, is also the oldest source of written Afrikaans used by the *Woordeboek van die Afrikaanse Taal*.

41. Syntagmatic relations are possible combinations that lexical items might have with one another where the particular items have semantic relations with other lexical items that are rather predictable, i.e. wedding + cake, marriage + proposal, wedding + anniversary and marriage + counselling. Paradigmatic relations on the other hand include synonyms, antonyms, complementary pairs, opposites, homonyms, part-whole relations, ordered series and unordered series.

42. Van Wyk (ed.), *Etimologiewoordeboek van Afrikaans* (Stellenbosch: Buro van die WAT (*Woordeboek van die Afrikaanse Taal*), 2003), 175.

43. Odendal and Gouws, *Verklarende Handwoordeboek van die Afrikaanse Taal*, 1,181.

44. Van Wyk, *Etimologiewoordeboek*, 505.

45. De Vries and Tollenaere, *Etymologisch Woordenboek* (Utrecht: Het Spectrum, 1983), 320.

46. Odendal and Gouws, *Verklarende Handwoordeboek van die Afrikaanse Taal*, 1,181.

47. Van Wyk, *Etimologiewoordeboek*.

48. Dr Frikkie Lombaard from the only comprehensive dictionary in Afrikaans, *Die Woordeboek van die Afrikaanse Taal* (WAT), indicated that the definitions of *huwelik* and *eg* will be changed to refer to two people instead of a man and a woman in the revision of the dictionary.

49. Prinsloo, *Afrikaanse Spreekwoorde en waar hulle vandaan kom* (Kaapstad: Pharos, 2004), 284: a variation on the Dutch saying *over de puthaak vrijen*, referring to the first courtship between young people at the village well, as moral codes forbade this at home. A marriage over the well hook implies the same lack of commitment that existed between young people at the village well.

50. Prinsloo, *Spreekwoorde en waar hulle vandaan kom*, 41.

51. Odendal and Gouws, *Verklarende Handwoordeboek van die Afrikaanse Taal*, 262

52. Prinsloo, *Spreekwoorde en waar hulle vandaan kom*, 11.

53. Prinsloo, *Spreekwoorde en waar hulle vandaan kom*, 82.

54. Prinsloo, *Spreekwoorde en waar hulle vandaan kom*, 156.

55. Prinsloo, *Spreekwoorde en waar hulle vandaan kom*, 45.

56. In Afrikaans the compound word *huweliksbootjie* the 'Hymem's Boat' or 'marriage boat' is often used in figurative speech to indicate difficulty, e.g. *die huweliksbootjie is in gevaar* 'the marriage boat is in danger', *in troebel water* 'in murky water' and finally *op die rotse* 'on the rocks' to indicate the end of a marriage.

57. Prinsloo, *Spreekwoorde en waar hulle vandaan kom*, 384.

58. Prinsloo, *Spreekwoorde en waar hulle vandaan kom*, 362.

59. Prinsloo, *Afrikaanse Spreekwoorde en Uitdrukkings* (Pretoria: J.L. van Schaik, 1997), 31.

60. WAT database: *Die Suidwester* 29 November 1953, 6.

61. Prinsloo, *Afrikaanse Spreekwoorde en Uitdrukkings*, 132.

62. Also see Pamela Khanakwa's chapter in this volume.

63. Prinsloo, *Spreekwoorde en waar hulle vandaan kom*, 270.

64. Prinsloo, *Spreekwoorde en waar hulle vandaan kom*, 280.

65. Prinsloo, *Spreekwoorde en waar hulle vandaan kom*, 281.

66. Prinsloo, *Spreekwoorde en waar hulle vandaan kom*, 315.

67. Prinsloo, *Spreekwoorde en waar hulle vandaan kom*, 403.

68. See note 40.

69. *Afrikaans-Engels/English-Afrikaans Woordeboek/Dictionary* (Cape Town: Pharos, 2010).

70. WAT database, entered in 1963.

71. Elsabé Brink's work on the ideology of the *volksmoeder* is also of relevance here as it explains how the Nationalist ideology intertwined with religion to come up with the ideal woman in whom loyalty to husband, family, church and the state were regarded as the ultimate characteristics. E. Brink, 'Man-Made Women: Gender, Class and Ideology of the *Volksmoeder*', in C. Walker (ed.), *Women and Gender in Southern Africa to 1945* (Cape Town: David Philip, 1990), 273–92.

72. Unfortunately, many of the examples in the database do not have dates for when they were entered.

73. WAT database, entered in 1983.

74. WAT database, *Die Burger*, 25/5/1963, p. 25.

75. Odendal and Gouws, *Verklarende Handwoordeboek van die Afrikaanse Taal*, 660.

76. A. Davids, 'Some Lexical Aspects of Cape Muslim Afrikaans'. Lexikos 2 (1992), 39–62.

77. Suid-Afrikaanse Akademie vir Wetenskap en Kuns, *Afrikaanse Woordelys en Spelreëls (AWS)* (Kaapstad: Pharos, 2009), 332.

78. WAT database, entered 1968.

79. WAT database, *Die Vaderland*, 17 May 1983, 8.

80. Once more Brink's work on the ideology of the *volksmoeder* resonates. Brink, 'Man-Made Women'.

81. Prinsloo, *Annerlike Afrikaans* (Pretoria: Protea Boekehuis, 2010).

References

Online Sources

'Community Histories of Cape Town: The Cape Malay'. *South African History Online*. Retrieved 8 October 2012 from http://www.sahistory.co.za/people-south-africa/cape-malay.

'Eerste Saamblytrust vir Ongetroude Paartjies in Suid-Afrika'. 26 April 2012. Retrieved 11 March 2014 from http://www.link2media.co.za/index.php?option=com_content&task=view&id=15771&Itemid=12.

Interviews

Mrs Suaad Bower. Telephone interview. 15 October 2012
Prof. Farid Esack. Department of Religion Studies, University of Johannesburg. 23 October 2012.
Mrs Amina Linneveldt. Telephone interview. 23 October 2012.
Dr Frikkie Lombaard. Buro van die Woordeboek van die Afrikaanse Taal, Stellenbosch. 28 March 2014.

Published Works

Afrikaans-Engels/English-Afrikaans Woordeboek/Dictionary. Cape Town: Pharos, 2010.
Brink, E. 'Man-Made Women: Gender, Class and Ideology of the *Volksmoeder*', in C. Walker (ed.), *Women and Gender in Southern Africa to 1945*. Cape Town: David Philip, 1990, 273–92.
Buro van die Woordeboek van die Afrikaanse Taal, PO Box 245, Stellenbosch, 7599.
Coontz, S. *Marriage, A History: How Love Conquered Marriage*. London: Penguin Books, 2005.
Davids, A. 'Some Lexical Aspects of Cape Muslim Afrikaans'. *Lexikos* 2 (1992), 39–62.
de Villiers, J. 'Storm in Kerk oor Saambly', *Rapport*. 15 December 2009.
Die Vaderland. 17 May 1983.
De Vries, J. and F. de Tollenaere. *Etymologisch Woordenboek. Waar komen onze woorden vandaan?* Utrecht: Het Spectrum, 1983.
Erasmus, C. 'Die Vergestalting van die Sleutelkonsep *Huwelik* in Agaat deur Marlene van Niekerk'. M.A. dissertation. Auckland Park: University of Johannesburg, 2012.
Evans, V. and M. Green. *Cognitive Linguistics: An Introduction*. Mahwah Lawrence Erlbaum, 2006.
Ifversen, J. 'About Key Concepts and How to Study Them'. *Contributions to the History of Concepts* 2(2) (2009), 65–84.
Jackson, N. 'Gay Predikant Geskors Omdat Sy met Haar Lewensmaat Trou'. *Beeld*. 17 February 2010.
Koselleck, R. 'Crisis', trans. M.W. Richter, *Journal of the History of Ideas* 67(2) (2006), 357–400.
Lakoff, G. and M. Johnson. *Metaphors We Live By*. Chicago: University of Chicago Press, 1980.
Odendal, F.F. and R.H. Gouws (eds). *HAT. Verklarende Handwoordeboek van die Afrikaanse Taal*. Midrand: Perskor, 2000.
Posel, D. and S. Rudwick. 'Marriage and ilobolo [Bridewealth] in Contemporary Zulu Society', *African Studies Review* 2 (2014), 51–72.
Prinsloo, A.F. *Afrikaanse Spreekwoorde en Uitdrukkinge*. Pretoria: J.L. van Schaik, 1997.
———. *Afrikaanse Spreekwoorde en Waar Hulle Vandaan Kom*. Kaapstad: Pharos, 2004.
———. *Annerlike Afrikaans*. Pretoria: Protea Boekehuis, 2010.
Republic of South Africa. Immorality Act (Act no. 5 of 1927).
———. Prohibition of Mixed Marriages Act (Act no. 55 of 1949).
———. Immorality Amendment Act (Act no. 21 of 1950).
———. Group Areas Act (Act no. 51 of 1950).
———. Marriage Act (Act no. 25 of 1961).
———. Amended Immorality Act (Act no. 57 of 1969).
———. Immorality and Prohibition of Mixed Marriages Amendment Act (Act no. 72 of 1985).

———. Constitution of the Republic of South Africa (Act no. 108 of 1996).
———. Domestic Violence Act (Act no. 116 of 1998).
———. Customary Marriages Act (Act no. 120 of 1998).
———. Civil Union Act (Act no. 17 of 2006).
Scully, P. *Liberating the Family? Gender and British Slave Emancipation in the Rural Western Cape, South Africa, 1823–1853*. Cape Town: David Philip Publishers, 1997.
'South Africa and Polygamy: Swimming Against the Tide'. *The Economist*. 28 April 2012.
Spilsbury, L. *Same-Sex Marriages*. New York: The Rosen Publishing Group, 2012.
Statistics South Africa. 'Statistical Release P0307. Marriages and Divorces'. 2011.
Suid-Afrikaanse Akademie vir Wetenskap en Kuns. *Afrikaanse Woordelys en Spelreëls (AWS)*. Kaapstad: Pharos, 2009.
Van der Merwe, H.J.J.M. *Patriotwoordeboek*. Nuwe reeks Nr. 3. Pretoria: J.L. Van Schaik: 1968.
Van der Merwe, I.J. and J.H. Van der Merwe (eds). *Linguistic Atlas of South Africa: Language in Space and Time*. Stellenbosch: Sun Press, 2006.
Van Wyk, G.J. (ed.). *Etimologiewoordeboek van Afrikaans*. Stellenbosch: Buro van die Woordeboek van die Afrikaanse Taal, 2003.
Vaughan, M. 'Which Family? Problems in the Reconstruction of the History of the Family as an Economic and Cultural Unit', *Journal of African History* 24(2) (1983), 275–83.
Versluis, J.-M. 'Pa's Meer Afwesig By Kinders'. *Beeld*. 27 June 2012.

Marné Pienaar is professor of linguistics and head of the Department of Afrikaans at the University of Johannesburg. Her research interests include semantics and translation and interpreting studies. She is the co-author of *Veeltalige Vertaalterminologie/Multilingual Translation Terminology* (Pretoria: Van Schaik, 2010). She is a member of the board of the *Woordeboek van die Afrikaanse Taal* (the only comprehensive dictionary for Afrikaans) and serves on the Language Commission of the South African Academy for Art and Science.

CHAPTER 5

Male Circumcision among the Bagisu of Eastern Uganda

Practices and Conceptualizations

PAMELA KHANAKWA

Male circumcision involves the operation and removal of the foreskin and it has a wide range of sometimes interrelated dimensions in different parts of the world, including hygiene, biomedical, religious and cultural. For some Oceanic societies and several ethnic groups in Africa, the practice has deep roots as a rite of passage into adulthood and is therefore an important marker of hierarchy and social differentiation. Indeed, anthropologists view it as a practice through which significant aspects of social identity are inscribed upon the human body, such as gender, generational or social and sexual maturity. While most scholars agree on these generalities, the specific contexts, procedures, meanings and rituals accompanying circumcision vary greatly over time and space.

Among the Bagisu, who inhabit the Bugisu territory located at the western foothills of Mount Elgon in Eastern Uganda (see Map 5.1), *imbalu* 'male circumcision' is a ritualized practice that embodies pain and marks transition from male childhood to manhood.[1] It is performed in public without anaesthesia, and the candidate's ability to withstand pain without any show of emotion is a signifier of his manhood and masculine status. While pain is very central, the concept and practice of *imbalu* also encompasses a whole host of rituals, performance and related social attributes. However, this is not to say that *imbalu* is a uniform rite of passage emblematic in some way of Gisu ethnic tradition. Rather, it has been debated, contested and reimagined as part of historical dynamics in colonial through postcolonial Uganda.

Notes for this section begin on page 132.

Map 5.1 Bugisu, Eastern Uganda

Practice and Conceptualization of *Imbalu*

The Lugisu word *imbalu* has two meanings, namely a long, sharp knife and male circumcision. When the Bagisu talk about circumcision, they use the phrase *khu khwingila imbalu*, meaning to enter or to join *imbalu*. The broader meaning being that one who 'enters' *imbalu* joins the social category of men (*basaani*) and also displays ideal masculinity.[2] Please note that I use the term 'masculinity' as defined by Stephan Miescher and Lisa Lindsay: 'a cluster of norms, values, and behavioral patterns expressing explicit and implicit expectations of how men should act and represent themselves to others'.[3] Also, the term 'manhood' as used here refers to the Bagisu notion of ideal male adulthood. In cultural terms, being a man among the Bagisu means first and foremost that one has undergone ritualized anaesthesia-free circumcision and endured the pain without any show of fear. Secondly, it means that he has married and produced children.

Available Gisu historical records drawing on circumcision year names (*kamengilo*)[4] suggest that the Bagisu or Bamasaaba have practised *imbalu* since at least 1800 and probably earlier.[5] The practice has deep social meaning, for it creates hierarchical and social differentiation through marking generational, gender, manhood and political distinctions in society. On average, boys undergo circumcision when aged between 16 and 18 years.[6] The operation is performed publicly, in courtyards (*tsintsanyi*) within homesteads where anybody, including men, women and children, can watch. It is done by specialist surgeons (*bakhebi*, sing. *umukhebi*) who do not administer any form of anaesthesia. During the operation strict discipline is imposed on and through the body and mind, as onlookers expect candidates not only to remain still and silent but also to refrain from showing any emotions, including involuntary responses such as flinching, blinking or even moving their eyes.[7] The demand for an emotionless mask while one's foreskin and subcutaneous tissue are cut away without anaesthesia is especially onerous, and yet critical to one's attainment of ideal manhood and display of masculinity.[8]

Endurance of circumcision pain reflects manliness and heroism, and as such it is celebrated.[9] In the past, during the operation, Bagisu elders narrate, as the *mukhebi* chopped off (*khurema*) the foreskin and continued to carefully cut the subcutaneous tissue, onlookers in the audience murmured *awoo awoo, abwenewo abwerewo* ('there, there' – imparting the meaning 'remain firm in that position, do not move or flinch').[10] To evaluate their performance, onlookers watch candidates closely for any telltale signs (such as blinking, flinching, moving lips or eyes) that may suggest a candidate's failure to withstand pain. However, emphasis on enduring pain should not be misconstrued to mean that no candidate showed signs of fear or suffering. Both written and oral evidence confirm that there have been candidates who failed to endure the pain and suffered lifelong consequences for doing so, including being beaten by the onlookers and subsequently treated with scorn.[11] In extreme cases such people might commit suicide rather than endure the contempt and humiliation.[12] Displaying any sign of fear, including involuntary trembling and blinking, is said to reflect 'womanliness' and 'cowardice'.[13] Bagisu associate manliness with strength and bravery and womanliness with weakness and cowardice, a clear indication of a violent patriarchal power structure. They believe that candidates who display fear bring shame and bad luck not only to themselves but also to their immediate families and clans in general. As such, elders use potential humiliation to threaten and psychologically prepare the young for circumcision pain.

Imbalu is said to separate boys from men. Irrespective of age, as long as a male is not yet circumcised, members of the community consider him to be a 'boy child' and treat him accordingly as of low and insignificant status.[14] Until the early postcolonial period, such a person did not qualify to enjoy the entitlements of male adulthood, such as owning land within the community and joining the 'council of men', where he would take part in the political affairs of the community.[15] Moreover, the Bagisu believe that *imbalu* links men to their ancestral world and only circumcised men make it to that world when they die. On the contrary, they believe that if an uncircumcised man dies his shadow returns to destroy his living kindred.[16] To avert such misfortune, they perform posthumous circumcision.

European missionaries and colonial officials who arrived in Bugisu in the first quarter of the twentieth century were struck by the 'brutality' and 'primitivity' with which the Bagisu performed *imbalu*. They condemned the practice and attempted to appropriate it through evangelization, medicalization and Western education. However, as colonialism took shape, *imbalu* became a contested terrain not only between the Bagisu and the Europeans but also among the emerging socially differentiated sections of Bagisu. While some of them embraced European attempts to modify *imbalu*, others negotiated the fraught currents of social change by redeploying the cultural practice in socially significant ways. As they debated and reimagined the practice, Bagisu cultural ideologues sustained the language of *imbalu* and focus on enduring pain. This produced a form of discourse that underlay changes and continuities in both the practice and concept.

Conceptualizations of Christian Missionary Intervention

In January 1901, Rev. W.A. Crabtree and his wife, both members of the Church Missionary Society (CMS), arrived in central Bugisu and established a mission station at Nabumali where they gave biblical instruction and taught reading, writing, arithmetic, singing and sewing. Initially, both of them had been based at Gayaza in Buganda, central Uganda, but they left for a holiday in Eastern Uganda in November 1900. On arrival in Bugisu, the Crabtrees were struck by the culture, which was different from what they had seen in Buganda. Unlike the Baganda, the Bagisu had no centralized political authority, their dressing covered only genitals, leaving men and women almost naked, and they also practised male circumcision in a very 'barbaric' manner. Rev. and Mrs Crabtree felt the urgent need to evangelize the Bagisu and so they asked the Bishop of Uganda to grant them permission to stay at Nabumali, to establish a mission station and carry on with evangelization.[17] By 1903, the Crabtrees had constructed a church, school and dispensary at Nabumali, where they had acquired a group of followers. In September of the same year they were joined by Rev. J.B. Purvis and his wife, who arrived in Nabumali to continue the evangelization project. Purvis was equally critical of the local customs and what he considered witchcraft and sorcery.[18]

The missionaries and colonial officials condemned *imbalu*, in part because it contradicted the European concept of 'circumcision'. Whereas the Jews had practised male circumcision for religious reasons as far back as the Middle Ages or even earlier, most Europeans did not perform this practice until the nineteenth century, when the medical establishment defined it as a hygienic procedure. Circumcision arose in England during the early part of the nineteenth century as a 'cure' for masturbation and treatment for conditions local to the penis including phimosis, balanitis and penile cancer. During the late Victorian times, circumcision was promoted and widely spread in English-speaking countries for purely medical reasons. Nonetheless, there was opposition against it from those who considered arguments for it fallacious.[19] Coming from such a background, the missionaries must have been shocked at the 'barbaric' nature of *imbalu*, especially its publicness, the absence of anaesthesia, use of unsterilized knives and performance of accompanying 'heathen' rituals as well as the 'obscene' circumcision dance.

Missionaries objected to naked male Gisu bodies parading in open locations where men, women and children alike watched as the *bakhebi* performed the operation. They confused the naked male bodies involved in *imbalu* with nude bodies.[20] Against the background of Victorian era England, in which public nakedness was considered obscene, the missionaries thought that displaying naked male bodies was immoral. But Bagisu men and women did not consider the uncircumcised male body as an adult body capable of nudity. As a matter of fact, John Roscoe (a CMS missionary) observed in 1924 that, 'Before initiation a boy went naked, but when his initiation was complete, he was entitled to wear the dress of a full-grown man', which would cover the genitals.[21] In the first quarter of the twentieth century, uncircumcised boys in Bugisu could be naked without offending any sensibilities, but adults could not.

In an effort to fight against the 'immoral' display of naked male bodies, Christian missionaries in Bugisu introduced circumcision enclosures in 1934. These were made of poles, sticks and dry banana leaves and they formed a kind of curtain, meant to make circumcision a private affair and to segregate it by gender and age. Rev. Edrisa K. Masaba, himself a product of missionary education, who later became the first Mugisu Anglican bishop in Uganda, spearheaded the initiative of constructing circumcision enclosures.[22] He joined the Church Missionary Society school at Nabumali in 1912 and became the first Mugisu to join the Theological College at Mukono in 1921. From Mukono, Masaba returned to Nabumali, where he worked both as a teacher and a church deacon.[23] By the early 1930s, he had become instrumental in promoting the European civilizing project and his involvement in the introduction of circumcision enclosures is testimony to this.[24] Because concealing circumcision candidates from the public was new in the history of Bugisu, the elders named the cohort of men circumcised in 1934 as Banabizagati, meaning 'those circumcised in enclosures'.

Missionary efforts to conceal the operation not only ameliorated their anxieties about nudity and nakedness, but also separated the initiates from the widest array of social entanglements at play in the fully public version. This was part and parcel of the missionary interest in crafting a converted African body as an atomized one whose primary relationship was with the Christian God and not with various forms of African sociality or community. The missionary emphasis on the candidates' privacy undermined the public experience of *imbalu*, in which the publicness was important precisely because it involved women and children, alongside men, as witnesses to a candidate's crucial moment of self-determination.

Beyond the display of naked bodies, missionaries and colonial officials were opposed to what they regarded as 'immoral' and unchristian rituals that accompanied circumcision. These included ritual sacrifices, ancestral worship and beer drinking, as well as 'immoral' dancing.[25] There were two types of local beer including *indali* and *busela* and both were quite intoxicating.[26] For the Bagisu, beer drinking was a social activity and a major component of any ceremony, including circumcision, where both adults and youths drank freely. Beer was so central to circumcision ceremonies that in the event of inadequate grain to brew, elders would postpone the ceremony in the given year. The Bagisu's concept of beer drinking shocked the missionaries. Purvis was particularly surprised that some of the Bagisu elders working on the mission-building project could ask for up to two weeks off to go and drink beer. He was convinced that beer drinking was 'a source of great evil in the country'.[27] In addition, the missionaries condemned the *imbalu* dance because they thought it was obscene and sexually provocative. The dance brought together men, women and children, who danced freely through the days and nights before the actual operation. To the missionaries' eyes, *imbalu* dance promoted immorality.

The social aspects of *imbalu* as well as the performance of the operation shaped missionary, colonial and early postcolonial concerns about the practice. Both Europeans and some Bagisu like E.K. Masaaba attempted to modify the practice, but *imbalu* muddled through amid contestations. It was confronted by different ideas and forces at different moments of colonial and early postcolonial Uganda but it continued to survive as a concept and a practice provoking social and semantic change.

The Vocabulary of Medicalization of *Imbalu*

In 1938, as part of the European civilizing project, colonial officials and Christian missionaries attempted to appropriate *imbalu* through medicalization. This initiative involved the administering of anaesthesia and use of medical personnel as opposed to the *bakhebi*, who in cultural terms were eligible to perform the operation and ensure a proper stamp of manhood in the form of a circumcision cut. In addition, medical circumcision was done privately in hospital with no public audience to sanction the boy's critical moment of self-actualization.

The first instances of medical circumcision took place at Bubulo Health Centre in 1938, where boys were said to have been circumcised lying on wooden beds while facing the ceiling. Although the statistics are not available, it is likely that the numbers were small because of the local opposition to the new initiative. Medical circumcision marked a significant shift in the practice of *imbalu* in terms of both space and procedure. For the first time, Bagisu boys could now be circumcised in hospital, away from the ancestral courtyard (*khulwanyi*). This shift influenced the naming of the cohort of all Bagisu men circumcised in 1938 – *Nalubawo* (derived from *lubawo*, 'a piece of wood') – irrespective of where they were circumcised. Initially, it referred to the entire cohort of men circumcised in 1938, but later, *Nalubawo* or *bekhulubawo*, 'those of the wooden board', came to have a connotation of contempt for all those circumcised in hospital. *Nalubawo* was derived from the fact that in hospital, as opposed to traditional circumcision, candidates were circumcised while lying on the wooden surgical beds. From Bubulo, medical circumcision spread to other health centres like Nyondo, Mbale and Bududa.[28] Henceforth, both European and Bagisu missionaries urged Bagisu men and women to take their sons to the hospitals for circumcision.[29]

The missionary efforts to medicalize *imbalu* rested less on ignorance of *imbalu* than on a considered analysis of the threats it posed to their evangelical and civilization project. Its 'brutality' and 'heathen' nature stood in stark contrast to their view of morality and Christianity.[30] Both the early missionaries and colonial officials who worked in Bugisu during the first three decades of the twentieth century saw the Bagisu's belief system, which was partially, but importantly, manifested in the practice of *imbalu*, as an obstacle to missionary evangelization and establishment of colonial rule respectively. In 1909, Purvis lamented: 'Masaba is one of those mission fields where mental, moral, and spiritual progress will be slow'. He blamed this on the locals' belief system.[31] He was convinced that the 'belief in witchcraft [was] one of the greatest and most dangerous powers in the land',[32] and it 'interfere[d] very considerably with missionary effort'.[33] The ritual practices prominently manifested at circumcision ceremonies were among those Europeans considered to be witchcraft.

In his study on medical mission in South-Eastern Tanzania, Terence Ranger noted the Europeans' assumption that Western medicine work would be 'a weapon in a more direct and militant confrontation with heathenism'.[34] No doubt, this assumption informed the European introduction of medical circumcision in Bugisu. The missionaries considered that medicalized circumcision would eliminate the 'barbaric' practices associated with *imbalu* and thereby open the way for Western civilization. It would not only convert 'heathen' practices into medical ones, but would also eliminate social 'evils' that accompanied the practice. They imagined that emulating Western values while discarding the 'primitive' cultural practice was a step towards civilization and progress. Medical circumcision, which included the administration of anaesthesia and which was performed without *imbalu* dance, beer drinking or relevant rituals, was a clear attempt at eliminating obstacles to European civilization.[35]

Response to Medicalized Circumcision

The medical initiative elicited varied responses. While some Bagisu embraced it, others rejected it outright and used terms that formulated a counterdiscourse to express their contempt. Adherents of tradition contemptuously referred to it as *imbalu ye mwi dwalilo* 'hospital circumcision' or *imbalu ye Bazungu* 'circumcision of Europeans', as opposed to *imbalu ye Bagisu* 'circumcision of Bagisu' or *imbalu ing'ene* 'the real circumcision'. To the missionaries and medics the surgical operation was circumcision. To the traditionalists, however, the medical initiative could not be equated to *imbalu* because it merely involved the surgical operation, leaving out significant aspects of the traditional practice.

Interviews with Bagisu elders confirmed that those who welcomed it did so because it offered an alternative to the severe and painful *imbalu*.[36] In the 1940s and 1950s, some elders would advise boys who seemed likely to fear traditional circumcision to go to hospital.[37] Mundu (not his real name) – born in 1932 and circumcised in hospital in Bubulo in 1952 – asserted that he preferred hospital circumcision because: 'my heart wanted [it]'.[38] Mundu was not willing to explain why his heart 'wanted' hospital circumcision. However, it is likely that he was not prepared for the pain of *imbalu*. His unwillingness to explain his choice derives from the fact that some Bagisu men and women denigrated those who opted for the medical initiative.[39]

Some Bagisu also embraced hospital circumcision because it was cheaper than traditional circumcision.[40] Usually, circumcision ceremonies were costly because they involved big feasts with large amounts of food and beer for relatives, friends, in-laws and members of one's age set as well as domestic animals like bulls and bucks for sacrificial rituals. For this reason, families preferred to hold ceremonies in years with good harvests. In cases of severe food shortage, like during the famine of 1918, elders would postpone circumcision ceremonies.[41] In the 1930s, Bugisu suffered severe famines owing to locust invasions.[42] The impact of the famines on family resources vis-à-vis the high expenses of *imbalu* ceremonies shaped local thoughts and influenced people's circumcision options.[43] For some Christian families, medical circumcision provided an alternative to the unchristian *imbalu* rituals. However, without the big feasts and beer parties, hospital circumcision eliminated a major social aspect of *imbalu*, making it an individual and private affair.

Unsurprisingly, champions of *imbalu* rejected medical circumcision. They did so in part, at least, because it compromised their understanding of the concept of 'circumcision' and its associated cultural values. In interviews conducted between 2008 and 2010 some Bagisu men reiterated the centrality of enduring circumcision pain in the attainment of proper manhood and identity. In explaining why he preferred 'traditional' circumcision to hospital circumcision, Joseph Weyusha, born in 1960 and circumcised in his grandfather's courtyard in 1972, narrated in English:

> Getting circumcised in hospital at that time was regarded as an act of cowardice. You would look like a real coward, worse than a woman. The community members regarded you as a person who was so fearful that [you] could not stand and brave the pain of *imbalu* in public. It is fear that drove people to hospital for circumcision. At that time, the culture was still very strong and anybody who got circumcised in hospital could not come before or join the *basinde* as the latter danced in preparation for *imbalu*. People would chase away such a person. They could not allow him to come near *basinde* during the circumcision dance. You would look like an outcast in society because you would be banned from participating in the *imbalu* celebrations where all other people would be dancing and having fun. That factor alone made us feel that we needed to get circumcised *khulwanyi* [on the traditional courtyard].[44]

Charles Siango, born in 1940 and circumcised in the traditional courtyard in 1952, reinforced Weyusha's assertion. He explained:

> I opted for traditional circumcision because I wanted my fellow Bagisu to respect me. I wanted to get the ego of being a Mugisu man and to show that a *musani* [circumcised man] does not cry. I wanted to join the council of circumcised men and participate not only in *malwa* [beer] drinking but also in other cultural affairs of the community. Bagisu men who were circumcised in hospital were not respected because by going to hospital they had demonstrated that they were cowards. In fact we considered them outcasts and teased them because they had not got the proper deep Gisu circumcision cuts.[45]

These two narratives underscore the centrality of pain as a key component of *imbalu*. Weyusha and Siango were circumcised twenty years apart – and several decades after Purvis and Roscoe's observations of 1909 and 1924 respectively – yet both men were keenly aware of the social consequences associated with medical circumcision. *Imbalu* pain signified manhood and, as such, circumcision devoid of pain was not real *imbalu* and could not mark one's transition into male adulthood.

Medical circumcision created a new category of men, along with new terms for them – *baari* 'fearful ones', *babengilila mwi dwalilo* 'those circumcised in hospital', *bekhulubawo* 'those circumcised on a piece of wood', *baakhasi* 'women' – that threatened Bagisu constructions of manhood and masculinities. From the late 1930s onwards, circumcision *per se* was not enough to make a man – the type of circumcision also counted. For the adherents of ritualized circumcision, only proper *imbalu* and associated components produced 'masculinized' men, while medical circumcision created 'feminized' men. Thus, following the introduction of medical circumcision, one could be circumcised and yet not be considered a real man because such a person had had the benefit of anaesthesia. *Imbalu* ideologues disparaged the hospital alternative by placing circumcision debates at the centre of constructions of gendered male bodies and masculinities. They derided those circumcised in hospital for being 'cowardly' and 'womanly'.

As the narratives of Weyusha and Siango confirm, advocates of *imbalu* employed derogatory language and hurled insults at those who were circumcised in hospital because the medical initiative contradicted the Gisu concept of circumcision, in particular, the centrality of pain. They referred to them as *baari* 'cowards', *baafu* 'deceased', meaning those who were 'killed' by anaesthesia before circumcision,[46] or *baakhasi* 'women', equating them with femininity, which they perceived as weak. Bagisu men and women in the late 1930s and early 1940s must have been shocked at the fact that anaesthesia could have such an effect on human bodies. They presumed that the circumcision candidates were hit on the head so that they could 'die' during the operation.

The open contempt for those circumcised in hospital brought to light debates about what it meant to be a Mugisu man. Adherents of *imbalu* framed medical circumcision as an option only for those who could not prove their manliness. As Weyusha explained, 'the cultural setting demands that you must come and demonstrate to everybody that you are transitioning from childhood to adulthood through braving *imbalu* in public. This is what makes you a Mugisu man'. However, 'if you [show] cowardice and go to hospital, then it means that you are fearing and so you are not even worthy [of] being called a Mugisu'.[47] By using such derisive language, *imbalu* ideologues sought to exclude those circumcised in hospital from officiating in cultural rituals and participating in the political affairs of the Bugisu 'nation'. This nation began to take shape in the colonial context, following the emergence of tensions between the Bagisu and non-Bagisu, with *imbalu* being the central distinguishing as well as uniting concept.[48] Advocates of *imbalu* hoped that using such language would propel other members of the Bugisu community to conform to the culturally acceptable way of transforming boys into responsible adult men who would participate in building, reproducing and protecting the Bugisu nation against threats from their non-circumcising neighbours and the wider Ugandan colonial state. They did not trust that men circumcised in hospital, who had succumbed to foreign ideas, could be relied on to defend and protect their community against foreign intrusion.

Bagisu elders also opposed medical circumcision because, contrary to the cultural demands of standing firm and upright during the *imbalu* operation, in the hospitals, boys were circumcised while lying on the wooden surgical beds. Under traditional ritualized circumcision, the only candidates who were circumcised while lying down were those who had been so frightened during the operation that other men had to hold them on the ground for the surgeon to complete his work.[49] Such candidates were said to have failed to 'stand *imbalu*' and consequently suffered lifelong insults for their weakness. Some of the common jibes included *kila warya imbalu* 'no wonder you feared *imbalu*' or *bona kwesi baambila asi oku* 'look at this one who was held down', meaning that he failed to stand independently and had to be held in place by other men for the surgeon to complete the circumcision operation. Furthermore, no young woman wanted to marry a man who had displayed fear, for she would suffer the potential humiliation of being referred to as the wife of a coward. However, by the early 1940s, following the introduction of hospital circumcision new jibes emerged. An example is: *kila watsya khukona khu lubaawo* 'that is why you went to lie on a piece of wood' – instead of standing upright and withstanding pain like a real man.[50] Cultural promoters, especially courtyard-circumcised men, used this disparaging language when referring to those circumcised in hospital in order to undermine their social standing and shun them from engaging in debates with 'real' men. These jibes produced a new discourse about *imbalu*.

There were also some Bagisu who rejected medical circumcision on the premise that those who performed the operation were neither Bagisu nor qualified to do the job. According to the culture, only *bakhebi* (specialist local surgeons) were qualified to perform the operation. They took on the practice after themselves withstanding the pain of traditional circumcision, marrying and producing children, and thereafter undergoing the relevant rituals and apprenticeship to become *bakhebi*.[51] They had to prove that they were viable for both biological and social reproduction lest they brought bad luck (i.e. infertility) to circumcision candidates during the operation. Not everybody could become a *mukhebi*: only those who possessed *kumusambwa* 'spirit' of circumcision had the power and legitimacy to perform the operation.

In contrast, possession of *kumusambwa kwe imbalu* was not a consideration in performing medical circumcision. Any medic who had acquired the relevant knowledge and training could do it. This brought the masculinity of those circumcised in hospital into question. Men and women derided and contested their masculinity and respectability by referring to them as having been circumcised by 'women'.[52] Reference to circumcision by 'women' was derogatory. Among the Bagisu, like the amaXhosa, it was a taboo for boys to be circumcised or even to have their circumcision wounds nursed by a woman.[53] Women were strictly forbidden from performing the operation, and were not even permitted to be helpers or apprentices to the local surgeons. Their task was to watch as the qualified men did their job. Furthermore, only knowledgeable and properly circumcised men could examine the wounds during the healing process. By having women nurses perform the operation and tend the wounds, medical circumcision introduced women into what was otherwise a men's domain. This further alienated medical circumcision from the concept of *imbalu* as it contravened the cultural value of the practice. In this way, it placed gender struggles at the centre of circumcision debates.

Secondly, being circumcised in a hospital could also mean that the surgeons were not 'proper' men in the eyes of the Bagisu men and women. By the 1940s, medics at health centres in Bugisu either came from non-circumcising communities like Buganda or from among the few Bagisu who had had a Western education and converted to Christianity. They did not have the spiritual power and legitimacy to circumcise Bagisu boys. Bagisu elders were angry that such people who neither had the cultural expertise nor understood the cultural value of circumcision were carrying out the operation.

Therefore reference to circumcision by a 'woman doctor' was language that champions of *imbalu* used to contest the manhood status of those circumcised in hospital, regardless of the biological sex of the surgeon. This language was effective in demeaning their social standing because, within Bugisu, it was unheard of for a woman to carry out circumcision. Such a possibility was outside the popular conceptualization of *imbalu*. Whereas it was ideal in the European conceptualization of circumcision to have medical professionals perform the operation, this was against the norm among the Bagisu. Having non-Bagisu and perhaps uncircumcised medics perform circumcisions in hospital was incompatible with the concept of *imbalu*.[54]

Some elders further opposed hospital circumcision because they claimed that the medics performed incomplete or shallow circumcision, where they removed only a small part of the foreskin. This worried some men and women, as they feared that in the long run, 'the foreskin would grow again, covering the penis and thus making one look as though they had not been circumcised'.[55] Seperiya (circumcised traditionally in 1940) explained that at the time of his circumcision people used to criticize hospital circumcision because 'the doctors just used to stitch the foreskin without proper circumcision'.[56] In addition, Matsanga (a Mugisu circumcision surgeon who was circumcised in 1962) pointed out that, 'in hospital, doctors used a pair of scissors and simply pinched off a small part of the foreskin'. Moreover, he added, 'doctors also stitched the circumcision wound'. This was different from *imbalu* where 'there is no killing pain, no stitching, and the scar is deeper – approximately one inch'.[57] Matsanga seems to have confused the depth and length. What he meant is that up to approximately one inch of foreskin was removed as well as the underlying tissue. The *bakhebi* marked off that spot using the thumbnail and the assistant surgeon pulled and stretched the foreskin lengthwise to enable the surgeon cut off that part.

The difference in the surgical tools, procedure and depth as well as length of the cuts meant that the scars of those who were circumcised by medics in hospital looked different from those of men circumcised by *bakhebi*. Emphasis on a particular size and shape of the circumcision scar suggests that *imbalu* was also a significant marker of Bagisu men's physical identity. No wonder that elderly and knowledgeable men closely watched and supervised the operation to ensure that the *mukhebi* made a proper cut, removing an adequate portion of the foreskin and underlying tissue. After observing *imbalu* operations in Bugisu, Roscoe, in his 1924 ethnography, noted that, 'old people examined the member to see that the work was properly done'.[58] If the cutting was not properly done, there would be a correction to ensure that the mistake was fixed.[59] The scar signified the experience of cutting. Having the correct scar allowed its possessor to claim the power and standing produced by that affective dimension of *imbalu* in a way that lasted and travelled far more easily than the public memory and scrutiny of an individual's actual performance.

The introduction of medical circumcision, among other things, heightened Bagisu sensibilities about experiencing pain as well as attaining the accepted shape and depth of the scar. Elders did not approve of hospital scars because they gave a different shape that did not conform to the physical mark of *imbalu*. Against this backdrop, getting a proper *imbalu* scar became critical to the advocates of cultural distinction.

Attempts to Appropriate *Imbalu* through Formal Education

Issues of pain, legitimacy of surgeons and proper cuts became important enough to compel missionaries to concede the use of anaesthesia. In the early 1940s, they introduced a new, anaesthesia-free form of circumcision to school premises (*imbalu ye khwisomero*). This was performed by select *bakhebi* at both Protestant and Catholic mission stations including Nabumali, Bulucheke, Nyondo and Butiru.[50] Under the new form, school authorities prohibited candidates from performing the relevant pre- and post-circumcision rituals like brewing beer, smearing yeast and chime as well as having *bakhebi* wash hands of initiates three days after circumcision.[61] They tried to appropriate the rite and conduct it in a new Christian direction by replacing the 'heathen' rituals with prayers.[62] Henceforth, the new form of circumcision was mandatory for schoolboys and especially trainee clergy whom missionaries intended to keep away from the 'evil' *imbalu* rituals and yet ensure that they experienced the pain and got proper cuts, as these were central to their social recognition as men.[63]

Although it combined some elements of both the cultural and medical forms, school circumcision did not conform to the totality of *imbalu*. Its architects ignored the accompanying rituals that were crucial to educating and preparing boys for male adulthood responsibilities and inculcating a loyalty to the interests of their clan in particular, as well as to the Bugisu community as a whole. Those circumcised at school experienced pain and got proper cuts but missed out on the elaborate manhood rituals. In this way, school circumcision fell short of the educational role of *imbalu*. The authorities did not impart the relevant cultural knowledge to the new generation of men circumcised at school and this threatened the social reproduction of society.

Interestingly, some trainee clergy thought that school circumcision met the requirements of *imbalu* because it was performed by *bakhebi* who did not administer any form of anaesthesia. They regarded endurance of pain and getting proper cuts as the critical aspects of Gisu manhood and entitlement to related responsibilities. As one retired clergyman who was circumcised at school in 1946 narrated, 'even as young boys training to become clergy, we did not go for hospital circumcision because we wanted to demonstrate to our people that we could withstand the pain of traditional *imbalu*. We did not want them to despise us'.[64] Such men focused on the importance of experiencing pain and getting a proper scar but disregarded the accompanying rituals. Unsurprisingly, some of them became critical of, and shunned the *imbalu* rituals. They promoted a modified approach to *imbalu* in which they emphasized only the shape of the scar.[65]

However, some Bagisu elders disapproved of school circumcision precisely because it lacked the totality of the cultural attributes that they deemed crucial in initiating the boys into manhood. The exclusion of parents and relatives from the preparations, as well as the relocation of the candidates to non-ancestral school grounds compromised the security of the boys and exposed them to dangers of bewitchment. Elders feared that bewitchment could cause the boys to display fear and even fail to procreate.[66] By 1950 school circumcision had become increasingly unpopular because some candidates circumcised on school premises had displayed signs of fear, including fainting and touching the hands of *bakhebi* or the circumcision knives in an attempt to stop the operation. The latter was the most heinous offence and the candidates' fathers had to pay fines in the form of goats, sheep and chickens to the local surgeons.[67] Elders also criticized school circumcision for eliminating the *imbalu* dance that psychologically prepared the candidates for the pain. Some of the songs that accompanied the dance contained lyrics that warned the candidates about the pain and the dangers of fearing circumcision. Also, during the dance, elders assessed the forcefulness of the candidate's rhythmic stamping of the ground: they thought that the 'more energetic and stylistic' dancer was better prepared than one whose dancing was less energetic.[68] The absence of these aspects reduced school circumcision to a physical operation and elders opposed it because they did not regard it as *imbalu*. Owing to local opposition, the missionaries abandoned this option in 1950, less than a decade after its introduction.

However, that did not mark the end of official attempts to use formal schooling to regulate the practice and thereby change the concept of *imbalu*. In 1954 members of the African Local Government drew up a circumcision calendar in which they allocated only two days (18 and 19 August) for the circumcision of all schoolboys in the entire Bugisu region. By contrast, they allocated thirty-seven days (8 August to 14 September) for the circumcision of village boys, with each sub-county being assigned a date.[69] Allocating only two days, close to the beginning of term holidays, for the circumcision of schoolboys was a deliberate effort to restrain them from engaging in the *imbalu* dance and related pre-circumcision rituals. This move upset some parents who lamented that the limited dancing time affected the candidates' preparation and ability to withstand pain.[70] Moreover, separating the circumcisions of schoolboys from that of village boys created another layer of differentiation contrary to the norm – *imbalu* was a leveller, supposed to bring people together and create a social brotherhood between those circumcised in the same year.[71]

In a further attempt to appropriate *imbalu*, in 1958 the Bugisu District Council passed a by-law aimed at controlling and 'improving' the practice. The architects of the by-law reiterated the separation of the circumcision of village boys from that of schoolboys and also banished the latter from joining in the village ceremonies, which included dancing, brewing beer and performing cultural rituals.[72] In sharp contrast with the popular emphasis on the centrality of pain, the by-law provided for the private circumcision of schoolboys either at hospitals, dispensaries and aid-posts or at their fathers' homes. In effect, these modes of circumcision offered youths a variety of ways to avoid the more established demands of public *imbalu* championed by its supporters. The by-law also outlawed forcible circumcision and provided a legal framework for reprimanding violators. It laid a basis for the arrest and prosecution of people who engaged in coercing others into circumcision. This was potentially problematic because promoting *imbalu*, including the use of coercive means, was the social responsibility of those Bagisu men and women who believed that grown-up yet uncircumcised males brought misfortune – including death – to society.

In spite of the by-law, in the mid-1960s, some men constituted themselves into *ad hoc* circumcision task forces, and pursued and forcibly circumcised defaulters, whose numbers were perceived to be increasing, especially among those who had emigrated or attained formal schooling.[73] On 5 August 1966, in a letter to the District Commissioner of Bugisu, Mutambo, a veterinary assistant in Mbale, reported that some chiefs were involved in forcing Bagisu men into circumcision and that he himself was a target of the circumcision enforcers' activities. He wrote: 'I am not circumcised myself, just because I do not see the importance of it and I have had mobs troubling me since 1964'.[74] Formal education had allowed him to get a civil service job and, therefore, Mutambo did not consider circumcision relevant to his adulthood responsibilities. By contrast, circumcision enforcers argued that *imbalu* was a cultural debt that every Mugisu male had to pay or else misfortunes would befall the community. Some of them equated the enforcement of *imbalu* to the stringent law on tax collection that led to the arrests and imprisonment of defaulters.[75] Concerned Bagisu men enforced circumcision, in part, because they wanted to ensure the social reproduction of their community. Forced circumcision was so rampant in 1966 that the elders named the cohort of men circumcised in that year as *Muwambe*, meaning 'capture, catch or hold him'.[76] Initially, this name referred to the entire cohort irrespective of how individuals had been circumcised. In the subsequent years, however, *muwambe* became a derogatory term referring only to those who were captured and forcibly circumcised after some years of evading.

From the 1930s to 1960s, competing concepts of circumcision underlay struggles over *imbalu* in Bugisu. These concepts diverged, in particular, over the centrality of pain, the shape of the scar and the social meaning of circumcision. In cultural terms, *imbalu* was a way of marking individual transition to male adulthood, through elaborate preparations and the experience of pain, but with at least a semblance of choice – only those deemed ready to withstand pain were put forward. The introduction of medical circumcision reduced the practice to the physical operation only. Then, school circumcision emphasized the experience of pain and shape of the circumcision scar but denuded it of the cultural practices central to *imbalu*. By the 1960s *imbalu* had become, in part, a forcible process aimed at policing the boundaries of the group – one was either a circumcised Mugisu man or not a Mugisu at all. Interestingly, forcible circumcision was also denuded of cultural context, but nonetheless had little resemblance to school circumcision.

Attempts to Appropriate *Imbalu* for Ethnonationalism

In an effort to establish themselves politically in the late colonial and early postcolonial contexts some Bagisu intellectuals appropriated *imbalu* and brought it to the fore in their struggles with their non-circumcising Bagwere neighbours, with whom they had a longstanding territorial conflict dating back to the early 1900s. In 1954, in an attempt to resolve the conflict, the colonial authorities split Mbale District on the basis of the two groups to create Bugisu and Bukedi districts with Mbale as a separate entity belonging to neither district.[77] This decision heightened tensions between the two factions, resulting in violent incidents in which Bagisu forcibly circumcised Bagwere men as they struggled to restrain them from occupying what they considered to be Bugisu territory.[78] The conflict culminated in demonstrations and riots in 1954, 1956 and 1962, in which violent acts lay at the centre of territorial struggles. No doubt the creation of districts upset prevailing patterns of wealth and patronage, including access to land, marketing of cash crops like coffee, collection and use of tax revenue and access to social services like health and education.[79]

On the eve of Uganda's independence, as they pressed the colonial state to resolve their conflict with the Bagwere, some Bagisu 'intellectuals' including members of Bugisu District Council used *imbalu* to mobilize Gisu-wide support against foreigners. During these intense struggles, reference to *imbalu* translated into the moral duty of every Mugisu man and woman to give political support to the struggle to save Bugisu land. They intimidated the non-circumcising Bagwere by arguing that Bugisu land had boundary markers which could only be identified by *basaani*, implying that the uncircumcised (*basinde*) did not have the legitimacy to debate land issues. *Imbalu* became a political tool that Bagisu 'intellectuals' intimately tied to ideas of land tenure.[80]

Between the 1930s and 1960s, competing conceptions of circumcision provided sites of struggles that were simultaneously over constructions of masculinities, authority, legitimacy and land tenure. These struggles were part of a larger struggle of defining and defending a cultural institution that set the Bagisu apart from other ethnic groups in the multi-ethnic modern Ugandan nation state. *Imbalu* was central to the construction of 'Gisu-ness' and it provided a strong platform from which people voiced their grievances.

Conclusion

By focusing on the Bagisu's conceptualization of circumcision as embodying pain, the chapter shows how configurations of *imbalu* and performances of this pain were challenged, reaffirmed, contested, negotiated and sustained among the Bagisu in different historical contexts. *Imbalu* had a complex social meaning for the Bagisu: it was a signifier of generational and social differentiation with endurance of pain being the ultimate test of manhood. But it also included the transmission of adult knowledge to new generations. Missionary efforts to appropriate it through medicalization and formal schooling met with strong resistance because they did not conform to the totality of *imbalu* as understood by adherents to the traditional practice. In the early postcolonial period, some Bagisu men and women used it to police the boundaries of their nation. They did this by pursuing and forcibly circumcising defaulters.

In spite of the contestations and various attempts to appropriate it, *imbalu* persisted, not merely because its adherents clung to their culture, but so they could also appropriate and use that culture as a mobilizing resource. There was continued competition over the meaning of the concept of circumcision; competition that endures into the present. Perhaps unpacking the social meaning of *imbalu* helps explain the enduring appeal and significance of the practice among some Bagisu in colonial and post-independence Uganda. Certainly, unpacking the social meaning of the concept brings to light the many different voices that have participated in shaping it, and the ways in which the competing conceptualizations of circumcision in the past enable us to understand the particular forms it takes in the present. This conceptual history approach to a practice is especially powerful in de-essentializing that which is presented as timeless tradition.

Notes

I am grateful to David Schoenbrun, Emily Callaci, and Andreana Prichard for their critical comments. I thank my informants in Bugisu who enlightened me on debates surrounding imbalu. Funding for this research was provided by the ACLS African Humanities Program Postdoctoral Fellowship; the Program of African Studies, the Roberta Buffet Center for International and Comparative Studies and the Graduate School at Northwestern University. I thank the Uganda National Council of Science and Technology for research clearance to conduct fieldwork for this project.

1. The terms Bagisu and Bugisu have a deeper history that should not detain us here. As used here, Bagisu (sing. Mugisu) refers to the people of the Bugisu region and their language is Lugisu. Available records suggest that these terms are a creation of the twentieth century. Under the leadership of Semei Kakungulu, Baganda colonial agents who arrived in the region at the turn of the twentieth century used the term Bageshu (sometimes Bagesu or Bagishu) to distinguish the Bantu-speaking people living on the western slopes of Mount Elgon from the other groups on the mountains and plains. In the past, the region was referred to as Masaaba (referring both to the eponymous ancestor, Masaaba, and associated with Mount Masaaba), the people Bamasaaba and the language Lumasaaba. Indeed, early missionaries and colonial officials in Eastern Uganda used the terms Bamasaaba and then later Bagesu and Bagishu to refer to the people now known as Bagisu. The terms Bugisu and Bagisu, which I use in this chapter, were adopted by members of the African Local Government of Bugisu District as it was created in 1954. Gisu is used as an adjectival form to refer to a something associated with Bugisu or Bagisu.

2. *Basaani* refers to circumcised men as opposed to *basinde* who are not.

3. L.A. Lindsay and S.F. Miescher, 'Introduction: Men and Masculinities in Modern African History', in L.A. Lindsay and S.F. Miescher (eds.), *Men and Masculinities in Modern Africa* (Portsmouth: Heinemann, 2003), 4.

4. *Kamengilo* refers to the names given to cohorts of men circumcised in a given year. Such names are derived from what elders perceived to be important events.

5. Andeera Khaukha, 'The Tribal Circumcision Periods', undated unpublished paper in author's possession; Mayegu, Wamimbi and Wawomola, 'Circumcision Year Names (*Kamengilo*) in Masaba and their Meanings', *Uganda Journal* 39 (1980): 58–75.

6. There were variations in the past. J.B. Purvis, *Through Uganda to Mount Elgon* (New York: American Tract Society, 1909), 277 says that boys were circumcised when aged between 16 and 18 years; J. Roscoe, *The Northern Bantu: An Account of Some Central African Tribes of the Uganda Protectorate* (Cambridge: Cambridge University Press, 1915. Reprint London: Frank Cass & Co. Ltd, 1966), 184 gives the age as 14 years; J. La Fontaine, 'The Social Organisation of the Gisu with Special Reference to their Initiation Ceremonies' (Ph.D. dissertation, University of Cambridge, 1957), 16 says between 18 and 22 years old.

7. See J. Roscoe, *The Bagesu and Other Tribes of the Uganda Protectorate* (Cambridge: University Press, 1924), 31.

8. On the use of pain to construct ideologies, see E. Scarry, *The Body in Pain: The Making and Unmaking of the World* (New York: Oxford University Press, 1985).

9. Several studies on *imbalu* reinforce the centrality of pain. Among others, see La Fontaine, 'The Social Organisation of the Gisu', 16; S. Heald, *Controlling Anger: The Anthropology of Gisu*

Violence (Athens: Ohio University Press, 1998), 60; S. Heald, *Manhood and Morality: Sex, Violence, and Ritual in Gisu Society* (London: Routledge, 1999); V. Turner, 'Some Comparative Notes on Gisu and Ndembu Circumcision Symbolism', Unpublished conference paper, Puberty and Joking Conference, Makerere University, Kampala, 2–6 December 1966, 20; N.J.E. Mukhwana, '"Imbalu" the Gisu Initiation Rite: Implications for Understanding African Religion and Christian Acculturation', (Ph.D. dissertation, University of Pittsburgh, 1991); W.J.F. Khamalwa, *Identity, Power, and Culture: Imbalu: Initiation Ritual among the Bamasaba of Uganda* (Bayreuth: Breitinger, 2004), 92.

10. Interview with T.W., 15 September 2008; see also Mukhwana, '"Imbalu" the Gisu Initiation Rite', 292.

11. Purvis, *Through Uganda*, 271–72; Roscoe, *The Bagesu*, 32.

12. J. Roscoe, *Twenty-Five Years in East Africa* (Cambridge: Cambridge University Press, 1921), 238.

13. Interview with Ewayo, 13 November 2008.

14. For comparison see P. Aggleton, '"Just a Snip"?: A Social History of Male Circumcision', *Reproductive Health Matters* 15(29) (2007), 15–21.

15. For a detailed discussion see La Fontaine, 'The Social Organisation of the Gisu', 194. Also note that in the postcolonial period some individuals who had not undergone *imbalu* held important national political offices.

16. Heald, *Manhood and Morality*, 155.

17. My ideas here have been informed by R.C.C. Mafabi-Madaba, 'The History of Women's Education in Bugisu', (graduating research paper, Makerere University, Department of History, 1973), 3–4. In her research, she read the C.M.S. proceedings from 1899 to 1930. Unfortunately, I have not been able to access this source.

18. Purvis, *Through Uganda*, 298.

19. For British debates on circumcision, see *The British Medical Journal* 2(3903) (1935), 822–23.

20. Purvis mentions that he met nude youth in Bugisu. See Purvis, *Through Uganda*, 292

21. Roscoe, *The Bagesu*, 5.

22. Mayegu, Waminbi and Wawomola, 'Circumcision Year Names', 70.

23. Mafabi-Madaba, 'The History of Women's Education', 14.

24. Mafabi-Madaba and oral sources suggest that Archdeacon and later Bishop Masaba continued with the struggle against ritualized circumcision through the 1970s.

25. Purvis, *Through Uganda*, 271.

26. Purvis, *Through Uganda*, 338–39.

27. Purvis, *Through Uganda*, 338.

28. Interview with Ewayo, 13 November 2008, Bumufuni; Interview with Nangalama, 16 July 2010, Bubulo.

29. Mafabi-Madaba observes that in 1954, while at Nabumali, Archdeacon Masaba addressed Bagisu school boys and girls about circumcision. It is very likely that he sought to discourage the ritual practice. In 2008, a retired clergyman (who worked with Bishop Masaba and was circumcised in 1946 at school in Nabumali without the relevant rituals) narrated how Bishop Masaba worked hard to promote circumcision with prayers as opposed to rituals. Interview with C.W., 26 September 2008, Mbale.

30. See R. Mustafa Abusharaf, '"We Have Supped So Deep in Horrors": Understanding Colonialist Emotionality and British Responses to Female Circumcision in Northern Sudan', *History and Anthropology* 17(3) (2006), 223. In regard to female circumcision in Sudan, Mustafa Abusharaf argues that the British used coercion to redress wrongs committed in the name of tradition. They did so because they presumed that they had moral superiority over the colonial subjects.

31. Purvis, *Through Uganda*, 335.

32. Purvis, *Through Uganda*, 345.

33. Purvis, *Through Uganda*, 350.

34. T.O. Ranger, 'Godly Medicine: The Ambiguities of Medical Mission in Southeastern Tanzania, 1900–1945', in S Feierman and J.M. Janzen (eds), *The Social Basis of Health and Healing in Africa* (Los Angeles: University of California Press, 1992), 258.

35. My analysis is partly informed by T. Asad's argument: 'On Torture, or Cruel, Inhuman and Degrading Treatment', *Social Research* 63(4) (1996), 1091.

36. Interview with Bwayo, 13 November 2008. Born in 1922 and circumcised traditionally in 1942: 'White people sympathized with us because of the pain of *imbalu* so they introduced *imbalu* of the hospital'.

37. Interview with Seperia, 14 November 2008, Busiu.

38. Interview with Mundu, 13 November 2008.

39. It is common knowledge in Bugisu that men circumcised in hospital shy away from discussing this topic for fear of being humiliated.

40. Interview with C.W., 26 September 2008.

41. Mayegu, Wamimbi and Wawomola, 'Circumcision Year Names' note that in 1919 *imbalu* was delayed until 1920 because of the famine of 1918.

42. Mayegu, Wamimbi and Wawomola, 'Circumcision Year Names', 70–71; Wangusa, *Upon this Mountain* (London: Heinemann, 1989), 118.

43. This resonates with Derek Peterson's study of central Kenya where he found out that some Kikuyu boys opted for medical circumcision in 1912 because their families did not have goats and sheep to pay circumcision fees to the local surgeons. *Creative Writing: Translation, Bookkeeping, and the Work of Imagination in Colonial Kenya* (Portsmouth: Heinemann, 2004), 55.

44. Interview with J.W., Mbale, 15 November 2008.

45. Interview with S.W., Bumutoto, Mbale, 26 June 2009.

46. During her 1953–1954 fieldwork in Bugisu, La Fontaine learnt that in some areas, men and women referred to those circumcised in hospital as *baafu*. La Fontaine, 'The Social Organisation of the Gisu', 57.

47. Interview with J.W., 15 November 2008, Mbale.

48. Bagisu men and women regarded *imbalu* as a marker of ethnic identity separating them from their non-circumcising neighbours like the Bagwere, Padhola, Iteso, Banyole, as well as the Baganda colonial agents who arrived in Bugisu in the early 1900s. See Purvis, *Through Uganda*, 271. In November 1914, a Muganda author, S.B.N. Balubuliza wrote in *Ebifa mu Buganda* that the Bagisu cherished the practice of male circumcision and very much despised non-circumcised men. See also P. Khanakwa, 'Introduction' in 'Masculinity and Nation: Struggles in the Practice of Male Circumcision among the Bagisu of Eastern Uganda, 1900s to 1960s' (Ph.D. dissertation, Northwestern University, Evanston, 2011). Note that new sources have enabled me to revisit my argument on the construction of the Gisu nation.

49. Interview with Mwasame, 14 December 2008, Bumoni.

50. Interview with Nangalama, 16 July 2010, Bubulo.

51. Interviews with circumcision surgeons: Matsanga, 14 November 2008; Abdu Maikuma, 14 December 2008; Sowedi Mwasame, 14 December 2008; Interview with Bwayo, 13 November 2008, Bumufuni; see also 'The Making of a Local Circumcision Surgeon', *New Vision*, 10 March 2007.

52. Interview with Seperiya, 14 November 2008.

53. L.S. Funani, *Circumcision Among the amaXhosa: A Medical Investigation* (Braamfontein: Skotaville Publishers, 1990).

54. For other studies on the medicalization of African practices during the colonial period and how the gender of the medical practitioners informed the way the locals responded to and attended the new medical facilities, see Ranger, 'Godly Medicine', 276; N.R. Hunt, *A Colonial Lexicon: Of Birth Ritual, Medicalization, and Mobility in the Congo* (Durham: Duke University Press, 1999), 8.

55. Interview with T.M., September 2007, Mukono; See Aggleton, 'Just a Snip' for an interesting case of decircumcision.

56. Interview with Seperiya, 14 November 2008.

57. Interview with Matsanga, 14 November 2008.

58. Roscoe, *The Bagesu*, 32.

59. Some Bagisu men narrate the ordeal of having undergone correction circumcision in the 1940s but they are also quick to point out that it gave them the proper cut. Interview with C.G.W. (not his real name), September 2008.

60. Interview with Seperiya, 14 November 2008.
61. Interview with Webisa, 10 December 2008.
62. Interview with C.W., 16 September 2008.
63. Both Webisa, who was circumcised at Namakhoola primary school in 1944, and Wawomula, who was circumcised at Butiru primary school in 1948, explained that they did not stand on the traditional ancestral courtyard for circumcision because by that time circumcision at school was compulsory for schoolboys. Interview with Webisa, 10 December 2008; Interview with Wawomula, 8 April 2009.
64. Interview with C.W., 26 September 2008.
65. Three informants who were circumcised at school in the 1940s revealed that they preferred hospital circumcision, and indeed took their sons to hospital to surgeons whom they trusted to ensure a proper circumcision cut. E.W. had seven of his sons circumcised in hospital and only one in the traditional manner.
66. Interviews with Wawomula, 8 April 2009 and Webisa, 10 December 2008.
67. Interview with Siango, 26 June 2009, Bumutoto.
68. Wangusa, *Upon this Mountain*, 58.
69. 'African Local Government Circular, Circumcision Arrangement for 1954', in La Fontaine, 'The Social Organisation of the Gisu', Appendix I, 270.
70. J. La Fontaine, 'The Power of Rights', Man, new series 12(3/4) (1977), 426.
71. P.M. Masolo, Circumcision', unpublished Katigondo research paper 1979–1980 (Katigondo National Major Seminary) explains that while conducting research on *imbalu* in Butiru, 1978, he noticed that some village boys did not follow the circumcision programme because they did not want to be identified as being village boys. They wanted to be associated with schoolboys who, by then, were getting circumcised in December and village boys in August.
72. Mbale Archives, 'Regulations for Control and Improvement of Bugisu Circumcision Ceremonies', 1958.
73. Archival records reveal forcible circumcision of a vet assistant, teachers and sons of a civil servant in 1966.
74. Mbale Archives, confidential, from Mutambo Veterinary Department to the District Commissioner, Bugisu, 5 August, 1956.
75. Interview with Munyanda, 7 April 2009, Mbale.
76. Mayegu, Wamimbi and Wawomola, 'Circumcision Year Names', 71.
77. For further details see *Report of the Commission appointed to Review the Boundary between the Districts of Bugisu and Bukedi* (Entebbe, 1962); P. Khanakwa, 'Inter-Communal Violence and Land Rights: Bugisu-Bugwere Territorial Boundary Conflict', *MISR Working Paper 6* (2012); Khanakwa, 'Masculinity and Nation'; S.R. Karugire, *A Political History of Uganda* (Nairobi: Heinemann Educational Books, 1980), 175–76; F.G. Burke, *Local Government and the Politics in Uganda* (New York: Syracuse University Press, 1964), 204–07.
78. See 'Report of the Commission appointed to Review the Boundary', 14.
79. Bagwere complained of discrimination by Bagisu including being turned away by gatemen at Mbale hospital and denial of education bursaries. See 'Report of the Commission appointed to Review the Boundary'.
80. Wamimbi, 'History of Bamasaaba' (unpublished manuscript, 1962), 19.

References

Primary sources

African Local Government Circular. 'Circumcision Arrangement for 1954', in La Fontaine, *The Social Organisation of the Gisu*, Appendix I, 270.
Correspondence in *The British Medical Journal*. 2(3903) (1935), 822–326.
Ebifa mu Buganda. 94, Buddo, November 1914.

Mbale Archives. 'Regulations for Control and Improvement of Bugisu Circumcision Ceremonies', 1958.
Mbale Archives. 1966. Confidential, from: Mutambo, Veterinary Department to the District Commissioner, Bugisu, 5 August 1966.
National Archives A46/262: Uganda Protectorate: Annual Report of the Provincial Commissioner on the Eastern Province for Year 1923. Entebbe.
New Vision, 7 October 1986.
New Vision, 10 March 2007.
Report of the Commission appointed to Review the Boundary between the Districts of Bugisu and Bukedi. Entebbe, 1962.

Interviews

Abdu Maikuma. 14 December 2008. Bumoni.
Matsanga. 14 November 2008. Busiu.
Situma Munyanda. 7 April 2009. Mbale.
Sowedi Mwasame. 14 December 2008. Bumoni.
Nangalama. 16 July 2010. Bubulo.
Seperiya. 14 November 2008. Busiu.
Charles Siango. 26 June 2009. Bumutoto.
Bwayo Sipande. 13 November 2008. Bumufuni, Bubulo.
Canon Wakiro. 26 September 2008. Senior Quarters, Mbale.
Timothy Wangusa. September 2007; 15 September 2008. Uganda Christian University, Mukono
Leo Wawumula. 8 April 2009. Naakhupa.
Esawi Webisa. 10 October 2008. Buwabwala.
Joseph Weyusha. 15 November 2008. Mbale.

Other Sources

Aggleton, P. '"Just a Snip?": A Social History of Male Circumcision', *Reproductive Health Matters* 15(29) (2007), 15–21.
Asad, T. 'On Torture, or Cruel, Inhuman and Degrading Treatment', *Social Research* 63(4) (1996), 1,081–109.
Burke, F.G. *Local Government and the Politics in Uganda*. New York: Syracuse University Press, 1964.
Funani, L.S. *Circumcision Among the amaXhosa: A Medical Investigation*. Braamfontein: Skotaville Publishers, 1990.
Heald, S. *Controlling Anger: The Anthropology of Gisu Violence*. Athens: Ohio University Press, 1998.
———. *Manhood and Morality: Sex, Violence, and Ritual in Gisu Society*. London: Routledge, 1999.
Hunt, N.R. *A Colonial Lexicon: Of Birth Ritual, Medicalization, and Mobility in the Congo*. Durham: Duke University Press, 1999.
Karugire, S.R. *A Political History of Uganda*. Nairobi: Heinemann Educational Books, 1980.
Khamalwa, J.P.W. *Identity, Power, and Culture: Imbalu: Initiation Ritual among the Bamasaba of Uganda*. Bayreuth: Breitinger, 2004.
Khanakwa, P. 'Masculinity and Nation: Struggles in the Practice of Male Circumcision among the Bagisu of Eastern Uganda, 1900s to 1960s'. Ph.D. dissertation. Evanston: Northwestern University, 2011.
———. 'Inter-Communal Violence and Land Rights: Bugisu-Bugwere Territorial Boundary Conflict'. *MISR Working Paper* 6 (2012).
Khaukha, A. 'The Tribal Circumcision Periods'. Unpublished paper in author's possession, undated.
La Fontaine, J. 'The Social Organisation of the Gisu with Special Reference to Their Initiation Ceremonies'. Ph.D. dissertation. Cambridge: University of Cambridge, 1957.
———. 'The Power of Rights'. *Man* (new series) 12(3/4) (1977), 421–37.

Lindsay, L.A. and S.F. Miescher. 'Introduction: Men and Masculinities in Modern African History', in L.A. Lindsay and S.F. Miescher (eds), *Men and Masculinities in Modern Africa*. Portsmouth: Heinemann, 2003, 1–32.

Mafabi-Madaba, R.C.C. The History of Women's Education in Bugisu'. Graduating research paper, Makerere University, Department of History, 1973.

Mayegu, A., G.M.W. Wamimbi and L. Wawomola. 'Circumcision Year Names (*Kamengilo*) in Masaba and Their Meanings', *Uganda Journal* 39 (1980): 58–75.

Masolo, P.M. 'Circumcision'. Unpublished student research paper. Katigondo National Major Seminary, 1979-80.

Mukhwana, N.J.E. '"Imbalu" the Gisu Initiation Rite: Implications for Understanding African Religion and Christian Acculturation'. Ph.D. dissertation. Pittsburgh: University of Pittsburgh, 1991.

Mustafa Abusharaf, R. 'We Have Supped So Deep in Horrors: Understanding Colonialist Emotionality and British Responses to Female Circumcision in Northern Sudan', *History and Anthropology* 17(3) (2006), 209–28.

Peterson, D. *Creative Writing: Translation, Bookkeeping, and the Work of Imagination in Colonial Kenya*. Portsmouth: Heinemann, 2004.

Purvis, J.B. *Through Uganda to Mount Elgon*. New York: American Tract Society, 1909.

Ranger, T.O. 'Godly Medicine: The Ambiguities of Medical Mission in Southeastern Tanzania, 1900–1945', in S. Feierman and J.M. Janzen (eds), *The Social Basis of Health and Healing in Africa*. Los Angeles: University of California Press, 1992, 256–82.

Roscoe, J. *The Northern Bantu: An Account of Some Central African Tribes of the Uganda Protectorate*. Originally published by Cambridge University Press, 1915. Reprint, London: Frank Cass, 1966.

———. *Twenty-Five Years in East Africa*. Cambridge: University Press, 1921.

———. *The Bagesu and Other Tribes of the Uganda Protectorate*. Cambridge: University Press, 1924.

Scarry, E. *The Body in Pain: The Making and Unmaking of the World*. New York: Oxford University Press, 1985.

Turner, V. 'Some Comparative Notes on Gisu and Ndembu Circumcision Symbolism'. Unpublished conference paper: Puberty and Joking Conference, Makerere University Kampala, 2–6 December 1966.

Twaddle, M. '"Tribalism" in Eastern Uganda', in P.H. Gulliver (ed.), *Tradition and Transition in East Africa: Studies of the Tribal Element in the Modern Era*. Berkeley: University of California Press, 1969, 193–208.

———. *Kakungulu and the Creation of Uganda, 1868–1928*. London: James Currey, 1993.

Wamimbi, G.M. 'History of Bamasaba'. n.p., 1962.

Wangusa, T. *Upon This Mountain*. London: Heinemann, 1989.

Whiting, J.W.M., R. Kluckhohn and A. Anthony. 'The Function of Male Initiation Ceremonies at Puberty', in E. Maccoby, T.M. Newcomb and E.L. Hartley (eds), *Readings in Social Psychology*. New York: Henry Holt, 1958, 359–70.

Pamela Khanakwa is a historian and lecturer in the Department of History, Archaeology and Heritage Studies at Makerere University, Kampala. She received her Ph.D. in African history from Northwestern University, Evanston, United States in 2011 and won a postdoctoral fellowship to the American Council of Learned Societies on the African Humanities Program in 2013. She has also worked as a research fellow at the Makerere Institute for Social Research. She is currently working on a book manuscript and her research interests include masculinities, ethnic nationalism and land struggles in Eastern Uganda.

CHAPTER 6

The Concept of 'Land' in Bioko

'Land as Property' and 'Land as Country'

Ana Lúcia Sá

The island today known as Bioko was named Flor Formosa, 'Beautiful Flower', by Fernando Pó when he arrived there in 1472. The Spanish colonial government then gave it the name of the Portuguese navigator and after independence, in 1969, the first president, Francisco Macías Nguema Biyogo, named the island after himself. Teodoro Obiang Nguema changed the name to Bioko, a Bubi royal, after the coup d'état of 1979 in which he succeeded his uncle Francisco Macías to the presidency. The island's colonial history began with these acts of naming and with the slave trade that followed the arrival of the Europeans in the fifteenth century. European powers recognized the island as a Portuguese possession until 1778, when it was given to Spain by the Treaty of El Pardo and formed part of the Spanish Territories in the Gulf of Guinea (see Map 6.1).

To the Bubi people, the inhabitants in 1472, the island did not belong to Portugal or Spain, nor was it called Flor Formosa or Fernando Pó. Its name was Eri or Ìchùla and it *belonged* to the Bubi. I emphasize the word *belonged* because this link between the Bubi people and an entire territory that they identified as theirs was noted by the Austrian cartographer Oscar Baumann in 1888, in *Fernando Póo und die Bube*: 'In every Bubi, with the exception of those who live near Santa Isabel, a feeling of derision or irritation is produced, when someone tries to convince them that Itschulla (the island of Fernando Pó) belongs not only to them, but also to the king of Spain'.[1] Baumann conceived of the island according to European political and economic references of spatial organization, where the notion of property is central.[2] The island belonged to the Bubi, meaning that they as a collective owned it and had the right to occupy

---

Notes for this section begin on page 155.

Map 6.1 Bioko, Equatorial Guinea

the territory and use the land. But, according to colonial claims by Fernando Pó the island belonged to a singular actor, the head of a state, being the private property and a commodity of Spain.

This chapter analyses the tensions created in the Bubi conceptualization of 'land' by the introduction of an exogenous and colonial concept of 'property' on the island of Fernando Pó (or Ìchùla or Bioko). In this chapter, I discuss the semantic field of 'land' in terms of the economic concepts of the agricultural life of the Bubi and their entanglement with concepts of the colonial economy, especially those central to the export-oriented economy, such as the 'plantation', showing how the colonial notion of 'property' became relevant to the Bubi people. The appropriation of a colonial symbol such as the plantation is key to understanding the tensions created in the conceptualization of 'land' in the Bubi context. I examine the entanglements between different perceptions of 'land' and 'property', the association between 'land' and 'country' and the use of colonial instruments by Bubi people to claim their rights over the land and to actively resist colonialism.

Each section of the chapter corresponds to a historical moment relevant to our understanding of the transformations of and the tensions in the concept of 'land' on Bioko. First, I explain the meaning of the 'island' and the beginning of colonization, coinciding as it did with the emergence of a centralized Bubi political system in the nineteenth century. Then I explain the introduction of the concept of 'property', linked to the plantation system, and the tensions this introduced to the island after 1904, when the regulation of property was systematized. Finally, the third section of the chapter is devoted to the impact that the new concept of 'property' had among the Bubi, taking as an illustration of these entanglements a 1931 letter signed by a collective called 'sons of the country' (*hijos del país*). This document was sent to the newly created Commissary of the Republic in the colony with the aim of changing the entire colonial system on their island.

The letter from the 'sons of the country' was written in a context of change and was an act of resistance to colonial encroachment. It was also an attempt by members of Bioko's autochthonous society to change their future, a future that was imagined using the new instruments provided by the colonizer, such as petitions and the language of law. The letter demonstrates the rapid appropriation of the colonial language and of colonial concepts by a group that did not constitute a political, social or economic elite, but was rather a group whose land and country were being occupied.

Bubi Political and Spatial Organization at the Dawn of European Colonization

In Bubi, the word *ichùla* has two meanings: 'island' and 'country'.[3] This is the island that belonged to the Bubi, according to Baumann. Bubi settlement patterns elucidate their relationship with their territory. According to tradition, their settlements were first located near the sea, but were moved inland to avoid kidnappings by slave traders in the sixteenth century.[4] Reconstructing the social and political institutions on the island before the fourteenth century, Jan Vansina describes the settlements as composed of Houses ('large household establishments' that were the heart of the settlement) inhabited for only part of the year.[5] If we consider the residence of the matriclan to be the Bubi House, the Spanish term *aldea* 'village' that was used in colonial writings is not an accurate description. These settlements were composed of patrilocal residences of matrilineal families and were called *lòbáó*. The word *kàrìchòbɔ̀* was used to name both the mother's matrilineal and the father's matrilineal clans, and has the etymological meaning 'maternal house'.[6] All the descendants of one mother belonged to the *kàrìchòbɔ̀*. The matriclan's property, understood as being that of the common ancestor, consisted of palm groves and agricultural products; control over these was inherited within the matriclan. The *bòtúkù* 'chief' ruled in the name of the common ancestor.[7]

Each *lòbáó* was autonomous and had its own *bòtúkù*. In the nineteenth century, the Bubi moved to a centralized system, coinciding with the colonial occupation of land on the island. The foundation of the city of Clarence (Malabo) by Fitz William Owen in 1827 was central to that occupation. Owen sought to use the city as a base to prevent the slave trade in the Bight of Bonny (Biafra).[8] The Spanish missionary and ethnographer Amador Martin del Molino explains that the foundation of Clarence marked the beginning of Bubi awareness of the existence of a colony in their land because the English bought land from Bubi chiefs to build the city and settle its limits.[9] Martin del Molino argues that the English arrogated 'Bubi territory' that was also 'Spanish territory'.[10] This means that the Bubi territory was a Spanish colony, in a moment when they were witnessing the building of an imperial space by a third party.

The city was strange to the Bubi and they called it *ǹpɔ̀tó* 'place of the foreigners', foreigners with whom they traded palm oil. This was also the time of the formation of a creole society on the island whose members were collectively known as the Fernandinos. They were freed people from Cape Coast, Freetown and Calabar, among other places, who were employed to build the city and stayed on, engaging in commerce and trading with the Bubi. The Fernandinos began to acquire farms on the shore and it was them, along with Santomeans, who introduced cocoa to the island.[11]

In parallel with the colonial construction of spaces and institutions on the island, the Bubi developed their own spaces and institutions, most notably a monarchy. In his work, Vansina viewed the Bubi monarchy as one of the 'unusual institutions' that resulted from 'an unusual degree of isolation' of the island.[12] Around 1835–45, Moka (or Mokaata), the chief of Riabba, one of the Bubi settlements in the south of Bioko, successfully claimed authority over the whole island, becoming a *bòtúkù bóté* 'great chief', and in so doing created the Bubi monarchy. The institution of the monarchy is best understood not as a result of isolation, as argued by Vansina, but rather as a response to the increased presence of foreign powers and foreign actors and the consequent need for protection and resistance.[13]

Moka was seen by other Bubi chiefs as the symbolic figurehead of their autochthonous political institutions, while the Europeans called him 'king'.[14] Paths led from every direction to Riabba, now the centre of Bubi political power, paths that Moka could close.[15] The word 'path' has two correspondences in Bubi, *bòsèkà* 'trail, road, and track' and *bòsɔ̀é* 'road, path'. Foreign travellers used the Spanish expression *camino bubi* 'Bubi footpath' in their texts denoting the specific paths in the interior of the island that led to Riabba.[16]

Moka conceded greater entry into 'Bubi space' to the foreigners than had occurred previously. It was, for example, during his reign that the Claretians, the Congregation Missionary Sons of the Immaculate Heart of Mary, started their mission on the island. The king gave them permission to build a mission and plant a farm on his lands in the bay of Riabba/Concepción (Bubi/colonial names), but he considered himself as the ruler of the foreigners in *his* lands. He ruled his territories, not Spain.[17] The Claretians, however, went on to play a significant role in the colonization of the island. They were not only in charge of evangelization, but also farmed products for the export-oriented colonial economy. In particular, they insisted on linking the education of the autochthonous people who laboured on cocoa plantations.[18]

Moka died in 1899. In 1900 European powers signed the Treaty of Paris inaugurating effective Spanish colonization over Spanish Guinea. In Bioko, the power struggle created by Moka's death resulted in the legitimate heir, Moka's oldest brother Malabo, losing to Esáasi Eweera, a 'secondary chief' and an opponent to the growing presence of foreigners in the island.[19] Eweera is still remembered in Bioko as a figure who resisted colonial occupation.

Esáasi Eweera's reign was short (1899–1904), ending with his death in colonial custody, and colonial documents present him as a violent rebel who acted against the missionaries in Concepción. The governor praised the police because they had contributed to ending the 'ridiculous legend of the Bubi kings and opening the way to the progress and to the civilization in the southern part of the island'.[20] The monarchy was belittled and presented as part of the 'barbaric' and 'sterile life' that needed to be destroyed to open up the island and its inhabitants to 'progress', 'civilization', 'empire of the law', 'church' and, ultimately, the 'truth'.[21] Although it reveals a European conception of linear time and justifies the use of violence, the letter also stresses the existence of an effective Bubi political power and of a territory over which Esáasi Eweera ruled.

In his report attached to the governor's letter, first lieutenant José de la Torre Rey wrote that Esáasi Eweera, his wives and children and the inhabitants of Riabba (in total almost fifty people) were forced to recognize King Alfonso XIII as the only sovereign and to travel to the capital, Santa Isabel, as a sign of obedience to Spain. Eweera died in the city, having refused medication or food.[22] After Esáasi Eweera's death in 1904, the 'Bubi state' went into decline.[23] His successor, Malabo Lopelo Melaka, held only symbolic power until his death in 1937. This, then, is what 1904 means to the Bubi people: the loss of their island and the onset of transformations in the Bubi organization of their territory. The concept of 'property', analysed hereinafter, was an essential element of the tensions around the reconceptualization of 'land' after Eweera's death and around colonial occupation.

The Introduction of the Colonial Concept of 'Property' in Bioko

The first two decades of the twentieth century were crucial in the submission, or as the Spanish called it 'pacification', of the Bubi people. In addition to being the year of Esáasi Eweera's death, 1904 also saw the introduction of a law that regulated the Spanish colonization of land, establishing by whom and how this could be achieved. The Royal Decree of 11 July 1904 regulated property and its registration in the colony, with reference to the role of the state, the exploitation of land by individuals and what the colonial government considered to be 'native property'. It was permeated by the development of colonial wealth, the notion of utility, of usable land, whether in terms of public works or products that would benefit the colonial economy. The tensions created by different kinds and concepts of 'property' in the island are the focus of this section.

In an unsigned document from the Ministry of State – the metropolitan institution in charge of the Spanish Territories in the Gulf of Guinea – called 'Notes on Projects to Colonize Guinea, 1903–06', the land on Bioko was divided into three categories, emphasizing the need to protect it as the main source of wealth:

> I. The lands occupied by the autochthonous population and over which they have the right of occupation, that, in addition of being fair, it is practical to respect it scrupulously.
> II. The already registered land, or those notarially known as private property.
> III. The lands that actually are of public domain or vacant; and those occupied or exploited by the state.[24]

The first had to be respected with regards to the 'first occupant', although they could be sold or rented with the permission of the colonial authority. The Spanish law on property applied to the other two categories and they had to be registered. The Royal Decree thus stipulated what was considered to be the property of the state, private property and native property. State property included the 'assets' (*bienes*) of common use, like rivers, beaches, and pathways, among others, spaces that established the territory as a place of movement under the control of the state.[25] Control of the pathways encompassed control over Bubi footpaths and roads, *bòsèkà* and *bòsòé*. These were important elements in the conceptualization of the territory, because they linked the settlements and enabled the movement of goods and people that lived outside of the colonial laws.

The state also controlled the land that could be assigned as private property or exploited by private individuals and companies who obtained concessions of land. The concession of land by grants was made according to the interests of the state, such as the cultivation of export crops or other crops required in the colony.[26] In the export-oriented colonial economy, cocoa was the preferred crop. Having obtained a lease, settlers could exploit the land for some years, paying taxes, and at the end of the period the land could be embargoed and auctioned. The original owners had to pay if they wanted to recover their land. When they could not afford the payment, the state could start a new auction process.

According to the colonial state, 'native property' consisted of the 'lands that have been demarcated as the property of tribes, villages or native familiar groups' and that were not the private property of the state.[27] Land tenure and respect for 'traditional rights' to land had to be upheld, according to Chapter IV of the Royal Decree, and colonized peoples could not be stripped of possession of the 'lands they usually occupy'.[28]

The notion of occupation of the lands was central to what the colonial state considered native property. The division between occupied and empty land determined what was considered as land to be used by the state and controlled in the name of a bright, future, colonial economy. Associated with the tangible occupation of the land is the notion of the collective.[29] Implicit within this notion of collective property is the colonial imposition of a particular and foreign notion of community, of common law and of common property. For the Bubi, a lòbáó was a settlement of a patrilocal residence of the matriclan; in the colonial perspective it was considered a village. The lòbáó was a specific form of housing, worship and farming that had specific rules of land tenure, property and inheritance that were neither understood nor taken into account by the colonial government.

The definition of native property and its demarcation was in the hands of the colonial government, which in turn drew on colonial anthropological works. In those anthropological texts, farmed land and houses were considered familiar or 'communal familiar' property.[30] Historically, however, agricultural lands – whose designations depended on the goods farmed – were distributed by the bàtúkkù 'chiefs' to heads of households and were not the 'property' of the family. The Bubi verb àbbà means 'to distribute, to allocate, to give' and the place where goods are distributed is the ǹ'àbbà. As seen before, Riabba is also the toponym where the bòtúkù bóté, the 'great chief', of the Bubi monarchy lived. Metaphorically, it is the place where lands and other goods were distributed by the highest authority. The only type of land that families had that could be inherited was palm groves. The family expressed possession with the verb òkkáà 'to have, to own', which can be applied to goods, real estate or values. The inherited patrimony, the kà'ó (which also means 'treasure') is linked to the descendants.

The Bubi people viewed palm oil trees as 'property'; palm oil plantations were communal property that belonged to the extended family. But central to this concept of 'property' was that it remained within the matriclan and so uterine nephews inherited the management of the palm oil groves on the death of the head of the family. The owners of the products of the trees, however, were the women of the matriclan. Despite the introduction of cocoa plantations, palm oil trees remained an important part of the economy.[31] At the end of the nineteenth century, each village had its palm oil groves and lands for crops were 'temporarily colonized in certain seasons'. Every village also had its 'beach', a place on the shore where they sold the palm oil, which was an important site for commercial transactions with foreigners.[32]

As we can see, the clash between different notions of 'property' in this context is notable. Furthermore, in Bubi, what can be translated as 'property' in the sense imposed by the colonial government is the concept of *kà'ó*, which has an association with the registration (of property) (*ilè'ó*) introduced under Spanish colonization.

The conception of 'property', in the *lòbáó* and the matriclan, as belonging to the family contrasted with the concept of native property developed by the colonial government. Following the imposition of the Spanish concept of common property, what was individual or familiar property came to be considered collective, with no accordance to the respect they claimed to have for the customary law on family and inheritance. This can be seen in articles eleven and twelve of the Royal Decree, which determined that the governor general of the colony had the competency to delimit the land of the 'tribes, villages or indigenous familiar groups'. That is, it was the colonial agent who assigned 'native property'.

Using these property laws we can trace an evolution in the colonial notion of 'native property' and an intensification in the actions of the colonial state. The Royal Decree of 27 September 1907 on the 'Demarcation of Native Farms', for example, stipulated that the colonial authorities were in charge of assigning (distributing, delimiting) 'native properties' to those who had not already established them.[33] With the Royal Decree of 21 May 1920, 'villages' were delimited along with farmland designated for the population, an accomplishment achieved with the assistance of the chiefs. The lands that the government determined to belong to each 'village' were 'communal properties' and they had to be registered in the Property Registry in the name of 'tribe, village of familiar group'.[34] Native property under an individual name was not recognized until 1944, and even then was limited to four hectares.[35]

So, in summary, what the colonial government gradually considered to be 'native property' was not in accordance with its proclaimed respect of 'native law'. As we have seen, in customary law what could be considered as property was linked to the *lòbáó* and the matriclan, namely the *kà'ó*, or matrilineally-inherited patrimony. The Bubi inheritance system was not taken into account in the colonial simplification of entitlement to lands in the name of a collective actor or of an individual. Another significant aspect is the fact that what the colonial state considered to be native property was the land that was not usable in terms of colonial profitability – the land that served the purpose of subsistence for villagers – again without considering the *lòbáó* and the matriclan.

Furthermore, under this system 'native property' had to be communal. The law stipulated what was communal, what was part of the colonial economy and what was the role of colonial agents in these determinations and their enforcement. By linking property to territory, the Spanish colonial regime assumed that the island belonged to Spain and thus that they could determine the use of the land and occupy 'native property' in the name of colonization. As Juan María Bonelli Rubio (Governor of the Spanish Territories of the Gulf of Guinea, 1943–49) indicated in a reflection on property rights, the right of property is not an 'absolute right', since this belongs only to God, so humans have the usufruct of the land to benefit humanity.[36] The colonial state reserved the right to determine what was of benefit to humanity.

Another tension linked to the colonial creation of 'native property' was the state's ignorance of Bubi concepts of arable lands. Bubi has words for different kinds of arable lands and plantations: *bùíà* means 'farm, forest, field'; 'farm' can also be designated by the word *èpátà* and *òbám*. Importantly, the different words that mean 'farm' specify the goods cultivated: *èpátà* means 'farm' but also 'cocoa plantation'. *Bùíà* means 'farm', but also 'yam farm [not plantation]', and *èbèrí* is a 'farm of yams and eddoe [Dioscorea esculenta]'.[37]

In 1911, the yam yield in Mussola was celebrated with a song: 'we beat the white, we are happy, we are strong'.[38] Thus the ritual of the agricultural cycle was linked to a celebration of the capacity for resistance to the colonial state and its agents. With this song, the Bubi asserted that the colonialists could not strip them of their institutions, festivities and connection to the land. Victory was linked to resistance in the act of keeping the land to farm products for their subsistence and not for the subsistence of the colony. On this point, the distinction made between 'farm' and 'plantation' in Bubi is notable, a distinction between the harvesting of local products associated with specific rituals and the harvesting of cocoa in plantations. Different spaces of experience overlapped in the situation of conflict and with the victory over the victors and their impositions.

'Land' Linked to 'Property', 'Farm' and 'Plantation'

The Spanish colonization of Bioko was a colonization of the land, which meant control of the usufruct of the goods provided by the soil. The development of plantations was a priority for Spanish politics and practices in the colony. The occupation of the land, profiteering of the goods and submission of the people all had their anchor in the plantation. The plantation can be understood as the pivot of the colonization of the island once called Fernando Pó. It was a new kind of space and social relations, based on race and labour, and had implications for how the Bubi related to the land. The plantation economy brought with it other categories of plantation systems (techniques, actors and conceptualizations). These new categories helped shape the concept of 'land' and its related concepts in Bubi.

From the Spanish perspective the barbarism of the colonized people would be overcome by the trio of 'education, agriculture and Christianity', rather than through 'education, industry and Christianity' as in the Gold Coast.[39] The three notions, in this conceptualization, included work. Since the beginning of religious colonization by the Claretians, missionaries had taught agricultural work, especially cocoa farming. The aim was to transform the autochthones from owners of their land into expert farm workers for colonial owners.[40]

In this setting, the colonial government created institutions that established racial discrimination and regulated the development of the colonial economy: the *Curaduría Colonial* 'Colonial Trusteeship', 1901, and the *Patronato de Indígenas* 'Tutelage of the Natives', 1904. It claimed these institutions were to 'protect' the colonized peoples and to promote Hispanization among the *indígenas*. These are the black colonial subjects in a model following the Law of the Indies of the Spanish colonization of America. The *Patronato*, after 1928, divided the autochthonous population into the emancipated (partially or fully, i.e. those who were able to partially or fully manage their lives) and the non-emancipated (i.e. those who were under the tutelage of the *Patronato*).[41] The non-emancipated could be recruited to work on the plantations.[42]

The need for a workforce on the plantations was a concern from the beginning of colonization. Labourers (*braceros*) were mainly recruited in other West African colonies and in continental Guinea, but one of the preoccupations of the governors after Esáasi Eweera's death was to make Bubi people work on plantations. Diego Saavedra, governor in 1906, wrote in his memoirs that the 'Bubi from the mountain' believed that the 'farms of the white' would never get to the mountains, and considered that space 'more of their own, more of their property'.[43] Because of this, they were diligent in farming. He acknowledged that there were two spaces on the island, pronominalized as 'ours' and 'theirs'. The Bubi space was that of those living outside the influence of the colonial government and its authority, independent and peaceful in 'their forests'. It was the space of those who did not create animosity, but who also did not 'help', or who were not useful for colonial work. That is, those who were not useful for the purposes of the Spanish rule over those territories.[44]

The governor after Saavedra, when Spanish colonization was intensified, Ángel Barrera y Luyando (1906–07, 1910–24), was an enthusiastic proponent of Spanish colonial subjects labouring on the plantations. In a letter to the Ministry of State, Barrera y Luyando explained the need to impose such labour on the autochthones. For him, work was a means to civilize people and bring progress in order that they abandon their 'primitive state':

> Several efforts have been made in the past years to force the Bubi to work without great results, since only a very small part of them work, always finding defenders of the poor little Bubi that present them as proprietors, because special care was

taken for many years to turn them into landowners of one hectare, on the basis of which it is impossible for them to subsist, but which serves as an excuse to defend the idleness of those who pompously qualified as landowners.[45]

This quote reflects the tensions within the colonial system, the system that created the legal concept of 'landowner', which collided with the need for a labour force that could not be hired among the proprietors.

Barrera y Luyando felt it was important to gather the chiefs and agree with them the boundaries of their 'small plantings', plantings that were to be worked only by women. The men should be hired to work on colonial properties near their villages. This situation, in his mind, was advantageous for the Bubi, 'because they live now isolated in the most intricate forest'. In the governor's mind, they needed to be 'concentrated' and 'protected', they needed to be under the control of the colonial state. But there was the complicating factor that they were landowners, too, under the colonial regulation of land tenure.

In an address to the Official Chamber of Agriculture of Fernando Pó in 1911, Barrera y Luyando criticized the colonizers who had preceded him, because they had taught the Bubi that 'with a hectare of land they can obtain profits enough to cover their needs', so they need not work on plantations.[46] This had resulted both in a lack of workers and in Bubi men insisting on a 'free and independent life in the woods'.[47]

Efforts to force the Bubi to labour on plantations were deeply resented. Mandatory work during the cocoa harvest was the leitmotiv of acts of rebellion, such as the Bubi revolt of San Carlos in 1906 and the armed uprising in Balachá of Riabba in July 1910. The latter resulted in the Decree of the General Government of 15 July 1910 that established mandatory work for non-landowning Bubi during the cocoa harvest.[48] This resistance to forced labour generated fears among colonial officials of further acts of resistance. On 6 July 1912, the governor general noted the possibility of a Bubi rebellion against colonial labour camps. People were moved by 'propagandists of subversive ideas'. The main reason, in his opinion, was that 'someone had taught them that the soil of the island belongs to them and therefore they alone had the right to work it to their advantage'.[49] Barrera y Luyando explicitly linked the notion of 'working the soil' to the 'ownership of the soil' and thus to the concept of 'property', which had to be registered, according to the Royal Decree of 11 July 1904.

This discourse allows us to see the ways in which the Bubi were victims of land expropriation and forced labour and also cash crop producers in their own right. But what is significant about Governor Barrera y Luyando's comment on work and property is that it highlights the clash between two different concepts of 'work' and 'land': the colonial one, expressed by Barrera y Luyando's interpretation of Bubi words, and the Bubi one, as it was transmitted to the governor. For the Bubi, the ownership of the land was linked to working the land and the usufruct of its products. For Barrera y Luyando, the land was owned by Spain as the colonial power. He used the concepts presumably transmitted by Bubi interlocutors and integrated them into a colonial discourse on 'land', 'property' and 'working the land'. In the interest of the colonial socio-economic system, 'property' was combined with 'land' and with 'labour'.

It was also combined with colonial bureaucracy through registration. The land registry was established in the colony in 1858, when the concept and existence of private property was introduced.[50] The registry remained relevant in the colony, despite the anomalies, mistakes, absences and imprecise knowledge of boundaries, the despoliation of 'indigenous tribes from their lands' and the need for total revision recognized in the 1920s by the government of the Spanish Territories in the Gulf of Guinea.[51] In 1926, the colonial government felt the need to regulate property registries on Fernando Pó. The Spanish inspector and register of property, José Luis Serrano Ubierna, established the 'Bases for the Reorganization of the Registry of Property of Santa Isabel of Fernando Pó'. Alongside Governor Miguel Núñez de Prado (1926–31), he sought to apply the laws emanating from the metropolis strictly and gather the *lòbáó* in 'strategic places', assigning to them 'the necessary land for them to live'. With this, 'native families are dispossessed of the lands in their possession'.[52] There were, however, difficulties in registering what was called 'native property' because of overlapping names and inconsistencies between autochthonous and baptismal names.

Another issue was the linkage between *owning land* and *producing products* in an export-oriented agricultural economy. With the regulation of property on the island, alongside a more effective colonial presence, the concept of 'property' started to assume an important role in the way Bubi conceptualized their relation to land and their detailed concepts of 'arable lands'. It became important for the Bubi to own a parcel of land according to colonial ideas and regulations. Thus, *èpátà* 'cocoa plantation' was increasingly a way of farming that could be used to pre-empt the colonial expropriation that was interrupting family inheritance. These tensions were even more acute when considering the introduction of another concept related to land in the Bubi context: the concept of 'farmer' (*agricultor*).

The 'Sons of the Country' and the Creation of 'Land' as 'Future'

In this process of transformation of perceptions of 'land', of 'land' as 'property' and of 'products' as 'property', cocoa held a disproportionate role. Cocoa was intimately linked with colonial considerations of what agriculture meant. As Bravo Carbonel stated, cocoa was associated with the 'development of the agricultural spirit', of a rational agriculture, among the Bubi as colonial subjects.[53] This provoked changes in the way property was considered in both the colonial and Bubi contexts, as we can see in this section, where I analyse the concept of 'farmer' (*agricultor*) drawing on written documents by colonial subjects. In so doing I explore the relationship between 'farmer', 'property' and 'country' in a letter signed by eleven 'sons of the country' and titled 'Propositions of the Sons of the Country. The Bubi' (*Proposiciones de los hijos del país. Los Bubis*), Santa Isabel, 28 August 1931.

Under Spanish colonial rule in Bioko, the concept of 'farmer' (*agricultor*) contrasted with that of 'labourer' (*bracero*) on the plantations. A farmer was an agent of colonization with the specific attribution of developing colonial agriculture. The concept of 'farmer' referred, from the beginning of the twentieth century, to a person for whom others worked, and was related to the labour shortage on the island, especially during the cocoa harvest.[54] The colonizers defined 'farmers' as those whose work benefitted colonial agriculture and who were responsible for and/or in possession of plantations.[55] The element of possession is important, because it mediates particular concepts and constructions such as 'each farmer should have the right to hire' a labour force, and a person who 'owns land' or 'farmer proprietor'.[56]

The Bubi who were educated in the Claretian missions knew how to farm cocoa and some were assisted by the missionaries to acquire small plots of land, meaning that the plots were recognized by the colonial state as private property.[57] These 'pieces of ground' (*terrenos*) could be obtained by submitting a request to the General Government of the colony, which claimed all 'empty' land as its property. In this regard, the government considered the Bubi to be Spanish.[58] Despite this legal definition of Bubi as Spanish with regard to this category of property, we need to take into account the arbitrary nature of the law in a racist colonial system and the privilege granted to the European settlers. Although in theory the law protected the property of Bubi individuals and what was considered 'native' and 'communal property', the reality was different, as we can see from documents reporting abuses by settlers and the dysfunction of the *Patronato de Indígenas*.

In Spanish, *indígena* means 'native', 'autochthonous', but the term acquired other meanings through the process of colonization. *Indígena* was a central concept in the justification of the occupation of land in an epoch when there was a distinction between those who should be under the tutelage of the *Patronato* (i.e. the non-emancipated *indígenas*) and those who could manage their own social and economic life, i.e. the 'emancipated'.

There are a number of reported cases of abuse of *indígenas* by European colonizers. These include the appropriation of their property by deception and the abuse of the 'credulity and unawareness' of the *indígenas*.[59] This was an ongoing situation and, in 1931, following the change of regime in Spain and the birth of the Second Republic, people presenting themselves as *indígenas* addressed letters of complaint to the colonial authorities. They claimed participation and representation in the colonial language, Spanish, and used colonial instruments, such as the concepts of *indígenas* or the 'registry of lands', to react against the colonial regime. The following examples are testimonies of a time marked by the plantation system and narrate the experiences of the colonized in relation to the colonial state. This was during a period when the colonized population was divided into 'emancipated' and 'non-emancipated' *indígenas*.

Lands recognized as property of the *indígenas* by the state were in the hands of European settlers, because they rented or acquired at auction lands whose owners could not pay the taxes demanded of them. This was a means, legitimized by the colonial government, for Europeans to occupy land. Having acquired access to the land, settlers registered it in their names, preventing the *indígenas* from recovering their property. This also prevented the Bubi from having the usufruct of the goods produced on their land.[60] Abuses of this kind were deeply resented by those who had lost their land and they disputed the right of settlers to that land. The institution charged with resolving these disputes was the *Patronato de Indígenas*, an institution that acted in favour of the colonial system and was characterized by arbitrary decisions that shored up the right of settlers to expropriate with impunity the property of *indígenas*.

Groups of *indígenas* used the *Patronato* in their internal disputes, appropriating the colonial system and the colonial definition of 'property'. This was the case for Miguel Boabisaha, a Bubi farmer from Basupu del Oeste, in 1931.[61] He owned eight hectares of land with a friend, near Basupu, that was expropriated in 1919 by *Sociedad de los Sres Benso y Hermanos*, a company that had behaved similarly with regards to the land of other Bubi farmers in Basupu. Boabisaha also narrated another expropriation and use of his land by an *indígena* of Fang origin, Manuel Bakale, legalized by the *Patronato* to collect a debt owed by Boabisaha's family. Boabisaha had farmed about two hectares of cocoa and this was a key element of his argument because property rights were symbolically linked to cocoa farming in the colonial context.

Complaints such as these existed because *indígenas* in Bioko felt that their voices were not heard under the monarchy; they felt outcast and sought to be included. Rather than question the legitimacy of Spanish colonization or metropolitan decisions over the island, they questioned the methods applied in the colony, including those used to determine the inheritance of land. The petitioners were aware that the change in the political regime in the metropolis could benefit them, so they tried to change the future using the means created by the colonial regime itself: the institutions and the concepts that created Spanish colonial subjects. The colonial notion of 'property' was, as noted, a key element in the arguments of those who saw their lands expropriated. 'Land' was already linked to 'property' but this association acquired a more complex dimension when the notion of 'country' (*país*) became entangled with the concept of 'land' (*tierra*).

The combination of 'land' as 'property' and 'land' as 'country' in the creation of a present future is the guiding idea of the document 'Propositions of the Sons of the Country. The Bubi' (hereinafter 'Propositions'). This document belongs to a set of petitions to the Commissary of the Republic that were delivered to the Director General of Morocco and the Colonies, at the beginning of the Spanish Second Republic, a time of change and of hope for an end to the abuses of the monarchical colonial regime.[62] It was signed by eleven people with a unitary collective statement: 'The Bubi'. This collective was created under colonial circumstances and the acknowledgement of their experiences in the past and present colonial time led them to aspire to transformations in the future. They anticipated a new political and historical moment for their country.

The collective actors described themselves as 'sons of the country' (*hijos del país*), natives (*naturales*) and farmers (*agricultores*). The phrase 'sons of the country' expresses autochthony; it had been used as a synonym for natives in a colonial decree on native property in 1868.[63] In 'Propositions' this naming is also a means of opposing themselves to other groups that had submitted petitions to the colonial government, groups who *were not* from the *country*, a word that can be expressed in Bubi as *ìchùla* 'island' or *bɔ̀bà*, which also means 'soil' and 'land'. The word *país*, in Spanish, reflects the association of land, autochthony and property that guides the argument of the letter and the reflection on historical time. The petitioners hoped to join the past (when the island and the land belonged to the Bubi) and the future (with the island and the land as a 'country').[64]

The letter writers self-identified with the soil. In the letter they entangled the concept of 'land' as a symbol for 'roots' (*raíces*) and that of 'land' as a commodity (*producto, bien*), with both expressions used as a means of identification:

> In the Colony, those who must be properly called farmers are the sons of the country, that means: the Bubi; the books of the Property Registration can prove it. // Usually today we can find extensive properties of Europeans, but in almost all of them there are Bubi plantations, that they were forced to abandon, because earlier the Bubi did not know what it meant to legalize a piece of land.

The colonial concepts of 'farmer' and 'proprietor', in isolation or in association, generated tensions in the Bubi socio-economic perception of 'working' and 'owning the land'. They were used by these Bubi petitioners in a context where land had become commoditized, and they asserted themselves as owners of 'Bubi plantations' (*plantaciones bubis*) inside 'properties of Europeans' (*propiedades de europeos*). The 'plantation' was the symbol they used to try to recover their lands, which had increasingly been in foreign hands since the foundation of Clarence. That is, this is the history of the Bubi people since the beginning of a definitive European colonial presence on the island. With this document and their statement of the injustices they had suffered, they tested the colonial concept of 'property' that guided the occupation of land. By farming cocoa, they asserted their right to regain their lands.

The 'sons of the country' narrated the histories of Bubi landowners who had been forced to abandon their land when European settlers produced documents proving their title. They were able to do so because those Bubi farmers had not obtained state recognition of land ownership. The Bubi farmers were thus forced to move and to start new farms (*fincas*) inland. European settlers used the institutions of the colonial state to register land in violation of Bubi rights to it. The 'sons' also exposed European plunder of property and of cocoa farmed by Bubi people. This created a cycle of indebtedness for the Bubi farmer that started from underpayment for his cocoa crop, which led to an inability to pay taxes and thus to the auctioning of his lands. In their words, this was a 'fatal deceit'. They asserted that because they were deceived, they were proprietors of land in the hands of Europeans. They did this through expressions such as 'Bubi owner of that farm' (*bubi propietario de dicha finca*), 'owner of the farm' (*dueño de la finca*) or 'Bubi properties' (*propiedades bubis*).

The tension in the concept of 'property' between the Bubi and the colonizers emerged because of the expropriation of land by auction or other means, as shown by the phrase used in the 'Propositions': 'the auction is always hidden from the owner of the farm, until some months later, when he realizes that his farm doesn't belong to him'. But another tension in the concept of 'property' created by the expression 'sons of the country' is its connection to the concept of *indígena*. The etymology of *indígena* is 'native', yet the term itself is a colonial creation. By linking *indígena* to the expression 'sons of the country', the authors of the letter drew on the semantics of emancipation and restituted to the word its original meaning. By being *indígenas*, they asserted themselves as the first inhabitants of the island, depriving the word of its colonial meaning, which was the basis for colonial discrimination of Spanish subjects.

The argument of the document was grounded in the assumptions that the authors were autochthonous, that they had lands that had been turned into plantations, that they worked those lands, and that therefore the lands were rightfully theirs. As such they, and other Bubi, should be able to recover the lands from European settlers, in the name of an 'equal justice, without distinction of colours or races, things that never occurred so far'.

In the petition, acknowledging the racial discrimination that characterized the Spanish colonial system, the authors began by recognizing the Spanish colonial power over 'these lands of Guinea', but ended by showing that it was not necessary. They used a set of adjectives of familiarity and confidence (such as 'adopted son' or 'close friend') and invoked the Spanish 'civilizing mission'. In so doing, they dismantled the language of colonialism and civilization, at the same time that they sought to change the structures and institutions of the Spanish colonial system.

The 'sons of the country' also used the term 'colony' strategically: 'colony', without an adjective, referred to the Spanish presence on the island; the 'actual Colony', with a capital C, was used when discussing 'Bubi agriculture in the

Colony', to emphasize that the Bubi were the only people on the island who could be called farmers. They created a tension in the concept of 'farmer', with respect to its meaning in Spanish, as 'the person who works the land', and its colonial meaning as 'the person who owns the land'.

They demonstrated that the colonial system could be reformed or it could, ultimately, be ended and substituted with newly created autochthonous institutions. As an example, they proposed the creation of the position of 'native mayors' in the Bubi settlements. These mayors would serve, they proposed, as intermediaries between the autochthonous people and the state and could govern the villages without European intervention and without replacing the chiefs. Furthermore, they proposed reform of colonial institutions. As such, they were inscribing modern state institutions onto their expression of country. In particular, they advocated the elimination of the *Curaduría Colonial* and reform of the *Patronato de Indígenas*. The latter should be a *Tribunal Indígena* 'Native Court' that could enable dialogue between the autochthonous people and Europeans settlers.

The 'sons of the country' wanted to bring about an end to the historical moment that they were living in, a moment that included the dispossession of their lands. They wanted to bring about a new period in which they would have a voice and the ability to act and which would give greater weight to the views of the 'sons of the country' and the will of the people. They proposed changing, through legal means, the most imperative aspect of the colonial system: education, work and land. The future-oriented nature of the petition expressed their expectations as well as their memories of the recent past of loss, of the time when the island was not subject to colonial rule. The 'sons of the country' wanted to recover their lands so as to change the future and make a country without 'undoing' the past, in the same way that 'decolonization does not simply "undo" the past', as shown by Pierre-Philippe Fraiture in this volume.

Conclusion

The most significant crops produced by the Bubi people were yam and eddoe. The arable lands where they farmed these crops (*bùíà* and *èbèrí*, respectively) weren't considered the property of the matriclan, in contrast to the palm groves and the agricultural products of land that was being *used*, although not *owned*. Bubi ways of conceiving 'property' and 'inheritance' were challenged by the progressive occupation of arable lands from the first half of the nineteenth century. The regulation of property and its registration in the colony by the 1904 Royal Decree was connected to the export-oriented colonial economy, which privileged cocoa and imposed a Spanish concept of private and public property. The coexistence and tensions between autochthonous and colonial concepts of 'property' had implications for the way that the terms 'farm' and 'plantation' were used by Bubi people and for the way that they could reclaim access to – and ultimately repossession of – their land. The cocoa farm began to have a name in Bubi, èpátà. which also had the meaning 'farm'.

The 'plantation' was the central concept and practice of the colonization of Bioko. The tensions created by the plantation economy are especially relevant to our understanding of the conceptualization of 'land' on the island. The linkage between the introduced concept of 'property' and the lands used to produce first cocoa, and later all crops, was the means by which the Bubi claimed access to the land they were progressively losing.

When addressing the new political power in the metropolis in 1931, a group of Bubi people declared themselves to be 'sons of the country'. They did so in opposition to the foreign settlers who were occupying their lands. They asserted themselves as the only ones who could be called 'farmers', linking the working of the land to ownership of it. As farmers, possible proprietors and as 'sons of the country' this group expressed the meanings of 'land' as 'soil' and as 'country', as in the Bubi word bɔ̀bà, and restored the original meaning to the Spanish words *indígena* and *agricultor* used in the colonial context. This was a means to present the arbitrariness of the colonial system, built as it was on the plantation system and racism.

The 'sons of the country' used their relationship to the land to test institutions, colonization and the justification for Spanish rule. It is worth emphasizing that the group did not constitute an elite. In contrast to the major examples of groups that used the written word to resist colonialism, they were not large landowners, nor political activists, nor any other group of status. Instead they were a group of people who knew the power of the written word, who had parcels of land that were being progressively occupied in the name of colonization and who used modern ways of fighting the arbitrariness of colonialism.

The colonial concept of 'property' established tensions in the concepts of *indígena*, 'labourer' and 'farmer'. But this concept ceased to belong to the colonizer; it was appropriated and contested by the colonized. Writing in a time of hope due to the change of regime in the metropolis, the 'sons of the country' wanted to create a future and to produce a different historical narrative based on the transformations in the concept of 'land' introduced to Bioko by the colonial system and the plantation economy.

Notes

I thank José Francisco Eteo Soriso (National University of Equatorial Guinea) for his explanations of concepts in the Bubi language and for sharing the Bubi orthography used in this chapter. I also thank Yolanda Aixelà (Spanish National Research Council) and Nuria Fernández Moreno (Spanish National University of Distance Education) for sharing bibliographies and for discussions that helped clarify some idiosyncrasies of Bubi society.

1. My translation from the Spanish edition of *Fernando Póo und die Bube*: O. Baumann, *Una Isla Tropical Africana, Fernando Poo y los Bubis* (Madrid: SIAL, 2012), 177.
2. 'Property' is a nuclear concept in Western perspectives on spatial organization, see for example J. Tully, *A Discourse on Property, John Locke and His Adversaries* (Cambridge: Cambridge University Press, 1980). S. Elden, 'Land, Terrain, Territory', *Progress in Human Geography* 34(6) (2010), 799–817, develops the association between 'territory' and 'property', while explaining the etymology of the word 'territory' in English and the Latin languages.
3. For the meanings of the words in Bubi and their translation into Spanish I follow J. Bolekia Boleká, *Diccionario Español – Bubi* (Madrid: Akal, 2009). Bolekia Boleká uses the *esso* variety, spoken in his home village, Baney. For the transcription of the words in Bubi, I use the unified alphabet for the languages of Equatorial Guinea, developed by Equatoguinean linguists and anthropologists in the National University of Equatorial Guinea with the aim of being used in the writing of the African languages of the country.
4. Baumann, *Una Isla Tropical Africana*, 153; J. Vansina, *Paths in the Rainforests: Toward a History of Political Tradition in Equatorial Africa* (Madison: University of Wisconsin Press, 1990), 139; J.F. Eteo Soriso, 'Ecología, economía tradicional y simbolismo de los pueblos de Guinea Ecuatorial', in J. Aranzadi (ed.), *II Jornadas de Antropología de Guinea Ecuatorial* (Madrid: Universidad Nacional de Educación a Distancia, 2011), 109.
5. Vansina, *Paths in the Rainforests*, 72, 140.
6. J.F. Eteo Soriso, 'Los Ritos de Paso Entre los Bubi' (Ph.D. dissertation, Barcelona: Universidad Autónoma de Barcelona, 2013), 124.
7. Eteo Soriso, 'Ecología, economía tradicional y simbolismo', 93; A. Martin del Molino, *La Ciudad de Clarence, Primeros Años de la Actual Ciudad de Malabo, Capital de Guinea Ecuatorial, 1827–1859* (Madrid, Malabo: Instituto de Cooperación para el Desarrollo, Centro Cultural Hispano-Guineano, 1993), 218.
8. Following the foundation of Port Clarence there was a 'significant migration by West Africans' to the island (Vansina, *Paths in the Rainforests*, 145). On the foundation of Port Clarence, see Martin del Molino, *La Ciudad de Clarence*, and I. Sundiata, *From Slavery to Neoslavery: The Bight of Biafra and Fernando Po in the Era of Abolition, 1827–1930* (Madison: University of Wisconsin Press, 1996).
9. Martin del Molino, *La Ciudad de Clarence*, 22–26, 36–37.
10. 'Foreign body', 'Bubi territory' and 'Spanish territory' are expressions of Martin del Molino, *La Ciudad de Clarence*, 39, 66.
11. For the Fernandinos, see Sundiata, *From Slavery to Neoslavery*, especially Chapter 6, 'The Cocoa Economy', 90–118, and Martin del Molino, *La Ciudad de Clarence*, 94–116.
12. Vansina, *Paths in the Rainforests*, 137, 144–45.
13. For details on the development of the Bubi monarchy, see I. Sundiata, 'State Formation and Trade: The Rise and Fall of the Bubi Polity, c. 1840–1910', *International Journal of African Historical Studies* 27(3) (1994), 505–23; N. Fernández Moreno, 'Bubi Government at the End of the 19th Century: Resistance to the Colonial Policy of Evangelization of the Island of Bioko, Equatorial Guinea', *Nordic Journal of African Studies* 22(1/2) (2013), 23–48.
14. In the 1940s A. de Unzueta y Yuste, *Geografía Histórica de la Isla de Fernando Poo* (Madrid: Instituto de Estudios Africanos, Consejo superior de Investigaciones Científicas, 1947), 245 and C. Crespo Gil-Delgado, *Notas para un Estudio Antropológico y Etnológico del Bubi de Fernando Poo* (Madrid: Instituto de Estudios Africanos, Consejo superior de Investigaciones Científicas, 1949), 180, state that Moka had a precarious hold on authority and only ruled nominally, especially in the northern part of the island. Martin del Molino, *La Ciudad de Clarence*, 220, highlights the symbolism of Moka among the chiefs.
15. These are described in Baumann, *Una Isla Tropical Africana*, 64, as a 'muddy path that meandered through the thick and humid forest'. When travelling on the island, Baumann wanted to meet King Moka, although he was a white man and therefore an 'evil devil' who could not enter the village.

16. See Baumann, *Una Isla Tropical Africana*, 64, and J. Más, *En el País de los Bubis* (A Coruña: Ediciones del Viento, 2010).

17. On this, see Fernández Moreno, 'Bubi Government at the End of the 19th Century', 34–39.

18. J. Bravo Carbonel, *Fernando Póo y el Muni, Sus Misterios y Riquezas, Su Colonización* (Madrid: Imprenta de Alrededor del Mundo, 1917), 223–24; Crespo Gil-Delgado, *Notas para un Estudio Antropológico*, 177. On the history of the evangelization of Spanish Guinea see, for example, Fernández Moreno, 'Bubi Government at the End of the 19th Century', or M.L. de Castro and M.L. de la Calle, *La Colonización Española en Guinea Ecuatorial (1858–1900)* (Barcelona: CEIBA, 2007).

19. Expressions by Crespo Gil-Delgado *Notas para un Estudio Antropológico*, 176, 179.

20. Archivo General de la Administración (AGA). Africa-Guinea. (15) 4 Box 81/6273. Folder of the Ministry of State, Colonial Section, file number 59. Dispatch 278 from the Governor General José de Ibarra Autrán to the Ministry of State, Colonial Section, handwritten in Santa Isabel, 26 July 1904. I translated this quote and all other quotes from documents of the Archivo General de la Administración (General Archive of the Administration, Alcalá de Henares, Spain), thereinafter AGA.

21. AGA. Africa-Guinea. (15) 4 Box 81/6273. Folder of the Ministry of State, Colonial Section, file number 59. Report of the first lieutenant Jose de la Torre Rey, dispatch 440 of the General Government of the Spanish Territories of Western Africa, 13 December 1904, responding to the Royal Order 461 of the Ministry of State of 21 October 1904.

22. The mystery around Esáasi Eweera's death was a point of tension between the colonial government and the metropolis. In the colony they reiterated that Esáasi Eweera died of natural causes, although the disease was unspecified; in the metropolis the Ministry of State (Royal Order 461 of the Ministry of State of 21 October 1904) believed that 'it is not the same to surprise a Bubi king in perfect health and in conditions of hiding and defending himself as to capture him ill and ailing to the point of needing to transport him in a hammock'. The references on the death of Esáasi Eweera are Unzueta y Yuste, *Geografía Histórica de la Isla de Fernando Poo*, 248; Crespo Gil-Delgado, *Notas para un Estudio Antropológico*, 181–182; L. García Cantús, 'El comienzo de la masacre colonial del pueblo Bubi. La muerte del Botuko Sás, 1904', in J. Martí Pérez and Y. Aixelà Cabré (eds), *Estudios Africanos, Historia, Oralidad, Cultura* (Barcelona: CEIBA, 2008), 7–26.

23. His death was the 'beginning of the colonial massacre of the Bubi people', according to García Cantús, 'El comienzo de la masacre colonial del pueblo Bubi', 3–9.

24. AGA. Africa-Guinea. (15) 4 Box 81/6413.

25. The Royal Decree of 11 July 1904, Chapter II, Article 2, in J.M. y Núñez de Prado, *La Propiedad en la Guinea Española* (Madrid: Imprenta de la Ciudad Lineal, 1929), 38.

26. The Royal Decree of 11 July 1904, Chapter VI, in Bravo Carbonel, *Fernando Póo y el Muni*, 348–51.

27. The Royal Decree of 11 July 1904, Chapter II, Article 3, in Núñez de Prado, *La Propiedad en la Guinea Española*, 39.

28. The Royal Decree of 11 July 1904, Chapter IV, 'On the Indigenous Property', Article 10, in Núñez de Prado, *La Propiedad en la Guinea Española*, 41. The Royal Decree of 12 November 1868, Article 17, in A. Yglesias de la Riva, *Política Indígena en Guinea* (Madrid: Instituto de Estudios Africanos, Consejo Superior de Investigaciones Científicas, 1947), 239 states as 'property of the sons of the country' the lands they farm and the area occupied by their buildings inside the population.

29. The collective property is that of *villages* and *families*, Yglesias de la Riva, *Política Indígena en Guinea*, 245.

30. It is common language on property in European sources, with expressions such as 'chief owner of the lands', 'chief proprietor' of houses or 'lands that belonged to the chief'. See Martin del Molino, *La Ciudad de Clarence*, 22, 25; G. Tessmann, *Los Bubis de Fernando Poo* (Madrid: Sial, 2009), 196; Gil-Delgado, *Notas para un Estudio Antropológico*, 100, 137, 164.

31. Eteo Soriso, 'Ecología, economía tradicional y simbolismo', 104–6.

32. Baumann, *Una Isla Tropical Africana*, 153.

33. Núñez de Prado, *La Propiedad en la Guinea Española*, 46.

34. Núñez de Prado, *La Propiedad en la Guinea Española*, 44–45.
35. On this, see A. Campos Serrano, *De Colonia a Estado: Guinea Ecuatorial, 1955–1968* (Madrid: Centro de Estudios Políticos y Constitucionales, 2002), 61–64.
36. J. Bonelli Rubio, *El Problema de la Colonización* (Madrid: Dirección General de Marruecos y Colonias, 1944), 5.
37. Described by the Bubi anthropologist Eteo Soriso in *Los Ritos de Paso Entre los Bubi*. The Bubi used both yams and eddoes in fertility rituals and celebrations of life stages.
38. AGA. Africa-Guinea. (15) 4 Box 81/6271. Report 631 of the General Government of the Spanish Territories of the Gulf of Guinea, 6 July 1912, signed by Ángel Barrera y Luyando.
39. As we can see in Pieter Boele van Hensbroek's chapter in this volume.
40. P. Ferrer Piera, *Fernando Póo y Sus Dependencias* (Barcelona: A. López Robert, 1900), 200, wrote in the beginning of the twentieth century that the 'beautiful aspect of the education' was to teach the colonized peoples the agriculture of subsistence, but not to make them proprietors.
41. Information from J. Bolekia Boleká, *Aproximación a la Historia de Guinea Ecuatorial* (Salamanca: Amarú Ediciones, 2003), 74–87, and D. Ndongo Bidyogo, *Historia y Tragedia de Guinea Ecuatorial* (Madrid: Editorial Cambio 16, 1977), 37–38, 55. The emancipated were black colonial subjects who could (in relative terms, given the racist nature of colonialism) acquire a status similar to that of white Spanish. The 'fully emancipated' could own properties. For more details on the *Patronato de Indígenas*, see R. Sánchez Molina, '*Homo infantilis*: asimilación y segregación en la política colonial española en Guinea Ecuatorial', *Revista de Dialectología y Tradiciones Populares* 57(2) (2002), 105–20.
42. At first, the Bubi were excluded from this second category that could be required to perform mandatory work. According to the Native Labour Regulation of 6 August 1906 (Section II, Chapter I, Article 24, in Bravo Carbonel, *Fernando Póo y el Muni*, 356), all residents in the island of Fernando Pó who don't have 'property, legal and known occupation or do not appear domiciled in the special registries' are subject to the tutelage of the Curaduría and obliged to work, with the exception of the Bubi, 'without prejudice of authorizing the contracts whenever they lend themselves to this'.
43. AGA. Africa-Guinea. (15) 18 Box 81/8200. There are no references to any publishing house, but it is a printed book.
44. AGA. Africa-Guinea. (15) 4 Box 81/6417. Dispatch 537 'About works that are being made among the Bubi', Santa Isabel, 15 September 1906, addressed to the Ministry of State, signed by Diego Saavedra.
45. AGA. Africa-Guinea. (15) 4 Box 81/6417. Document 497 of the General Government of the Spanish Territories in the Gulf of Guinea, letter directed to the Ministry of State, 15 November 1910, signed by Ángel Barrera y Luyando.
46. The same idea is presented by the Spanish settler Más, *En el País de los Bubis*, 124, in a work first published in 1920 that related his experience in the island in the beginning of the twentieth century: 'Since only a small part of the island is farmed, they hide themselves in the forests and make their villages, distributing the field' and having their needs covered.
47. AGA. Africa-Guinea. (15) 4 Box 81/6409. Addressed to the Official Chamber of Agriculture of Fernando Po, 14 January 1911.
48. For the events of 1906, see Unzueta y Yuste, *Geografía Histórica de la Isla de Fernando Poo*, 250. The rebellion of Balachá, also known as *Guerra Bubi* 'Bubi War', was commanded by a chief, Lubá, in opposition to plantation work and resulted in the death of colonial police officers and of Lubá himself. The rebellion of Balachá is described in the *Boletín de la Camara Oficial Agrícola* (Official Bulletin of the Agricultural Chamber, Year IV, Number 7), reproduced in Bravo Carbonel, *Fernando Póo y el Muni*, 197–202. It is also the subject of a document by the Ministry of State, Colonial Section, 29 September 1910 about the dispatches of the General Government on 25 July and 1 August 1910 (AGA. Africa-Guinea. (15) 4 Box 81/6276).
49. AGA. Africa-Guinea. (15) 4 Box 81/6271. Document 631 (report) of the General Government of the Spanish Territories of the Gulf of Guinea, signed by Ángel Barrera y Luyando.

50. Núñez de Prado (*La Propiedad en la Guinea Española*, 17) gives a brief history of the legal antecedents of the 'private property' in the colony since 1858, highlighting the Bylaw of 12 November 1897 that stipulates the need to register the granted lands.

51. AGA. Africa-Guinea. (15) 4 Box 81/6420. Dispatch 580 from the Presidency of the Council of Ministers, General Direction of Morocco and Colonies, to the Governor General of the Spanish Territories of the Gulf of Guinea, titled 'Copying a Part of the Report of the Extraordinary Visit to the Registry of Property' ('Trasladando una parte del informe de la visita extraordinaria efectuada en el Registro de la propiedad'), 18 August 1926. Núñez de Prado (1929, 19–20) recognizes that the books of register of the properties are not updated, have mistakes and have missing sheets.

52. AGA. Africa-Guinea. (15) 4 Box 81/6421. Report by José Luis Serrano Ubierna of his 'extraordinary visit' to the colony, dated 12 July 1926, titled in Spanish 'Bases para la reorganización del registro de la propiedad de Santa Isabel de Fernando Póo'.

53. Bravo Carbonel, *Fernando Póo y el Muni*, 57–58, 121–23.

54. As in Ferrer Piera, *Fernando Póo y Sus Dependencias*, 200.

55. AGA. Africa-Guinea. (15) 18 Box 81/8095. Memorandum of the works made by the Permanent Council of the Delegation of the Official Agricultural Chamber of Fernando Pó since its constitution until 31 December 1923, presented to the General Assembly of 20 February 1924.

56. AGA. Africa-Guinea. (15) 18 Box 81/7722. The expressions can be found in documents signed by 'farmers' in the folder 'Requests to Hire Labourers from Other Colonies, 1928'. There are European 'farmers', such as the company Cunha Lisboa, Limitada, but also Bubi 'farmers' and 'proprietors', such as José Mao or Gabriel Boricó.

57. AGA. Africa-Guinea. (15) 4 Box 81/6340. Copy of the presentation of the Agricultural Section of the Spanish Africanist Association about the way of recognizing wills in Fernando Pó. They quote the opinion of the missionary Father Luna about the Bubi educated in the missions, that they can properly farm the cocoa and have access to the property of land.

58. As we can see on a manuscript 'Nominal List of the Gentlemen Who Have Requested Lands of this General Government', according to the respect of the conditions of the Royal Decree of 11 July 1904. There are petitions by French, English, Portuguese, Liberian, Spanish and, among them, some Bubi referred to only with one name: 'Sube (bubi)', 'Blacki (bubi)' or 'Lluvet (bubi)'. AGA. Africa-Guinea. (15) 4 Box 81/6426.

59. Document of study of the dispatches of the Governor General 7, 21 and 88 of 1911 and identification of problems of the Colonial Section of the Ministry of State, Madrid, 3 May 1911. AGA. Africa-Guinea. (15) 4 Box 81/6271.

60. Information in a letter by Claudio E. Ricardo Burnley to Ricardo Ferrer, Commissar of the Government of the Spanish Republic, AGA. Africa-Guinea. (15)4 Box 81/6426. The letter (written in Santa Isabel on 12 August 1931) is in the folder of the Presidency of the Council of Ministers, General Office of Morocco and the Colonies.

61. The letter by Miguel Boatisaha of 5 September 1931 is document 32 of the folder 'Judicial Competences. List of Subjects in Favour of Other Authorities' of 1931. AGA. Africa-Guinea. (15) 4 Box 81/6340.

62. AGA. Africa-Guinea. (15) 4 Box 81/6426. The document is in the folder of the Presidency of the Council of Ministries, General Office of Morocco and Colonies. There are other petitions of *indígenas*, such as 'Tribe One from Punta N'Bonda, Petitions of Considerations and Improvements' or 'In the Name of the Main Chiefs and All the *Indígenas* of the Continent, Making Different Requests of Social, Political and Economic Orders'.

63. See Yglesias de la Riva, *Política Indígena en Guinea*, 239.

64. On the notions of experience and horizon of expectation, see R. Koselleck, *The Practice of Conceptual History: Timing History, Spacing Concepts*, trans. T.S. Presner (Stanford: Stanford University Press, 2002).

References

Primary Sources

Archivo General de la Administración (AGA; General Archive of the Administration), Alcalá de Henares, Spain. Collection Africa-Guinea. Boxes (15) 4 81/6271, 81/6273, 81/6276, 81/6340, 81/6409, 81/6413, 81/6417, 81/6420, 81/6421, 81/6426 and (15) 18 81/7722, 81/8095, 81/8200.

Other Sources

Baumann, O. *Una Isla Tropical Africana, Fernando Poo y los Bubis: Relato del Viaje Efectuado a Expensas de la Imperial y Real Sociedad Geográfica de Viena*. Trans. E. Reuss Galindo. Madrid: SIAL, 2012.
Bolekia Boleká, J. *Aproximación a la Historia de Guinea Ecuatorial*. Salamanca: Amarú Ediciones, 2003.
———. *Diccionario Español – Bubi*. Madrid: Akal, 2009.
Bonelli Rubio, J. *El Problema de la Colonización*. Madrid: Dirección General de Marruecos y Colonias, 1944.
Bravo Carbonel, J. *Fernando Póo y el Muni, Sus Misterios y Riquezas, Su Colonización*. Madrid: Imprenta de Alrededor del Mundo, 1917.
Campos Serrano, A. *De Colonia a Estado: Guinea Ecuatorial, 1955–1968*. Madrid: Centro de Estudios Políticos y Constitucionales, 2002.
de Castro, M.L. and M.L. de la Calle. *La Colonización Española en Guinea Ecuatorial (1858–1900)*. Barcelona: CEIBA, 2007.
Crespo Gil-Delgado, C. *Notas para un Estudio Antropológico y Etnológico del Bubi de Fernando Poo*. Madrid: Instituto de Estudios Africanos, Consejo Superior de Investigaciones Científicas, 1949.
Elden, S. 'Land, Terrain, Territory', *Progress in Human Geography* 34(6) (2010): 799–817.
Eteo Soriso, J.F. 'Ecología, economía tradicional y simbolismo de los pueblos de Guinea Ecuatorial', in J. Aranzadi (ed.), *II Jornadas de Antropología de Guinea Ecuatorial*. Madrid: Universidad Nacional de Educación a Distancia, 2011, 85–119.
———. 'Los Ritos de Paso Entre los Bubi'. Ph.D. dissertation, Barcelona: Universidad Autónoma de Barcelona, 2013.
Fernández Moreno, N. 'Bubi Government at the End of the 19th Century: Resistance to the Colonial Policy of Evangelization of the Island of Bioko, Equatorial Guinea', *Nordic Journal of African Studies* 22(1/2) (2013), 23–48.
Ferrer Piera, P. *Fernando Póo y Sus Dependencias*. Barcelona: A. López Robert, 1900.
García Cantús, L. 'El comienzo de la masacre colonial del pueblo Bubi. La muerte del Botuko Sás, 1904', in J. Martí Pérez and Y. Aixelà Cabré (eds), *Estudios Africanos, Historia, Oralidad, Cultura*. Barcelona: CEIBA, 2008, 7–26.
Koselleck, R. *The Practice of Conceptual History: Timing History, Spacing Concepts*. Trans. T.S. Presner. Stanford: Stanford University Press, 2002.
Más, J. *En el País de los Bubis*. A Coruña: Ediciones del Viento, 2010.
Ndongo Bidyogo, D. *Historia y Tragedia de Guinea Ecuatorial*. Madrid: Editorial Cambio 16, 1977.
Martin del Molino, A. *La Ciudad de Clarence, Primeros Años de la Actual Ciudad de Malabo, Capital de Guinea Ecuatorial, 1827–1859*. Madrid: Instituto de Cooperación para el Desarrollo, Centro Cultural Hispano-Guineano, 1993.
Núñez de Prado, J.M. *La Propiedad en la Guinea Española*. Madrid: Imprenta de la Ciudad Lineal, 1929.
Sánchez Molina, R. '*Homo infantilis*: asimilación y segregación en la política colonial española en Guinea Ecuatorial', *Revista de Dialectología y Tradiciones Populares* 57(2) (2002), 105–20.

Sundiata, I. 'State Formation and Trade: The Rise and Fall of the Bubi Polity, c. 1840–1910', *International Journal of African Historical Studies* 27(3) (1994), 505–23.

――― (ed.). *From Slavery to Neoslavery: The Bight of Biafra and Fernando Po in the Era of Abolition, 1827–1930*. Madison: University of Wisconsin Press, 1996.

Tessmann, G. *Los Bubis de Fernando Poo*. Trans. E. Reuss. Madrid: Sial, 2009.

Tully, J. *A Discourse on Property, John Locke and His Adversaries*. Cambridge: Cambridge University Press, 1980.

de Unzueta y Yuste, A. *Geografía Histórica de la Isla de Fernando Poo*. Madrid: Instituto de Estudios Africanos, Consejo superior de Investigaciones Científicas, 1947.

Vansina, J. *Paths in the Rainforests: Toward a History of Political Tradition in Equatorial Africa*. Madison: University of Wisconsin Press, 1990.

Yglesias de la Riva, A. *Política Indígena en Guinea*. Madrid: Instituto de Estudios Africanos, Consejo Superior de Investigaciones Científicas, 1947.

Ana Lúcia Sá has a Ph.D. in sociology, and is a guest assistant professor at ISCTE-University Institute of Lisbon and an associate researcher in African studies at the Centre for International Studies, University Institute of Lisbon. After working extensively on the discourses of Angolan intellectual elites on the building of the nation in Angola, her research is now focused on the discourses of social scientists from West Central Africa about the representations of the continent, cultural diversity and the decolonization of knowledge. The context receiving most attention in her current research is Equatorial Guinea, regarding the representation of its social, cultural and political idiosyncrasies.

CHAPTER 7

Conceptualizing 'Land' and 'Nation' in Early Gold Coast Nationalism

PIETER BOELE VAN HENSBROEK

On 24 May 1898, a crowd gathered in Cape Coast harbour to say farewell to a delegation of the Aborigines' Rights Protection Society (ARPS) as they set sail for London. They were to protest to the Secretary of State for the Colonies, Joseph Chamberlain, against the recent land bills of the Gold Coast governor. The ARPS had raised funds all over the Gold Coast and there had been much agitation because it was felt that the bills undermined a central prerogative of the indigenous Gold Coast rulers, namely to allocate land. The Aborigines' Rights Protection Society – one of the first 'modern' organizations in nineteenth-century Africa – had been formed a few months before, uniting kings, 'chiefs', businessmen and members of the educated elite. In one of the earlier protests 'a noisy crowd' had protested in Cape Coast. On another occasion, a meeting of indigenous rulers in the Gold Coast Methodist Church in Cape Coast was reported in *The Gold Coast Aborigines* newspaper to have ended in a joint prayer in which even the 'heathen cane bearers' of the kings participated: 'O Lord of heaven and earth ... Thou has given us our lands which we inherited from our forefathers ... But the Government under whom it hath pleased Thee to place us, after depriving our native Rulers of most of their powers and authority, are now bent on despoiling us of our individual ancestral rights in our land'.[1]

The land bills formed the tipping point for developing discontent, the result of West Africa being confronted on a dramatic scale by European power, business, religion and language, in the last decades of the nineteenth century. It was then – starting for the British from 1874 – that European powers rapidly extended their control inland beyond trading stations, resulting in almost

---

Notes for this section begin on page 179.

complete European control of Africa by the year 1900. The Gold Coast agitations against the land bills were like a laboratory in which indigenous understandings of 'land' and 'authority' were forcefully advanced and at the same time reconceptualized and translated into the English language, thereby producing several ideas and concepts that would be guiding points for African nationalists throughout the twentieth century.

The aim of this chapter is to reconstruct the discourses and actions of the Gold Coast intellectuals and political organizations in these struggles against the land bills, bringing out their historical importance and their innovative character, in particular by gradually elaborating the concept of a Gold Coast nation. By choosing this focus, and by using an approach of conceptual history, this chapter seeks to correct available interpretations of early Gold Coast nationalism as (conceptually) a case of 'importation' of Enlightenment notions from Europe, and as (socially) the activities of a westernized, educated elite of 'Black Englishmen'. Some have even dismissed them as sell-outs, as 'deserters of their fatherland's cultural heritage'.[2] I hope to show the contrary, namely that the struggle against the colonial land bills (and other bills) involved a home-brewed, innovative reframing of concepts, identities and political horizons, and that this was the joint creative and courageous work of a broad range of actors in Gold Coast society.

The Gold Coast was considered, in the nineteenth century, to cover what is now Southern Ghana, the zone between the Asante empire and the sea, including Fanti (Akan),[3] Ga and Ewe speaking peoples who engaged mostly in agriculture (see Map 7.1).[4] Towards the end of the century, the Gold Coast had an estimated population of around one million in a variety of kingdoms. Transit trade with Asante from the seaports was a major point of tension with Asante military power a continual threat to the Fanti. From the mid-nineteenth century, the British took over coastal forts from other European powers and expanded 'legitimate trade' in the place of the slave trade.[5] Logging and mineral exploitation was on the rise in the last decades of the nineteenth century and the liberal granting, by indigenous kings, of concessions for such activities was one of the reasons for the colonial government to advance the land bills.[6]

The main indigenous political actors in the Gold Coast were the kings, supported by their council and advisors consisting of 'linguists' (see below) and, increasingly, also by those with a Western education (the 'educated elites'). An early marker of British-Gold Coast relations was the Bond of 1844, a voluntary agreement of three points in which the kings delegated some of their judicial powers to British courts. In order to deal with the Asante on the one hand and the British on the other, the remarkable, but failed, Fanti Federation was formed in 1868 and in 1871 it formulated the Mankessim Constitution, an ambitious modernization programme that included infrastructural works and 'the daily attendance of all children between the ages of eight and fourteen' at 'national schools'.[7] In Cape Coast and Accra, an African middle class of traders, lawyers,

Map 7.1 The Gold Coast in the Nineteenth Century

journalists and administrators developed. Their 'educated elite' lifestyle was oriented towards British middle-class culture, with church communities, debating societies, fashion trends, 'Letters to the Editor' in local newspapers, etc. The Gold Coast enjoyed a lively public sphere, including an African-owned press (in English), cultural and educational societies such as the *Mfantsi Amanbuhu Fekuw* 'Fanti National Political Society' (1889) and the Mfantsi National Education Fund (1902). Initially, the educated felt a strong link with the imperial undertaking, involving the idea of a partnership in a grand abolitionist mission of civilizing and Christianizing the African continent. Education, industry and Christianity would replace 'barbarism'.[8] Around 1870, the high tide of so-called mid-Victorian optimism, Gold Coast Africans were preparing to lead the local church hierarchy, to spread modern education and media and to establish modern African states.[9] It should be noted that within this world view there was no necessary contradiction between being African and being oriented towards Britain, thus being a 'Black Englishman', because joining in British civilized life was seen simply as a means of joining in the universal development of humanity in which Africa and Africans could very well play a big role in enriching the future path of human civilization. Kings and educated people alike saw no necessary contradiction between 'our country and the Queen'.[10] Yet a competing view on African civilization, which was gaining ground in West Africa in the 1880s, was defended at the time by the flamboyant Liberian Edward Wilmot Blyden, with his spirited arguments for a uniquely 'African personality' and a distinct African development path.[11]

However, ideas of white superiority and new 'scientific' theories of race spread from Europe in the second half of the nineteenth century. The British Empire obtained global hegemony, and quinine and other medicines made possible the actual colonization of West Africa (earlier the proverbial 'white man's grave'). The educated elite, many of them dependent upon formal employment, were gradually excluded from all higher positions in the administration and suffered increasing ridicule from the British, who depicted them as half-baked, hybrids and 'trousered niggers'.[12] This 'betrayal of the educated elite' led to interesting reactions among them, such as a reorientation towards African roots. Movements for cultural self-consciousness propagated the adoption of African rather than Christian names, or African rather than European ways of dressing, and promoted education for Africans. The disenchantment with the British civilizing mission led not only to a cultural awakening and self-searching, but also to much public debate, divergent positions and political activity.

Within this context of potential conflict and tensions the colonial land bills of 1894 and 1897 sparked unprecedented political and intellectual activity, aligning kings, traders and educated elites in a modern oppositional organization, the Aborigines' Rights Protection Society (ARPS). In the following decades, the ARPS always played a leading role in politics. But a rift developed between indigenous Gold Coast rulers and the educated elite in the first decades of the twentieth century. This rift formed a second terrain of conflict alongside that with the British on the land bills. The divergent ideas of indigenous rulers and the educated elite became visible in the early 1920s in the clashes between the prominent King Ofori Atta and the lawyer and journalist Joseph Casely Hayford over who truly represented the Gold Coast nation. This chapter takes the ARPS and its struggles in the 1890s about the power to allocate land as a starting point to trace conceptual innovations in subsequent decades, innovations that finally resulted in the 'nationalist' agenda of the National Congress of British West Africa (NCBWA) in the early 1920s.

In order to understand this interesting transition period it is not enough to write a political history of events, institutions and persons. The 'doing' and 'thinking' of actors are guided by their perceptions of their situation and their interests, and by their fears, dreams and ideals. All these perceptions and drivers are shaped by the concepts available to them. A powerful strategy for including these cognitive dimensions in our analyses has been proposed by the historian Reinhart Koselleck in his approach to conceptual history. In this approach, the bumpy and crooked trails of social and political struggles can be traced via transformations in the meaning of the key concepts used to articulate them. Such transformations of meaning do justice to the actors' action perspective, and at the same time show how this perspective is part of broader contemporary discourses on social and political issues.[13]

Starting with the land bills means starting with the concept of 'land' and its related concepts. Initially the notion of 'land' referred to the concrete soil one could stand on, toil, or dig in, the land allocated by local kings to be used for agriculture. In the struggle against the land bills the notion of 'land' acquired a second meaning, namely country, nation, or fatherland. This double meaning makes the genealogy of the notion of 'land' a particularly powerful instrument for mapping social, cultural and political transitions in the Gold Coast, because this second meaning is what makes nationalism an imperative. The sources I use for reconstructing this transition period are books by key public intellectuals in the Gold Coast and African contributions to local newspapers. There is little doubt about the choice of the key historical texts and authors. Intellectuals like John Mensah Sarbah, Attoh Ahuma, J.E. Casely Hayford, J.W. de Graft Johnson and J.B. Danquah were considered prominent men of letters as well as key political figures and participants in public debate. The reader today will be captured by their thorough argumentation, extensive empirical work and elegance of formulation. Studying these classics in African legal and political thought is an exercise of thorough hermeneutics, i.e. reconstructing the meaning which the historical actors themselves gave to their world (in this case the idea of 'land') and to their practices (their struggles). Hermeneutics here tries to uncover the action perspective of actors; it traces the text's 'positive heuristics' (suggesting certain options) and 'negative heuristics' (what it disregards).[14]

The second pillar of this study is a quantitative analysis of local newspapers. This enables me to trace the concepts used in direct public action and to check, albeit within limitations, the representativeness of the texts of the key political authors. The digital resource of African newspapers in the World Newspaper Archive provides a useful database for such an analysis. This database allows both the counting of hits of particular words or collections of words (token frequency) and to check the sentences in which the word was used (type frequency), in order to make sure that the concept was actually used in a sense relevant for the study.[15] The method is nevertheless not perfect. Some relevant newspapers are missing from the database, such as *The Gold Coast Methodist Times*, which was very outspoken in the struggle against the colonial land laws. In addition, many single issues of newspapers are missing. The word counts made from the database are thus not absolute counts and not exact. Nevertheless, assuming that the distribution of missing issues is random, they can show the direction of change in the use of the concepts over time. A further limitation is that the newspapers are often old and the print setting not easily legible, such that there will be mistakes in automatic identification of the search words in the digital count. Despite these shortcomings, the information from the newspapers proves to be very useful and the counts show a remarkable synchronicity with results from the hermeneutical study.

Using these newspapers to track public discourse requires some reflection on their status and role. There are reliable studies of the early press in West Africa, which reconstruct not just the titles, but also ownership, circulation, editorship and impact.[16] The very first newspapers (usually weeklies) were government gazettes and appeared early in the nineteenth century. But from 1857, African-owned papers developed (the first issue of *The West African Herald* appeared in handwritten form!). Each title had a rather short lifespan and they were not financially sustainable, with circulations of just two hundred copies on average. With a population of about one million in the Gold Coast of which (in the 1880s) only one out of a thousand could read English well, papers were necessarily an enterprise for the elite, a fact also expressed in the family background of the owners and chief editors.[17] But they involved critical journalism and public debate, harbouring so much criticism of the government that attempts were made to start controlling the press.[18] One of the editors stated the aims of his paper as providing 'a source of inspiration to the rising youth in matters relating to the political enfranchisement of the Gold Coast'.[19] The main papers (all African-owned) mostly existed successively: *The West African Herald* (1857–73), *The Gold Coast Times* (1874–85), *The Western Echo*, later *Gold Coast Echo* (1885–90), *The Gold Coast Chronicle* (1890–1901), *The Gold Coast People* (1891–94), *The Gold Coast Methodist Times* (1894–98), *The Gold Coast Independent* (1895–98), and *The Gold Coast Aborigines* (1898–1902).[20] Although circulation was low, the spread of the newspapers and their impact seems to have been considerable.[21]

Conceptualizing 'Land' before the Land Bills

The focus in this chapter is on changing conceptualizations of 'land'. In particular, the aim is to trace discourse about 'land', that is the ways in which key public actors (writers and readers) perceived the meaning of 'land' and the system of land governance in the Gold Coast. As such, the ways in which land was actually used or its socio-economic value are of secondary interest and will not be addressed in detail, although of course they are the backdrop against which these debates played out.[22]

Descriptions of the Akan system of land management, by key authors such as Sarbah, Casely Hayford and Danquah, contradict the common view that in 'traditional' Africa land was owned communally. Casely Hayford, for instance, states that: 'there is a keen pleasure in the sense of possession. *My* land, *my* house, as distinguished from *your* land, *your* house'.[23] The authors agree that, in the Akan system, land ownership had three forms: self-acquired or private, family and 'stool' property.[24] The stool was the ruling authority but not the owner of all land. Ownership could be transferred, for instance through sale, but in the case of stool or family ownership this could not be done by the king or family head alone, as such a decision was subject to consultation and agreement by a much larger circle of stakeholders. Land acquired by an individual was at the disposal of the owner, and could also be sold by that person; however, upon the passing away of the individual owner the property was not inherited by an individual heir but reverted to become the property of the family. As Sarbah noted, '[i]f land is free today in the hands of its acquirer, it will tomorrow resume its fetters in the hands of his heirs'.[25] The family allocated the land resources that it controlled according to need among its members. All land belonged, in this system, to a person or some collectivity.[26]

The political structure of Akan societies was said by these authors to relate in a specific way to land. It was considered to consist of federations of units at ever higher levels, up to the level of the state or the 'union of states'. Families were units, and families tracing their origin to a common ancestor formed a unit of families, which confederated again at a higher level under a paramount chief or king. Native states or kingdoms could again confederate. This is the way in which Casely Hayford describes the centuries-old great Asante political unit: not as an empire or centralized state but as a 'union'. However, authority at these higher levels did not include the right to dispose of or expropriate the lower levels where ownership of the land was vested: 'the King, *qua* King, does not own the lands of the State'.[27] The 'stool' (king or 'chief') controlled only the stool lands, and even here important decisions about these required the consent of a large circle of councillors. Danquah states: 'the highest prince becomes *ex officio* supreme lord of the lands', and 'the occupant of the stool acts like a "trustee" for the members'.[28] In this way, the king represented all the owners in the kingdom, making it a territorial whole.

How, then, was the relation between the individual and the land conceived of by these authors? We can understand it as a series of interrelated assumptions. First, to be a member of the community was related to 'land' because 'a native of the soil has the right to cultivate land within the locality of his residence'.[29] The use-right of land was central to the concept of belonging to a community. Second, a community was a collection of landowners and land users. Third, the territory of a community was the sum of all their lands; a kingdom or 'native state' as a territorial unit derived from the lands of the inhabitants. Fourth and conversely, their 'democratized' right to access to these lands via their family affiliations was constitutive of their group membership, their 'citizenship'. The persons as family members (and thus as legitimate claimants of use-rights) constituted together 'the people'.[30]

Thus, land-use rights both derived from and underlay group membership.[31] And the community consisted of landowners. As a result when these owners expanded their lands, the political community covered a larger territory.

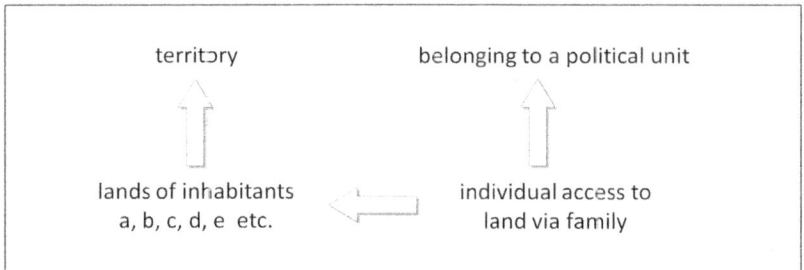

Figure 7.1 Linkages between the concepts 'territory', 'land', 'access to land', 'political identity'

Collective territory was the result of, rather than pre-fixed by, control over lands. The centrality of persons as claimants of land-use rights can be represented as in Figure 7.1.

If this reconstruction is correct, then the 'political' unit was not directly constituted as controlling a certain bounded territory (or a 'fatherland' as 'the' country of 'the people X') as in the Weberian idea of a state. This is why the arrow between political unit and territory is missing. The territory of the unit was simply the result of the lands controlled by the members forming that unit.[32]

In the conceptualization sketched here, the concept of 'land' does not have a direct territorial and political meaning; it is far removed from the notion of a nation. Rather, a political unit was simply comprised of the lands of the inhabitants. In the texts, and most especially in John Mensah Sarbah's *Fanti Customary Law* (1897), the arrangements related to land are discussed in a remarkably matter-of-fact manner. 'Land' is simply an item discussed under the chapter on property, and the quite elaborate and detailed Akan laws and customs are spelled out without suggesting an overall political significance of land-as-territory.

At this point critical questions can be raised about the status of these reconstructions of the indigenous system by Gold Coast intellectuals. Their 'description' unavoidably involves several translations, such as framing in the English language, using legal vocabulary, formulating their writing (at least in part) for an audience of British administrators, while operating themselves not in the regular Akan system but in the coastal towns of the Gold Coast. This need for translation raises classical questions of the commensurability of African and European worlds.[33] Interestingly, the authoritative intellectuals of the Aborigines' Rights Protection Society (ARPS), like Sarbah and Casely Hayford, hardly ever report problems of 'translation' or of systematic misrepresentation when rendering the indigenous system in the English language. John Mensah Sarbah describes the aim of his project as being to 'reduce into writing the customary laws and usages of the Fanti, Ashanti, and other Akan inhabitants of the Gold Coast', and 'to state the Customary Law in a few simply worded statements'.[34] Only J.B. Danquah, the later leader of the nationalist movement, in his encyclopaedic description in *Gold Coast: Akan Laws and Customs and the Akim Abuakwa Constitution* (1928) refers to the 'theoretical difficulty' of describing the Akan system in words like democracy, monarchy etc.[35] But Danquah sees no major difficulties in grasping the original meanings: 'Akim Abuakwa stands out prominently as one of the few Akan States whose dialect has remained unadulterated and pure throughout the period of Anglo-European contact with the Gold Coast. Consequently the institutions and customs as practiced in that country still retain to a very large extent their original meaning and significance'.[36]

A critic may object that the denial of translation problems by these authors is to be expected because, as 'brokers' between the British and indigenous populations, their role depended upon the assumption of translatability.[37] They claim to represent the African voice. As such, making a point of limited translatability would run against their interests. However, the biographical data on the educated elite authors suggest otherwise. They undeniably combined excellent command of the British system with deep, first-hand knowledge of indigenous legal systems. Remarkably, all of the four leading educated elite authors (Sarbah, Casely Hayford, de Graft Johnson and Danquah) themselves derived from so-called 'stool traditions'. They belonged to the families that provided one of the most central office holders in the Akan system, namely the Kyiame or so-called 'linguist', who was the 'living encyclopaedia' of the indigenous law of a community. These office holders, who were generally succeeded by their sons, were the oral legal experts of the council in addition to being the mouthpieces of the king and moderators of council meetings.[38] Of course, this biographical fact does not eliminate the problem of translatability itself; even the best possible emic understanding does not guarantee the success of the translation of this understanding into a different language. However, if we have to rely on interlocutors to map indigenous systems of land governance, then these specific educated elite authors are our best choice.

The Press

The conceptualization of 'land' by key intellectual leaders can be compared with the conceptualization used in newspaper discussions in order to test their representativeness for the larger Gold Coast political discourse at the time. For this purpose, I analyse one of the first newspapers in the Gold Coast, *The Gold Coast Times*, which started publication in 1874.[39] With 162 issues searchable in the digital African Newspaper Archive for the 1874–85 period, it provides a good resource for concept mapping. My strategy was to count and check hits for a range of notions (viz. 'land', 'soil', 'territory', 'state', 'nation', 'country', 'native', 'people', 'aborigines', as well as key combinations, such as 'our land', 'our nation', 'our country', 'sons of the soil', 'natives of the soil', 'natives of the colony', 'Fanti Nation' and 'Gold Coast Nation'). One remarkably low result is for 'soil', which yielded only thirty-five hits for the entire period and those mostly refer to its practical utility (e.g. 'chalky soil', 'virgin soil'). The notion of 'land' itself scored only up to twenty hits per year in the 1870s, but then rose rapidly in 1881, up to 282 in total, in discussions about foreign companies gaining concessions. In the context of those discussions we find, for instance in 1881, the expression 'the soil is ours' as well as some hits on 'our land' (four), 'aborigines' (five) and even 'our country' (fourteen) and 'natives of the colony' or 'natives of the country' (twenty-one). There are no hits for 'fatherland', 'nation', 'territory', nor for 'sons of the soil', 'our nation', 'our people', 'Fanti nation' or 'Gold Coast nation'. The conclusion seems to be that, at least until 1881, there is little evidence in the newspapers that 'land' had anything more than the socio-economic meaning of the soil to be cleared, planted, privately acquired or sold.

Thus, both sources (books and newspapers) suggest that until the 1880s (and, if we look at Sarbah's work, for at least a decade after that), the notions of 'land' and 'soil' were predominantly used to refer to the physical soil that can be planted or owned, without political connotation. Typically, in this early period, even the intensifying concerns about increasing British usurpation of indigenous sovereignty could be worded in terms such as 'not an inch of land beyond the gates of their Forts' and 'not an inch of land which it can point to as British soil', thus using again the practical, physical connotation of the term even while hinting at the issue of loss of sovereignty in Fanti territories.[40]

Conceptualizing 'Land' in the Aborigines' Rights Protection Society Agitation of the 1890s

Within the more political expressions of the Aborigines' Rights Protection Society (ARPS) and the emerging press discussions on the land bills in the 1890s, 'land' and its related concepts rapidly became charged with political and cultural meaning. The claim of the colonial government via the Crown Lands Bill (1894) to 'waste lands', and the restrictions placed on indigenous power holders' ability to allocate lands, were perceived as threatening the basis of authority at all levels in the indigenous system, even as threatening the very way of life of Gold Coast communities. Given the intimate relation between group membership and land-use rights and between indigenous views of authority and guardianship over land distribution procedures, explained above, the threats were real. I map this field of contestation by starting from the key concepts used and the transformations of their meaning in political expressions in political texts and in newspapers.

The long row over the various land bills involved lively debates and political organization that were quite exceptional in the early stages of the colonial presence in Africa. In this context, the issue of the reduced command of *Omanhene*, 'kings and paramount chiefs', over the distribution of land became increasingly formulated in terms of 'nation', of 'unity', of 'our people'. Notions that were frequently used from the mid-1890s onwards are 'natives', 'nation', 'aborigines', 'native community', 'fatherland', 'aboriginal race', 'sons of the soil', 'natives of the soil', 'our people', 'native state' and 'Gold Coast nation'. The people are described not as just members of a specific 'kingdom' or 'native state', but as part of a larger political identification, of a 'fatherland' or a 'nation'.[41] This shift in conceptualization was achieved by linking *people* to *land* in a more abstract manner than the connection to land through family, cultivation or ownership. In this new conceptualization, 'land', so to speak, does not belong to you; you belong to a land. Such a connection between people and territory (person to place) is implicit in the new notions used, such as 'native', 'aboriginal', 'indigenous' and 'native of the soil'. For instance 'native' suggests a person with a specific geographical or political anchoring (one could not speak of being a native of one's own estate, it must minimally be a village or region – thus a symbolic or political unit). For the larger collective of people this anchoring is achieved via the notion of 'nation'. These are exactly the notions that we find being used increasingly after the mid-1890s. The outspoken newspaper editor, writer and preacher Attoh Ahuma (who took this Fanti name in place of his English one, S.R.B. Solomon) tried to forge the imagined link between people and land already in 1892 by stating 'We are all one, and natives of the same colony'.[42] In his *The Gold Coast Nation and National Consciousness* (1911), he cried out in capitals: 'WE ARE A NATION' adding, 'If we are not one it is time to invent one'.[43]

We see here that 'land' becomes the central concept in which a range of social, cultural, political and economic issues are expressed. It connects together several concerns: the gradual usurpation of the powers of the indigenous power holders, from the Bond of 1844 to the protectorate and beyond; the gradual cultural marginalization of everything indigenous as 'uncivilized'; the fear that the social fabric was endangered, and in particular that the positions of authority relating to the distribution of land, from family heads to kings, were threatened; the maintenance of the sophisticated framework of indigenous law, semi-formalized and reframed by the British in the form of Customary Law; the religious, spiritual dimensions of communities linked to the soil via ancestor relationships (as such already threatened by the advance of Christianity); and the changing landscape of elites, where the new urban professional class, the 'educated elite', carved out a 'national' space overarching the 'native states' spaces of the various kings.

The specific place connotations of the notions 'native', 'indigenous', 'aboriginal' and 'people of the soil' offer a useful edge for nationalist agitation. A geographical or territorial claim is automatically expressed through reference to place of birth or to local rootedness. It also automatically creates an opposition, in terms of groups, to those not 'aboriginal' to that place. Ironically, while 'native' and 'aboriginal' were, for the British, terms that excluded Africans from civilization, in the Gold Coast they obtained the opposite exclusion effect by defining a Gold Coast 'WE' against a British 'THEY'. Reference to 'land' thus served as a vehicle for political identification. Apart from the marking of a

'THEY' (the British), concepts like 'people of the soil' demarcated among the Africans a new collectivity, a new 'WE', at an overall, 'national' level.

The useful double reference of the notion of 'land' can be found in many statements in opposition to the land bills. For instance when Casely Hayford refers to 'the lands of the aborigines' that are alienated, the word 'lands' refers to the cultivatable plots (family lands and 'stool' lands in the framework of native states and the immediate issue in the land bills).[44] But the word 'aborigines' in the same expression connects it to land as common 'roots', to a community of those born in Fantiland or the Gold Coast and thus a more overarching unit of a 'fatherland'. The frequently used expressions of 'nation', 'national consciousness', 'people of the Gold Coast', 'natives of the soil', 'patriotic fire', 'fatherland' and so on, all refer to 'land' as Fantiland or the Gold Coast.[45] Thus we see that in the struggle over land-as-soil, the idea of land-as-country solidifies. But the two meanings remain connected internally; at least the idea of nationhood continues to tap into the notion of being 'sons of the soil' and controlling land distribution through indigenous institutions.

The Press

The key newspapers (often weeklies or fortnightlies) from the 1890s had a connection with the ARPS. They include *The Gold Coast People* (1891–98), *The Gold Coast Chronicle* (1894–1902), *The Gold Coast Methodist Times* (1896–98) and *The Gold Coast Aborigines* (1898–1902). Unfortunately in the digital African Newspaper Archive only *The Gold Coast Chronicle* (153 issues) and *The Gold Coast Aborigines* (138 issues) are included. For the later discourses between 1902 and 1922, the paper *The Gold Coast Leader* (891 issues), *The Gold Coast Nation* (313 issues) and *The Gold Coast Independent* (36 issues) are my sources.[46] My strategy was, again, to count and check hits for a range of notions (such as 'land', 'soil', 'territory', 'nation'), as well as key combinations (such as 'our land', 'our nation', 'sons of the soil', 'natives of the colony').

The newspapers confirm the remarkable change in discourse in the 1890s. Notions like 'nation', 'aborigines', 'natives of the Gold Coast/Colony' were frequently used, whereas they had been almost absent before. The notions of 'land' and 'soil' continued to be used, but now rarely in the simple physical sense. They were rather used with new meanings such as 'indigenous to the soil', 'the common good of the land', 'the soil is ours', 'claim to the soil of the colony'.[47] In *The Gold Coast Chronicle* in the 1890s, several political notions became more common, such as 'nation' (forty-two), 'aborigines' (twenty-seven), and 'natives of the colony' (thirty-seven).[48] From around 1900, identity-charged political notions became popular that had previously been infrequent (e.g. 'native', 'the country', 'our country'). In particular, if we look at *The Gold Coast Leader* (published between 1902 and 1922 with a large number of 891 searchable issues), we find an abundance of hits on 'land' (821), 'fatherland' (141), 'native' (2,218), 'our country' (448), 'patriotic' (361), and 'national spirit' (1,884).[49] However, the notion of 'self-determination', which became popular in nationalism in the twentieth century, scored only a few hits (and only after 1918 when it was made internationally topical by U.S. President Woodrow Wilson).

The Nationalist Discourse of the National Congress of British West Africa (NCBWA) after 1919

In the first decade of the opposition to the land bills by the Aborigines' Rights Protection Society, land was the focus of political and public attention in two ways. First, the land bills urged Africans to explicate their system of land tenure and political authority. Second, as explained above, land united the different political units in the Gold Coast into one movement, claiming that people in the Gold Coast as a unit ('the Gold Coast people') should manage their own affairs, thus propping up the idea of Fantiland or the Gold Coast itself as a nation, a 'land'. There is an irony here, because in order to defend their authority at the 'native state' level of the Omanhene 'stool' to distribute parcels of land, the various peoples in various local states presented themselves as one nation, as Fantiland or the Gold Coast, as belonging to one shared 'fatherland'. However, if such 'national unification' of local states were to have been successful, then of course the same local Omanhene (king or paramount chief) whose sovereign powers were defended in the struggle against the land bills, would again have lost part of his authority to the new structures of a Fanti or Gold Coast overall national state system. The educated elite (journalists, lawyers, etc.) were very closely linked with the indigenous rulers and defended the rulers' prerogative to allocate land, but their political project was more that of constructing the larger political unit, overarching all the indigenous states. This 'national' project was first framed in the form of Fantiland or the Gold Coast, later in that of a united Gold Coast and Ashanti, and after 1920 by the NCBWA as a West African Union.

The same irony emerges in the uses of the concept of 'land'. In the 1890s struggles against the land bills, the land issue was in the first place conceptualized in terms of land-as-cultivatable-soil, land as a social-economic (and spiritual) asset under Omanhene control. But in the process of the struggle of kings and educated elites together, the concept of 'land' was used more often in a political sense, as 'nation', as the fatherland of a consolidated people who were characterized by similar indigenous institutions of governance. This political meaning of 'land' establishes far-reaching conceptual connections, such as with the notion of a bounded territory, of the people as a collective identity – a nation, of elected representation in government, and, finally, of self-determination of that people in 'its' bounded territory. The frequently used notions of 'sons of the soil', 'nation', 'fatherland' and 'patriotism' all embody such connections. Although both the Omanhene and the educated elite shared the same programme in the ARPS, their stake was different: land-as-soil was the domain of the Omanhene, and land-as-nation that of the educated elite. In an overall Gold Coast nation the elites would be the 'natural' leaders. Gradually, this difference created a new fault line of political struggle, in this case not between British and African leaders, but between African traditional leaders and the educated elite.

The conflict between traditional rulers and the educated elite evolved partly because of the parallel British policy of increasing inclusion of traditional rulers in the colonial system and exclusion ('betrayal') of the educated elite, as described above. The British decided, as part of 'indirect rule' and to limit opposition, to work with the traditional rulers rather than with the elites. The authority of the native rulers to administer justice in the native tribunals and to allocate land became protected by the various, hotly debated, Native Administration Bills (1919, 1922, 1927), but the price they paid was to become office holders of a kind in the British administration, working under British authority. Part of the price was also the gradual undermining of the position of these rulers themselves, because in the colonial setting they became actors with executive power, thereby sacrificing the old idea of the chief-in-council, i.e. the idea that the indigenous ruler does not govern but represents the decisions of the council to those outside of it.[50] In the first decades of the twentieth century there was abundant discussion on a number of proposed bills in native jurisdiction and native administration; each time the respective roles of the indigenous rulers, the colonial administration and the educated elite were at issue.[51]

Parallel to the inclusion of the indigenous rulers was the exclusion of the educated elite with their role in the system becoming ever more limited. There was no longer any need for an intermediary between British and native authority, no place to engage in politics on behalf of the chiefs, not even for the lawyers to play a role in the juridical process in the native tribunals. The ARPS (comprising mostly of members of the educated elite) continued to defend the rights of the traditional authorities in most of the frequent clashes with the colonial authorities on new regulations, but the agenda of the educated elite drifted gradually away from that of the indigenous rulers.

The tension between the projects of the educated elite and traditional rulers is epitomized in conflicts between Nana Ofori Atta – the influential king of Akim Abuakwa – and J.E. Casely Hayford. Both were African representatives in the small, colonial Legislative Council of the Gold Coast. In discussions about the Native Jurisdiction Bills of 1919 and 1922, Casely Hayford argued that the consolidating colonial situation made a more direct political representation of the Gold Coast constituency necessary. He tried to turn the ARPS into an organization that could petition the colonial government directly 'on behalf of the people' This clearly clashed with the traditional rulers' fundamental claim to represent the people of the Gold Coast, and Ofori Atta actively worked against Casely Hayford's anticolonial actions. Partly because of the effective colonial divide-and-rule tactics, the NCBWA's petitioning was unsuccessful, as the government in London did not accept its members as representatives of the Gold Coast population.

The developments of the first quarter of the twentieth century thus ended the alliance between the educated elite and the indigenous rulers. It also marked the fading of a political horizon that had taken shape during the Fanti Federation of 1868 when an African future was conceived in terms of a vigorous African modernization that would start from indigenous institutions (a discourse of 'modernization from indigenous roots').[52] This vision itself had become much less realistic because, from the turn of the century, colonial rule had become a solid reality that could not be evaded. The rift between traditional rulers and the educated elite brought to the fore a tension that was already present in the very ideas behind the programme of the ARPS. These ideas included, on the one hand, the defence of traditional institutions and rulers from the onslaught of colonial rule and, on the other hand, the idea of modernizing these indigenous systems. In Sarbah's words, it called for 'adjusting the political institutions of a country to its existing stage of political growth'. In Casely Hayford's, 'it must be the work of the educated Native, if the British Government will trust him to do it. On what lines will we proceed? He will take the Native State System as he finds it, and develop and improve it on aboriginal lines, and on scientific principles'; this could result in 'a perfect system, which, properly developed and worked, would usher in a new civilization, the like of which the world has probably never seen'.[53] But political developments in the Gold Coast were pushed in a different direction, one that embedded 'traditional' rule in a colonial framework without the prospects for 'a new civilization'. Colonial control involved limiting of the rights of Africans and increasing the exploitation of mineral and forest resources, mainly by foreign companies. The vision of 'modernization from indigenous roots', comparable to Japan's path of indigenous modernization after the Meiji revolution, became more and more obsolete.

The new National Congress of British West Africa (NCBWA), founded in 1920 under the leadership of J.E. Casely Hayford (interestingly not restricted to the Gold Coast) developed a more general criticism of colonialism. It expressed a new modernist nationalist agenda, one of political mobilization for a system that would include elected representatives and a large degree of self-determination, such as control over natural resources like land, elections to select office-holders and obtaining independent status within the Commonwealth comparable to that of Australia or Canada.

This changing elite discourse can also be traced by mapping shifts in the use of the notion of 'land'. Its references become more clearly political, as well as socio-economic at a macro level. Casely Hayford spoke of ordinary Africans becoming 'squatters on their own lands', and 'hewers of wood and drawers of water unto his Caucasian protector and so-called friend'. He urged the 'aborigines of the country' to 'show spirit of nationality' and 'wreck the empire'.[54] Issues of land became part of what are now considered to be more classical discourses of social struggle, self-determination and nationalism. Such conceptualizations can be found in Casely Hayford's works as well as in the political documents of the NCBWA and in the press. The high frequency of use of the concepts 'our country', 'fatherland', 'patriotic', 'our nation' and 'national spirit' in *The Gold Coast Leader* between 1902 and 1922, as set out above, also confirm this shift towards nationalism. The notion of 'land' as used here refers not just to soil to cultivate, or the fatherland as a collective unit, but also to land as an economic factor – one of the several natural resources like forests and minerals that Africans lost control over through colonialism.

Conclusion

Central to the present study are the multiple meanings of 'land' in public discourses in the Gold Coast between the 1870s and the 1920s. Conceptualizations of 'land' took many forms, from land as physical soil or the terrain one can stand on, toil, fence and own – and also where the ancestors dwell – to land as a geographical division and administrative and political unit that can be plotted on a map and that is the domain of particular power holders and a source of cultural and political identification. Finally, 'land' was conceptualized as a natural resource, including minerals, waters or forests, which needed to be controlled by Africans. However different these meanings of the word were, they may be linked in various ways. For instance, ideas of land-as-soil and of land-as-national-territory tended to be charged with symbolic value as the focus of identity and spirituality, as in its designation as 'ancestral land', 'roots' or 'fatherland'. In the African discourses explored here, the link was expressed in notions such as 'natives of the soil', 'land of the aborigines', 'native community', 'aboriginal race', 'native state', 'indigenous' or 'spirit of nationality'. Conceptualizations of 'land' almost always relate closely to power, such as the power to distribute land as the core of the authority of power holders in indigenous systems, the power to define who is inside of the nation (and who is out) and who controls exploitation of natural resources.

The contested and often fragile status of nation and state in African countries today suggests that it would be worth investigating in detail the linkages between the notions of 'land' and 'nation' in other African 'national' histories compared to the Gold Coast case, as well as in more recent African histories, such as in the idea of nation building after independence (e.g. in African Socialism, *Ujamaa* and Consciencism), and also in contemporary discourses about authenticity, *Ubuntu*, or Azania. For instance, in the second half of the 1960s, leaders felt a strong need to elaborate the 'African' character of the independent nation states by making recourse to African traditions of sharing and of working together in agricultural production. These were translated in African socialist, 'one-party' systems in the late 1960s and 1970s into policies of state property of land rather than private ownership, justified by the claims that land was held collectively in African traditional practices.[55]

If we look at contemporary discourses, 'land' receives a central role in some alternative political discourses, such as in the Pan African Congress (PAC) of Azania, based in South Africa and inspired by Steve Biko. Their prime slogan is 'Izwe Lethu, The Land is Ours'. Here, the history of (South) Africa is depicted as essentially one of expropriation of Africans of their lands, and the key task for progressive politics is to regain control over their 'long alienated land' and reclaim the continent for the black race. The first text on the PAC website states:

> We Azanians only need to reclaim and utilise our land in the interest of Azania, the Azanian People and Africa. Restitution of the land insures the material basis for real democracy. The use of land is the key variable in determining the direction of the society. If the people control the land they will build a truly democratic egalitarian political economic system based on the direct political participation and control of the majority.[56]

Similarly, contemporary discourses on 'autochthony' in several countries, with the notorious consequences of exclusionary politics based upon criteria of origin of citizens, could be analysed by tracing the conceptions of 'land' and 'nation' involved.

In this chapter we have been able to trace the details of shifting political discourses of African actors in a way that a plain political or social historiography could not do. The conceptual history approach made it possible to map in detail the different positions of various types of actors, as well as the shifting horizon of struggles in the Gold Coast in the decades around 1900, finally moving towards a more standard nationalist-anticolonial perspective. One of the fruits of this analysis is to bring out the innovative nature of the Fanti Confederation and its 1871 Mankessim Constitution. Although killed off politically by the authorities of the protectorate within a few years, as a vision it was a true alternative to self-rule; the comparisons made by the actors themselves with the Japanese Meiji revolution, or with the different routes that Australia or Canada could take within the Commonwealth, were justified from this perspective. Another fruit of the analysis is the insight it offers into the resourcefulness of the notion of 'land' itself. The fact that it could mean 'soil' as well as 'nation' made it especially suitable for political discourse in the Gold Coast context of the land bills. Concepts like 'native', 'aboriginal' and 'indigenous' could delegitimize the claims of colonials by suggesting a natural bond between persons and their place of birth, and thus suggesting a natural claim to control over that place. But the main fruit of this exercise in conceptual history is to demonstrate that Gold Coast discourses involved a broad spectrum of actors in the Gold Coast and not a small 'alienated' elite; these were creative and innovative local discourses, rather than mere imports of European Enlightenment ideas, and may inspire contemporary thinking about the future of African nation states.

Notes

I acknowledge the Netherlands Organisation for Scientific Research (NWO) for financing the study 'Democratic Imaginations in Global Perspective', upon which this chapter builds; and the RIDE research group of the Faculty of Philosophy, University of Groningen.

1. *The Gold Coast Aborigines.* 22 October 1898. Quoted in F. Agbodeka, *African Politics and British Policy in the Gold Coast, 1868–1900: A Study in the Forms and Force of Protest* (Evanston: Northwestern University Press, 1971), 143.
2. E.A. Ayandele, 'James Africanus Beale Horton, 1835–1883: Prophet of Modernisation in West Africa', *African Historical Review* 4(3) (1971): 691 (quote); P.F. de Moraes Farias and K. Barber (eds). *Self-Assertion and Brokerage: Early Cultural Nationalism in West Africa* (Birmingham: University of Birmingham Centre for West African Studies, 1990).
3. Most Gold Coast authors use the word Fanti rather than Fante; I follow this usage.
4. G. Austin, *Labour, Land and Capital in Ghana: From Slavery to Free Labour in Asante, 1807–1956* (Rochester: Rochester University Press, 2005); Agbodeka, *African Politics and British Policy*; D. Kimble, *A Political History of Ghana: The Rise of Gold Coast Nationalism 1850–1928* (Oxford: Clarendon Press, 1963).
5. The British Slave Trade Act of 1807 abolished the slave trade. The West African Squadron then started policing the Atlantic coast to prevent the slave trade. The Slavery Abolition Act of 1833 abolished slavery in the whole empire.
6. Only from 1900 did cacao growing start to expand, and was only well-developed half a century later. Gareth Austin's classic study *Labour, Land and Capital in Ghana* traces this development and underscores that labour shortage, rather than land, was the major issue in cacao production.
7. For the Mankessim Constitution see, for example, 'Constitution of the New Fante Confederacy', *ModernGhana.com*, 5 February 2007. Retrieved 17 May 2015 from http://www.modernghana.com/news/123177/1/constitution-of-the-new-fante-confederacy.html.
8. The abolitionist project involved black missionaries who came from the American continent to Africa, such as Blyden and Crummel. They perceived human civilization as a great flow moving through the millennia from East to West around the globe, having initially passed Africa but now touching Africa in a magnificent Christianizing civilizing project. See E.W. Blyden, *Christianity, Islam and the Negro Race* (London: W.B. Whittingham & Co., 1887. Reprinted Edinburgh: Edinburgh University Press, 1967), K.A. Appiah, *In My Father's House: Africa in the Philosophy of Culture* (New York: Methuen, 1992) and P. Boele van Hensbroek, *Political Discourses in African Thought: 1860 to the Present* (Westport: Praeger, 1999).
9. Even the British Parliament adopted a plan to establish independent African states in West Africa (the Select Committee of Parliament 1865). In a spirited book, *West African Countries and Peoples, British and Native* (reprinted from 1868, New York: Cambridge University Press (digitally printed version), 2011), Africanus Horton produced a modernistic blueprint for West African independence, and in 1868 the Fanti kings formed the Fanti Confederation.
10. Even the critic Casely Hayford argued for a 'healthy imperial policy' (1903 subtitle). The fact that people in the Gold Coast in those days did not see a contradiction between supporting 'the Queen' and being a self-conscious African is expressed in a touching way in a letter by the important and combative King Ghartey IV of Winneba (to Brown, 28 July 1897), then seventy-seven years old: 'Hopefully, therefore, I fall in this battlefield with many wounds,

fresh and old, and deep scars of the Fanti Confederation. Kindly convey my last farewell to all true patriotic native Kings and friends of the country's cause. Be constitutional. God bless you, our country and the Queen'. [Quoted in F.L. Bartels, *The Roots of Ghana Methodism* (London: Cambridge University Press, 1965), 145.] The idea of a universal world history was not only popular in Africa in those days; see e.g. for the case of Japan, Toru Takenaka, 'The Domestication of Universal History in Meiji Japan', *Saeculum*, 63(1) (2013), 119–42.

11. Blyden, *Christianity, Islam and the Negro*; E.W. Blyden, *African Life and Customs* (London: C.M. Phillips, 1908).

12. P.D. Curtin, '"Scientific" Racism in the British Theory of Empire', *Journal of the Historical Society of Nigeria* 2(1) (1960), 40–51; P.D. Curtin, *The Image of Africa: British Ideas and Action, 1780–1850* (Madison: University of Wisconsin Press, 1964); Ayandele, *James Africanus Beale Horton*; V. Bickford-Smith, 'The Betrayal of Creole Elites, 1880–1920', in P.D. Morgan and S. Hawkins (eds), *Black Experience and the Empire* (Oxford: Oxford University Press, 2004), 194–227.

13. Koselleck uses the notion of 'Sattelzeit' to indicate world historical periods of historical and discursive transition; R. Koselleck, *Futures Past: On the Semantics of Historical Time*, trans. K. Tribe (Cambridge: MIT Press, 1985). The period described in the present chapter can be described as a Sattelzeit for Africa.

14. Keith Tribe, in his introduction to Koselleck's *Futures Past*, speaks of 'examining the experiences that they [concepts] both contain and make possible' (Koselleck, *Futures Past*, xv).

15. Because of the habit of the time of writing under a pseudonym, it is not always possible to ascertain if the contribution was from an African or a colonial writer.

16. K.A.B. Jones-Quartey counts as the classical author on the West African press. K.A.B. Jones-Quartey, 'Sierra Leone and Ghana: Nineteenth-Century Pioneers in West-African Journalism', *Sierra Leone Studies* 12 (1959), 230–44; K.A.B. Jones-Quartey, 'The Ghana Press', in *Report of the Press in West Africa* (Committee for Inter-African Relations, 1960), 32–56; K.A.B. Jones-Quartey, 'A Note of J.M. Sarbah and J.E Casely Hayford: Ghanaian Leaders, Politicians, and Journalists – 1864–1930', *Sierra Leone Studies* 14 (1960), 57–62; K.A.B. Jones-Quartey, 'The Gold Coast Press: 1822–1930, and the Anglo-African Press: 1825–1930 – The Chronologies', *Research Review* 4(2) (1967), 30–46. The most complete and useful overview, also giving data on circulation etc., is provided by Y. Mizobe, 'A Survey of Gold Coast (Southern Ghanaian) Newspapers in the Latter Half of the Nineteenth Century', *CASAS Occasional Paper* 28 (2007).

17. Mizobe, 'A Survey of Gold Coast (Southern Ghanaian) Newspapers'. See p. 32 for the estimate of 200, specific data per paper is on p. 21. He gives many details about readership, management and financial issues, and family background of editors (24–31). Although 'enrolment rate in primary and secondary education was approximately 1% of the total population of one million', being able to 'understand what they read' was far lower (19).

18. On press freedom in nineteenth-century West Africa, see Y. Twumasi, 'Press Freedom and Nationalism Under Colonial Rule in the Gold Coast (Ghana)', *Journal of the Historical Society in Nigeria* 7(3) (1974), 499–519. See also, Mizobe 'A Survey of Gold Coast (Southern Ghanaian) Newspapers', 28–32.

19. J.E. Casely Hayford, *Gold Coast Native Institutions: With Thoughts Upon a Healthy Imperial Policy for the Gold Coast and Ashanti* (reprinted from 1903, London: Frank Cass, 1970), 176. Jones-Quartey, 'A Note of J.M. Sarbah and J.E. Casely Hayford', 32 speaks of the press 'championing African Freedom'; Mizobe, 'A Survey of Gold Coast (Southern Ghanaian) Newspapers', 28 and 29 quotes criticisms like the Governor 'abusing his privilege' and practising 'tyranny' and 'oppression'.

20. Jones-Quartey, 'The Gold Coast Press', 30–46.

21. Most papers had eight or nine distribution agents in different towns in the Gold Coast, as well as some two in Lagos, Freetown, or Gambia, and one or two in England. Mizobe, 'A Survey of Gold Coast (Southern Ghanaian) Newspapers'.

22. Kimble, *A Political History of Ghana*; Agbodeka, *African Politics and British Policy*; Austin, *Labour, Land and Capital in Ghana*.

23. Casely Hayford, *Gold Coast Native Institutions*, 4.

24. J.M. Sarbah, *Fanti Customary Law: A Brief Introduction to the Principles of the Native Laws and Customs of the Fanti and Akan Sections of the Gold Coast, with a Selection of Cases Thereon Decided in the Law Courts* (London: W. Clowes, 1897. Reprint, London: Frank Cass, 1968).

25. Sarbah, *Fanti Customary Law*, 90.

26. The origins of the existing distribution of land is often traced back to capturing the land in a war situation where conquered lands were appropriated by the conqueror, or to settling on virgin forest grounds.

27. Casely Hayford *Gold Coast Native Institutions*, 44.

28. J.B. Danquah, *Gold Coast: Akan Laws and Customs and the Akim Abuakwa Constitution* (London: Routledge, 1928), 198.

29. Danquah, *Gold Coast*, 202.

30. Sarbah states: 'From the moment a tribal community settles down finally upon a definite tract of land, the land begins to be the basis of society in place of kinship'. J.M. Sarbah, *Fanti National Constitution: A Short Treatise on the Constitution and Government of the Fanti, Asanti, and other Akan tribes of West Africa, Together with a Brief Account of the Discovery of the Gold Coast by Portuguese Navigators, a Short Narration of Early English Voyages, and a Study of the Rise of British Gold Coast Jurisdiction, etc., etc.* (London: Frank Cass, 1968, first published 1906), 7.

31. These analyses of the educated elite intellectuals synchronize with those of legal anthropologists. Paul Bohannan compares such land relations to being a participant or shareholder in a company. P. Bohannan, 'Africa's Land', in G. Dalton (ed.), *Tribal and Peasant Economies* (Garden City, N.Y.: The Natural History Press, 1967. Reprinted from *The Centennial Review* 4(4) (1960), 439–49).

32. This reconstruction synchronizes with the well-known idea that prosperity (and power) in African societies depends upon authority over people (rather than assets or territory), i.e. the idea of 'wealth in people'. J.I. Guyer, 'Wealth in People, Wealth in Things – Introduction', *Journal of African History* 36(1) (1995), 83–90.

33. One of the Nestors of Anthropology of African Law, Prof. A.N. Allott, extensively discusses this issue in his *Law and Language* concluding that with good linguistic and anthropological input such understanding is possible. A.N. Allot, *Law and Language: An Inaugural Lecture Delivered on 2 March 1965* (London: School of Oriental and African Studies, 1965).

34. Sarbah, *Fanti Customary Law*, xi and ix.

35. Danquah, *Gold Coast*, 20.

36. Danquah, *Gold Coast*, 4.

37. de Moraes Farias and Barber, *Self-Assertion and Brokerage*.

38. Casely Hayford, *Gold Coast Native Institutions*, 68–72.

39. *The Gold Coast Times* was edited by James Hutton Brew, a Gold Coast businessman; it ended publication in 1885, only to be operational again between 1923 and 1940.

40. *The Gold Coast Times* 1875, March 30, and 1874 respectively.

41. Both Sarbah and Casely Hayford sometimes used the notion of 'tribe', but generally they preferred notions such as 'kingdom' or 'native state'.

42. *The Gold Coast Chronicle* (4 January 1892).

43. A. Ahuma, *The Gold Coast Nation and National Consciousness* (Liverpool: Marples, 1911; Reprint, London: Frank Cass, 1971), 1.

44. Casely Hayford, *Gold Coast Native Institutions*, xiii and in many other texts.

45. Frequently used terms in Casely Hayford *Gold Coast Native Institutions*, e.g. xvi, 8, 180, 316.

46. *The Gold Coast Chronicle* (1890–1901, in African Newspaper Archive from 1894) was edited by T. Laing and J.E. Casely Hayford. *The Gold Coast Leader* (1902–22 in the archive) was edited by J.E. Casely Hayford, J. Brown, Attoh Ahuma, J. Buckman and G. Acquah. *The Gold Coast Nation* (1912–20 in the archive) was edited by Attoh Ahuma. *The Gold Coast Independent* (1918–22 in the archive) was edited by J.J. Akrong and D.G. Tackie (Jones-Quartey, 'The Gold Coast Press', 30–46).

47. Although I build my evidence related to the newspapers from word counts, it can be helpful also to give relevant quotes. In *The Gold Coast Chronicle* of 14 March 1895, p. 3, an author calling himself 'Indignant', speaks of 'the soil is ours', 'the natives of the Colony', 'our country', and 'the natives of the Gold Coast'. *The Chronicle*'s 29 March 1897 issue, p. 2 gives a spirited critique of the Lands Bill using expressions like 'Her Majesty did not lay any claim to the soil of the Colony which belonged to the people of the Gold Coast', and 'you become mere squatters on your own soil ... hewers of wood and drawers of water'; p. 3 speaks of 'the land of the native tribe'.

48. E.g. *The Gold Coast Aborigines* (1 January 1898) p. 3 speaks of 'the welfare of the country'; the issue of 8 January speaks on pp. 2 and 3 of 'indigenous to the soil', 'give up their lives for their Country', 'the interest of the Country', 'the 'spirit of unity' and 'obligation to the country and ... duty to the fatherland', 'this dear fatherland'.

49. E.g. *The Gold Coast Leader* of 5 July 1902, p. 1 mentions 'God has given you your country, and He has given us ours'; on p. 2 the article 'What's in a Name' reads almost like a regular twentieth-century nationalist discourse, speaking of 'natives of the soil', 'as a people', 'countrymen', 'the nation' and complains about 'The hereditary rights of our kings and chiefs, our public and even private men ... arbitrarily trampled upon'.

50. A classical study on the position of the chief is K.A. Busia, *The Position of the Chief in the Political System of Ashanti: A Study of the Influence of Contemporary Social Changes on Ashanti Political Institutions* (Reprinted from 1951. London: Frank Cass, 1968).

51. See B.M. Edsman, *Lawyers in Gold Coast Politics c. 1900–1945: From Mensah Sarbah to J. B. Danquah* (Uppsala: University of Uppsala, 1979); and Kimble, *A Political History of Ghana*.

52. Boele van Hensbroek, *Political Discourses in African Thought*, 58–61.

53. Sarbah, *Fanti National Constitution*, 149; Casely Hayford, *Gold Coast Native Institutions*, 250 and 254.

54. J.E. Casely Hayford, *Ethiopia Unbound: Studies in Race Emancipation* (Reprinted from 1911. London: Frank Cass, 1969), 98 and other places on 'Hewers of wood'. See also, Casely Hayford, *Gold Coast Native Institutions*, 15, 24 and Chapter 8 for use of other terms quoted.

55. These claims were in fact already refuted convincingly in the earliest discussions about these policies in the 1960s; see for instance Busia, *The Position of the Chief in the Political System of Ashanti*.

56. Pan Africanist Congress (PAC) of Azania, 'Road to Pan-Africanism: Pan-African Perspective Home Page'. Retrieved 20 April 2011 from http://www.panafricanperspective.com/pac/index.html. Interestingly, the concept of land as the core of African self-determination is here detached from reference to 'traditional' indigenous institutions such as analysed in detail by Sarbah or Danquah one hundred years before. Reference to these authors also cannot be found in PAC writings.

References

Newspapers

The Gold Coast Aborigines (1898–1902).
The Gold Coast Chronicle (1890–1901).
The Gold Coast Independent (1895–98).
The Gold Coast Leader.
The Gold Coast Methodist Times (1894–98).
The Gold Coast Nation.
The Gold Coast People (1891–94).
The Gold Coast Times (1874–85).
The West African Herald (1857–73).
The Western Echo, later *The Gold Coast Echo* (1885–90).

Websites

Pan Africanist Congress (PAC) of Azania, 'Road to Pan-Africanism: Pan-African Perspective Home Page', http://www.panafricanperspective.com/pac/index.html

World Newspaper Archive, http://www.crl.edu/collaborations/global-resources-partnerships/news/world-newspaper-archive

Other Works

Agbodeka, F. *African Politics and British Policy in the Gold Coast, 1868–1900: A Study in the Forms and Force of Protest*. Evanston: Northwestern University Press, 1971.

Ahuma, A. *The Gold Coast Nation and National Consciousness*. 1911. Liverpool: Marples; reprint, London: Frank Cass, 1971.

Allott, A.N. *Law and Language: An Inaugural Lecture Delivered on 2 March 1965*. London: School of Oriental and African Studies, 1965.

Appiah, K.A. *In My Father's House: Africa in the Philosophy of Culture*. New York: Methuen, 1992.

Austin, G. *Labour, Land and Capital in Ghana: From Slavery to Free Labour in Asante, 1807–1956*. Rochester: Rochester University Press, 2005.

Ayandele, E.A. 'James Africanus Beale Horton, 1835–1883: Prophet of Modernisation in West Africa', *African Historical Review* 4(3) (1971), 691–707.

Bartels, F.L. *The Roots of Ghana Methodism*. Cambridge: Cambridge University Press, 1965.

Bickford-Smith, V. 'The Betrayal of Creole Elites, 1880–1920', in P.D. Morgan and S. Hawkins (eds), *Black Experience and the Empire*. Oxford: Oxford University Press, 2004, 194–227.

Blyden, E.W. *Christianity, Islam and the Negro Race*. 1887. London: W.B. Whittingham & Co.; reprint, Edinburgh: Edinburgh University Press, 1967.

———. *African Life and Customs*. London: C.M. Phillips, 1908.

Boele van Hensbroek, P. *Political Discourses in African Thought: 1860 to the Present*. Westport: Praeger, 1999.

Bohannan, P. 'Africa's Land', in G. Dalton (ed.), *Tribal and Peasant Economies*. Garden City, N.Y: The Natural History Press, 1967. Originally published in *The Centennial Review* 4(4) (1960), 439–49.

Busia, K.A. *The Position of the Chief in the Political System of Ashanti: A Study of the Influence of Contemporary Social Changes on Ashanti Political Institutions*. 1951. Reprint, London: Frank Cass, 1968.

Casely Hayford, J.E. *Gold Coast Native Institutions: With Thoughts Upon a Healthy Imperial Policy for the Gold Coast and Ashanti*. 1903. Reprint, London: Frank Cass, 1970.

———. *Ethiopia Unbound: Studies in Race Emancipation*. 1911. Reprint, London: Frank Cass, 1969.

———. *The Truth About the West African Land Question*. 1913. Reprint, London: Frank Cass, 1971.

Curtin, P.D. '"Scientific" Racism in the British Theory of Empire', *Journal of the Historical Society of Nigeria* 2(1) (1960), 40–51.

———. *The Image of Africa: British Ideas and Action, 1780–1850*. Madison: University of Wisconsin Press, 1964.

Danquah, J.B. *Gold Coast: Akan Laws and Customs and the Akim Abuakwa Constitution*. London: Routledge, 1928.

Edsman, B.M. *Lawyers in Gold Coast Politics c. 1900–1945: From Mensah Sarbah to J.B. Danquah*. Uppsala: University of Uppsala, 1979.

Guyer, J.I. 'Wealth in People, Wealth in Things – Introduction', *Journal of African History* 36(1) (1995), 83–90.

Horton, J.A.B. *West African Countries and Peoples, British and Native* (reprinted from 1868), New York: Cambridge University Press (digitally printed version), 2011.

Jones-Quartey, K.A.B. 'Sierra Leone and Ghana: Nineteenth-Century Pioneers in West-African Journalism', *Sierra Leone Studies* 12 (1959): 230–44.

———. 'The Ghana Press', in Committee for Inter-African Relations (ed.), *Report of the Press in West Africa*. Ibadan: University College, 1960, 32–56.

———. 'A Note of J.M. Sarbah and J.E Casely Hayford: Ghanaian Leaders, Politicians, and Journalists – 1864–1930', *Sierra Leone Studies* 14 (1960): 57–62.

———. 'The Gold Coast Press: 1822–1930, and the Anglo-African Process: 1825–1930 – The Chronologies', *Research Review* 4(2) (1967), 30–46.

Kimble, D. *A Political History of Ghana: The Rise of Gold Coast Nationalism 1850–1928*. Oxford: Clarendon Press, 1963.

Koselleck, R. *Futures Past: On the Semantics of Historical Time*, trans. K. Tribe. Cambridge: MIT Press, 1985.

Mizobe, Y. 'A Survey of Gold Coast (Southern Ghanaian) Newspapers in the Latter Half of the Nineteenth Century', *CASAS Occasional Paper* 28 (2007).

de Moraes Farias, P.F. and K. Barber (eds). *Self-Assertion and Brokerage: Early Cultural Nationalism in West Africa*. Birmingham: University of Birmingham Centre for West African Studies, 1990.

Sarbah, J.M. *Fanti Customary Law: A Brief Introduction to the Principles of the Native Laws and Customs of the Fanti and Akan Sections of the Gold Coast, with a Selection of Cases Thereon Decided in the Law Courts*. 1897. London: W. Clowes. Reprint, London: Frank Cass, 1968.

———. *Fanti National Constitution: A Short Treatise on the Constitution and Government of the Fanti, Asanti, and other Akan tribes of West Africa, Together with a Brief Account of the Discovery of the Gold Coast by Portuguese Navigators, a Short Narration of Early English Voyages, and a Study of the Rise of British Gold Coast Jurisdiction, etc., etc*. 1906. Reprint, London: Frank Cass, 1968.

Takenaka, T. 'The Domestication of Universal History in Meiji Japan', *Saeculum* 63(1) (2013), 119–42.

Twumasi, Y. 'Press Freedom and Nationalism Under Colonial Rule in the Gold Coast (Ghana)', *Journal of the Historical Society in Nigeria* 7(3) (1974), 499–519.

Pieter Boele van Hensbroek holds a doctorate in political philosophy from the University of Groningen. He has worked at the University of Zambia and is currently deputy director of Globalisation Studies Groningen. He also coordinates the (inter-faculty) development studies minor programme and teaches social and political philosophy at the Faculty of Philosophy. He researches intellectual histories in the non-Western world, especially in Africa and Asia, as well as theories of democracy and of cultural citizenship.

CHAPTER 8

An Untimely Concept

Decolonization and the Works of Mudimbe, Mbembe and Nganang

Pierre-Philippe Fraiture

How has decolonization featured in the works of Valentin-Yves Mudimbe, Achille Mbembe and Patrice Nganang, and to what ends? These are the two main questions under scrutiny in this chapter. The task is quite problematic because 'decolonization' remains a vague notion in which ideas of independence, agency, sovereignty and freedom intersect. In the fields of culture and politics, there is no doubt that 'decolonizers' were active well before the official termination of colonialism and were able to imagine, in the midst of colonialism, postcolonial futures. The concept of decolonization conjures up intriguing temporal issues and upsets our understanding of historical sequences. Equally, however, one needs to take seriously Ramon Grosfoguel's view that the 'heterogeneous and multiple global structures put in place over a period of 450 years' did not disappear overnight and that, in many ways, 'we continue to live under the same colonial power matrix'. Indeed, Grosfoguel contends that 'with the juridical-political decolonization we moved from a period of "global capitalism" to the current period of "global coloniality"'.[1]

Nonetheless, there seems to be a consensus among lexicographers with regards to the meaning of the verb 'decolonize' and its associated noun 'decolonization'. Invariably, their explanations focus on two opposite sides, a colonizing power and a colony, and on the withdrawal of the former from the latter, which, as a result of this process, becomes independent.[2] In his otherwise scrupulously detailed *Dictionnaire historique de la langue française*, Alain Rey is equally expeditious: *décoloniser* and *décolonisation* are swiftly

Notes for this section begin on page 202.

glossed over under the main entry *colon* from which, alongside other words such as *colonial, colonisateur, colonialiste* or *colonialisme*, they are shown to have derived: 'Whilst the historical period of colonialism was entering its final stage, compounds designating the collapse of this system started appearing: **DÉCOLONISER** tr. V. (1963) preceded by **DÉCOLONISATION** f. n. (1952)'.[3]

What is interesting in this brief attempt to define these terms is the author's inability to consider them as part of an ongoing phenomenon which, at the time of publication of his *Dictionnaire historique* (in 1998), was still unfolding, concretely so if one thinks of Hong Kong and Macau (1997 and 1999 respectively). These definitions fail to render the dynamic nature of decolonization and, more importantly, to translate its long-term historical shifts and mutations beyond its first appearance in 1952. Given the global nature of the process, it is surprising that Rey fails to mention the wider linguistic context in which decolonization was inscribed and the fact that quasi-identical words appeared in English and other languages. Indeed, Dietmar Rothermund traces the first occurrence of decolonization in 1932 in an encyclopaedia entry on 'empire' by the German economist Moritz Julius Bonn.[4] Rothermund shows that Bonn would later use the analogous concept of 'counter-colonization' in *The Crumbling of Empire: The Disintegration of World Economy*[5] in order to 'characterize the movements of subject peoples who wished to put an end to colonial rule as well as the trend of global development, which led to the demise of colonial empires ... in the years of the Great Depression'.[6]

With regards to dictionary definitions, one has the impression that 'decolonize', to refer briefly to Zeno Vendler's aspectual features of verbs, has a clear endpoint and generates instantaneous effects. In reality, its temporal aspects are rather more complex, generating effects that are either dynamic (and thus without any discernible endpoint) or incremental.[7] There is, what is more, the issue of the prefix 'de-' which implies a reversal and the undoing of an initial situation and process (colonialism/colonization). This initial site is, however, hardly a stable point of departure. Indeed, colonization is a concept that also resists strict definitions. The prefix cancels, therefore, a process that cannot be unequivocally defined. In these circumstances, it is difficult to rely exclusively on dictionaries to identify what the cancellation entails and what decolonization really *is* since colony and colonization, along with some of their compounds such as 'anticolonial',[8] have remained contested and evolving concepts. The colonial situation was so complex and diverse that colony itself never retained an absolute primacy in the colony-related semantic field, which includes a great variety of terms such as plantation, protectorate, dominion, overseas territories, and, of course, empire. Finally, there are two other questions that these dictionary definitions fail to address: who are the agents of decolonization and what are the objects – decolonize is after all a transitive verb – of their decolonization? This chapter will examine this very crucial issue of agency and assess how it can contribute to a better understanding of concepts of political and intellectual freedom and sovereignty in a post-independence Africa.

Decolonization in Postcolonial Thought

The concept of decolonization is inextricably linked to those of colonization and colonialism. There is therefore a sense that the aforementioned 'withdrawal' or 'undoing' cannot quite bypass the intellectual landscape that contributed to the emergence of European imperialism and that the colonial is residually present in the 'decolonial', a rather unusual word, which seems nonetheless to have gained a certain currency.[9] From the end of the 1970s onwards, postcolonial studies engaged with the 'othering' excesses of European modernity. At the same time, postcolonial scholars attempted to identify, in the period preceding political independence, examples of critical agency on the part of colonized people. By doing so, they highlighted these people's ability to imagine, well before the demise of colonialism, the future of their own sovereignty. By parenthesis, it is perhaps useful to add that the adjective 'postcolonial', as opposed to 'post-colonial', not only refers to the aftermath of colonialism but is also used to explore how future liberation was conceived of in the colonial past.[10] The paradox often highlighted by postcolonial scholars is that European expansion largely took place after the Enlightenment and the French Revolution. This historical moment coincided with the rise of the individual and demands for a higher degree of personal freedom but relied nonetheless on a two-tier conception of humanity in which some ethnicities were deemed to be more human, that is, more worthy of civil rights and liberties, than others. Many anticolonial thinkers – for instance Sartre and Fanon – articulated their fight from the perspective of this denied humanity and argued throughout the 1950s that the cancellation of the colonial system would provide the basis for the emergence of a 'new man'.[11]

The word 'man' – yet another unstable concept – provides a telling example of this difficulty to think outside of (or to 'unthink')[12] the intellectual framework and the array of universal concepts developed as a result of the French Revolution. Anticolonial thinkers and fighters schooled in the French republican system – e.g. Ho Chi Minh, Aimé Césaire and Léopold S. Senghor – used to make frequent references to the wording and spirit of the 'Declaration of the Rights of Man and of the Citizen' to militate for the restoration of their own dignity as *men* and for the independence of their own people. In *Provincializing Europe*, Dipesh Chakrabarty attempts to 'find out how and in what sense European ideas that were universal were also, at one and the same time, drawn from very particular intellectual and historical traditions that could not claim any universal validity'.[13] Chakrabarty explores the enduring power of concepts forged by European social scientists in the wake of the Enlightenment but argues that their translocation into other places, and into languages such as his own native Bengali, produces a supplement and indeterminacy that defy translation.[14] This point will be examined again in the final part of this chapter.

Throughout his study, Chakrabarty also demonstrates that this European corpus and repository of concepts – 'citizenship, the state, civil society, public sphere, human rights, equality before the law, the individual'[15] and many others – are both 'indispensable' *and* 'inadequate' in 'helping us to think through the experiences of political modernity in non-Western nations'.[16] He remarks that it is not his intention to discard this European intellectual legacy but rather to examine 'how this thought – which is everybody's heritage and which affects us all – may be renewed from and for the margins'.[17] Chakrabarty argues, however, that European concepts were for a very long time borrowed uncritically and that their alleged universal value remained unchallenged. This was, for instance, the case of nationalist elites in newly decolonized countries who embraced the historicist categories of European thought and 'rehearsed to their own subaltern classes … the stagist [i.e. developing in neat stages] theory of history on which European ideas of political modernity were based'.[18] Indeed, Chakrabarty argues that 'most modern third-world histories' are invariably underpinned by a 'transition narrative … of which the over-riding (if often implicit) themes are those of development, modernization, and capitalism',[19] a view echoing Pieter Boele van Hensbroek's analysis (in this volume) of Ghanaian elites and their attempt to become 'Black Englishmen'.

As a result of this reliance upon European historicism and on a set of ideas that are fundamentally parochial,[20] third-world nationalists' self-perception has been more often than not dominated by the idea that this transition has remained 'incomplete',[21] that their 'now' is still a 'not yet',[22] that their present is still lingering in an 'imaginary waiting room',[23] and that their history is a 'figure of lack',[24] forever linked, as suggested by Ngũgĩ wa Thiong'o, to a past that, somehow, is still living now: 'Even today, years after achievement of political independence, the African continent is often identified as Anglophone, Francophone, or Lusophone'.[25] Indeed, albeit about India, *Provincializing Europe* can be applied to decolonization in sub-Saharan Africa. African decolonization, as will be shown via the works of Valentin Mudimbe, Achille Mbembe and Patrice Nganang, has often been experienced, contested, read and imagined within, and sometimes against, this historicist/stagist logic of transition narratives in which neat ideas of temporality (precolonial, colonial, postcolonial) are favoured over more complex examinations. Each of these three intellectuals has devoted a significant part of his writing career to the legacies of colonial and African traditions on the postcolonial here and now. Their works also provide a rich network of propositions to grapple with the depth of decolonization, a concept which, like that of crisis as analysed by Reinhart Koselleck, cuts 'across short- and long-term processes' and 'promises misery and crime, but also salvation and cleansing'.[26]

A unifying narrative can be traced between these three individuals and their search for agency: they operate at the intersection of several disciplines, they are from the African diaspora and have published in European languages (French, English and German) and they belong to a growing body of African intellectuals absorbed by American academia. *Sortir de la grande nuit. Essai sur l'Afrique décolonisée* by Mbembe and *Manifeste d'une nouvelle littérature africaine. Pour une écriture préemptive* by Nganang will be explored in this analysis to define the ways in which these two thinkers relate to Mudimbe, the eldest member of this trinity.[27] The terms *sortir*, *décolonisée*, *nouvelle* and *préemptive* are indicative of a shared focus on temporal ideas of shifts, transitions and transition narratives. The two authors indeed attempt to articulate the political (Mbembe) and the literary (Nganang) modalities of a passage to an epistemologically rejuvenated Africa that will be, according to Mbembe, 'afropolitan', 'post-racial' and, for Nganang, 'post-genocidal'. Beyond the differences of corpus and approaches, these two essays, ultimately, examine the multilayered nature of the concept of decolonization in its relation to agency; they dialogue therefore, sometimes explicitly, with Mudimbe, the only representative of the trinity who is in a position to provide first-hand testimonies on the passage from the colony to the 'postcolony'.[28]

Like Mudimbe, Mbembe and Nganang have adopted a 'writerly' style and have also practised a return to the speaking 'I' behind the scientific investigation; or, to put it differently, they have scrutinized Africa from the point of view of their own traumatic and violent experiences. In *Sortir de la grande nuit*, Mbembe shows, in 'À partir du crâne d'un mort. Trajectoire d'une vie' ('From a dead man's skull. Trajectory of a life'), how the ethnic cleansing perpetrated by Ahmadou Ahidjo's regime directly affected his own family and, eventually, led to his own exile from Cameroon.[29] In his manifesto, Nganang refers to the same historical context of political and ethnic oppression in order to shed light on the links between his own life, his academic projects – in France and in Germany – and the very personal significance of the pre-emptive role that he would like to ascribe to African literature.[30] Like Mudimbe, Mbembe and Nganang have explored the potential of autobiography as a tool to challenge the epistemological basis of the postcolony and a means to assert their own agency. Mbembe examines identity politics in France and in sub-Saharan Africa and Nganang defines new tools to read African literature. Both scholars approach decolonization as a process involving subtle temporal connections. In the constant interferences between past, present and future, the past is both a haunting presence – a network of traces in the present – but also a toolkit to rethink the present.

Decolonizing Africa: Fifty Years On

Sortir de la grande nuit and *Manifeste d'une nouvelle littérature africaine* offer implicit and explicit perspectives on Mudimbe's legacy and show that decolonization has generated yet another quarrel between the ancients and the moderns. In a first stage, Mbembe's project to consider sub-Saharan Africa as the terrain of a rejuvenated humanity will be compared to Fanon's, and indeed Mudimbe's, attempts to flesh out the contours of a postcolonial and decolonized world. I shall then examine how and why Mbembe and Nganang dialogue with one another, especially as Nganang's reflection, in his manifesto, relies heavily upon two other essays by Mbembe ('Necropolitics'[31] and 'African Modes of Self-Writing'[32]). Finally, the analysis will focus on Mudimbe's art criticism in *The Idea of Africa* in order to examine the way in which he responds retroactively to the charges levelled against him by Nganang and, to a lesser extent, Mbembe.[33] A common concern can be identified in their writings: African decolonization, a notion that has undergone significant transformations since it was first used by Moritz J. Bonn and then, much more visibly, by Third World intellectuals at the height of the Cold War. The three authors are engaged in a cacophonic conversation: they tap into the same anticolonial ideas, draw upon one another's views but also contradict each other. In this discussion, they reflect upon colonial exclusions, express their disillusionment with the African present and muse about the extent, but also the limit, of their own present and future agency.

Achille Mbembe

In *Essai sur l'Afrique décolonisée*, Mbembe argues that the African decolonization was a non-event that paved the way to the introduction of a neocolonialist order orchestrated by France itself.[34] This idea of a failed decolonization is not new and, in fact, it predominantly informed Mudimbe's scholarly work and novels from the 1970s to the publication of *The Invention of Africa*. Mbembe, therefore, is attempting to demonstrate that the past militancy of canonical thinkers and writers such as Fabien Éboussi-Boulaga, Mongo Béti, Yambo Ouologuem, Cheikh Hamidou Kane, Léopold Sédar Senghor and, above all, Fanon, still constitutes a valid set of ideas to elucidate the present and probe decolonization, a process that he regards as incomplete. This essay can also be read as a tribute to postcolonial theory and to the critique that Chakrabarty himself conducts in *Provincializing Europe*. Mbembe explores, through the Haitian and Liberian cases, the extent to which these countries have remained subjugated by discursive and epistemic conditions established before the abolition of slavery. Like the early Mudimbe, he advocates the urgency of decolonizing knowledge.[35] He remarks that in order to 'open up the future to everyone', it is necessary to radically critique the conditions that have perpetuated the reproduction of 'submissive relationships developed during the imperial era between indigenous populations and colonisers and ... between the West and the rest of the world'. He is of the view that the creation of the 'democracy of tomorrow' will be underpinned by a deconstruction of the 'imperial knowledge which, in the past, made possible the domination of non-European societies'.[36]

This examination of colonial servitude and focus on the transformative steps that should form the basis for the construction of an autonomous selfhood is reminiscent of the utopian climate that prevailed in the 1950s and 1960s, in texts by Sartre and Fanon and in some of Mudimbe's early works such as *L'Autre face du royaume*.[37] This brings about an alternative trinity, Sartre-Fanon-Mudimbe, which deepens the complexity of the Mudimbe-Mbembe-Nganang trinity. What is surprising is this constant focus on a symbolic rebirth of 'man', both 'singular' and 'universal'. There is here a Sartrean leitmotiv that has been recurrently exploited, first by Fanon and then Mudimbe. This idea, expounded by Sartre in his *Plaidoyer pour les intellectuels*,[38] considers 'man' as a future possibility for, as Mudimbe would also argue, 'man is the future of man'.[39] This word 'man', despite its gendered and masculinist connotations, needs to be understood in the sense of 'human'. This new human is 'singular' because 'situated' and belongs to the universal because her or his rebirth will coincide with the emergence of a raceless humanity. Behind Mbembe's ideas, one can detect the influence of the Marxism-inflected historical dialectics as it had been poeticized by Sartre in 'Orphée noir'.[40] Mbembe's text therefore embraces a promethean tone whose traces are to be found in our second invented trinity (Sartre-Fanon-Mudimbe). *Sortir de la grande nuit* is in many respects a political manifesto. Its title is a direct tribute to Fanon's passionate revolutionary call in the conclusion of *Les Damnés de la terre*: '*La grande nuit dans laquelle nous fûmes plongés, il nous faut la secouer et en sortir*'.[41] The English translation very deftly renders the sense of tragedy that a successful orphic ascent will imply: 'We must shake off the heavy darkness in which we were plunged, and leave it behind'.[42]

Just fifty years after decolonization Mbembe advocates for Africa an analogous rebirth. His essay, however, is not merely repetitious of Fanon's words and views. Mbembe's main exigency, that is, the establishment of a 'truly post-racial democracy',[43] retains the universal dimension promoted by Fanon but is sustained by a less dualistic conception of geopolitical configurations. Mbembe's Africa is recast in a global and mostly transatlantic network of exchanges. His *Afrique décolonisée* lies at the crossroads between America, the Caribbean, Cameroon and South Africa. The book also provides a bleak assessment of contemporary France, which has not been able to shake off the discursive weight of its 'long imperial winter'.[44] This largely depressing portrayal of France is not just an end in itself; it serves also as a pretext to examine contemporary Africa. He identifies the mimetic relationship between France's false universalism, colonial ideology and the *réflexe indigéniste*[45] adopted by African national leaders after independence, a point which reiterates the main thrust of Mudimbe's *Invention of Africa*, and further upstream, Fanon's thoughts on the link between revolution and indigenous cultures.[46]

Mbembe, however, contends that there is more to contemporary Africa than this internalization of imported models. The essay is a manifesto of sorts, which quite programmatically seeks to map out in the present *singular* characteristics that could contribute to the underlying *universal* goal that it is pursuing. He identifies across the continent a series of signs that could constitute the building blocks of 'new cartographies', opposed to the *anciennes cartographies*,[47] as he announces that it is time now 'to move to something else'.[48] These signs of the present from which, Mbembe hopes, a not too distant future will emerge, are, paradoxically, also to be found in Africa's past. This remapping of the continent has been aided by the gradual atomization of the African nation state and capitalism, two interconnected models introduced as a result of the demise of European empires. States are no longer able to impose regulatory frameworks to control the development of transnational commercial networks initiated by rich and powerful but (in theory) still non-autonomous territorial enclaves.[49] Ironically, this new post-national African modernity marks the presence of a precolonial model of exchange and communication; it also bears witness to Africa's 'historical difference', a phrase that Chakrabarty uses to contend that 'historical time is not integral' but 'out of joint with itself'.[50]

Mbembe does not romanticize this former geography but argues, however, that African precolonial networks were not dependent on the idea of strict frontiers and sovereignties and had the merit of generating multi-ethnic relations.[51] This programme is not fully developed and has in many ways a utopian and messianic dimension, as he collects here and there signs indicating that the old logics that had fed and legitimized colonialism and the 'postcolony' are receding. To qualify this new post-racial modernity, he uses the expression *afropolitaine*. He argues that the prime site of this emerging afropolitanism is the African city and shows that South Africa constitutes the most successful example of this new trend.[52] The afropolitan city is a site of political and cultural creativity in which conventional racial markers of Africanity are challenged in favour of a more creolized political and societal project.[53]

Ultimately, *Sortir de la grande nuit* is driven by an idealist agenda (and also a high degree of wishful thinking), which championed the emergence of a *universalisme lateral*.[54] This type of universalism is predicated on the idea that if blacks and whites are to walk together again on the 'paths of humanity', they will need to surmount – the word *dépassement* is used here to imply this dialectical movement – 'the radical opposition between the self and the foreigner'.[55] This *dépassement* is what the author seeks. I have highlighted here the close relationship between Mbembe and Mudimbe and their common adherence to a type of political and epistemological militancy partly inflected by dialectical materialism and its underlying 'transition narrative' (Chakrabarty). Mudimbe's *The Invention of Africa*, although primarily a vast epistemological survey, is also a manifesto. In his conclusion, Mudimbe hopes that present signs of emancipation will provide 'the starting point of an absolute discourse'.[56] Mudimbe's survey – his 'geography of African gnosis'⁵⁷ – measures the present against the past, and in so doing, implicitly anticipates the shape of the future. This strategy informs Mbembe's effort to 'identify in the present the power of the future'.⁵⁸ This perspective is challenged by Patrice Nganang.

Patrice Nganang

The focus on temporality is equally paramount in Nganang's *Manifeste*. The book proposes a reflection on the fleeting meanings of such concepts as past, present and future and their (in)ability to inform African literatures and the power of these texts to comment on African decolonization. Nganang's text is avowedly a manifesto: it demands the rapid transformation of the theoretical tools that have hitherto helped scholars to read African literatures. Nganang militates for the emergence of a new scholarship and, in doing so, questions performatively, that is, via a petulant, disrespectful and sometimes incantatory style, the generic divides between scholarship and political activism. He proposes to excavate out of a corpus situated in the past – for example Soyinka, Tutuola and Césaire – the contours of his new and 'pre-emptive' African writing. The enterprise amounts therefore to an attempt to disrupt traditional concatenations, genealogies, historic-critical segmentations and to challenge the prevalence of 'transition narratives' and 'stagist' conceptions of history. The theoretical instruments used by Nganang in this manifesto are unusual. The book is underpinned by a number of references to the works of canonical German philosophers such as Hegel, Nietzsche, Heidegger, Adorno and Benjamin. This constant recourse to German philosophy consolidates the weight and significance of the adjective *nouvelle* in the title as Nganang's literary call to arms is also intended as an effort to break away from the habit of interpreting African novelists with francophone theorists.

This book can be read as a rejection of canonical postcolonial models and as an endeavour to constitute a 'new grammar' and take on board the new *philosopheme* of our time,⁵⁹ defined largely by the Rwandan genocide of 1994, a catastrophe that generated a *nouvelle épistémologie*.⁶⁰ Nganang uses the term 'tragedy' to refer to this *philosopheme*, which, he contends, is informed by a *principe destructif-créatif*.⁶¹ Like Adorno, who famously asked whether it was not 'barbaric' to write poetry after Auschwitz,⁶² Nganang tries to ascribe a new place to novelists in a post-genocide Africa. The rejection at work in this essay is explicitly directed towards the Sartre-Fanon-Mudimbe trinity. Nganang deplores that African literature and its critique have been living 'in Sartre's shadow'.⁶³ African writers and thinkers, he remarks, have been the recipient of what he names, a 'transcendental loan', that is, a borrowed set of conditions of possibility that have enabled them by proxy to know the world, to write and philosophize.⁶⁴ What is at stake in Nganang's criticism of Sartre is the latter's examination of the necessary relation between literature and political commitment in his literary manifesto *Qu'est-ce que la littérature?*[65] Nganang's interpretation is heavily indebted to 'Commitment', Adorno's text examining Sartre's thesis on literature.[66] Adorno mostly objects to the idea that, as Sartre puts it 'the writer deals with meanings',[67] that is, puts meanings into words, which can be translated into action and which reflect meanings outside the world of literature. Adorno criticizes the mechanical dimension of such a transaction; Sartre's position deprives the work of art of its indeterminacy, autonomy and, it is also argued, of its genuine ability to challenge a prescribed order.

Nganang embraces Adorno's perspective and 'negative dialectic'. Against the Sartrean conception of commitment, he claims that literature should have a *conscience prévisionnaire* and become therefore an instrument to pre-empt future catastrophes.[68] This new African literature will be able to 'see the beginning of that which, elsewhere, dug the bottomless well of crime'.[69] This pre-visionary perception is rooted in African reality and emerges 'from the morbid hole of the mass graveyard' left behind by the Rwandan genocide and years of dictatorship.[70] This new literature is to be found in the abyss of African negativity, that is, in a realm which is no longer solely governed by reason but ruled by life and death, categories that Nganang borrows from Mbembe's 'Necropolitics',[71] an essay which 'assumes that the ultimate expression of sovereignty resides, to a large degree, in the power and the capacity to dictate who may live and who must die'.[72]

Nganang argues throughout his essay that the new African literature should expose the ways in which death informs the tragedy at the heart of African everyday life. He contends that by taking this 'negative route' writers will retain their artistic autonomy, disclose reality, the reality of African suffering, and, beyond this particular focus, reveal human suffering in its universality.[73] In this respect, Soyinka, Tutuola and Césaire are described as pre-visionary and 'post-genocide'[74] writers. Césaire was able to deterritorialize suffering.[75] His *Cahier d'un retour au pays natal* is 'post-national' because it transcends spatial and temporal boundaries and is able to conjure up 'the universal historicity of the profound disaster against which African subjects define themselves today'.[76]

With regard to the pre-visionary dissidence of these writers, Nganang adopts a number of intriguing temporal perspectives, as the most accomplished proponents of this African literature of the future are, paradoxically, in the past. He contends, a point resonating with Chakrabarty's critique of stagist historicism, that their writings question conventional timelines; in their works, Nganang envisages the past from the perspective of its ability to generate conceptual blueprints for possible futurities. Pre-visionary writing is 'more original than the origin itself'[77] and enables its readers to see the 'future of violence'.[78]

Pre-visionary consciousness needs therefore to be understood within the specific genre, the manifesto, in which it is employed. Nganang also uses it polemically to mark the divide between his *nouvelle littérature africaine* and (in his eyes) the outmoded anticolonial and postcolonial critique as expressed in the works of Sartre, Fanon and Mudimbe. With regards to the latter, Nganang contends that his philosophical 'patience' did not prevent the Rwandan tragedy: 'It is not in the limitless labyrinth of the African library that, one night, evil took place but on an ordinary African street'.[79] Although Nganang highlights the scientific merits of *The Invention of Africa*, he argues that its most conclusive finding, that is, Africa is the West's discursive object, is no longer useful in a post-genocide era. Nganang also remarks, as I noted earlier, that Mudimbe's essay concludes on an optimistic note as he foresees in the midst of the 'geography of African gnosis', encouraging signs of a new discursive dawn. This 'happy ending' does not ring true with Nganang's ambition to think negatively for 'hope resides henceforth in the negation'.[80]

However, Mudimbe has not always been the proponent of a 'positive' dialectics. He is in many ways also a 'negator'. Nganang's analytical weakness resides in his hasty, and certainly, impatient treatment of Mudimbe's thought. Mudimbe is only a representative, albeit prominent, of African philosophy; he can hardly be regarded as its spokesperson. Nganang establishes nonetheless an irrelevant analogy between African philosophy's lack of pre-visionary capability and Mudimbe, described as the most patient of all African philosophers, who 'was asleep when corpses were piling up in his backyard'.[81]

Beyond Afro-Radicalism and Nativism

This reductive view of the relationship between African philosophy and Mudimbe mainly results from Nganang's reading of 'African Modes of Self-Writing', another essay by Achille Mbembe.[82] Echoing Chakrabarty's critique, according to which 'the narratives of "modernity"' are 'almost universally' used to describe 'a certain "Europe" as the primary habitus of the modern',[83] Mbembe contends that African thinkers have not been able to free themselves from the very instruments that facilitated and justified African colonization, that is, the dualistic logic implied in the opposition between 'custom' and 'civilization' (and its various cognates: civil society, the state and Christianity). He also shows that African criticism has only been able to define its struggle through 'a construction of the self understood in terms of both victimhood and mutilation'.[84] The main thrust of Mbembe's critique of African thought rests on the argument that the 'civilization' vs. 'custom' binary opposition has generated two major African discourses:

> The first of these is what might be termed *Afro-radicalism*, with its baggage of instrumentalism and political opportunism. The second is the burden of the metaphysics of difference (*nativism*). The first current of thought – which liked to present itself as 'democratic', 'radical', and 'progressive' – used Marxist and nationalist categories to develop an imaginaire of culture and politics in which a manipulation of the

rhetoric of autonomy, resistance, and emancipation serves as the sole criterion for determining the legitimacy of an authentic African discourse. The second current of thought developed out of an emphasis on the 'native condition.' It promoted the idea of a unique African identity founded on membership of the black race.[85]

Mbembe ascribes to these two currents the failure of African philosophy to deal with its past and present, to construct a future and to yield any systematic framework to account for 'human misfortune and wrongdoing'.[86] He notes that the proponents of Afro-radicalism have always shied away from facing African co-responsibility for slavery and colonialism. About the nativists, he remarks that their exclusive model runs counter to Afropolitanism and its underlying ambition to contribute to the edification of a 'post-racial' African *polis*.

Nganang's argument is built upon analogous premises as he underscores the utter ineffectiveness of these two currents in the context of the Rwandan genocide: Afro-radicalists used the victimization argument to prove their innocence, whereas nativists were confronted with their own shame since the identity argument had been employed by the perpetrators to legitimize ethnic massacres.[87] At this stage, it is important to point out that Mudimbe's *patient* exegesis of Africanist epistemology is linked by Nganang to the efforts of Afro-radicalists to delve into 'Belgian colonial dichotomies'[88] in order to explain the present and escape responsibility, which for Nganang and Mbembe is the sign of their ongoing dependency. Nganang contends therefore that Mbembe's essay succeeded where that of Mudimbe in *The Invention of Africa* 'stalled'.[89] He contends that, unlike Mudimbe, Mbembe is truly dissident because, via his interrogation of the present's tragedy, he embraces Adorno's negative thought.[90]

At this point, it would be useful to return to the ways in which decolonization is conceptualized by these three authors. What unites them is an ambition to link African decolonization to epistemological renewal. Indeed, a continuum can be traced between Mudimbe's *Odeur du père* ['The Father's Scent'], Mbembe's *Sortir de la grande nuit* ['Exit from the Long Night'] and Nganang's 'transcendental loan'. Like the early Mudimbe, Mbembe contends that one needs to reconnect with the thought of Fanon and Sartre and their insistence on existential freedom and rejection of racial determinism. Nganang, however, adopts a different temporal perspective as he posits that the dialectical progression informing Sartre's description of decolonization does not do justice to the complexities of this process. He argues that answers to Africa's inability to decolonize itself must be looked for in the past, a point that overlaps with Mbembe's focus on African pre-colonial political and commercial practices, and that strategies adopted by Africans to cope with 'necropolitics' (Mbembe) should also offer blueprints for a better future.

The rest of this text will probe further the opposition that Nganang establishes between Mbembe and Mudimbe with regards to 'negative thinking' and then show how Mudimbe offers a sort of retroactive response in 'Reprendre'. There is a striking resemblance between the epistemological survey conducted by Mbembe in 'African Modes of Self-writing', above all in relation to the dismissal of nativism and Afro-radicalism, and Mudimbe's work. In his main essays, and from the onset of his writing career,[91] Mudimbe has invariably taken to task the advocates of fixed identities and those, such as Nkrumah and Nyerere, who called upon Marxism – a fundamentally European (and 'provincial') doctrine – to declare the uniqueness of African nations.[92] Given this clear overlap, it is surprising that Mbembe, and Nganang after him, reduce Mudimbe's philosophical input to the epistemological description of the 'colonial library', 'a pre-existing library' in which 'a self that claims to speak with its own, authentic voice always runs the risk of being condemned to express itself in a pre-established discourse that masks its own, censures it, or forces it to imitate'.[93]

Mbembe announces his intention to go beyond this epistemological description and to 'propose ways out of the dead end into which [afro-radicals and nativists] have led reflection on the African experience of self and the world'.[94] Mbembe's essay is therefore also prescriptive and can be regarded as a manifesto offering tools to read the present, transform the future and *sortir de la grande nuit*. He contends that the analogy between slavery, colonization, apartheid and the Holocaust is entirely justified because these events 'are all characterized by an expropriation of the self by unnameable forces', and 'indict life on the pretext that origin and race are the criteria of any kind of valuation'.[95] Mbembe argues that 'new African practices of the self' must be achieved away from the former enslavement to geography and ideas of 'a lost identity that must at all costs be found again'.[96] These practices, 'whose theory and vocabulary remain to be invented' are 'sculpted by cruelty'.[97] Kourouma's *Allah n'est pas obligé* constitutes, according to Mbembe, an example of these new practices that Nganang locates also in *Sozaboy* by Saro-Wiwa.[98] Survivors rather than victims, these characters 'have to invent an art of existing in the midst of despoliation'.[99]

Creation as Survival in '*Reprendre*'

It is true that this perspective does not inform *The Invention of Africa*, which is more concerned with pre-established Western modes of thinking and metanarratives and their impact on African scholarship throughout history up to the present. However, it would be erroneous to reduce Mudimbe's work to the sole excavation of the colonial library. In novels such as *Entre les eaux*, *Le Bel immonde*, and *Shaba Deux*, he has also teased out how this violence has inflected the construction of African subjects.[100] Like Nganang's post-genocide Africans, Mudimbe's characters blur the divide between innocence and guilt, victims and perpetrators, as they experience the integration of Africa into, as Nganang puts it, 'simple but guilty humanity'.[101] He has also explored the ways in which daily practices, rooted in everyday violence, inform the African here and now and offer creative examples of survival. As explained in *On African Fault Lines*,[102] he owes the use of the word 'invention' to *L'Invention du quotidien* (translated as *The Practice of Everyday Life*).[103] The survivors on whom Mudimbe, Mbembe and Nganang focus are inventors of novel cultural practices borne out of the horrors of wars, genocides *and* decolonization, an evolving and multi-directional concept that cannot be reduced to the mechanical definitions of dictionaries.

'Reprendre' is an essay dedicated to artistic creation in Congo-Zaire and elsewhere in sub-Saharan Africa. Mudimbe demonstrates here that the relation between colonialism and decolonization cannot be reduced to a simple logic of 'withdrawal'. His approach does not replicate the patterns of transition narratives as described by Chakrabarty. Instead he argues that the present repeats the past but also generates a supplement. This focus on a repetition, which does not quite replicate the previous stage, is reminiscent of a translational process and the relationship between a source text and its translation when the purity of the original is submitted to the partial cannibalization of the vernacular.[104] Mudimbe argues that a particular cult of alterity that developed before decolonization had a major impact on local artists' aesthetic sense and, ultimately, on their ability to articulate creative responses to very local events.[105] He does not intend here to provide a full historical overview of this aesthetic evolution: rather than focusing on 'causal successions', he remarks that his aim is to highlight 'new artistic thresholds [and] displacements of inspirations'.[106] The main argument made in this essay is that the 'radical reconversion of African arts' undertaken 'in the colonial settings' neither generated a clear-cut withdrawal from the past, nor produced a neat and regimented reordering and assimilation of aesthetic practices.[107]

In this discussion, Mudimbe focuses on the significant role played by Pierre Romain-Desfossés in mentoring Katangese artists during the colonial period. Mudimbe does not condemn Romain-Desfossés, but presents him as a man who, albeit paternalistic, was above all pursuing an aesthetic agenda. His energy and 'missionary zeal' rested upon the conviction that local artists needed to reconnect with their African (in fact 'Nilotic') personality and move away from the 'uniformizing aesthetics of White masters'. He contended that Congolese artists were the recipients of a type of 'aesthetic unconscious', shared by all sub-Saharan Africans, and took it upon himself to 'awaken in his students this ancient, unchanging aesthetic memory'.[108] His teaching was therefore based on a cult of alterity and a belief in 'an innate African artistic imagination ... radically different from that of Europe'.[109] What Mbembe, after Fanon, called *réflexe indigéniste* became the backbone of an aesthetic philosophy that advocated the return to the primitive basis of a purer collective past. This artistic position, and above all the inverted racism that it suggests, has, however, become much more than just an instrument for the dissemination of nativist theses. 'Reprendre' is in this respect suitably ambiguous and demonstrates that aesthetic decolonization cannot be reduced, as in the dictionary definitions, to a straightforward 'withdrawal'. The indigenist aesthetics that Romain-Desfossés revived was adopted by his pupils but also reprised, recaptured or adapted by subsequent generations of artists in Zaire and elsewhere on the continent. The adoption-adaptation pair renders the deliberate indeterminacy contained in the French verb *reprendre*.

Mudimbe demonstrates that Romain-Desfossés's 'Nilotic etiquette' never retained any fixity and went through a number of 'displacements'.[110] This issue of displacement is central in Mudimbe's thinking and is linked to the relationship between the global and the local, the universal and the specific. By way of Michel de Certeau's opposition between 'place' and 'space', he often shows the ways in which the transposition and the transformation from the one to the other occur. Certeau argues that, 'The law of the "proper" rules in the place: the elements taken into consideration are *beside* one another, each situated in its own "proper" and distinct location. ... A place is thus an instantaneous configuration of positions. It implies an indication of stability'.[111] He adds that his element of order and stability is absent from 'space':

> ... in relation to place, space is like the word when it is spoken, that is, when it is caught in the ambiguity of an actualisation, transformed into a term dependent upon many different conventions, situated as the act of a present (or of a time), and modified by the transformations caused by successive contexts. In contradistinction to the place, it has thus none of the univocity or stability of a 'proper'.[112]

Romain-Desfossés's aesthetic order is a 'place' that became displaced or spatialized. The invention of new cultural practices results from these displacements that have affected, according to Mudimbe, the whole spectrum of art production in sub-Saharan Africa. He remarks that the notion of heritage has remained important but that artists have consistently refused to define their works through this exclusive link with tradition. He contends that contemporary African artists 'consciously relate to earlier African art', but 'know how to distort it, how to submit it to their own creative process'.[113]

Mudimbe explores the characteristics of popular art whereby this tendency to call upon and distort tradition also operates. A popular artist such as Tshibumba Kanda-Matulu, for instance, engages with tradition, adopts its seemingly naïve techniques and teases out the symbolic significance of local mythological figures such as the Mami Wata. On the surface, Tshibumba Kanda-Matulu complies with the aesthetic agenda of the Mobutu regime and its desire to promote authenticity.[114] Beyond these superficial marks of compliance, Kanda-Matulu's works nonetheless displace the stable and orderly thrust of this indigenist programme. With regards to popular artists such as Kanda-Matulu, Mudimbe argues that their works witness 'a practice of everyday life':[115]

> In many respects, popular arts, mostly paintings, are structured as *histoire immédiate*, in Benoît Verhaegen's expression; they are literally a capturing of ordinary, banal

stories and events (a market, a drinking party, a political event), of violence and tragedy (a civil war and assassination), or of mythological motifs ... Here technical flaws become marks of originality. The artist appears as the '*undisciplinable*' hero, challenging social institutions, including art practices, particularly academic ones. Yet this 'deviant', who sometimes attacks both a tradition and its modern currents, incarnates clearly the locus of their confrontation.[116]

Ultimately, the formal distortions that are identified here are the signs of a rebellion whereby the present is reinvented with fragments from the past *and* the present. The concept of 'invention' is therefore far from being limited to the construction of the colonial library in which Africanists would proverbially proceed to order, catalogue and magic up their own version of Congolese culture. Mudimbe suggests that 'invention' transcends the 'tension between the within and the without',[117] a point made by Roy Wagner in *The Invention of Culture*.[118] In his use of the concept, Mudimbe, who admits to having read Wagner's book several times,[119] intends to go beyond the simplistic opposition between creators and epigones, originals and copies and demonstrate that the 'repetition of the same' is never completely repetitious and generates its own creative displacements.

Conclusion

It is worth exploring further why the writings of these three authors cannot be reconciled with the historicist understanding of decolonization as a process in which 'withdrawal' is followed by 'independence'. As intimated by Ana Lúcia Sá in her examination of the concept of property among Bubi people, old colonial tenets can sometimes be re-appropriated and adapted to express very local (postcolonial) interests. Mudimbe, Mbembe and Nganang all agree with Dipesh Chakrabarty's views regarding the disproportionate prevalence of European thought among academics in the humanities and the social sciences in postcolonial countries: 'The everyday paradox of third-world social science is that *we* find these theories, in spite of their inherent ignorance of "us", eminently useful in understanding our societies'.[120] Chakrabarty's use of words such as 'Europe' and 'European' is of course not literal: they are employed as 'hyperreal' shorthand terms, since he focuses on a climate of conceptual subservience 'whose geographical referents remain somewhat indeterminate'.[121] By the same token, one could argue that the provincializing of Europe started in Europe itself at the time of decolonization, and that our three authors have been the critical interlocutors of a debate conducted by some European thinkers who were engaged in bringing down the barriers between the West and the rest. Mudimbe's deep familiarity with Foucault, Lévi-Strauss and Sartre (he once qualified the former as the 'unhappy historian of the Same'),[122] Mbembe's frequent engagement with Foucault, Derrida and

Certeau, and Nganang's recurrent reference to Adorno's negative dialectics all bear witness to the fact that the old humanism and its historicist prejudices became the major target of post-war Continental thought. Mbembe, Nganang, but also Mudimbe, are all exploring the possibility of identifying universal figures in their own singular settings.

Decolonization, as it is understood here, is not a rejection of the West but a process underpinned by the realization that the West was able to canonize, universalize its languages and literatures. What is also at stake is the West's ability to export its reason which, although it was not 'always self-evident to everyone, has been made to look obvious far beyond the ground where it originated'.[123] Nganang's and Mbembe's insistence on suffering as a possible terrain from which the contours of a rejuvenated African subject can be drawn results from this attempt to extend the definition of decolonization to a realm that is not solely ruled by Enlightenment rationalism and the autonomy of the subject.

The three African authors considered in this study adopt also a number of temporal perspectives that disrupt the tripartite conception of African history (precolonial, colonial, postcolonial). This point of view is not in itself new, as it constituted one of the foundational gestures of postcolonial studies and their early proponents' ambition to identify, not just in their present but also in the colonial past, local figures that had contributed to the collapse of the imperial edifice. Nganang claims that the works of writers such as Tutuola, Soyinka and Césaire should help perceptive readers to pre-empt future genocides because they bore witness to the fact that the future had already taken place. By this he argues that violence – yet another universal arch-figure – possesses an uncanny tendency to repeat itself under parochial guises (in Rwanda and Biafra for instance). Although Mbembe's 'emergence from the long night' does not quite escape historicism and the idea of a 'not yet' to be completed in the future, his examination of the African situation in Cameroon and in South Africa is also an attempt to retrieve fragments of the future in the past. His reference to other communal and political practices is reminiscent of the rationale behind Chakrabarty's project:

> To attempt to provincialize this 'Europe' is to see the modern as inevitably-contested, to write over the given and privileged narratives of citizenship other narratives of human connections that draw sustenance from dreamed-up pasts and futures where collectivities are defined neither by the rituals of citizenship nor by the nightmare of 'tradition' that 'modernity' creates.[124]

Mudimbe is, for his part, also reluctant to read decolonization as a process underpinned by a strict logic of rupture with a 'before'. Decolonization does not simply 'undo' the past. The idea of *reprendre* is akin to a translational process and the displacements that it invariably elicits. It is undeniable that Congo, like other colonial territories worldwide, was submitted to assimilation in the fields of culture, politics and religion. Concepts, techniques, genres and rituals were imposed and transposed in contexts that were far remote from the place where they had first originated (Europe). The translation, however, did not result in a straightforward restoration of the original and the return of an unadulterated sameness. Something was lost but also gained. Sartre was right to say that the assimilated elite in colonized countries (the so-called *évolués*) were 'walking lies'.[125] In his derogatory use of this expression, Sartre may however have failed to see that their deception was in fact a creative process and a refusal to adhere to the letter of the source text, for translations always produce a supplement that is no longer reducible to the *provincial* logic of the original. *Reprendre*, the French verb that Mudimbe does not translate, captures this moment of invention in which the original meaning is both taken over (one of the meanings of *reprendre*) but also submitted to an act of reprisal, a word deriving from the Italian *ripresaglia*, itself etymologically linked to the Latin verb *reprendere*.[126] In the light of these semantic interferences, decolonization cannot be a *de*colonization (the 'withdrawal' mentioned earlier) but is a process whereby colonization is reprised, that is, repeated, translated, taken over, displaced *and* retaliated against.

Notes

1. Cited in S.J. Ndlovu-Gatsheni, *Coloniality of Power in Postcolonial Africa: Myths of Decolonization* (Dakar: CODESRIA, 2013), 3.

2. Pronunciation: /diːˈkʊlənʌɪz/ (also **decolonise**). Definition of **decolonize**. V*erb [with object]* (of a state): withdraw from (a colony), leaving it independent. This definition from the online Oxford Dictionaries (http://oxforddictionaries.com/definition/english/decolonize?q=decolonize, consulted on 4 May 2013) reflects this consensus.

3. A. Rey (ed.), *Le Robert: Dictionnaire historique de la langue française* (Paris: Le Robert, 1998), 805–06. All translations are mine unless otherwise stated.

4. D. Rothermund, *Routledge Companion to Decolonization* (London: Routledge, 2006), 1. I am grateful to Ana Lúcia Sá for drawing my attention to this study.

5. M.J. Bonn, *The Crumbling of Empire: The Disintegration of World Economy* (London: George Allen & Unwin Ltd, 1938).

6. Rothermund, *Routledge Companion to Decolonization*, 1.

7. Z. Vendler, 'Verbs and Times', *The Philosophical Review* 66(2) (1957): 143–60. I am grateful to Axel Fleisch for drawing my attention to this author.

8. See R. Girardet, *L'Idée coloniale en France de 1871 à 1862* (Paris: Éditions de la Table ronde, 1972), where the French historian discusses the development of the term from the early nineteenth century to decolonization. Jean-Baptiste Say (7–8) was anticolonial because he argued that colonial expansion would be too costly for France and he advocated instead a global order (and market) in which all nations would be free to compete against one another; Édouard Drumont (61–62), in the wake of figures such as Count Gobineau and Gustave Le Bon, on the other hand, rejected colonialism because he feared that the enterprise would encourage racial miscegenation and weaken the specific features of each race. These two types of early anticolonialism were very different from the anticolonial thought and movements that developed from the 1930s onwards.

9. See W.D. Mignolo and A. Escobar (eds), *Globalization and the Decolonial Option* (London: Routledge, 2010) and W.D. Mignolo, *The Darker Side of Western Modernity: Global Futures, Decolonial Options* (Durham: Duke University Press, 2011).

10. On this definitional uncertainty, see the sustained discussion on the entry 'postcolonialism/postcolonialism', in B. Ashcroft, G. Griffiths and H. Tiffin, *Key Concepts in Post-Colonial Studies* (London: Routledge, 1998), 186–92.

11. Anticolonial intellectuals and militants such as Sartre, Fanon, but also Cabral and Che Guevara, were the heirs of a tradition that held the 'Declaration of the Rights of Man' in high esteem. In the immediate post-war era, the word 'man' had not been challenged yet for its sexist connotations. See: D. Bahri, 'Feminism in/and Postcolonialism', in N. Lazarus (ed.), *The Cambridge Companion to Postcolonial Literary Studies* (Cambridge: Cambridge University Press, 2004), 199–220.

12. See E. Shohat and R. Stam, *Unthinking Eurocentrism: Multiculturalism and the Media* (London: Routledge, 1994).

13. D. Chakrabarty, *Provincializing Europe: Postcolonial Thought and Historical Difference*, with a new preface by the author (Princeton: Princeton University Press, 2007 [2000]), xiii.

14. Chakrabarty, *Provincializing Europe*, xiii–xiv.

15. Chakrabarty, *Provincializing Europe*, 4.

16. Chakrabarty, *Provincializing Europe*, 16.

17. Chakrabarty, *Provincializing Europe*, 16.

18. Chakrabarty, *Provincializing Europe*, 9.

19. Chakrabarty, *Provincializing Europe*, 31.

20. Chakrabarty, *Provincializing Europe*, x.

21. Chakrabarty, *Provincializing Europe*, 31.

22. Chakrabarty, *Provincializing Europe*, 8.

23. Chakrabarty, *Provincializing Europe*, 10.

24. Chakrabarty, *Provincializing Europe*, 32.

25. Ngũgĩ wa Thiong'o, *Something Torn and New: An African Renaissance* (New York: Basic Civitas Books, 2009), 9.

26. R. Koselleck, 'Crisis', trans. M.W. Richter, *Journal of the History of Ideas* 67(2) (2006): 388.

27. A. Mbembe, *Sortir de la grande nuit. Essai sur l'Afrique décolonisée* (Paris: La Découverte, 2010); P. Nganang, *Manifeste d'une nouvelle littérature africaine: pour une écriture préemptive* (Paris: Éditions Homnisphères, 2007).

28. See A. Mbembe, *On the Postcolony* (Berkeley: University of California Press, 2001).

29. Mbembe, *Sortir de la grande nuit*, 31–53. This very autobiographical account is an amplification of a previously published article: A. Mbembe, 'Ecrire l'Afrique à partir d'une faille', *Politique Africaine* 51 (1993), 69–97.

30. In the third letter of P. Nganang, *La République de l'imagination. Lettres au benjamin* (La Roque-d'Anthéron: Vents d'ailleurs, 2009), he looks up to the figure of Ruben Um Nyobé to find hope for a better future: 'La Voix d'Um: lettre troisième', 45–69.

31. A. Mbembe, 'Necropolitics', trans. L. Meintjes, *Public Culture* 15(1) (2003), 11.

32. A. Mbembe, 'African Modes of Self-Writing', trans. S. Rendall, *Public Culture* 14(1) (2002), 239–73.

33. V.-Y. Mudimbe, *The Idea of Africa* (Bloomington: Indiana University Press, 1994).

34. Mbembe, *Sortir de la grande nuit*, 58.

35. See V.-Y. Mudimbe, *L'Odeur du père: essai sur des limites de la science et de la vie en Afrique noire* (Paris: Présence africaine, 1982).

36. Mbembe, *Sortir de la grande nuit*, 113.

37. V.-Y. Mudimbe, *L'Autre face du royaume. Une Introduction à la critique des langages en folie* (Lausanne: L'Age d'homme, 1973).

38. J.-P. Sartre, *Plaidoyer pour les intellectuels* (Paris: Gallimard, 1972).

39. Mudimbe, *L'Autre face du royaume*, 136.

40. J.-P. Sartre, 'Orphée noir', in L.S. Senghor (ed.), *Anthologie de la nouvelle poésie nègre et malgache de langue française*, avant-propos de C.-André Julien (Paris: Presses Universitaires de France, 1948), ix–xliv.

41. F. Fanon, *Les Damnés de la terre*, preface by J.-P. Sartre (Paris: Maspero, 1961), 239. In 'Ecrire l'Afrique à partir d'une faille', Mbembe uses also the term *nuit* to refer to the African postcolonial present.

42. F. Fanon, *The Wretched of the Earth*, preface by J.-P. Sartre, trans. C. Farrington (London: Penguin Books, [1961] 2001), 251.

43. Mbembe, *Sortir de la grande nuit*, 114.

44. Mbembe, *Sortir de la grande nuit*, see Chapter IV: 'Le long hiver impérial français', 121–72.

45. Mbembe, *Sortir de la grande nuit*, 229.

46. V.-Y. Mudimbe, *The Invention of Africa: Gnosis, Philosophy, and the Order of Knowledge* (Bloomington: Indiana University Press, 1988). Fanon, *The Wretched of the Earth*, specifically the chapter 'On National Culture', 166–99.

47. Mbembe, *Sortir de la grande nuit*: 'Anciennes et nouvelles cartographies', 174–80.

48. Mbembe, *Sortir de la grande nuit*, 229–37.

49. Mbembe, *Sortir de la grande nuit*, 180–91.

50. Chakrabarty, *Provincializing Europe*, 16.

51. Mbembe, *Sortir de la grande nuit*, 180.

52. Mbembe, *Sortir de la grande nuit*, 233.

53. Mbembe, *Sortir de la grande nuit*, 226.

54. Mbembe, *Sortir de la grande nuit*, 241. A concept first developed by M. Merleau-Ponty in 'De Mauss à Claude Lévi-Strauss' (1959), republished in *Éloge de la philosophie* (Paris: Flammarion, 1989). See also: J.-G. Bidima, 'Philosophies, démocraties et pratiques: à la recherche d'un "universalisme latéral"', in *Critique* 771/772, special issue 'Philosopher en Afrique' (2011), 672–88. I would like to thank Pieter Boele van Hensbroek for drawing my attention to this article.

55. Mbembe, *Sortir de la grande nuit*, 241.

56. Mudimbe, *The Invention of Africa*, 200.

57. Mudimbe, *The Invention of Africa*, 200.

58. Mbembe, *Sortir de la grande nuit*, 241.

59. Nganang, *Manifeste d'une nouvelle littérature africaine*, 27.

60. Nganang, *Manifeste d'une nouvelle littérature africaine*, 136.

61. Nganang, *Manifeste d'une nouvelle littérature africaine*.

62. 'To write poetry after Auschwitz is barbaric'. T.W. Adorno, *Prisms*, trans. S. Weber and S. Weber (Cambridge, Massachusetts: MIT Press, 1981), 34.

63. Nganang, *Manifeste d'une nouvelle littérature africaine*, 57–82.

64. On this crucial issue, see also K. Wiredu, *Cultural Universals and Particulars: An African Perspective* (Bloomington: Indiana University Press, 1996), 136.

65. J.-P. Sartre, *Qu'est-ce que la littérature* (Paris: Gallimard, 1948).

66. T.W. Adorno, 'Commitment', in R. Taylor (ed.), *Aesthetics and Politics*, trans. F. McDonagh (London: Verso, 1980 [1977]), 75–89.

67. Cited in Adorno, 'Commitment', 76.

68. Nganang, *Manifeste d'une nouvelle littérature africaine*, 289.

69. Nganang, *Manifeste d'une nouvelle littérature africaine*, 295.

70. Nganang, *Manifeste d'une nouvelle littérature africaine*, 46.

71. Nganang, *Manifeste d'une nouvelle littérature africaine*, 46–47.

72. Mbembe, 'Necropolitics', 11.

73. Nganang, *Manifeste d'une nouvelle littérature africaine*, 68–72.

74. Nganang, *Manifeste d'une nouvelle littérature africaine*, 158.

75. Nganang, *Manifeste d'une nouvelle littérature africaine*, 159.

76. Nganang, *Manifeste d'une nouvelle littérature africaine*, 157.

77. Nganang, *Manifeste d'une nouvelle littérature africaine*, 115.

78. Nganang, *Manifeste d'une nouvelle littérature africaine*, 256.

79. Nganang, *Manifeste d'une nouvelle littérature africaine*, 38–39.

80. Nganang, *Manifeste d'une nouvelle littérature africaine*, 36.

81. Nganang, *Manifeste d'une nouvelle littérature africaine*, 40.

82. A. Mbembe, 'African Modes of Self-Writing', 239–73.
83. Chakrabarty, *Provincializing Europe*, 43.
84. Mbembe, 'African Modes of Self-Writing', 271–72.
85. Mbembe, 'African Modes of Self-Writing', 240–41.
86. Mbembe, 'African Modes of Self-Writing', 239.
87. Nganang, *Manifeste d'une nouvelle littérature africaine*, 45.
88. Nganang, *Manifeste d'une nouvelle littérature africaine*.
89. Nganang, *Manifeste d'une nouvelle littérature africaine*, 42.
90. Nganang, *Manifeste d'une nouvelle littérature africaine*, 43.
91. See, V.-Y. Mudimbe, 'Physiologie de la négritude', *Études Congolaises* 5 (1967): 1–13.
92. In *The Invention of Africa*, Mudimbe's appraisal of the 'Arusha Declaration' is, however, positive. *Ujamaa* is translated as 'communalism'. (Mudimbe, *The Invention of Africa*, 95.)
93. Mbembe, 'African Modes of Self-Writing', 257.
94. Mbembe, 'African Modes of Self-Writing', 242.
95. Mbembe, 'African Modes of Self-Writing', 259.
96. Mbembe, 'African Modes of Self-Writing', 269.
97. Mbembe, 'African Modes of Self-Writing', 269.
98. A. Kourouma, *Allah n'est pas obligé* (Paris: Seuil, 2000); Mbembe, 'African Modes of Self-Writing', 269; Nganang, *Manifeste d'une nouvelle littérature africaine*, 272; K. Saro-Wiwa, *Sozaboy: A Novel in Rotten English* (Port Harcourt: Saros, 1985).
99. Mbembe, 'African Modes of Self-Writing', 262.
100. V.-Y. Mudimbe, *Entre les eaux* (Paris: Présence Africaine, 1973); V.-Y. Mudimbe, *Le Bel immonde* (Paris: Présence Africaine, 1976); V.-Y. Mudimbe, *Shaba Deux. Les Carnets de Mère Marie-Gertrude* (Paris: Présence Africaine, 1989).
101. Nganang, *Manifeste d'une nouvelle littérature*, 30.
102. V.-Y. Mudimbe, *On African Fault Lines: Meditations on Alterity Politics* (Scottsville: University of KwaZulu-Natal Press, 2013), 75.
103. M. de Certeau, L. Giard, and P. Mayol, *L'Invention du quotidien* (Paris: Union Générale d'Éditions, 1980).
104. See S. Bassnett and H. Trivedi, 'Introduction: of Colonies, Cannibals, and Vernaculars', in S. Bassnett and H. Trivedi (eds), *Post-Colonial Translation: Theory and Practice* (London: Routledge, 1999), 1–19.
105. V.-Y. Mudimbe, '"*Reprendre*": Enunciations and Strategies in Contemporary African Arts', in S. Vogel (ed.), *Africa Explores. 20th Century African Art* (Munich: The Centre for African Art and Prestel, 1991), 276–87. I use here the expanded version of this essay as published under the same title in *The Idea of Africa* (Bloomington: Indiana University Press, 1994), 154–208.
106. Mudimbe, *The Idea of Africa*, 155.
107. Mudimbe, *The Idea of Africa*, 156.
108. Mudimbe, *The Idea of Africa*, 156.
109. Mudimbe, *The Idea of Africa*, 159.
110. Mudimbe, *The Idea of Africa*, 156.
111. M. de Certeau, *The Practice of Everyday Life*, trans. S. Rendall (Berkeley: University of California Press, 1984), 117.
112. de Certeau, *The Practice of Everyday Life*, 117.
113. Mudimbe, *The Idea of Africa*, 163.
114. On this artist, see: J. Fabian, *Remembering the Present: Painting and Popular History in Zaire* (Berkeley: University of California Press, 1996).
115. Mudimbe, *The Idea of Africa*, 167.
116. Mudimbe, *The Idea of Africa*, 174–75 (my emphasis). Mudimbe's long-standing admiration for the work of Benoît Verhaegen testifies to an analogous ambition to explore the territories where decolonization and the practice of everyday life intersect. Verhaegen's *Rébellions au Congo* chronicled the development of a number of rebellions that occurred throughout the newly-independent country in 1964. What is interesting is not so much the historical events *per*

se as the way in which these poorly equipped rebels, who were eventually defeated by the Armée Nationale Congolaise, bricolaged new popular myths that have retained their currency to the present.

117. Mudimbe, *On African Fault Lines*, 74.
118. R. Wagner, *The Invention of Culture* (Chicago: University of Chicago Press, 1981 [1975]).
119. Mudimbe, *On African Fault Lines*, 75.
120. Chakrabarty, *Provincializing Europe*, 29.
121. Chakrabarty, *Provincializing Europe*, 27.
122. Mudimbe, *The Invention of Africa*, 34.
123. Chakrabarty, *Provincializing Europe*, 43.
124. Chakrabarty, *Provincializing Europe*, 46.
125. J.-P. Sartre, 'Preface', in F. Fanon, *The Wretched of the Earth*, 7.
126. Rey (ed.), *Le Robert. Dictionnaire historique de la langue française*, 3,190–91.

References

Adorno, T. 'Commitment', in R. Taylor (ed.), *Aesthetics and Politics*, trans. F. McDonagh. London: Verso, 1980 [1977].
———. *Prisms*, trans. S. Weber and S. Weber. Cambridge, Massachusetts: MIT Press, 1981.
Ashcroft, B., G. Griffiths and H. Tiffin. *Key Concepts in Post-Colonial Studies*. London: Routledge, 1998.
Bahri, D. 'Feminism in/and Postcolonialism', in N. Lazarus (ed.), *The Cambridge Companion to Postcolonial Literary Studies*. Cambridge: Cambridge University Press, 2004, 199–220.
Bassnett, S. and H. Trivedi (eds). *Post-Colonial Translation: Theory and Practice*. Routledge: London, 1999.
Bidima, J.-G. 'Philosophies, démocraties et pratiques: à la recherche d'un "universalisme latéral"'. *Critique* 771/772, special issue 'Philosopher en Afrique' (2011), 672–88.
Bonn, M.J. *The Crumbling of Empire: The Disintegration of World Economy*. London: George Allen & Unwin Ltd, 1938.
de Certeau, M., L. Giard and P. Mayol. *L'Invention du quotidien*. Paris: Union Générale d'Éditions, 1980.
———. *The Practice of Everyday Life. Volume II: Living and Cooking*, trans. T.J. Tomasik. Minneapolis: University of Minnesota Press, 1988.
de Certeau, M. *The Practice of Everyday Life*, trans. S. Rendall. Berkeley: University of California Press, 1984.
Chakrabarty, D. *Provincializing Europe: Postcolonial Thought and Historical Difference*. Princeton: Princeton University Press, 2007 [2000].
Fabian, J. *Remembering the Present: Painting and Popular History in Zaire*. Berkeley: University of California Press, 1996.
Fanon, F. *Les Damnés de la terre*, preface by J.-P. Sartre. Paris: Maspero, 1961.
———. *The Wretched of the Earth*, preface by J.-P. Sartre, trans. C. Farrington. London: Penguin Books, 2001 [1961].
Girardet, R. *L'Idée coloniale en France de 1871 à 1862*. Paris: Éditions de la Table ronde, 1972.
Koselleck, R. 'Crisis', trans. M.W. Richter, *Journal of the History of Ideas* 67(2) (2006), 357–99.
Kourouma, A. *Allah n'est pas obligé*. Paris: Seuil, 2000.
Mbembe, A. 'Ecrire l'Afrique à partir d'une faille', *Politique Africaine* 51 (1993), 69–97.
———. *De la Postcolonie. Essai sur l'imagination politique dans l'Afrique contemporaine*. Paris: Karthala, 2000.
———. *On the Postcolony*. Berkeley: University of California Press, 2001.
———. 'African Modes of Self-Writing', trans. S. Rendall, *Public Culture* 14(1) (2002), 239–73.
———. 'Necropolitics', trans. L. Meintjes, *Public Culture* 15(1) (2003), 11–40.

———. *Sortir de la grande nuit. Essai sur l'Afrique décolonisée*. Paris: La Découverte, 2010.
Merleau-Ponty, M. *Éloge de la philosophie*. Paris: Flammarion, 1989.
Mignolo W.D. and A. Escobar (eds). *Globalization and the Decolonial Option*. London: Routledge, 2010.
Mignolo, W.D. *The Darker Side of Western Modernity: Global Futures, Decolonial Options*. Durham: Duke University Press, 2011.
Mudimbe, V.-Y. 'Physiologie de la négritude', *Études Congolaises* 5 (1967), 1–13.
———. *L'Autre face du royaume. Une Introduction à la critique des langages en folie*. Lausanne: L'Age d'homme, 1973.
———. *Entre les eaux*. Paris: Présence Africaine, 1973.
———. *Le Bel immonde*. Paris: Présence Africaine, 1976.
———. *L'Odeur du père: essai sur les limites de la science et de la vie en Afrique noire*. Paris: Présence Africaine, 1982.
———. *The Invention of Africa: Gnosis, Philosophy, and the Order of Knowledge*. Bloomington: Indiana University Press, 1988.
———. *Shaba Deux. Les Carnets de Mère Marie-Gertrude*. Paris: Présence Africaine, 1989.
———. '"Reprendre": Enunciations and Strategies in Contemporary African Arts'. First published in S. Vogel (ed.), *Africa Explores: 20th Century African Art*. Munich: The Centre for African Art and Prestel, 1991, 276–87.
———. *The Idea of Africa*. Bloomington: Indiana University Press, 1994.
———. *On African Fault Lines: Meditations on Alterity Politics*. Scottsville, South Africa: University of KwaZulu-Natal Press, 2013.
Ndlovu-Gatsheni, S.J. *Coloniality of Power in Postcolonial Africa: Myths of Decolonization*. Dakar: CODESRIA, 2013.
Nganang, P. *Manifeste d'une nouvelle littérature africaine: pour une écriture préemptive*. Paris: Éditions Homnisphères, 2007.
———. *La République de l'imagination. Lettres au benjamin*. La Roque-d'Anthéron: Vents d'ailleurs, 2009.
Ngũgĩ wa Thiong'o. *Something Torn and New: An African Renaissance*. New York: Basic Civitas Books, 2009.
Rey, A. (ed.). *Le Robert. Dictionnaire historique de la langue française*. Paris: Le Robert, 1998.
Rothermund, D. *Routledge Companion to Decolonization*. London: Routledge, 2006.
Saro-Wiwa, K. *Sozaboy: A Novel in Rotten English*. Port Harcourt: Saros, 1985.
Sartre, J.-P. 'Orphée noir', in L.S. Senghor (ed.), *Anthologie de la nouvelle poésie nègre et malgache de langue française*. Paris: Presses Universitaires de France, 1948, ix–xliv.
———. *Qu'est-ce que la littérature?* Paris: Gallimard, 1948.
———. *Plaidoyer pour les intellectuels*. Paris: Gallimard, 1972.
Shohat, E. and R. Stam. *Unthinking Eurocentrism: Multiculturalism and the Media*. London: Routledge, 1994.
Vendler, Z. 'Verbs and Times', *The Philosophical Review* 66(2) (1957), 143–60.
Verhaegen, B. *Rébellions au Congo*. Brussels: Centre de recherche et d'information socio-politiques, 1966.
Wagner, R. *The Invention of Culture*. Chicago: University of Chicago Press, 1981 [1975].
Wiredu, K. *Cultural Universals and Particulars: An African Perspective*. Bloomington: Indiana University Press, 1996.

Pierre-Philippe Fraiture is professor of French at the University of Warwick, U.K. He is the author of *Le Congo belge et son récit francophone à la veille des independences. Sous l'empire du royaume* (L'Harmattan, 2003), *La Mesure* de l'autre. Afrique subsaharienne et roman ethnographique de Belgique et de France (1818–1940) (Honoré Champion, 2007), and VY Mudimbe: Undisciplined Africanism (Liverpool University Press, 2013). He is the editor of a special issue of the *International Journal of Francophone Studies* on 'Francophone African Philosophy and the Aftermath of the Empire' (2015) and is co-editing, with Daniel Orrells, *A VY Mudimbe Reader* to be published by Virginia University Press in 2016. He is currently working on a monograph on decolonization and African philosophy.

Index

Aborigines' Rights Protection Society (ARPS), 162, 165, 169, 171–74
Adorno, Theodor, 194, 200–201
African press, 55, 166–67, 170–71
Afrikaans language, 8, 10, 50–51, 57, 59, 65, 91–93, 99–107
Afro-Asiatic language family, 4. *See also* specific languages
Afro-radicalism, 195–96
agency, 12–13, 73, 85, 186–87, 189, 190
agricultor. *See* farmer, concept of *(agricultor)*
Ahidjo, Ahmadou, 189
Ahuma, Attoh, 166, 172
Akan language, 6
Akan system of land management, 167–70
Alfonso XIII, King of Spain, 142
amaMfengu, 81–82
Amended Immorality Act (1969), 93, 108
apartheid policies, 96, 108, 197
Arbeit, concept of, 62
ARPS. *See* Aborigines' Rights Protection Society
Asante people, 163
Ateker Eastern Nilotic languages, 21, 26, 28, 30, 31, 33, 39–40
Ateso language, 26, 28, 30, 31, 38, 39
Atta, Ofori, King of Akim Abuakwa, 165, 175–76

Bagisu men, circumcision of, 13–14, 115–32; masculinity and, 116–18, 123–26; use of terms, Bagisu/Bugisu, 132n1. *See also* circumcision, concept of *(imbalu)*
Bagwere people, 130–31
Bamasaaba people, 117, 132n1. *See also* Bagisu.
Bantu languages, 21, 26, 33–38, 40–42
Barrera y Luyando, Ángel, governor of Bioko, 147–48
Bastin, Yvonne, 33, 34
Batshidi people, 50
Baumann, Oscar, 138
beggar, concept of, 30
belonging, concept of, 2
Biko, Steve, 178
Bioko, 4, 13, 138–40; colonial concept of property in, 143–46, 155; map, *139*; naming of, 138. *See also* Bubi people; land, concept of
Biyogo, Francisco Macía Nguema, 138
black press. *See* African press
Blyden, Edward Wilmot, 165
Bonatz, Brother, 77
Bond (1844), Gold Coast, 163
Bonelli Rubio, Juan María, governor of Bioko, 146
Bonn, Moritz, 190
borderlands, concept of, 74–75
bridewealth *(lobola)*, 96, 103–4
Brink, Elsabé, 112n71
Bubi language, 4

Bubi people, 13, 138–39; Hispanization of, 147; monarchy, 141; plantation labour, 146–49; settlement patterns, 140–42, 144; as sons of the country, 150, 152–55. *See also* land, concept of
Buganda, 41–42
Bugisu, 13–14, 115, 120, 124, 126–31; famines, 122–23; map, *116*; use of terms, Bagisu/Bugisu, 132n1. *See also* Bagisu men, circumcision of
Busoga, 42

Cape Malay Muslims, 92, 96–97
Casely Hayford, Joseph E., 165, 166, 167–68, 169, 173, 175–77
cattle-killing movement, 55, 61, 64, 82
cattle raids, 76–77
Certeau, Michel de, 199, 200–201
Césaire, Aimé, 215, 196
Chakrabarty, Dipesh, 195, 200; *Provincializing Europe,* 187–88, 190
Chamberlain, Joseph, 162
Christian missionaries, 15–16, 24, 74, 77–79, 84, 118–20, 127–28, 142, 147
Church Missionary Society (CMS), 118
circumcision, concept of *(imbalu)*, 2, 13–14, 15, 115; appropriation for ethnonationalism, 130–31; appropriation through education, 127–30; appropriation through medicalization, 121–22; enforced, 129–30; *imbalu* dance, 119, 120, 122, 123, 128–29; masculinity and, 116–18, 123–26; missionary intervention, 118–20, 127–28, 131; practice and conceptualization, 116–18, 129; response to medicalization, 122–27, 131; as ritual, 115, 119–20, 121, 122, 127–29, 131–32; social meaning, 131
citizen, concept of, 2, 5
Civil Union Act (1998), South Africa, 95, 108
CMS. *See* Church Missionary Society
cocoa trade, 143, 144–45, 147, 153
cohabitation *(saambly),* 95, 98–99, 101, 105–7, 108, 109
colony, concept of, 153–54, 186
Comaroff, Jean, 50, 52, 63
Comaroff, John, 50, 52, 63

conceptual history in Africa: agency and, 12–13, 73, 85; defined, 1, 15, 22; language and, 3–5, 43; methodologies, 2, 16, 73, 165–66; oral societies and, 23–24; temporality and, 186. *See also* specific concepts
Cooper, Frederick, 74
country and land, concepts of, 151–52
Crabtree, Mrs. W. A., 118–19
Crabtree, W. A., 118–19
crisis, concept of, 23, 188
Crown Lands Bill (1894), Gold Coast, 171
Curaduría Colonial, Spain, 147, 154
Customary Law, 172
Customary Marriages Act (1998), South Africa, 95, 108

Danquah, J. B. D., 166, 167, 168, 170
'Declaration of the Rights of Man and of the Citizen', 187
decolonization, concept of, 2, 12, 15; agency and, 186–87, 189, 190; definitions, 185–86; as failed, 190, 196; global capitalism and, 185; in postcolonial theory, 187–89; as process, 196. *See also* Mbembe, Achille; Mudimbe, Valentin-Yves; Nganang, Patrice
de Graft Johnson, J. W., 166
Derrida, Jacques, 201–202
domestic relationship, defined, 98
Domestic Violence Act (1998), South Africa, 98, 108

Eastern Nilotic languages, 21, 26, 28, 29–33, 41–42
Eastern Uganda, 10, 14, 42; linguistic landscape, *25,* 25–26. *See also* circumcision, concept of; poverty, concept of; wealth, concept of
eclecticism, 1, 191
eg, concept of, 94, 99–101, 106–7, 109
Ehret, Christopher, 7
English language, 6, 57, 80
Erasmus, Cecilia, 96
Eri, 138. *See also* Bioko
Esack, Farid, 97
ethnic cleansing, 189
ethnicity and gender, 7
Evans, Vyvyan, 94

Ewe language, 163
Eweera, Esáasi, 142

Fanakalo pidgin language, 63
Fanon, Frantz, 187, 191, 196
Fanti Federation (1868), 163, 176, 178
farmer, concept of *(agricultor),* 150–55
fatherland, concept of, 166, 171–72, 173–75, 177
Feierman, Steven, 14
Fernandinos, 141
Fields-Black, Edda, 7
findig/finden, use of term, 11
Flor Formosa, 138–39. See also Bioko
Foucault, Michel, 200–201
Franciscan friars, 24
French republican system, 187
frontier, concept of, 74

Ga language, 163
Ganda language. See Luganda language.
Geeraerts, Dirk, 27, 28–29
gender: associated traits, 117–18; in division of labour, 77–78; ethnicity and, 7; language and, 40–41, 42, 105–6; power and, 21, 79–80; in proverbs, 102; segregation by, 119; slavery and, 92. See also masculinity, concept of
Gisu, 14. See also Bagisu
Gisu, use of term, 132n1. See also Bagisu men, circumcision of; Bugisu
Glen Grey Act (1894), South Africa, 83
go berega, concept of, 57, 63
God, concept of, 74
go dira, concept of, 57, 63
Gold Coast, 6, 147, 162–67; Akan system of land management, 167–70; ARPS agitation, 165, 171–74; educated elite, role of, 6, 163–65, 169, 175, 176–77, 178–79; land bills, 162–63, 171, 173, 174, 178; map, 164; nation, concept of, 163; NCBWA nationalism, 174–77; newspapers, impact of, 166–67, 170–71
Gold Coast Methodist Church, 162, 166
grammaticalization theory, 9
Great Lakes Bantu languages, 26, 28–29, 40
Great Trek (1835-1846), 92
Green, Melanie, 94
Grey, George, 79

Grosfoguel, Ramon, 213
group identity, concept of, 13–14
Gwere language. See Lugwere language

Handwoordeboek van die Afrikaanse Taal (HAT), 100
Hanks, William, 24, 27
Harries, Patrick, 54
Hegel, Georg Wilhelm Friedrich, 24
Hopkins, A. G., 21–22
Hountondji, Paulin, 206
huwelik, concept of, 94, 99–101, 106–7, 109

Ìchùla, 138; use of term, 140. See also Bioko
identity politics, 3, 7, 189
Ifversen, Jan, 93–94, 95
imbalu. See circumcision, concept of *(imbalu)*
IMF. See International Monetary Fund
Immorality Act (1927), South Africa, 93, 108
Immorality Amendment Act (1950), South Africa, 93, 108
indígena, concept of, 150–55
intellectual history in Africa, 1, 3, 23
isiNdebele language, 49, 53, 58, 59, 63
isiXhosa language, 11, 15, 49, 50, 53, 58–63, 75, 79, 84–85
isiZulu language, 53, 58, 59

Janzen, John, 14
Jolobe, J. J. R., 85

Kanda-Matulu, Tshibumba, 199–200
Karimojong language. See Ngakarimojong language
Karp, Ivan, 32
key concepts, 14; construction of meaning, 93–95; Koselleckian, 93, 95, 165–66; translatability of, 5–6. See also specific concepts
Kiswahili language, 3, 6, 20
knowledge: concept of, 2; encyclopaedic, 9, 94; lexical, 9, 94
Koselleck, Reinhart, 1, 2, 15, 50, 73; on crisis, concept of, 23, 188; on key concepts, 93, 95, 165–66; on mutability of language, 24; on Sattelzeit, use of term, 180n13; on translatability, 5
Kourouma, Ahmadou, 197

Kropf, Albert, 75
kujitegemea. *See* self-reliance, policy of *(kujitegemea)*

labour, concept of, 11, 50–51, 155; colonial system, 49, 52, 53–55, 60, 74, 80–81, 84, 142, 146–50, 155; isiXhosa, 76–77, 84–85; land and, 146–49; Nguni, 57–65; taxes and, 83–84; women and, 77–78, 80–82, 83, 85, 92. *See also* work, concept of

land, concept of, 2, 4, 6, 13, 15, 140, 166; arable, types of, 146, 154; country and, 151–52; expropriation and, 151, 153; governance and, 167–71; harming, 14; healing, 14; individual/group rights, 168–69; land bills, 162–63, 171, 173, 174, 178; nation and, 171–72, 173, 174–75, 177; native rights to, 144–46, 149, 171–73, 177; plantation system and, 140, 146–49, 155; as property, 139–40, 143–46; registry, 149, 154; sons of the country and, 150, 152–55; stool property, 167–68, 170, 174

Landau, Paul, 24, 27, 74

language: borrowing in, 26, 50–51, 65; change in, 9–12, 24; colonial dictionaries, 75, 76–77; conceptual history and, 3–5; identity politics and, 3; oral vs. written, 4, 24, 62; words-and-things methodology, 7, 8. *See also* linguistics; specific languages

Law of the Indies, 147

Lévi-Strauss, Claude, 200–201

Lindsay, Lisa, 116–17

linguistics, 2; change in, 9–12, 24, 73; classifications, 28–29; cognitive, 9, 10, 24; cultural, 64, 73; data, 3, 8, 9–10, 15, 49–50, 52, 53, 55–57, 63–64; diversity in, 3–4, 5, 6, 7–8, 21, 25, 51; historical, 3, 4–5, 8, 10, 27, 55–56, 74; methodologies, 7, 10–11, 51–52, 63–65; semantic meaning and, 6, 7, 24, 56. *See also* specific concepts; specific languages; specific regions

literacy, 25

literary scholarship, 2

lobola. *See* bridewealth *(lobola)*

logging industry, 163

Lotuko-Maa language, 31

Luganda language, 24, 33, 34, 35, 36, 37, 40, 41

Lugisu language, 15, 116, 132n1

Lugwere language, 26, 28, 33, 34, 35, 36, 37, 40, 41

Lusoga language, 26, 28, 33, 34, 35, 36, 40, 41

Maa language, 31, 38, 39

male circumcision. *See* circumcision, concept of *(imbalu)*

Maleka, Malabo Lopelo, 142

Mankessim Constitution, Gold Coast, 163, 178

maro. *See* polygamy

marriage, concept of (Afrikaans), 2, 8, 15, 41; civil, 95, 96; cohabitation, 95, 98–99, 101, 105–7, 108, 109; conventional, 91, 95; customary, 95, 96; definitions and etymology, 99–101; domestic relationship, defined, 98; interracial, 93, 95; legal language and practices, 91, 95–99; overview, 91–93, 107–9; polygamy, 91, 92, 95, 96–97, 100–101, 108; proverbs and expressions, 101–5, 108; same-sex, 91, 93, 94, 95–98, 100–101, 108; slaves and, 92; syntagmatic and paradigmatic relations, 105–7. *See also eg*, concept of; *huwelik*, concept of; *trou*, concept of

Marriage Act (1961), South Africa, 95, 108

Martin del Molino, Amador, 141

Masaba, Edrisa K., 119–20, 133n24, 133n29

masculinity, concept of, 13–14, 115, 116–18, 123–26

Masters and Servants Act (1856), South Africa, 76, 79–81, 83

Maya language, 24

Mbembe, Achille, 12, 185, 188, 201; "African Modes of Self-Writing," 195–97; *Essai sur l'Afrique décolonisée*, 190, 191; "Necropolitics," 194; *Sortir de la grande nuit*, 189–90, 191–92

McLaren, James, 75, 76

meaning: change in, 27; construction of, 93–95; enduring, 7–8; lexical, 7–8; semantic, 6, 7, 24, 56; source of, 51; translation and, 5–6. *See also* specific concepts

Meischer, Stephan, 116–17
Menze, L. E., 85
Mfengu. *See* amaMfengu
Mfantsi Amanbuhu Fekuw, 164
Mfantsi National Education Fund, 164
millenarian prophesy. *See* cattle-killing movement
mineral industry, 163
Mkapa, Benjamin William, 204
Mobutu regime, 199
Moka, chief of Riabba, 141–42
Mombasa, 74
Moravian missionaries, 75, 77–79
Mqhayi, Samuel E. K., 84
Mudimbe, Valentin-Yves, 12, 185, 188; *On African Fault Lines,* 198; *L'Autre face du royaume,* 191; *Le Bel immonde,* 197; colonial library and, 197, 200; on concept of invention, 197–200; *Entre les eaux,* 197; on failed decolonization, 190; *The Idea of Africa,* 190; *The Invention of Africa,* 190, 191, 195, 196, 197, 199–200; legacy of, 189–90; *Odeur de père,* 196; "Reprendre," 198–200, 202; *Shaba Deux,* 197
multilingualism, 4, 61

nakedness, 119
nation, concept of, 163, 166, 171–72, 173, 174–75, 177
National Congress of British West Africa (NCBWA), 165, 174–77
national identity, concept of, 2
Native Administration Bills (1919, 1922, 1927), Gold Coast, 175
nativism, 195–96
NCBWA. *See* National Congress of British West Africa
Ndebele. *See* isiNdebele language.
Ngakarimojong language, 28, 30, 31, 32, 39, 40
Nganang, Patrice, 12, 185, 188, 200–201; *Manifeste d'une nouvelle littérature africaine,* 189–90, 193–95; on Mbembe, 195–96
ngoma healing, 14
Nguema, Teodoro Obiang, 138
Ngũgĩ wa Thiong'o, 188
Nguni languages, 5, 10, 49–55, 57–65
Nietzsche, Friedrich, 14, 23

Niger-Congo language family, 4. *See also* specific languages
Nilo-Saharan language family, 4. *See also* specific languages
Nilotic languages 11–12, 21, 26, 28
Nomvete, F., 84–85
North-Eastern Cape Frontier, map, 75
North Nyanza Bantu language, 21, 29, 33–38, 40–42
Núñez de Prado, Miguel, governor of Bioko, 149
Nyerere, Julius, 6, 12

oral societies, 4, 23–24, 26, 62, 75
Owen, Fitz William, 141

PAC. *See* Pan African Congress
palm oil trade, 141, 144–45
Pan African Congress (PAC), 178
paradigmatic relations, 105–7
Patrono de Indígenas, 147, 150, 151, 154
pauper, concept of, 30, 33, 34
plantation systems, colonial, 140, 146–49
Pó, Fernando, 138–39
polygamy, 91, 92, 95, 96–97, 100–101, 108
poor. *See* poverty, concept of
Posel, Dorrit, 96
postcolonial theory, 22; decolonization in, 187–89
poverty, concept of, 2, 4–5, 10–11, 22–23, 29–43; Eastern Nilotic, 29–33; happiness and, 32; North Nyanza, 33–38; social-ethnic identity and, 42
pragmatics and semantics, 94, 107
Prinsloo, Anton F., 105
Prohibition of Mixed Marriages Act (1949), South Africa, 93, 108
property, concept of, 139, 143–46; native property, 144–46, 149; plantation system and, 140, 146–49, 155; sons of the country and, 150, 152–55; stool property, 167–68, 170, 174
punishment, concept of, 23
Purvis, J. B., 119, 121

Ranger, Terence, 1, 15, 21–22, 122
reducción, 24
reed festival. *See umkhosi womhlanga* (reed festival)

Rey, Alain, 185–86
Rhodes, Cecil John, 83
Riebeeck, Jan van, 91
Romain-Desfossés, Pierre, 188–89
Roscoe, John, 119, 127
Rothermund, Dietmar, 186
Royal Decree (1904), Bioko, 143, 145, 154
Rudwick, Stephanie, 96
Rushana language, 26, 28
Rwanda, genocide in (1994), 193

saambly. See cohabitation *(saambly)*
Saavedra, Diego, 147
same-sex marriage, 91, 93, 94, 95–98, 100–101, 108
Sarbah, John Mensah, 166, 167–68, 169, 170–71, 176, 181n30
Saro-Wiwa, Ken, 197
Sartre, Jean-Paul, 187, 191, 193–94, 197, 200–201, 202
Schadeberg, Thilo, 33, 34
Schoenbrun, David, 27, 34
Scully, Pamela, 91–92
Searle, John, 93–94
semantics: borrowing in, 50–51, 65; change in, 9–11, 27, 56–57, 93; cognitive, 7–8, 9–10, 24, 94; comparative, 10; diachronic, 27, 56; linguistics and, 6, 7, 24, 56; pragmatics and, 94, 107; prototype theory, 27; translation and, 6. *See also* specific concepts
Senghor, Léopold S., 187
Serrano Ubierna, José Luis, 149
servant, use of term, 80–81
Setswana language, 50, 52
Shambaa history, 14
Shipton, Parker, 42
Siango, Charles, 123
siSwati language, 53
social constructivism, 93–94
social history in Africa, 1–2, 3, 22, 85
Soga language. *See* Lusoga language
Solomon, S. R. B. *See* Ahuma, Attoh
Southern Luo languages, 30–31
South Kyoga language, 26
Stompjes, Wilhelmina, 78
Strauss, Piet, 98
subjectification, 9
Swahili. *See* Kiswahili language

Swati/Swazi, see siSwati language
syntagmatic relations, 105–7

Tambookies, 58, 78, 81–83
temporality, 6–8, 15, 57, 187
Teso language. *See* Ateso language
Torre Rey, José de la, 142
translatability of concepts, 5–6, 75, 76–77
Treaty of El Pardo (1778), 138
Treaty of Paris (1900), 142
trou, concept of, 94, 99–107, 109
Tswana. *See* Setswana language
Turkana language, 30, 31, 32, 38, 39, 40

Uganda, 4–5, 21. *See also* Eastern Uganda
ujamaa, concept of, 2, 4, 6, 12, 15
ukuberega, concept of, 49, 51, 57, 63, 65
ukulobola custom, 78
ukuphangela, concept of, 49, 50–51, 57–60, 76–77, 85
ukusebenza, concept of, 49, 50–51, 56–61, 63–64, 63–65, 76–77, 85
umkhosi womhlanga (reed festival), 2
usable past, use of term, 21
van Onselen, Charles, 54, 68n42

Vansina, Jan, 7, 56, 140, 141
Van Wyk, G. J., 99–100
Vaughan, Megan, 110n24
Vendler, Zeno, 186
Verwoerd, H. F., 102

Wagner, Roy, 200
water, concept of, 2
wealth, concept of, 2, 4–5, 22–23, 29–43; Eastern Nilotic, 37–40, 42; North Nyanza, 40–42
werk, concept of, 10, 57, 59, 62, 65, 103
werken, concept of, 57, 62
Weyusha, Joseph, 123
white superiority, ideas of 165
witchcraft, 121
Woordeboek van die Afrikaanse Taal, 100, 102

work, concept of, 2, 10, 11, 14–15, 149; cognates, 57, 58; colonial conceptual engineering, 79–85; conflicting meanings, 60–63; English definition, 80; isiNdebele, 49; isiXhosa, 49, 50, 53, 58–63, 76, 84–85; in Masters and Servants Act, 76, 79–81; Moravian, 75, 77–79; Nguni, 51, 57–65; in Xhosa fiction, 84–85. *See also* labour, concept of; *ukuphangela,* concept of; *ukusebenza,* concept of

Xhosa communities, 54–55, 64. *See also* isiXhosa language

Zuma, Jacob, 96
Zulu. *See* isiZulu language

MAKING SENSE OF HISTORY
Studies in Historical Cultures
General Editor: Stefan Berger
Founding Editor: Jörn Rüsen

Bridging the gap between historical theory and the study of historical memory, this series crosses the boundaries between both academic disciplines and cultural, social, political and historical contexts. In an age of rapid globalization, which tends to manifest itself on an economic and political level, locating the cultural practices involved in generating its underlying historical sense is an increasingly urgent task.

Volume 1
Western Historical Thinking: An Intercultural Debate
Edited by Jörn Rüsen

Volume 2
Identities: Time, Difference, and Boundaries
Edited by Heidrun Friese

Volume 3
Narration, Identity, and Historical Consciousness
Edited by Jürgen Straub

Volume 4
Thinking Utopia: Steps into Other Worlds
Edited by Jörn Rüsen, Michael Fehr, and Thomas W. Rieger

Volume 5
History: Narration, Interpretation, Orientation
Jörn Rüsen

Volume 6
The Dynamics of German Industry: Germany's Path toward the New Economy and the American Challenge
Werner Abelshauser

Volume 7
Meaning and Representation in History
Edited by Jörn Rüsen

Volume 8
Remapping Knowledge: Intercultural Studies for a Global Age
Mihai I. Spariosu

Volume 9
Cultures of Technology and the Quest for Innovation
Edited by Helga Nowotny

Volume 10
Time and History: The Variety of Cultures
Edited by Jörn Rüsen

Volume 11
Narrating the Nation: Representations in History, Media and the Arts
Edited by Stefan Berger, Linas Eriksonas, and Andrew Mycock

Volume 12
Historical Memory in Africa: Dealing with the Past, Reaching for the Future in an Intercultural Context
Edited by Mamadou Diawara, Bernard Lategan, and Jörn Rüsen

Volume 13
New Dangerous Liaisons: Discourses on Europe and Love in the Twentieth Century
Edited by Luisa Passerini, Liliana Ellena, and Alexander C.T. Geppert

Volume 14
Dark Traces of the Past: Psychoanalysis and Historical Thinking
Edited by Jürgen Straub and Jörn Rüsen

Volume 15
A Lover's Quarrel with the Past: Romance, Representation, Reading
Ranjan Ghosh

Volume 16
The Holocaust and Historical Methodology
Edited by Dan Stone

Volume 17
What is History For? Johann Gustav Droysen and the Functions of Historiography
Arthur Alfaix Assis

Volume 18
Vanished History: The Holocaust in Czech and Slovak Historical Culture
Tomas Sniegon

Volume 19
Jewish Histories of the Holocaust: New Transnational Approaches
Edited by Norman J.W. Goda

Volume 20
Helmut Kohl's Quest for Normality: His Representation of the German Nation and Himself
Christian Wicke

Volume 21
Marking Evil: Holocaust Memory in the Global Age
Edited by Amos Goldberg and Haim Hazan

Volume 22
The Rhythm of Eternity: The German Youth Movement and the Experience of the Past, 1900–1933
Robbert-Jan Adriaansen

Volume 23
Viktor Frankl's Search for Meaning: An Emblematic 20th-Century Life
Timothy E. Pytell

Volume 24
Designing Worlds: National Design Histories in an Age of Globalization
Edited by Kjetil Fallan and Grace Lees-Maffei

Volume 25
Doing Conceptual History in Africa
Edited by Axel Fleisch and Rhiannon Stephens

Volume 26
Divining History: Prophetism, Messianism, and the Development of Spirit
Jayne Svenungsson

Volume 27
Sensitive Pasts: Questioning Heritage in Education
Edited by Carla van Boxtel, Maria Grever, and Stephan Klein

Volume 28
Evidence and Meaning: A Theory of Historical Studies
Jörn Rüsen

Volume 29
The Mirror of the Medieval: An Anthropology of the Western Historical Imagination
K. Patrick Fazioli

Volume 30
Cultural Borders of Europe: Narratives, Concepts and Practices in the Present and the Past
Edited by Mats Andrén, Thomas Lindkvist, Ingmar Söhrman and Katharina Vajta

Volume 31
Contesting Deregulation: Debates, Practices and Developments in the West since the 1970s
Edited by Knud Andresen and Stefan Müller

Volume 32
Making Nordic Historiography: Connections, Tensions and Methodology, 1850–1970
Edited by Pertti Haapala, Marja Jalava and Simon Larsson

www.ingramcontent.com/pod-product-compliance
Lightning Source LLC
Chambersburg PA
CBHW072152100526
44589CB00015B/2199